The GMC CCKW Truck in U.S. Service

Historical Reference

Written by David Doyle

Squadron Signal Publications

Illustrations by Mike Canaday

About the Historical Reference Series

Volumes in the *Historical Reference* series bring you the results of in-depth research into primary documents, providing extensive information, direct from original sources, much of just now entering the published historical record. The wartime history of a particular type of aircraft, vehicle, or vessel is recounted systematically.

Hard cover ISBN 978-0-89747-724-6

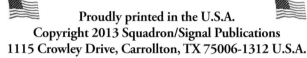

Proudly printed in the U.S.A.
Copyright 2013 Squadron/Signal Publications
1115 Crowley Drive, Carrollton, TX 75006-1312 U.S.A.

Military/Combat Photographs and Snapshots

If you have any photos of aircraft, armor, soldiers, or ships of any nation, particularly wartime snapshots, why not share them with us and help make Squadron/Signal's books all the more interesting and complete in the future? Any photograph sent to us will be copied and returned. Electronic images are preferred. The donor will be fully credited for any photos used. Please send them to:

Squadron/Signal Publications
1115 Crowley Drive
Carrollton, TX 75006-1312 U.S.A.
www.SquadronSignalPublications.com

Front cover: The GMC CCKW formed the backbone of the U.S. Army's tactical vehicle pool during World War II and well into Korea. The CCKW could be found on all fronts throughout the war, performing a variety of tasks from rear areas to the front line. At an unidentified port facility with a refinery and tank farm in the background, a sailor talks with the driver of an early-production CCKW. (General Motors)

Rear cover: The CCKW not only was the mainstay of U.S. Army transport during WWII, the truck was also widely used during the Korean War, particularly during the early stages. Here, a group of the veteran trucks move along the tortuous Yanggu Road, near Kwandae-ri in August of 1951. (National Archives)

Title page: Italian refugees from Velletri, Italy, are loaded in Fifth Army CCKWs at the waterfront at Anzio in June 1944. From there, they were scheduled to be evacuated by U.S. Navy ships to Naples. (National Archives)

Dedication

For every fighting man carrying a rifle on the front, or maneuvering a tank across a battlefield, six more soldiers provide support. Food, ammunition, weapons, clothing, medical treatment, and host of other goods and services had to be brought forward, most often in a truck. To those invaluable troops, and the legions of workers at home who built the trucks they used, this book is dedicated.

Contents

Introduction   4
Acknowledgments   4
Terminology   4

Section I - Production

Chapter 1	The ACKWX	5
Chapter 2	The Heart of the CCKW	19
Chapter 3	The CCKWX	30
Chapter 4	The CCKW is born	53
Chapter 5	Chevrolet CCKWs	75
Chapter 6	The CCW – the 6x4 variant	82
Chapter 7	War production begins	88
Chapter 8	AFKWX – Cab over Engine	95
Chapter 9	The Largest Truck Contract	98
Chapter 10	The Open Cab	112
Chapter 11	CCKWs for the Navy	125
Chapter 12	Cargo Dump Trucks	129
Chapter 13	Mid-Production AFKWX	139
Chapter 14	CCKW Production Continues	142
Chapter 15	The Composite Bed Introduction	157
Chapter 16	The End of the AFKWX	167
Chapter 17	Building the CCKW	170
Chapter 18	Air Transportable CCKWs	195
Chapter 19	Low Silhouette Trucks	218
Chapter 20	Charcoal-Gas Converter	226
Chapter 21	Accessory kits	233

Section II - Specialized trucks

Chapter 22	Army Air Corps	245
	Aerial Lift Trucks	
	Airfield Service Trucks	
	Bomb Service Trucks	
Chapter 23	Chemical Warfare Service	268
	Chemical Service Trucks	
	Decontamination Trucks	
	Flame Service Trucks	
Chapter 24	Corps of Engineers	281
	Air Compressors	
	Bolster Trucks	
	Fire Trucks	
	Cranes	
	Pipeline Construction	
	Reproduction Trucks	
	Shop, Motorized, General Purpose	
	Line Construction Trucks	
	Water Purification Trucks	

Chapter 25	Army Medical Service	319
	Clubmobile	
	Surgical Trucks	
	Optical Trucks	
Chapter 26	Ordnance Shop Trucks	337
Chapter 27	Signal Corps	361
Chapter 28	Unusual CCKWs	368

Section III – Field Use

Chapter 29	Field Use During WWII	373
	Continental U.S.	
	North Africa	
	European Theater of Operations	
	Pacific Theater of Operations	
	China-Burma-India	
Chapter 30	Interwar Period	486
Chapter 31	Korea	496
Chapter 32	Post-Korea	503

An open-cab CCKW-353 takes a happy-looking group of G.I.s to a Fifth Army rest center in Italy. It is not clear where this rest center was located, but from at least November 1944 through March 1945, the Fifth Army's rest center was at Montecatini Terme, Italy. There troops could wind down and recuperate in a relaxing environment after hard campaigning. (National Archives)

Introduction

The GMC was the mainstay of U.S. Army transport throughout World War II and well into the Korean War. With its straightforward design, the truck was easy to drive, easy to maintain, and relatively easy to produce. The result was a reliable truck that was available in large numbers. Originally built in cargo/personnel carrier and prime mover variants, the chassis was soon adapted for a myriad of special purpose trucks by the using services.

Since the last CCKW rolled off the assembly line in 1945 it has been the subject of numerous books and articles published around the globe. Lacking access to genuine General Motors documentation, previous authors were forced to resort to a certain amount of speculation, leaving many questions unanswered, and raising yet other questions.

The author of the present volume was blessed to have access to the surviving General Motors documentation. While in the seven decades from the end of CCKW production to the publication of this book, many documents have been lost or destroyed, those that remain have yielded a treasure trove of information – much of it previously unknown or forgotten with the passage of time. Regrettably, even after a decade of research through U.S. government archives as well as those of General Motors, some questions remain unanswered. Missing are two holy grails – the MTER – Motor Transportation Engineering Record – which would have associated the minutiae of any change in truck production to a serial number and manufacturing facility – and a complete listing associating each serial number to an army registration number.

However, GM's documents did provide a great deal of material relating to the sequence of production of these vehicles, their sales order numbers, and many serial numbers. Any such numbers that appear in this book can be trusted to not be speculation, but rather taken from GM documents.

Many of the surviving General Motors documents concerning GMC military trucks were compiled by the GMC Production Control Manager, R. A. Crist. Crist crafted a four-volume *War History* for GM internal use, of which only five copies were printed. A portion of his 29 January 1946 cover letter, written when the books were delivered, is quoted here for insight – the first of many times that Crist will be quoted in this volume: "This 'Story of Production' is essentially a history of facts, events, conditions, problems, situations, grief and accomplishment. It is supported by tables of figures, charts and a few pictures. . . . It is not the whole story of production as that will never be written, but the records are complete, the data and information accurate, the charts informative and interesting, and there is probably more data and information here than anyone can absorb unless you have lived this story as I have lived it.

"I wrote this entire history because it could not have been written by anyone else. With the possible exception of Mr. Hire I doubt if anyone will ever read it, but it is a great load off my mind and a burden off my aching war shoulders. At least I hope it will be of some value."

Terminology

As mentioned, virtually all of the material in *The GMC CCKW Truck in U.S. Service* is drawn from period documentation, much of it not previously available. A great amount of information in this book is directly quoted from those documents, which in some cases could be confusing to a reader not familiar with the way some terms, particularly abbreviations, have changed over time. For example, "DOD" when seen on these pages is referring to the Detroit Ordnance District, not the Department of Defense; and TAC is the Tank-Automotive Center, not the Tank-Automotive and Armaments Command.

The passage of time has also introduced new terminology – or slang. Despite reading literally thousands of pages of vintage General Motors and Army documents, as well as informal period communications, not once have I seen the term "Deuce and a half" used when referring to these 2½-ton trucks. Nor have I ever seen the term "tipper" used when referring to the GMC CCKW Cargo Dump truck, leading me to conclude that these terms were coined sometime after the fact.

Other terms introduced during the war never surfaced in thousands of pages of production records. Invariably, CCKW axles are internally referred to as "Chevrolet" and "Timken" – the latter sometimes referenced as Timken-Detroit or TDA. Never are they internally referenced as "Banjo" or "Corporation" for the former and "Split" for the latter, yet those are the terms used in the period manuals. It is my conjecture that this was a marketing/pride decision to avoid using the names of competitors. While there was far more cooperation within the General Motors family in the production of these trucks than most people realize – with not only GMC building the trucks, but Chevrolet assembling CCKWs in St. Louis and Baltimore, and also producing many components, and the Pontiac Motor Division crating CCKWs for export – the GMC name was the one that went on the truck.

Acknowledgments

Unlike most of what has been previously written, this book draws almost entirely upon primary source documents. Many of these documents are held by General Motors, access to which was arranged by Keith Nattrass, to who I am deeply indebted, and whose staff, including Larry Kinsel and Christo Dantini provided immeasurable help in bringing this project to life.

Jim Gilmore graciously provided copies thousands of additional pages of documentation found at the National Archives, which was added to the materials that had been located during the many trips taken by my wife Denise and I to this institution.

Tom Kailbourn, Bryce Sunderlin, Fred Coldwell, Tom Wolboldt, Jerry Cleveland, Steve Zaloga, Scott Taylor, and the late Fred Crismon all contributed immeasurably to the completion of this volume.

Dr. Larry Roberts with the U.S. Army Engineer School History Office opened his files for research, as did Kip Lindberg with the Chemical Corps Museum. The staffs of the Army Transportation Museum, Quartermaster Museum and Ordnance Museum were inordinately helpful.

Special thanks to my dear and long-suffering wife Denise, who carefully scanned thousands of pages of documents and photos for use in this volume. The entire staff at Squadron Signal Publications is owed a debt of gratitude for tackling this enormous project, and presenting the materials in a clear manner.

To everyone involved in this, a sincere "Thank You!"

Chapter 1

The ACKWX

When the U.S. Army Quartermaster Corps began developing its "Standard Fleet" of vehicles about 1928, one of the new creations was a 2½-ton 6x6. The approximately 60 vehicles of the Standard Fleet were broken into five groups, numbered I through V, with each group roughly corresponding to a weight class. Among to new designs in Group I, the lightest weight class of the groups, were two 2½-ton 6x6 vehicles. The fruits of this effort began to pay off in 1932 when the vehicles were rolled out of the shops of the Holabird Quartermaster's Depot. One, W3228, was powered by a Duesenberg J engine, while the other, W3229 was powered by a Lycoming engine. In time a Franklin air-cooled V-12 was also trialed in one of the vehicles. It is worthwhile to note that during this time one A.W. Herrington was employed by the Motor Transport Division of the Quartermaster Corps. While the so-called Standard Fleet did not enter mass production, the vehicles created were instrumental in defining future generations of U.S. Army tactical vehicles. The Standard Fleet had been created with the purpose of crafting vehicles built to wholly military specifications, using standardized components – as opposed to the previous process of buying commercial vehicles from a variety of manufacturers – vehicles that most closely fit the military's need, but rarely truly were what the Army wanted. Ultimately the Congress and the comptroller general of the United States decreed that the Army could not produce its own vehicles, as it had with the Standard Fleet, but rather had to rely on private enterprise for its future vehicle needs.

The shortcoming of high wheel loadings on four-wheel vehicles, even four-wheel-drive four-wheel vehicles, was becoming evident – namely, a lack of floatation. Those vehicles with dual rear wheels faired better than their four-wheeled counterparts, but frequent miring was still a problem. Accordingly, additional consideration was given to 6x6 trucks. In 1933 the Army procured a commercial 2½-ton 6x6 truck. Designated the TL29-6, this truck was manufactured by the Indianapolis-based Marmon-Herrington Company, one of the

principals of which was A. W. Herrington, by this time no longer in the service of the Army.

The TL29-6 was not without competition, however, as the Corbitt Motor Truck Company of North Carolina offered its 168-FD8 to the Army. While neither design was an outright failure, neither offered the Army what it wanted, at the price that it wanted to pay. At this point in time, powered front axles were still in their infancy, and vehicles utilizing them were limited-production, expensive specialist machines. However, these efforts had piqued the interest of the automotive titan General Motors's GMC Division.

GMC had its origins in the Rapid Motor Vehicle Company and the Reliance Motor Company, both Detroit-based independent truck manufacturers. W. C. Durant, who began assembling the corporate behemoth that would later become General Motors, purchased Reliance in 1908, and followed that with the purchase of Rapid in 1909. Reliance and Rapid formed the General Motors Truck Company, and the GMC logo first appeared in 1911.

A little over a decade later, on 8 July 1925 in the city of Chicago, the Yellow Truck and Coach Company was formed by John D. Hertz – later of rental car fame – who owned Yellow Cab. Hertz had purchased Lake Shore Motor Bus Company, which included American Motor Bus Manufacturing Company, in November 1922. The initial function of the firm was to provide buses for the Chicago Motor Bus Company, which Hertz also controlled. The firm soon also sold motor coaches to other bus operators. On 17 April 1923 American Motor Bus Manufacturing Company was sold to the also-Hertz-controlled Yellow Cab Manufacturing Company, and the bus-builder was promptly reorganized as the Yellow Coach Manufacturing Company. The firm's business prospered, with well over 2,000 units delivered between August 1923 and July 1925, about half of these going to Hertz-controlled firms, with the rest going to outside interests.

Hertz's success in his endeavors piqued the interest of Alfred P. Sloan, chairman of General Motors. On 8 July 1925 a merger of

The Quartermaster's Standard Fleet of vehicles included two nearly-identical vehicles in the 2½-ton 6x6 range. These were intended to serve as both truck and command/reconnaissance vehicles, and this Duesenberg-powered example, registration number W3228, was aptly suited for the latter, with an 80 MPH top speed. (Fred Crismon collection)

General Motors with Yellow Coach Manufacturing was announced. General Motors would get 60% of the new holding company, Yellow Truck and Coach Company, in exchange for the assets of General Motors Truck Company (GMC) and the obscure GM subsidiary of Northway Motor and Manufacturing Company. On 26 August 1925 the deal was consummated, and in March of 1927 the new firm acquired a 160-acre tract of land near Pontiac, Michigan, for the construction of a new truck and bus assembly plant. Trucks began leaving the assembly line of the new Pontiac plant on 5 January 1928. With 26 acres under roof, it was then the world's largest truck plant.

It was from this formidable position that General Motors entered into the Army 6x6 fray, offering the purpose-built model 4929. This truck was created in response to invitation for bid 398-38-31, which was awarded 8 December 1937. This stylish 1½-ton truck was created by joining an Oldsmobile 230 engine to a Chevrolet four-speed transmission in order to power Timken axles through a Wisconsin T32 transfer case. The front-end sheet metal was a Chevrolet pattern, and the truck chassis was a modified Yellow commercial unit. Utilizing such readily available components both lowered cost and sped production. In total, 229 of these trucks were built on contract 398-QM-6270, valued at $539,534.00. The last of these vehicles was delivered on the final day of May 1938.

Also in 1938 GMC's efforts to develop its own engine for use in commercial vehicles bore fruit with its 248-cubic-inch six-cylinder design. This engine would play as important role in future GMC military contracts, as did the model 4929 truck. The first military application of this engine was in eleven 2½-ton 6x6 trucks. One of these vehicles was built for export, while the remaining 10 were for the U.S. Marine Corps. Designated Model 4937, the truck cab and chassis (no body) shared a 155½-inch wheelbase, as well as the remainder of the powertrain, (apart from the engine) with the model 4929 trucks. The USMC contract was awarded on 29 August 1938, and the final Model 4937 was delivered on 27 January 1939.

In 1939 the Army issued solicitation for bid 398-40-2601939, and the die was cast for the truck that would ultimately become the ubiquitous CCKW. This specification increased the cross-country payload to 5,000 pounds, required a top speed of 45 m.p.h., and mandated the ability to climb a 3½-percent grade in direct drive. Studebaker and Mack responded to the solicitation, as did Yellow Truck and Coach. Yellow Truck and Coach assigned the new vehicle the model ACKWX-353, signifying: A– 1939 model year; C – conventional cab; K – selective front wheel drive; W – driven tandem axles; X – nonstandard (Timken) driveline; 353 chassis code. Bids were opened on 18 May 1939, and the contract awarded to GM on 15 June of the same year. Thirty-two of these trucks were delivered 4 January 1940 with one more on the 8th, all powered by the same 248-cubic-inch engine used in the 4929 and 4937. Thereafter the ACKWX-353 used an enlarged 256-cubic-inch version of the 1938 248-cubic-inch engine. While the GMC parts book indicates that the serial number range for these vehicles is ACKWX353-3604 through ACKWX353-6070, totaling 2,466 vehicles, GM's records indicate that 2,469 of these trucks were built under contract for the U.S. government (this includes the 33 trucks powered by the 248-cubic-inch engine). Fifty of these trucks, all powered by the 256-cubic-inch engine, were equipped with winches. A further single unit was built for the GM's demonstration purposes, and a 248-cubic-inch version with right hand drive was built for the French. Another 248-engine powered truck was also built for export, possibly to Switzerland, but by far the largest overseas order was 1,000 trucks, with the 256 engine, sent to Great Britain in 1941 on sales order 10000-999.

A very similar vehicle was also constructed at the Holabird depot, powered by a more modest Lycoming engine. This vehicle, registration number W3229, notably featured air brakes, as opposed to W3228's hydraulic brakes. (Fred Crismon collection)

Above: Congress effectively put the Army out of the business of building its own trucks, with private industry to supply vehicles moving ahead. This Marmon-Herrington TL29-6 was that firm's offering in the 2½ ton 6x6 range. (Fred Crismon collection)

Left: Corbitt, of Henderson, North Carolina, also courted the Army's business with their imposing 168-FD8, which featured a chrome radiator shell, very different from the austere looks tactical trucks would have a scant 10 years later. (Fred Crismon collection)

General Motors Truck entered in the government 6x6 market with this truck, their model 4929. Powered by an Oldsmobile 230 engine and utilizing a Chevrolet Cab, the vehicle epitomized the economies afforded by the massive General Motors corporate structure. (General Motors)

Above: The model 4929 exhibited two spare tires stowed vertically between the rear of the cab and the front of the cargo body, which would become a feature of the CCKW. A chrome placard lettered "General Motors Truck" was affixed to the side of the hood. (General Motors)

Right: The cargo body lacked reinforcing with the exception of the protruding frame at the front, top, and rear. The tandem axles were suspended from leaf springs; the spring seat and the torque rods are visible between the wheels. The door handle was chromed. (General Motors)

The model 4929 was equipped with sideboards fashioned from channel-section stakes and wooden slats. The troop seats are folded up against the stakes in this photo. The rear fender was braced, front and rear, by a steel strip welded to the fender and the bottom of the cargo body. (General Motors)

To the rear of the 4929's narrow, express body is a tailgate fitted with hold-open chains and a D-shaped opening on each side that served as a step when the tailgate was lowered. Between the bumperettes was a tow pintle. Above the license plate was a tail-light assembly. Firestone directional-tread tires were mounted. (General Motors)

Left: A brush guard fabricated from metal strips protected the 4929's radiator and headlight assemblies. A GMC logo is at the top center of the radiator grille. The stamped front fenders featured rather complex contours. The axles were Timkens, and the front one is clearly visible. (General Motors)

Below: Most of the 229 examples of GM's pioneer 6x6 were sent to units in the field. This artillery unit is employing a mixed lot of early 6x6 trucks, including at least two of the model 4929. (Author's collection)

Furthering the company's success in the market, eleven improved trucks were built. Given the model number 4937, ten of these trucks were delivered to the U.S. Marine Corps, while the eleventh was exported. All were powered by GMC's own 248 cubic inch displacement 6-cylinder engine. This example is carrying a test load of massive concrete blocks. (General Motors)

Above: The cab of the GMC model 4937 was the same type used on the model 4929, complete with chromed "General Motors Truck" placard and door handles. Visible below the rear of the running board is the vacuum-booster assembly. Up to September 1941, the booster was made by the Bragg-Kliesrath Division of Bendix. (General Motors)

Right: The 2½ ton 6x6 was further refined with the introduction of the ACKWX-353. The example shown here outside the Pontiac, Michigan plant on 29 September 1939 wears U.S. Army registration number 410673, the first assigned to an ACKWX-353. (General Motors)

While not the first 2½-ton 6x6 design built for the U.S. Government by General Motors, the ACKWX-353, shown here, was the first to be produced in a quantity over 1,000. While this was a small quantity compared to the hundreds of thousands of CCKWs to be built only a few years later, it was nevertheless many fold more than had been built of earlier GM models. (General Motors)

Above: The ACKWX incorporated a full-width cargo body, rather than the narrow express body used on the 4929. (General Motors)

Right: General Motors ACKWX-353 U.S. Army registration number 410673 displays its rear end and tarpaulin. Below the tailgate, at the center of the cross sill, was the door to a recessed toolbox, underneath which were the tow pintle and bumperettes. (General Motors)

11

On the outboard side of each of the bumperettes of the ACKWX-353 was an air coupling for operating the brakes of a trailer. To the left of the tool-box door was an electrical receptacle for powering a trailer's tail lights. (General Motors)

The ACKWX-353's bumperettes, right air coupling, tool-box door, and tailgate hinges are viewed from a different angle. The round holes were for recessed tail-light assemblies. (General Motors)

Factory-fresh ACKWX-353 registration number 410673 is viewed from the right rear. In this photo, the window flap on the rear closure of the tarpaulin has been secured in the open position. (General Motors)

The earliest examples of the ACKWX utilized the 248 engine and featured a fuel tank positioned under the seat, the filler of which can be seen here, just ahead of the spare tire, which has been swung down on its mounting. (General Motors)

Above: The spare tire of an early ACKWX-353 is shown in its stowed position under the front right corner of the cargo body. (General Motors)

Right: GMC ACKWX-353 registration number 410673 is observed from the front. The cab was the 1939-1940 GMC model 984. The brush guard was similar to the one used on the GMC models 4929 and 4937, complete with braces from the guard to the fender. (General Motors)

Later production trucks, such as this one, had the fuel tank relocated to a position suspended from the right frame rail, and utilized a 256-cubic inch 6-cylinder engine. This truck was delivered sometime prior to June 1940, when this contract W-398-QM-7479 was completed. (Fred Crismon collection)

Winches were furnished with fifty of the ACKWX-353 trucks (despite some sources leaving the impression only eight were so equipped), including this example. (Fred Crismon collection)

On 21 June 1940 GM delivered this truck, registration number 412337, one of only two ACKWX-352 trucks built without a winch. (Fred Crismon collection)

Right: The only other ACKWX-352 built was this winch-equipped model, registration number 410895, delivered 26 June 1940. (Fred Crismon collection)

Below: This truck, utilizing a convertible cab (cab model 1547) was the sole example of its type. It bore army registration number 412338. (Fred Crismon collection)

While the later CCKWX would host a variety of body types, and the CCKW itself a myriad of specialist bodies, the ACKWX-353 came in few varieties, including this stock rack version, of which 27 were built, all delivered between February and July of 1940. (General Motors)

The ACKWX-353s fitted with stock racks were designed to transport livestock. Several horses or cattle could be loaded aboard. Here, one of the two loading ramps is lowered. (General Motors)

Right: Both loading ramps are lowered on the ACKWX-353. A tarpaulin could be installed over the four bows inserted in the stock racks. Tie-down hooks for the tarpaulin lashings were on the side of the body. (General Motors)

Below: Through field maneuvers such as this one, where troops are constructing an encampment, the Army gained familiarity with its new fleet of all-wheel drive trucks. This experience would play an important part in refining the design of the vehicles, and how they could best be used. (Fred Crismon collection)

GMC ACKWX-353 registration number 413667 has been rigged for transporting litter patients in Hawaii in 1942. Eighteen litters were mounted, with the rails of the top two tiers of litters resting on the sideboards and the troop seats. (Fred Crismon collection)

Eight of the ACKWX-353 trucks built for the U.S. Army were delivered as cab and chassis only, without bed. At least some of these were used as the basis for the M3 mobile water-purification unit, shown here. (General Motors)

GMC ACKWX-353 U.S. Army registration number 60470 was fitted with the M3 mobile water-purification unit, housed in a shelter on the rear of the vehicle. (General Motors)

This Water Purification Unit, Mobile, M3, Model 1938 is mounted on a GMC ACKWX 6x6 chassis. With some refinements to equipment, body and truck chassis, the basic gear formed the backbone of the U.S. Army engineers water purification units during WWII. (Fred Crismon collection)

On Kodiak Island in the Aleutians, a GMC ACKWX-353, towing what appears to be an antiaircraft gun, leads a convoy transporting cargo. As harassment by Japanese aircraft was a possibility, the ACKWX is armed with a water-cooled .50-caliber machine gun in an antiaircraft mount in the cargo body. (National Archives)

Chapter 2
The Heart of the CCKW

While generally pleased with GMC's ACKWX, the Army felt that the truck was underpowered. This concern lead to a whirlwind effort to get more power out of the company's six-cylinder engine, and the result was an increase in displacement from 256 to 270 cubic inches. Remarkably, the engine was designed and a running prototype built in less than a month.

The 270 was the cornerstone upon which the CCKWX, CCKW, ACKW, and the DUKW were built. The 270 was also a key part of the GMC's post-WWII civilian truck line. The serial number for these engines, which is stamped into a pad near the distributor, begins "270." However, all 270s are not alike, not even all the military engines. In fact, the manuals list no fewer than 20 different variations of the 270. As the focus of this book is on the CCKW, the discussion below will largely be confined to the various engine models used on the CCKW and its predecessor, the CCKWX.

The GM part number initially assigned to the 270 initially installed in the CCKWX when production began in 1940 was SN-3063. This six-cylinder, valve-in-head engine with a 3 25/32-inch bore and 4-inch stroke was equipped with a 25-ampere generator. The model SN-3240

The heart of the Yellow Truck and Coach/GMC 6x6 is the 270 cubic inch, six-cylinder gasoline engine. Produced in no fewer than 20 variations, in addition to the CCKWX this engine also powered the cab-over AFKWX as well as the DUKW amphibian. (General Motors)

engine, which added crankcase ventilation and water bypass to the engine's features, replaced the 3063. These engines constitute what the July 1945 ORD 9 SNL G-508 refers to as the "first series engines."

The same manual lists three "second series" engines, with one of them being GM part number SN-3148, which began with engine serial number 270-43180. These engines are listed as being for the CCKW and CCW, rather than the CCKWX. This engine featured a 40-amp generator and steam relief tube connected to the radiator core. At engine serial number 270-159367, the engine model changed again, this time to SN-3168, reflecting the addition of water bypass. The third version of what GM dubbed the "second series" engine was the SN-3191, which began at serial number 270-211601, which added radio suppression.

As opposed to the multiple variations of first- and second-series engines, the third series is remarkably straightforward, with only one model, the SN-3199, introduced at serial number 270-219512. This engine had all the features of the SN-3191, 40-ampere generator, water bypass, radio suppression, plus added positive crankcase ventilation.

GM's fourth series of CCKW engines began with the model SN-3230, which represented a major evolution in the engine. Beginning with engine serial number 270-266551, the oil pan on the CCKW became an enlarged, two-piece, deep-sump unit. The use of this engine in the CCKW required a change in the truck chassis as well, since spring stops were required to prevent suspension travel from damaging the oil pan. GM began procuring the parts to build the first 78,607 trucks incorporating this engine in July 1942. That said, these trucks were not actually scheduled to begin production until May 1943.

True mass production requires dealing with numerous suppliers for vast quantities of materials and parts, all of which are bought for a specific purpose (as opposed to buying large volumes of screws, sheet steel, pistons, etc., and then hoping that some sort of order comes through that will permit the use, and sale, of finished goods including them). Complicating this issue further, each purchase order from the government requires that the product, in this case, trucks, meet certain clearly spelled out specifications. Subsequent changes require contract revisions. Thus, trucks ordered on older, unrevised purchase orders that did not call for the deep sump oil pan (and the concurrent changes in HydroVac, fuel tanks with enlarged fillers, etc.), and for which all the necessary parts had been ordered from GMs suppliers, had to be completed as well, resulting in what for us today seems like a protracted delay between the authorization and the implementation of the change in oil pan.

The next big change for the 270 engine resulted in the creation of GM part number SN-3431. The major change here was the carburetor. Up to this point, the 270 breathed through a Zenith 28AV11 carburetor, also used on a number of civilian trucks of the era. The downfall of this carburetor, from the military perspective, is that its diecast construction makes it relatively fragile and susceptible to damage when the truck is operating in rugged, off-road situations. The solution to this problem was the Zenith 30B11 cast-iron carburetor, the hallmark of the SN-3431. This change hit the CCKW assembly line at chassis number 321078, and appears to have been made near engine serial number 270-394484.

Many U.S. military vehicles of this era were plagued with vapor locking, and the CCKW was no exception. There was even a training film produced about this issue. In an effort to combat this problem, a new six-valve fuel pump, GM-153816, was introduced beginning at CCKW-394577, and engine serial number 270-524701. The model number assigned this engine was SN-3731.

It should be remembered that while the above information addresses the CCKW and CCKWX engines, these progressive changes were made in the remainder of the wartime military 270-engine families as well, resulting in three versions of AFKWX engines (SN3158, SN3220, and SN3381) as well as four varieties of DUKW engines (SN3214, SN3229, SN3380 and SN3477). The 1951-dated ORD 8, SNL G-508, however, lists additional engines in this family, with the SN4824 and SN4827 being named as CCKW engines, with the latter being noted as a replacement for all previous models, while the SN4841 and SN4844 are specified as AFKWX engines.

Yellow Truck and Coach, which in 1943 became GM Truck and Coach Division, built its engines in its Plant 4, in Pontiac, Michigan. Engine production occupied 102,638 square feet of this 324,683 square foot building in late 1941, the rest being consumed by the company's service department. General Motors had bought these buildings on South Saginaw St. (now known as Woodward Ave.) in April, 1937. The buildings had previously been part of the Wilson Foundry Machine Shop – Wilson Foundry of course is familiar for their work on jeep engines, which was carried out at another facility long after GM bought the properties discussed here.

A study conducted by GM, at the behest of the War Department in October 1941 revealed that Plant 4, working 22½ hours per day, could produce a maximum of 23 engines of 270 cubic inches displacement per hour, although the practical limitation was 21 engines per hour.

The blocks themselves were by the Pontiac Motor Company at their foundry operations on Montcalm St., only a few blocks away from Yellow's Plant 4. Cylinder heads were initially produced by Ferro Foundry in Cleveland, Ohio, but this was later supplemented with additional cylinder head casting by the Buick Motor Division of GM. From the standpoint of Yellow Truck and Coach, the limiting factor in engine production was the machining time required on the various engine components.

The documents furnished by General Motors to the War Department contemplated that truck assembly would be performed 5 days per week, on two shifts per day on three assembly lines, and one shift per day on a third assembly line (keep in mind at this time Yellow Truck and Coach was also still building non-military vehicles, and these figures reflect the goal of producing 600 trucks per day, combined military and civilian). In order to keep up with the demand for engines required for the planned scenario, engine operations would work three shifts, six days per week.

Even before Pearl Harbor, Yellow Truck and Coach anticipated that demand for the military 270 engine would soon outstrip the production capacity of Plant 4. To overcome this bottleneck, Yellow Truck and Coach executed a Purchase Order to Chevrolet Central Office, contracting Chevrolet's Flint engine plant to build the GMC 270. Under the agreement production would begin at Flint on 1 February 1942, with delivery at the rate of 110 per day.

Pearl Harbor changed the entire manufacturing landscape at General Motors, and for the United States as a whole. At a meeting in the office of Yellow Truck and Coach president Irving B. Babcock on New Year's Day 1942, it was decided that Chevrolet Flint should be tooled up to produce 700 of the 270 engines per day. This output was of course in addition to Yellow's own production capacity in Plant 4. It was also approved to spend $6 million to expand the capacity of Yellow Truck's plants 1 through 4 in Pontiac.

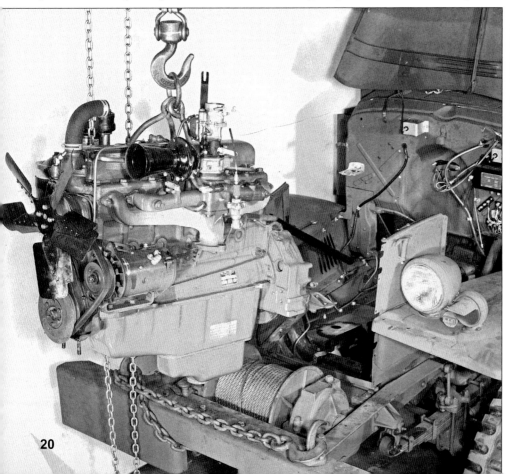

A mid-production 270, evidenced by the deep two-piece oil pan but retaining the diecast carburetor is suspended from a chain hoist near a CCKW engine compartment. This scene was posed during the creation of a maintenance publication. In official histories submitted to the War Department, both GMC and Chevrolet claim credit on the behalf of their engineers for enlarging the 256 engine to the 270 that powered the CCKW. Regrettably, the General Motors documents holding the key to this seem to have disappeared into the mist of time. (General Motors)

This 2nd series engine is being used as a training aid in the classroom of a GMC Army training school. The tall black oil filler tube is serving as a handy prop for the second student from the right. The crankcase oil breather can be seen on the top of the valve cover. (General Motors)

Left: That this is a third-series 270 engine is evidenced by the presence of both the shallow oil pan and the crankcase vent affixed to the top of the valve cover. Atop the oil filler pipe is an air filter, cleaning the air drawn into the crankcase. The oil dipstick enters the side of the block, just to the rear of the oil filler pipe. (General Motors)

Below: A conveyor line is feeding cylinder heads to the engine machine shop at GMC's Pontiac plant. Stacked in the background are hundreds of cylinder-blocks and cylinder heads. (General Motors)

GMC workers are machining cylinder heads on the engine-assembly line. Extensive use was made of roller conveyors to move assemblies from point to point. (General Motors)

A worker treats cylinder-head assemblies with a spray gun. His grease-covered apron suggests he was applying oil to the assemblies. (General Motors)

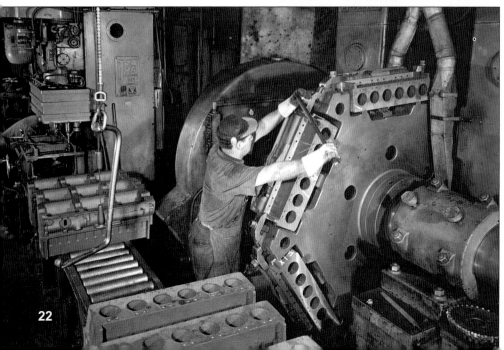

The bottleneck in production of the 270 engine at Plant 4 was limited machining capacity. In late 1941, 449 people labored in this facility building all of the GMC engines. (General Motors)

As the war wore on, the machining capacity itself was limited not only by limits of machine tool time, but also an ever-diminishing number of experienced laborers. (General Motors)

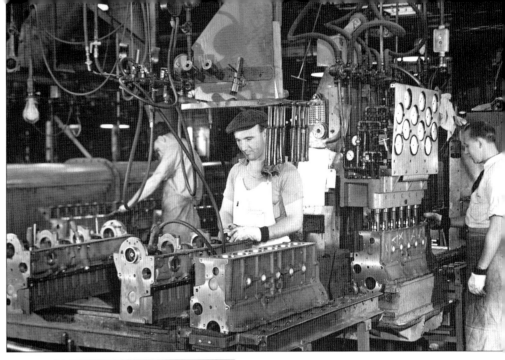

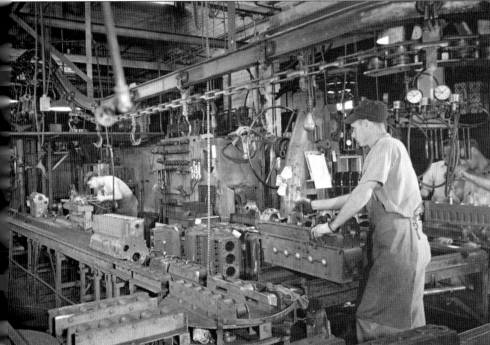

Machining of cylinder blocks is being undertaken on the line. In addition to the roller conveyors, there is an overhead, chain-driven conveyor with hooks. (General Motors)

A workers uses a press to install timing gears on camshafts. Camshaft gears have been installed on the camshafts on the rack to the left of center but not on the camshafts in the foreground. (General Motors)

GMC workers are machining pistons at the engine machine shop. Scores of pistons are visible, lined up to the left. (General Motors)

A series of check gauges on the table in front of him, an inspector checks the tolerances on 270 camshafts with a dial indicator. (General Motors)

In the crankshaft-assembly area, the machinist to the left is working on an assembly. More crankshafts are on the conveyor to the left, standing up on the floor to the right, and in racks in the center background. (General Motors)

An inspector checks crankshaft assemblies. The parts had to be checked for proper shape and dimensions and to make sure there were no previously undiscovered defects. He has a gauge in his hand and is checking the size of the journals. (General Motors)

Left: Workers are preparing engine blocks on the east end of the GMC engine assembly line. Hanging from hooks on the overhead conveyor are intake-manifold and exhaust-manifold assemblies. (General Motors)

Below: On this part of the engine assembly line, machinists are assembling bearing caps and engine blocks. The clutch housings have been installed on the rear ends of the three cylinder blocks between the two closest workers. (General Motors)

25

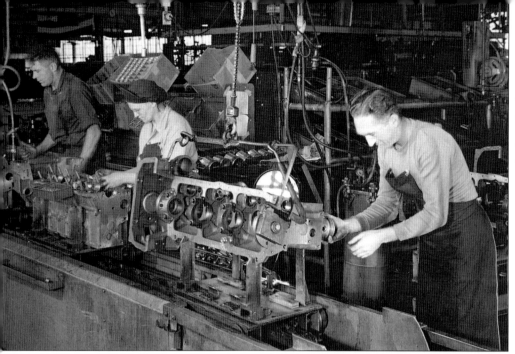

Workers are installing pistons and rods in cylinder blocks. The man to the right has a piston in his hand and is pushing it into the forward cylinder of a cylinder block lying on its side. (General Motors)

Right: A man lowers a crankshaft assembly into a cylinder block using an overhead hoist. Attached to the rear end of the crankshaft is the clutch flywheel, which will fit into the clutch housing. (General Motors)

Below: Cylinder block/clutch housing assemblies roll down a conveyor on the engine assembly line. The crankshafts and the flywheels have been installed in them and this man appears to be tightening the main bearing caps. In the background are work benches, parts bins, and one man's lunch bucket. (General Motors)

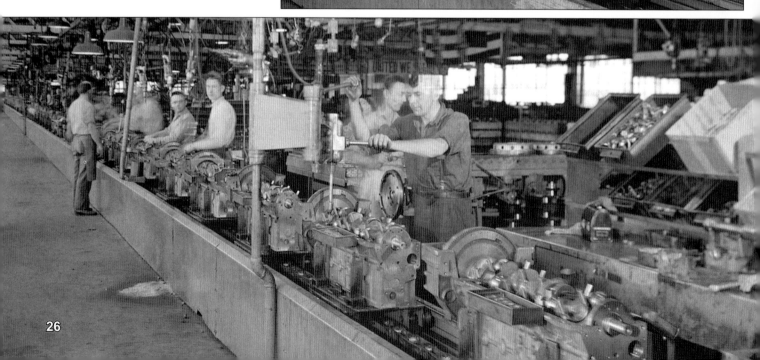

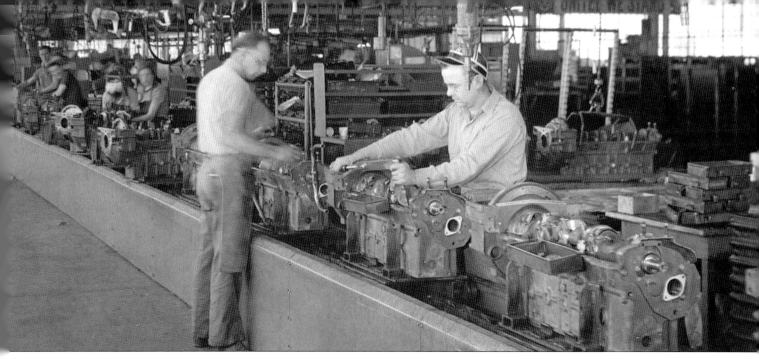

Above: A worker uses a torque wrench to tighten the main bearing caps. Timing gear housings have been installed on the fronts of the three closest cylinder blocks. In the background is a morale-boosting banner that reads, "United we stand." (General Motors)

Left: An assembly line worker installs a camshaft into the front end of a cylinder block. His left hand is holding the camshaft gear. On the rack to his right are stored a number of camshaft / camshaft-gear assemblies ready for installation. (General Motors)

After assembly the engines were sent through this second-floor paint booth, where they were given a coat of GMC's characteristic olive green. Not to be confused with the U.S. Army's olive green, GMC engine paint was glossy, and a notably different color. (General Motors)

Engines are nearing the end of the Yellow Truck and Coach assembly line. To the right the blocks have just had pistons installed. The engines in the foreground have been reversed, revealing the data plates on their sides. At center of the photo is the station where the heads are being installed. (General Motors)

The full extent of the assembly line on the top floor of Building 20 at GMC's Pontiac, Michigan, plant is in view, facing east. The engines in the foreground are nearing completion, although components such as carburetors and generators not yet installed. (General Motors)

Workers appear to be using L D Naptha, contained in the drums at left, to remove paint overspray from the data plates and the grooves of the pulleys of freshly painted engines. Presumably this approach was less costly than a laborious masking/unmasking process. (General Motors)

Above: Much of the engine sub assembly was done on the upper floors of plant three, but once largely complete the engines were sent via conveyor downstairs, where they were stored (banked, in GM terms) temporarily pending final assembly. The engine subassembly surge point is shown here. This operation is performed prior to most of the engine accessories, thus the engine with accessories was a multitude of colors. (General Motors)

Right: Starting with CCKW GMC serial number 321078 in February 1944, late-type GMC 270 3431 engine was installed in CCKWs. A key feature of this engine was the late-type, cast-iron Zenith Model 30B11 carburetor. Affixed to the lower part of the engine block was the serial-number plate. The 270 governor, the metallic device mounted directly under the carburetor, is clearly visible. (National Archives via Jim Gilmore)

Chapter 3
The CCKWX

With an established, reliable powerplant available in the form of the GMC 270, Yellow Truck and Coach responded to the government's invitation for bid number 398-41-7 with a redesigned truck.

Since GM's model designations include design year in their coding, the old-1939 code ACKWX (A – 1939 model year; C – conventional cab; K – selective front wheel drive; W – driven tandem axles; X – nonstandard [Timken] driveline; 353 chassis code) gave way to CCKWX. This reflected the 1941 model designation, code C, vs. the 1939 model designation of the ACKWX.

But the engine change and the model number change were not what the casual observer would notice upon approaching the truck. Rather, the extensively revised front-end sheet metal would draw attention to itself. While the cab appeared unchanged, since GMC continued to use a Chevrolet closed cab, there were some minor differences. The cab used on the ACKWX was the Chevrolet 984, while the CCKWX used the 1574 cab, which had a redesigned cowl. Chief among the visible differences between the two was the total absence of chrome trim on the latter. More noticeable was the newly-designed front clip, with the CCKWX introducing simplified fenders, a flat grille, and a nearly flat, rear-hinged hood. The new model was also ever so slightly longer than the old ones, the wheelbases of both the long and short trucks being increased two inches, from 162 and 143 inches for the ACKWX to 164 and 145 inches for the CCKWX. Whereas the later CCKW used different model suffixes, -352 and -353, to differentiate between these wheelbases, no such distinction was made for the CCKWX, all of which were simply CCKWX-353 models.

The responses for the invitation for bid were opened on 20 July 1940, and on 2 August contract W-398-QM-8266 was awarded by the Quartermaster Corps to Yellow Truck and Coach. This contract, worth almost $13 million, was for 5,948 of the new trucks.

At this point it is probably worthwhile to consider how vehicle production is viewed. The military tends to look at things from a contract point of view – and the contract specifies how a vehicle is to be equipped, a consideration that, in turn, is driven by its eventual use. The vehicle enthusiast tends to be interested in serial numbers or registration numbers. For Yellow Truck and Coach, however, the important number was the sales order number, most often referred to as the "TC number." Once Yellow Truck and Coach's way of looking at things as outlined above is understood, it makes these trucks' history clearer.

These numbers, which were issued after analyzing the contract,

A bevy of CCKWX trucks, along with the entire 3rd Division and 41st Division, pass in review at Fort Lewis, Washington on 7 May 1941. (General Motors)

grouped trucks into common lots. Then, both purchased components, such as Timken-Detroit axles, frames, winches, and Chevrolet cabs, were scheduled to arrive at the Yellow Truck and Coach plant, and the assembly line, in the proper quantities and at the proper time for efficient production. During the time period under discussion, it was Yellow Truck and Coach's practice to project material requirements 90 to 120 days in advance, and to release this material every 30 days.

Thus, on 15 August, just after the awarding of contract W-398-QM-8266, five sales order numbers were generated to encompass the 5,948 trucks on the contract. The contract, by the way, stipulated that GM would incur a financial penalty if these trucks were not shipped by 31 December 1940. To tie the "TC" numbers, which were vital to GM, to the serial numbers more familiar to the enthusiast, we need only look at the early CCKWX manual, GM publication X-14102. From it, we can learn the following:

TC61572 was issued for 4,160 long-wheelbase cargo trucks, serial numbers 001 through 4160, at $2,090.28 each.

TC61573 covered 298 short-wheelbase cargo trucks, serial numbers 4161 through 4326 at $2,126.85 each.

TC61574 provided for 1,316 long-wheelbase cargo trucks with winch, serial numbers 4327 to 5642, at $2,367.83 each.

TC61575 was for 135 short-wheelbase cargo trucks with winch, serial numbers 5643 to 5777, at $2,404.40 each.

TC61576 was for 171 long-wheelbase trucks with fuel tanker beds, serial numbers 5778 through 5948, at $2,505.21 each.

It may seem counterintuitive that the short-wheelbase models were more expensive than the long-wheelbase cargo trucks, but the contract specified that the short-wheelbase trucks, destined for use as artillery prime movers, be equipped with the more expensive high-traction differential gears, which limited slip.

All of these trucks would be built on Chassis Assembly Line #2 (of a total of three assembly lines) in the Yellow Truck and Coach plant. This line was converted in September 1940 for exclusive government 6x6 production. This conversion aimed at meeting the delivery requirements specified in the contract, which called for delivery of the trucks to begin on 6 October at a rate of at least 40 per day. By 30 October, 332 trucks had been built, as production was ramping up. By 4 November, 276 additional trucks had been completed. A further 700 trucks were built during the week of 4-8 November, thereafter the CCKWXs were built at a rate of 160 per day, working five days per week, except for the week of Thanksgiving. As a reslut, the 5,948 trucks were completed by 20 December. As a sidenote, also in December production began of 1,000 of the "older" ACKW-353 for the British government, with 200 of those trucks being completed that month.

Also, as with so many of the orders for the 2½-ton 6x6, there was a change order issued even before the CCKWX began production. This change specified that 34 of the trucks would be completed without the cargo bed, consisting of cab and chassis only. These trucks were completed and shipped prior to 11 December 1940.

Further complicating what would seem to be an orderly production process was the receipt of another contract, W-398-8275, which was entered into the production schedule on 9 August, just one week after the first CCKWX order.

With the sales order number 61573 nicely noted on the original negative, this image illustrates one of the 298 short-wheelbase non-winch trucks on the initial CCKWX order. (General Motors)

Demand increases

The ink had scarcely dried on the initial contract for the CCKWX when four days later a second contract was issued. Whereas the first contract was a result of competitive bidding, the second contract, W-398-QM-8275, was a negotiated deal. This contract was subsequently extended, first on 10 September 1940 and then again on 27 September, until the second contract totaled an 7,239 trucks.

Yellow Truck and Coach (GMC) was able to respond quickly and efficiently to this situation, grouping sales orders for like chassis together in the production sequence in some instances.

The new Sales Order (TC) numbers, dates and vehicle quantities and types were as follows:

TC62383	9 Aug 40	298	long-wheelbase cargo
TC62384	9 Aug 40	785	short-wheelbase cargo with winch
TC20313	10 Sep 40	24	long-wheelbase cargo
TC20314	10 Sep 40	40	long-wheelbase cargo with winch
TC20315	10 Sep 40	327	short-wheelbase cargo with winch
TC22908	27 Sep 40	2,250	long-wheelbase cargo
TC22909	27 Sep 40	1,080	short-wheelbase cargo
TC22910	27 Sep 40	1,611	long-wheelbase cargo with winch
TC22911	27 Sep 40	648	short-wheelbase cargo with winch
TC22912	27 Sep 40	105	long-wheelbase tank truck
TC22913	27 Sep 40	60	long-wheelbase stake truck
TC22973		11	long-wheelbase cargo

The pilot models of the long-wheelbase cargo trucks, with and without winches, for the government were completed the week of 30 September 1940, as was an engineering pilot for the short-wheelbase winch-equipped truck.

Mass production of the CCKWX was confined solely to long-wheelbase trucks without winches until the week beginning 11 November 1940, when 25 tank trucks were built. By that time 2,083 of the long-wheelbase cargo trucks had been built, and 1,458 of the cargos had been shipped (although the first 36 were shipped without beds, and 34 of those likely became water-purification trucks).

Production of the CCKWX remained confined to only long-wheelbase, non-winch cargo trucks and tankers until the week beginning 25 November 1940. By that time, 3,478 of the cargo trucks had been built, as had 70 of the tankers, with shipments totaling 2,853 of the former and 55 of the latter.

In the week beginning 2 December 1940, production shifted from the long-wheelbase non-winch cargo vehicle to the winch-equipped variant. The non-winch trucks received serial numbers 001 through 4160, equaling the number of such vehicles ordered on the initial

The CCKWX had a significantly different front clip from its predecessor, the ACKWX, employing the model 1547 cab with a redesigned cowl, and different fenders with less bulging contours. Chrome trim was eliminated. (General Motors)

contract.

Production of the winch-equipped long-wheelbase trucks carried though the week ending Saturday, 14 December. The serial numbers assigned to the total of 1,316 trucks of this type were 4327 through 5642. These trucks were joined by 25 more tankers, produced the week ending 14 December.

The week beginning 16 December marked the final production of long-wheelbase, winch equipped vehicles purely to satisfy the original contract, with 448 trucks being assembled. The serial numbers assigned to the total of 1,316 trucks of this type were 4327 through 5642.

Also produced the same week were 166 short-wheelbase cargo trucks, serial numbers 4161 through 4326; 134 short-wheelbase winch-equipped trucks, serial numbers 5643 through 5777, and 51 tankers. The serial numbers of the tanker trucks on the first order ran from 5778 through 5948, inclusive. For reasons unknown at this time, 133 of the short-wheelbase winch-equipped trucks originally on sales order TC61575 were moved to sales order TC62384, and thus became associated with contract W-398-QM-8275.

The start of the new order

With the issuance of Contract W-398-QM-8275, every indication was being given that genuine mass production of military vehicles had begun. For perspective, prior to 1 April 1941, American Bantam had delivered just 70 jeeps, while GMC had delivered thousands of 6x6 trucks, in multiple variations of length, accessories, and body types.

The Army, naturally, had only a passing familiarity with the vehicle as compared to General Motors' experience. The relatively small contracts issued previously, many of which went to relatively small producers, apparently led the military to some unrealistic expectations about speed and flexibility in manufacturing. Such expectations would be a source of recurring problems throughout CCKW production.

An internal GM document dated 1 November 1940 detailed some of the obstacles, specifying trouble points as "…the Timken Axle and Transfer Case situation, Budd bodies, increased 270 engine production, domestic orders, export military orders and our own government defense program vehicles."

General Motors – specifically Yellow Truck and Coach – was trying

The radiator opening of the CCKWX was square, as opposed to the graceful, civilian-type radiator grille of the ACKWX. A newly designed band-iron grille/brushguard with a GMC logo at the top center protected the radiator and the service headlights and marker lamps on the fender. (General Motors)

The design of the CCKWX's cargo body was similar to that of the ACKWX, featuring a recessed toolbox in the rear cross sill, bumperettes with a tow pintle between them, recessed tail lights, and a receptacle for a power connection to a trailer. (General Motors)

to build trucks to meet the Army's contract requirements, which included financial penalties for late deliveries. The trucks would be built in a sequence that both met those delivery requirements and made for efficient, repetitive, assembly-line work. This is why the trucks were built in blocks divided by wheelbase, presence of winch, and type of body, rather than an intermixing of all of the above.

The Army had naturally enough assigned blocks of registration numbers based on contract number and vehicle type. The result today is a situation that sometimes bewilders the enthusiast, with serial numbers and registration numbers not lining up in an obvious numeric, or chronological progression. Rather the progressions are maintained within each sales order – a piece of the puzzle not available to the public (or the military).

Production of the long-wheelbase non-winch truck resumed during the week beginning 23 December 1940, with the 298 newly contracted trucks, serial numbers 5949 through 6246, on sales order TC62383 being built, as well as 342 short-wheelbase, trucks, with winch. These 342 trucks were part of Sales Order 62384, which was for a total of 785 such trucks, which would carry serial numbers 6247 through 7031.

The last week of 1940 saw the 24 long-wheelbase, no-winch cargo trucks on TC20313 built. Their serial numbers were 7032 through 7055. Also rolling off the assembly line that week were 40 long-wheelbase trucks with winch, serial numbers 7056 through 7095, as well as the strange lot of 133 short-wheelbase winch-equipped trucks now on sales order TC62384.

The following week another 443 of these trucks were finished, completing sales order TC62384. Also completed this week was sales order TC20313 for 24 long-wheelbase, no-winch models, serial numbers 7032 through 7055, and TC20314, which was for only 40 long-wheelbase with-winch trucks, serial numbers 7056 through 7095.

CCKWX production continued in the first week of 1941, with trucks being delivered against the new contract. The first 1941-production trucks were 194 winch-equipped short-wheelbase trucks, which when combined with the 133 trucks built the week before, satisfied sales order TC20315. The serial numbers for the trucks on this sales order were 7096 through 7422. Also built that week were 81 long-wheelbase trucks without winch, built against sales order TC-22908 – a sales order for 2,250 such vehicles. Production to complete this sales order (serial numbers 7423 through 9672) was maintained into the first week of March, when production shifted to winch-equipped long-wheelbase models.

Initial assembly on sales order TC22910 began during the week starting 3 March 1941, when 246 of this model were built. During each of the following weeks 425 more trucks of the type were built, followed by 420 during the week ending 24 March. Output of the 1,621 trucks on sales order TC22910, serial numbers 10753 through 12363, ended with a final 95 units during the last week of March 1941.

Only 135 of the short-wheelbase trucks on the first CCKWX order were equipped with a winch, as this one, photographed at the Yellow Truck and Coach factory, is. (General Motors)

To finish out the week, production of short-wheelbase, non-winch trucks resumed, with 305 being completed toward sales order TC22909. The following week a further 400 such trucks were built, with the final 375 of this order being completed during the week beginning Monday, 14 April. The serial numbers assigned to this sales order were 9673 through 10752.

The winch-equipped brothers of these short-wheelbase trucks were built over a three-week period, starting during the week of 14 April, when 25 trucks of the type were built. The following week 420 more left the assembly line, with the final 203 trucks of the 648 trucks called for by sales order TC22911 being finished during the week ending 28 April 1941. These trucks were assigned serial numbers 12364 through 13011.

Produced the same week as those 203 short-wheelbase winch trucks was a small order of 11 long-wheelbase, no-winch cargo trucks that were constructed on sales order TC25173. These vehicles carried serial numbers 13177 through 13188.

As these data indicate, the vehicles' serial numbers do not increment sequentially relative to manufacturing dates, but rather, are related to the sales order numbers. Nowhere is this likely to be more evident than in the two final groups of CCKWX we will discuss.

Assembly of the 105 CCKWX tanker trucks called for by sales order 22912 began during the week ending 24 March, and continued at a rate of 25 per week until the week ending 21 April 1941, when the final five were finished. These trucks were assigned serial numbers ranging from 13012 through 13116 inclusive.

Sales order 22913, on the other hand, was for 60 CCKWX vehicles equipped with stock rack bodies. These trucks began production during the week beginning 13 January 1941, during which 25 were built. A like number were constructed the following week, and the final 10 were completed during the third week, which began on 27 January. Despite being built three months earlier than the previously mentioned tankers, the stock rack trucks bore GM serial numbers 13117 through 13176.

The week beginning 28 April 1941 marked the end of CCKWX production. Despite the relatively large number of sales orders involved, mechanically these trucks were fairly similar, all being powered by a Yellow Truck and Coach-produced 270 engine, driving through a Clark five-speed overdrive transmission, and a Timken-Detroit T79 transfer case, and riding on Timken-Detroit axles, and all delivered as assembled, operable vehicles. Inside, these trucks were just like the CCKWXs built on the first contract, and had a distinct similarity to civilian models, with an ash tray, comfortable seat and commercial instrument cluster. But with the introduction of the next model, the CCKW, things would begin to change, and also get a lot more complicated.

On short-wheelbase CCKWXs, two spare tires were stored in holders referred to as clamps between the cab and the cargo body. The clamps swung downward, making it easier to access the spares. In a sleeve below the clamps was the fuel tank. (General Motors)

The winch installation on a short-wheelbase CCKWX is displayed. Winches on these vehicles were shaft-driven from the power takeoff and were useful for a variety of applications, chiefly in recovering other vehicles or in self-recovery operations. (General Motors)

Although the rear of the CCKWX was very similar to that of the ACKWX, missing from the CCKWX were the air lines and couplings on the outboard sides of the bumperettes. A round reflector was mounted on the center rear of each of the mud flaps. (General Motors)

Newly minted short-wheelbase, winch-equipped CCKWXs are lined up at the factory, ready for delivery to the Army. U.S. Army registration numbers are visible on the vehicles in the front row: left to right they are 421343, 421619, and 421625. (General Motors)

Far more common, in fact, the most dominant variant of the CCKWX, is the long-wheelbase, no-winch cargo truck, as shown in this 7 November 1940 factory photograph. (Fred Crismon collection)

Long-wheelbase CCKWXs proceed along the assembly line. Whereas short-wheelbase CCKWXs had two vertically stored spare tires in clamps, the long-wheelbase vehicles had one spare tire in a swing-down holder to left rear of the cab. (General Motors)

On the GMC assembly line, a painter sprays a fuel tank for a long-wheelbase CCKWX while the worker to the right makes adjustments to the engine. On the table in the foreground is a socket set and lock barrels for the spare-tire holders. (General Motors)

37

The fuel tank is installed on the CCKWX in the foreground, and a painter in the pit below the truck is spraying the underside. Long-wheelbase CCKWs had a single fuel tank on the right side of the frame, as opposed to the short-wheelbase fuel tank that extended from side to side. (General Motors)

Assembly-line workers make final installations on a long-wheelbase CCKWX. The man at the top is adjusting the left windshield wiper. The regulator, the air cleaner and carburetor, and the hood hold-open strut are visible. Drop cloths protect the new paint. (General Motors)

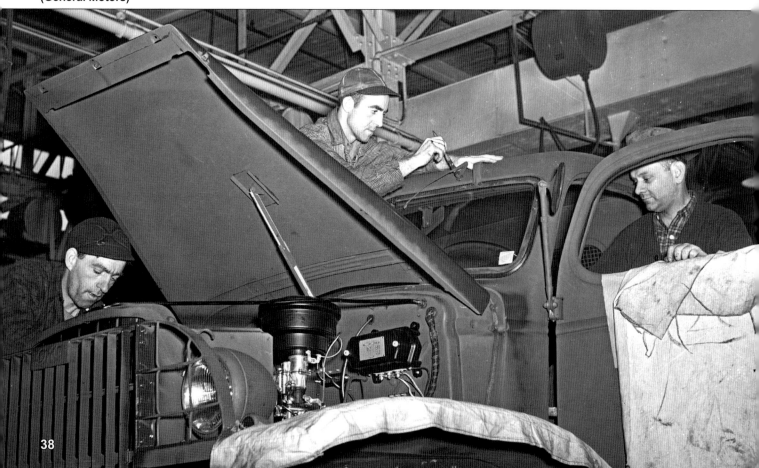

A painter uses a stencil to spray the U.S. Army registration number on a CCKWX at the GMC Truck & Coach factory. The device he is holding in his left hand prevented overspray on the hood. The dashboard with civilian instrument panel is visible. (General Motors)

CCKWX U.S.A. registration number 271739 receives some paint touchups under the front left fender. On top of the fender are the service headlight and the early-type blackout marker lamp. In raised letters on the winch gear case is "GARWOOD/DETROIT." (General Motors)

U.S. Army registration number 420866, a long-wheelbase CCKWX, is about ready for rollout. The strut for the rear-view mirror is mounted on the top hinge of the driver's door, but the mirror has not been installed yet. Stenciled on the center of the tarpaulin is "FRONT." (General Motors)

This view, like the following, was taken to show the articulation of the CCKWX suspension. Also clearly shown is the distinctive split differential housing used by the Timken-Detroit axles installed these trucks. (General Motors)

A total of 1,316 winch-equipped long-wheelbase cargo trucks like this one were included in the first contract, as compared to the 4,160 non-winch trucks sharing the same 164-inch wheelbase. (General Motors)

CCKWX registration number 421155 was a long-wheelbase version without a winch. Partially visible are the Timken axles that gave the CCKWX the "X" designation, that letter standing for a nonstandard driveline. The engine exhaust is visible below the spare tire. (General Motors)

Above: The same CCKWX is observed from the right side. From this angle, with the positioning of the driver's mirror not visible, the truck was virtually indistinguishable from an early long-wheelbase CCKW. Between the cab and the fuel tank was the battery box. (General Motors)

Right: An example of a CCKWX with the long wheelbase and a winch was U.S.A. registration number 419799. A tow chain equipped with a hook on the end, attached to the winch cable, was standard equipment for winch-equipped vehicles. (General Motors)

Left: Both the long- and short-wheelbase cargo trucks incorporated a stowage compartment beneath the tailgate at the rear of the truck. Also of interest are the reflectors, which were mounted on the rear mud guards on both the long and short-wheelbase CCKWX trucks. (General Motors)

Below: At $2,505.21 each, the most expensive of the early CCKWX were the fuel tanker trucks, like this one photographed in the snow outside the factory on the second day of December, 1940. (General Motors)

Bottom: The two tanks constituting the bed of these trucks had a combined capacity of 750 gallons of gasoline, whereas the chassis fuel tank held 40 gallons. (General Motors)

Above: Lockers at the rear of the tanker body held dispensing equipment, and as with the cargo trucks, a pintle hook was located between the rear bumperettes. (General Motors)

Right: The fuel tanks were elliptical in cross section. There was no toolbox in the cross sill, which was of a different design than that of the cargo-body CCKWX, but there were two holes in it for recessed tail light assemblies. (General Motors)

From the front, the tanker version of the CCKWX looked similar to the cargo version with the bows and tarpaulin not installed. However, the structures visible from this angle just aft of the cab were not the front of a cargo body, but separate front panels at the fronts of stowage racks for 5-gallon gas cans. (General Motors)

43

Left: On top of each tank on CCKWX tanker trucks was a filler cap. Each of the tanks had its own fuel outlet, so it could fuel two vehicles or refuel two liquid containers at a time. Two U.S.A. registration numbers are visible: 80386 and 80396. In the background are cargo trucks. (General Motors)

Below: The fuel-can stowage rack to the left side of the fuel tanks of the tanker CCKWX is visible from this angle. Stenciled on the outboard side of the "fins" atop the fuel tanks is the tanks' capacity, "375 GAL." These tanks dispensed fuel by means of gravity. (General Motors)

Bottom: This CCKWX tanker truck, photographed with a measuring stick planted next to it at what appears to be a desert proving ground, bears U.S. Army registration number 80536 on the hood. (Fred Crismon collection)

Above: As can be seen in this photo of CCKWX tanker registration number 80409, the tanker version retained the same placement of the long-wheelbase cargo truck's fuel tank and battery box, while the spare-tire clamps are as on the short-wheelbase cargo version. (Military History Institute)

Right: The arrangement of the left side of the tanker installation on the CCKWX was virtually the mirror image of that of the right side. The door of the rear storage boxes each had a piano hinge at the top. (Military History Institute)

Below: CCKWX tanker U.S. Army registration number 80409 is observed from the right rear quarter. At the center of the access door on the rear storage box on each side of the tanker was a latch-operating handle. (Military History Institute)

45

Because U.S. tanker trucks were the particular focus of enemy attacks, in the summer of 1942 plans were devised to camouflage tankers with bows and tarpaulins. A sample vehicle was converted from a CCKWX tanker by November of that year. (National Archives)

Camouflaging the CCKWX entailed installing four bow pockets to each side of the fuel tanks to hold four bows of the type used on 80-inch-wide cargo bodies. (National Archives)

Once a tarpaulin was rigged over the bows, the tanker could easily pass for a common cargo truck. As part of the modification, hooks were installed on the side sills for tying the tarpaulin lashings. (National Archives)

The "real" CCKWX cargo trucks had five bows supporting the tarpaulin, not four as were utilized with the camouflaged CCKWX tanker. However, it was believed unlikely that any enemy pilot or gunner would be sufficiently savvy to spot this minor difference. (National Archives)

A 17 November 1942 overhead view of a CCKWX tanker with the camouflage tarpaulin and bows installed reveals details of the tops of the hood and the cab, including the vent door at the center of the cowl, the hood hinges, and the slight V-shaped crease front-to-back at the center of the cab roof. (National Archives)

All 60 of the stock trucks were built in the first month of 1941, with the entire group of them being shipped during the week ending 27 January 1941. (General Motors)

CCKWX tanker trucks are being loaded from a dock onto a Liberty ship. The one in the process of being hoisted by tire slings was U.S. Army registration number 80525. The nearest one on the dock was 80518; note the pioneer tool rack on its left storage box. (General Motors)

48

It is perhaps indicative of the evolution within the U.S. army that the last batch of CCKWX production included 60 of these trucks, specially designed to transport livestock. (General Motors)

The cargo and tank trucks on the second order of CCKWX were indistinguishable from those on the first order, thus Yellow Truck and Coach did not dispatch their photographer to further document those variants. This truck, however, was representative of a new model, and was suitably photographed. (General Motors)

One of the 60 CCKWXs issued with stock racks is viewed from the front with the tarpaulin installed. The hood clamps above the service headlights were unfastened, perhaps so the hood could be raised to photograph the engine compartment. (General Motors)

One CCKWX fitted with the stock rack wore U.S. Army registration number 427946. The two ramps were fashioned from lateral wooden planks bolted to angle-iron frame members. A sliding bolt locked the two ramps together. (General Motors)

A somewhat "sexier" job was envisioned for the short-wheelbase trucks, that of artillery prime mover. All of the short-wheelbase CCKWXs were equipped with high traction differentials for this reason. The public relations department at GMC decades ago airbrushed the "GMC" moniker on the front bumper in this photo. (General Motors)

This Water Purification Unit, Mobile, M3, Model 1940, was mounted on a GMC CCKWX. This particular truck was one of a batch of 10 delivered in 1941. A total of 89 of the water purification trucks were ordered for the Corps of Engineers that year. (Chemical Corps Historian)

The water connections in these early trucks were on the side, and one is visible here just forward of and slightly above the rear side reflector. Later trucks had these connections in the rear. The large windows not only allowed light in (and, unfortunately, out) but also provided ventilation, important given that the crew was working with chlorine.

One of the lingering mysteries of CCKWX production are the 18 "wreckers" listed in the X-14102 manual. This photo, taken at Fort Holabird, shows one of the wrecker trucks, as identified by the Army registration number, which interestingly is painted in white, rather than the blue-drab that the factory used to apply registration numbers. (Military History Institute)

In early 1941 the Quartermaster Corps issued GMC contract W-398-QM-8796 for a one-off short-wheelbase CCKWX with a dump body. For this experiment, CCKWX serial number 13188 was selected. (General Motors)

This vehicle was designated the GMC CCKWX-353-L1 and was assigned U.S. Army registration number 428589. As befitted a short-wheelbase vehicle, two spare tires were stored on clamps mounted on top of the lateral gasoline tank. (General Motors)

The rear-tipping steel dump body was operated by a hydraulic cylinder. Because the vehicle was intended as a combination dump/cargo truck, the body was equipped with four pairs of bow pockets so bows and a tarpaulin could be rigged.

Chapter 4
CCKW Production Begins

By late 1940, the gathering clouds of war brought about an earnest effort to mobilize the nation's defenses. Naturally, this meant more trucks for the Army, and on 3 October 1940 a meeting was held in the Yellow Truck and Coach offices between various representatives of the company and Colonel Douglas Dow and Major Jones of the Quartermaster Corps. The Army requested this meeting in order to learn what difficulties would be encountered should the Army order a further 15,000 trucks with delivery required by 1 July 1941. This quantity would be in addition to those already on order.

To meet this demand, Yellow Truck and Coach would expect to produce 160 trucks per day. The men of Yellow Truck reported that the bottleneck in this production would be the axles supplied by the Wisconsin Axle Division of the Timken Detroit Axle Company. Not only was the capacity at Timken somewhat limited, that supply would have to be parceled out to numerous manufacturers of trucks, armored cars, and halftracks.

Less than a month later, on 29 October, Yellow Truck and Coach president Irving Babcock met with members of the management team and announced that the Army now wanted a projection of delivery of not 15,000 trucks, but 21,000 trucks by 1 July 1941. With the increase in numbers, more bottlenecks presented themselves. Budd, which supplied cargo bodies to Yellow Truck and Coach (and most

other military truck suppliers) would have difficulty supplying the needed 1,000 units weekly. Ferro Foundry, which supplied the heads for 270 engines as well as the Pontiac Foundry, which cast the block, would both struggle to meet the demand. A second source for frames, A.O. Smith, was lined up to augment Midland Steel. The axle situation, already projected at a deficit, would only become worse with the increasing demand. To overcome this hurdle, Yellow Truck and Coach looked for a second source for axles. They did not have to look far, rather only to their sister General Motors company, Chevrolet Gear and Axle.

Chevrolet produced hypoid gears almost exclusively, whereas Timken Detroit (Wisconsin) axles utilized plain spiral bevel gears. Early Army testing of all-wheel drive vehicles with hypoid gears was not successful, but GM engineers determined that those problems were caused by a lack of understanding on the part of other vehicle manufacturers. Those manufacturers used rear axle gear sets and simply reversed them – unfortunately the differential gear teeth themselves are manufactured so that they are to be driven on a particular side. By reversing the gear set, the teeth were then being driven on the wrong side, which lead to excessive wear and premature failure.

Chevrolet addressed this in its front axle design by using rear axle gears with the pinion rotation reversed and turning them upside down. This was then coupled to a transfer case that turned the front

Under the first contract for the CCKW, W-398-QM-9095, GMC produced a number of sales orders for 6x6 trucks; they had a mix of Timken and Chevrolet axles, and 33 of them had cargo bodies. This example, CCKW-353-A1 U.S.A. registration number 432344, was part of order number 200014; the A1 suffix indicated it had no winch (A) and had Timken axles (1). (General Motors)

driveshaft in a direction opposite of the rear driveshafts. The result of these changes was that the driving force was applied to the proper side of each gear tooth, and front differential life was then equal to that of the rear.

In anticipation of higher demand, Yellow Truck and Coach produced a pilot vehicle with Chevrolet transfer case and axles that was scheduled for testing by the Quartermaster Corps at Camp Holabird. This testing was to begin 25 November 1940, with the Army to give approval within 12 days, but no later than 7 December 1940.

On 26 November 1940 contract W-398-QM-9095 for 12,000 trucks was awarded to Yellow Truck and Coach. When company president Ira Babcock returned from Washington on 18 November, a meeting was held to further plan the 1941 production of the 6x6, which by then could no longer be considered non-standard, so the "X" was dropped from the model designation, with the vehicles becoming simply CCKW. The plan, as outlined in the 18 November meeting, was to produce 1,200 trucks per week, starting with the first week of March 1941. The parts to build these trucks would begin arriving in January, beginning with axles from Timken. In February Chevrolet axle deliveries would begin, at the rate of 250 sets per week. All of the Chevrolet axles at that time, as well as five out of six of the Timken axles, were to be equipped with high-traction gear sets. The axles equipped with high traction gears were to be used in all short-wheelbase trucks (and in later years, in the DUKW as well). As production shifted to long-wheel base trucks, obviously the axle delivery schedule was adjusted accordingly.

The articulation required within a driven front axle poses a special problem for vehicle designers – a simple universal joint will not suffice, as such a joint induces a change in velocity between the driven shaft and the driving shaft. If such a joint were actually used, the result would be a loss of control by the driver. Driven front axles must

instead use constant-velocity joints. Regardless of whether equipped with Timken or Chevrolet axles, the CCKW uses Bendix-Weiss style constant-velocity joints, but for a small group of about 3,000 trucks that utilized axles equipped with Rzeppa constant-velocity joints. Those axles feature an identification plate reading "Rzeppa."

Ironically, the very problem that the constant velocity joint eliminated was deliberately reintroduced, on a limited scale, in the high-traction differentials. A standard automotive differential transmits the power to the wheel with the least resistance to rotation, meaning that with one wheel on ice or in mud, and the other on dry surface, one wheel spins while the other does nothing and the vehicle does not move.

High-traction differential gear sets used in the CCKW, whether Chevrolet or Timken, utilize gear teeth cut with a very peculiar profile so that the roll ratio varies as the tooth profile goes in and comes out of mesh with the mating component – a situation which in normal circumstances would be considered an imperfect gear. This imperfection creates a torsional vibration within the axle that eventually makes the stationary wheel rotate.

The long- and short-wheelbase trucks finally got unique model designations (previously all the trucks of this general type had been designated CCKWX-353). The short-wheelbase trucks were designated CCKW-352, while the long-wheelbase trucks were CCKW-353. As before, Yellow Truck and Coach tended to classify the vehicles by their contract paragraph. The breakdown of the 12,000 vehicle order was as follows:

CCKW-353 long wheelbase, no winch, contract item1A - 5200
CCKW-352 short wheelbase, no winch, contract item 1B - 2800
CCKW-353 long wheelbase, with winch, contract item 1C - 1200
CCKW-352 short wheelbase, with winch, contract item 1D - 2800

The CCKW-353-A1 was a long-wheelbase (164 inches) vehicle with the model 1574 cab, the same cab used on the CCKWX. In fact, aside from the registration number on the hood, this vehicle was virtually indistinguishable from a CCKWX. (General Motors)

This order stood until 16 December 1940, when substantial changes were made, with the total increasing to 14,000 trucks. The modified order called for the following:

CCKW-353 long wheelbase, no winch, contract item 1A - 6000
CCKW-352 short wheelbase, no winch, contract item 1B - 3250
CCKW-352 short wheelbase, with winch, contract item 1D - 3250
CCKW-353 long-wheelbase tanker, no winch, contract item 1E - 1500

On 16 December 1940 Yellow Truck and Coach ordered 2,333 sets of axles from Chevrolet. Chevrolet would not be able to produce these axles until March, timing that required a change in Yellow Truck's production schedule. Midland Steel promised to start delivering the special frames required for the Chevrolet axles on 22 February 1941.

All of these issues were compounded on 23 December 1940 when the order was increased for a third time, with the total to be 28,000 trucks. Once again, the makeup of the order changed too. With this revision, the make up was:

CCKW-353 long wheelbase, no winch, contract item 1A - 11000
CCKW-352 short wheelbase, no winch, contract item 1B - 8250
CCKW-353 long wheelbase, with winch, contract item 1C - 4000
CCKW-352 short wheelbase, with winch, contract item 1D - 4750

Chevrolet's axle order was increased to 4,667 sets, and it was planned that all of these would be installed on long-wheelbase no-winch trucks. This greatly simplified production planning on the part of Yellow Truck and Coach by requiring only one additional frame type, and one new style of driveshaft set. Unfortunately, this plan soon fell apart.

Further, it was planned to allocate all of the high-traction Timken axles to the short-wheelbase trucks on this order. In order to execute this demanding production job, extensive revisions were made to the production plan. Production control manager R. A. Crist issued a memo on 31 December 1940, which contained the following information:

"With this memo we are delivering to you a revised chart covering the program on our 6x6 and 6x4 Government and British vehicles. This chart supersedes the one previously handed to you which should now be destroyed. This information is confidential."

"This new chart covers a total of 41,188 U.S. Government 6x6 Trucks; 1000 British 6x6s; 320 British 6x4 Searchlight jobs; and 149 U.S. Government 6x4 Searchlight jobs – making a total of 42,657 vehicles using the multiple wheel drive axles and transfer cases in the 6x6 type."

"Your attention is directed to the following points:

"(1) Orders have been placed with Chevrolet for a total of 4667 sets of transfer cases and high traction differential type axles, of which the first 2333 are to because on contract item 1-a, which the second order of 2334 is to be applied to item 1-b.

"(2) Only high traction differential type axles can be used in the short-wheelbase jobs; i.e., items 1-b and 1- d.

"(3) In order to fit the combined schedule of Timken high traction and standard gear axles and Chevrolet high traction axles to this new production program, using only high traction type in the short wheelbases and limiting the use of Chevrolet units to two models, it has been necessary to make a definite allocation of the weekly production of all three types of axles to the several different types of vehicles. We have tried to show this clearly on the chart, but if it is not clear to anyone, we will try to explain it so that there will be no chance for misunderstanding."

All the while these contracts were being issued, and production plans finalized, the Yellow Truck and Coach plant was building

On an early CCKW-353, the manner in which the tarpaulin was lashed to the steel body is exhibited. This also illustrates another of the many tread pattern tires that were mounted on these trucks. (General Motors)

CCKWX vehicles for the U.S. Army. These trucks, by contract, required Timken axles, with no stipulation for using the Chevrolet unit. This requirement created the situation outlined as point 6 of Crist's New Year's Eve memo:

"(6) It will also be noted that since Chevrolet axles and transfer cases are only to be applied to the new contract for 28,000 units, it will be necessary to build 200 trucks per week using the Chevrolet material against new contract during the month of March before the first contracts totaling 13,188 are completed. Thus, there will be an overlapping for four weeks of old and new specification vehicles."

Thus we see that during the month of March both the CCKWX and the CCKW were being built concurrently.

As we have previously discussed, Yellow Truck and Coach's sales order, or "T.C." number, was the guiding force for the production department. Sales order numbers for the 28,000 vehicle contract were assigned as follows:

4,750 CCKW-352 Short wheelbase, with winch, contract item 1D; TC-200017

3,990 CCKW-353 Long wheelbase, with winch, contract item 1C; TC-200016, all with Timken axles.

10 CCKW-353 Long wheelbase, with winch, contract item 1C; diverted to GM Export TC-15986-15995

8,250 CCKW-352 Short wheelbase, no winch, contract item 1B; TC-200015

The trucks on sales order TC-200015 were further divided, with 5,416 of these CCKW-352s having Timken axles and the remaining 2,834 trucks having Chevrolet axles. To distinguish the type of drivetrain, Yellow Truck and Coach assigned suffixes to the serial numbers, with A1 designating Timken axles, and A2 indicating Chevrolet axles. Winch-equipped trucks were assigned similar suffixes, B1 and B2, indicating axle type. Serial numbers CCKW-352-24189-A1 through CCKW-352-26522-A1, inclusive, were assigned to the Timken axle-equipped trucks, while CCKW-352-26523-A2

through CCKW-352-32438-A2 were used with the Chevrolet-axle trucks.

Making up the biggest group of trucks, however, were the 11,000 CCKW-353 no-winch vehicles, which were divided onto five sales orders:

TC-200096 covered 1,000 trucks with Chevrolet axles boxed for export to Alexandria.

TC-200150 covered 446 trucks with Timken axles for British Ministry of War Transport.

TC-200017 covered 33 trucks with Chevrolet axles, these trucks were completed with stake rack bodies rather than cargo bodies.

TC-200014 covered 9,520 trucks, 2,332 with Chevrolet axles and 7,188 with Timken axles. Of the trucks with Chevrolet axles, 1,072 were to be boxed for shipment, two unit pack, to Rangoon.

TC-200152 was for a single truck with Chevrolet axles, which Yellow's Engineering department converted to the pilot CCW 6x4.

Serial numbers CCKW-353-13189-A2 to CCKW-353-15521-A2, inclusive, were given to the long-wheelbase no-winch trucks with Chevrolet axles. These trucks carried registration numbers W-429270 through W-431602. The trucks with Timken axles were given serial numbers CCKW-353-15522-A1 through CCKW-353-24188-A1 inclusive, and registration numbers W-431603 through W-440236.

Like the CCKWX, all of these trucks featured the Chevrolet 1574 closed cab, except for 10 winch-equipped long-wheelbase Chevrolet -axle-equipped vehicles, which used the 1608 closed cab. These trucks carried registration numbers 452211, 452353, 452358, 452404, 452431, 4524335, 452466, 452483, 452490, and 452492. They are something of an anomaly, being produced much later (November 1941) than the other vehicles on sales order TC-200207 so to replace the 10 trucks diverted to GM Export from the original order.

But for these 10 trucks, all the vehicles contracted on W-398-QM-9095 were delivered prior to 20 August 1941.

The rear of an early CCKW-353 with split axles is shown. The U.S. Army registration number, 432344, is visible on the tailgate through the lashings below the tarpaulin. Details of the tread pattern are visible. (General Motors)

Right: In a frontal view of CCKW-353-A1 U.S.A. registration number 432344, the front Timken axle is clearly visible. Also in view is the rear-view mirror mounted on the upper hinge of the driver's door, a characteristic of the model 1574 cab. (General Motors)

Below: CCKW-353-A1 U.S. Army registration number 432525 is displayed without the bows and tarpaulin installed. This vehicle was equipped with Timken axles. (General Motors)

The same vehicle is viewed from the left rear. The flexible jackets fitted over the tailgate chains reduced the noise from chains clanging on the body and helped prevent paint chipping by the chains. (General Motors)

This CCKW-352-A1, registration number 443041, was part of GMC order number 200015. The cab remained the model 1574. As per the 352 designation, this was a short-wheelbase (145 inches) vehicle. (General Motors)

Left: GMC CCKW-352-A1 registration number 443041 is viewed from the right rear. CCKWs with winches received a B suffix, and those with Chevrolet axles had a 2 suffix. Of the CCKWs produced under GMC order number 200015, 5,416 were built with Timken axles and 2,834 had Chevrolet banjo axles. (General Motors)

Bottom: The model 1574 cab's positioning of the driver's rear view mirror on the top hinge of the door is clearly in view. The spare-tire clamps behind the cab of the short-wheelbase CCKWX carried over to the short-wheelbase CCKWs, as did the lateral fuel tank below the tire clamps. (General Motors)

In contrast to the tires seen earlier on CCKW-353-A1 U.S.A. registration number 432344, a different style of directional-tread tires was mounted on CCKW-352-A1 registration number 443041. (General Motors)

A specimen truck that GMC elected to photograph to represent order number 200016 was CCKW-353-B1 registration number 448813. This order comprised long-wheelbase vehicles with a 144-inch Budd-type cargo body, a front winch, and Timken axles. (General Motors via Bryce Sunderlin)

CCKW-353-B1 U.S. Army registration number 448813 is observed from the front. Under order number 200016, 4,000 CCKW-353-B1s were produced. These vehicles retained the model 1574 cab. The vertical sides of the winch-cable cutout in the bumper were rounded so the cable would not snag on them. (General Motors)

Right: The extended space between the front bumper and the front tires of winch-equipped trucks is shown in this view of CCKW-352 registration number 452775. (General Motors)

Below: CCKW-353-B1 registration number 448813 is observed from the right side. There were interruptions in the Army registration numbers for CCKW-353-B1s, representing ten long-wheelbase vehicles with winches diverted to G.M. Export. (General Motors)

Bottom: Another example from contract W-398-QM-9095 was CCKW-352-B1 U.S. Army registration number 452775, which was from GMC order number 200017, which included 4,750 short-wheelbase vehicles with Timken axles and a winch. (General Motors)

Left: On the first-contract short-wheelbase CCKWs and on subsequent orders of them, a feature that was not visible to the eye was high-traction gears in the differentials. This grew out of a November 1940 directive that all short-wheelbase CCKWs receive high-traction differentials. (General Motors)

Below: This photo and the following two document a CCKW-352-B1 from GMC order 200017 with no body installed. An army registration number was not painted on the vehicle. A front-mounted winch was standard on the CCKWs of this order number. (General Motors)

With no body installed, an excellent view is offered of the spare tire clamps and the lateral fuel tank of the short-wheelbase CCKW. The clamps were mounted on a sleeve-type enclosure in which the fuel tank rested. Details of the frame also are visible. (General Motors)

The inboard tire-clamp structures had triangular gussets at the bottom to reinforce their junction with the sleeve around the fuel tank. The top of the fuel tank is visible through the three round holes in the sleeve. (General Motors)

The Timken axle, left, as seen from the front was also called the split axle because of the joint between the halves of the differential housing. The Chevrolet axle, also called the corporation or banjo axle, had a round front with raised cross-hatching.

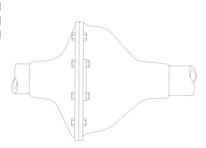
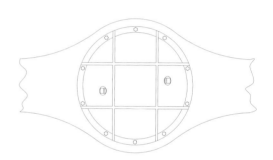

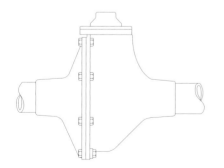
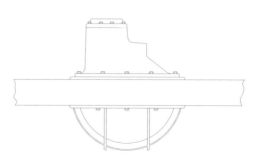

The differential housings of the Timken axle, left, and the Chevrolet axle, right are compared as viewed from above, with the flanges for the drive shaft to the top.

From the first CCKW contract on, the differentials of the long-wheelbase vehicles had standard gears, as shown to the left. In November 1940, a directive called for all short-wheelbase CCKWs to be equipped with high-traction gears, as shown to the right.

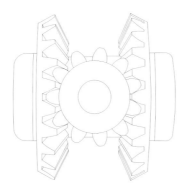 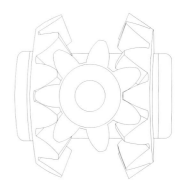

The tandem axles of a short-wheelbase vehicle from the first CCKW contract are viewed with the body removed. These are Chevrolet "banjo" or "corporation" axles, and would have been equipped with the high-traction gearing. To the lower right is the coil spring of the tow pintle assembly. (General Motors)

The same tandem axles and suspension are viewed from another angle. Two drive shafts separated by a pillow block mounted on the front tandem axle powered the rear tandem axle, permitting a drive-shaft configuration in the shape of a shallow V to get around the obstruction formed by the front tandem axle. (General Motors)

CCKWs equipped with Chevrolet axles also received a transfer case entirely different from the one used with Timken axles, and the two units were not interchangeable. Here, transfer cases for use with Chevrolet axles are under construction at Chevrolet's Toledo, Ohio, plant. (National Archives)

Right: This photo of a long-wheelbase CCKW of GMC order number 200014 was originally captioned to indicate that Goodrich tires (Silvertowns, on close inspection) were installed. These tires had one of several directional tread patterns seen on first-contract CCKWs. (General Motors)

Below: A long-wheelbase CCKW chassis is viewed from the right side. The tires were U.S. Special Service Master Grips, size 7.50-20. The battery, its box cover not installed, lies exposed to the front of the fuel tank. (General Motors)

A view into the left rear corner of the engine compartment of a first-contract CCKW-353 includes the Delco-Remy regulator to the right, which controlled the generator's voltage, and, toward the left, the carburetor and air cleaner. (General Motors)

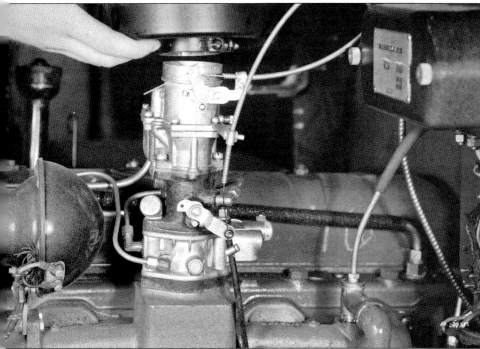

In this photo, the air cleaner has been detached from the top of the carburetor and is being held in place. The carburetor type was the Zenith downdraft, a double-venture design that maintained the correct depression ratio between the carburetor intake and the fuel bowl. (General Motors)

The right side of the engine compartment of a first-contract CCKW-353 is displayed. At the bottom is the distributor, above which is the ignition coil. Between the ignition coil and the oil cleaner at the bottom right are the dipstick and the oil-filler neck. (General Motors)

The following sequence of photos documents the process of boxing CCKWs for shipment overseas using procedures developed by the Army and major truck manufacturers by March 1942. Here, workers lift a steel cargo body from a first-contract CCKW-353. A very faint U.S. Army registration number, 432773, is on the hood. (General Motors)

Above: A steel cargo body is being hoisted from another first-contract CCKW-353. The registration number on the hood is indistinct but appears to be 432757. (General Motors)

Left: Workers are preparing steel cargo bodies for shipping. The procedure was to place one bed on its bottom and place another bed, oriented the other way and upside down, to straddle the lower bed. Then they were bundled together with steel strapping. (General Motors)

GMC workers are lifting a model 1574 cab from the frame of a CCKW. The vehicle's nomenclature plate has been tied to the grille: standard procedure when preparing a vehicle for boxing. (General Motors)

A model 1574 cab is being hoisted from a CCKW prior to boxing for shipment. Boxing trucks for shipment overseas both protected the vehicles from damage and allowed more units to be loaded in ships because the boxes could be stacked. (General Motors)

A GMC model 1574 cab is being prepared for boxing for shipment overseas. The regulator has been detached from the firewall and stored with other components in a box, and the wiring harness, starter and speedometer cables, oil-gauge line, and other lines will be reconnected during reassembly. (General Motors)

Two model 1574 cabs comprising a pack are sitting face-to-face on the wooden base of a box resting on a roller conveyor. The sides and top of the box will be installed soon. The civilian-style instrument panel is visible through the side window of the closer cab. (General Motors)

The ends and one side of a box for the two nearest cabs are installed. In the background, a workman stands next to a long box containing a CCKW chassis. In the left of that box, a louvered hood side panel is visible. (General Motors)

The chassis of a CCKW-353 earmarked for shipment is being readied for boxing. The tires are all mounted now but will be removed and stored on top of the chassis frame during the boxing process. (General Motors)

A CCKW-353 chassis is secured to the base of a box. Two-by-four legs support the front bumper, and steel strapping and blocking hold the frame and axles in place. The vehicle's nomenclature plate is affixed to the left headlight brush guard. (General Motors)

A CCKW-353 chassis is lowered to the base of a box in preparation for shipment. All of the tires, including the spare, have been dismounted and are strapped to the top of the chassis frame. Lying on the base of the box is the steering gearbox and shaft. (General Motors)

The fuel tank has been dismounted from the chassis and is secured to the base of the box to the front of the forward tandem axle. Cardboard served to keep the steel strapping from cutting into the tires. (General Motors)

Right: Carpenters in the foreground are fabricating a wooden assembly for a box while the carpenters in the background are installing the sides of a shipping box for a CCKW. The first U.S. Army specification for boxing trucks was ES-595 of 18 June 1941. Based on lessons learned, various revised specifications followed. (General Motors)

Below: A shipping box for a CCKW chassis is complete, and painters are spraying stenciled markings on the side. As seen on the box to the lower left, the markings included the dimensions, gross, tare, and net weights, and "Q.M.L.I. No 1/ CCKW-353." (General Motors)

Two CCKW steel cargo bodies are banded together as a bundle and are resting on a trolley prior to shipment. CCKW steel bodies, unlike cab and chassis assemblies, were sturdy and stackable enough to be shipped without boxing. They were shipped with two bodies secured to each other with steel strapping, with one body set upside down on the other and straddling it. (General Motors)

In a vintage color photo of a mechanic servicing the engine of a CCKW, the blackout marker light on the fender outboard of the headlight is the blue-louvered type that was used on CCKWs up to chassis number 41189, which, according to available data, included all trucks in contract QM-9095. (Library of Congress)

Some CCKW steel cargo-body bundles are loaded on edge on a railroad car while other dual-body units rest on the platform in the foreground. These units were arranged with one body turned in the opposite orientation from the other. (General Motors)

These two-body bundles are loaded into railroad cars flat instead of on edge as seen in the preceding photo. On the far end of the nearest body is the rear cross sill, with the housings for the tail light assemblies and the electrical receptacle visible. (General Motors)

GMC sales order 200015 included two chemical-tank CCKWs, including this one, U.S. Army registration number 444365. As this truck was part of contract QM-9095, it should have had blue-louvered marker lights, but quite clearly it has the later "cat's eye" marker lamps. (General Motors)

The same chemical-tank truck is viewed from the front, displaying its Timken front axle. It was based on a short-wheelbase CCKW. (General Motors)

The rear mud flaps of the chemical-tank truck were fastened to the rear cross sill and were cut out to accommodate the rear tail lights. (General Motors)

On top of the tank of the CCKW chemical truck was a manhole cover and two fixtures that appear to have been valves, with the one to the rear smaller than the one to the front. (General Motors)

The chemical tank fit tightly to a walkway with diamond tread around the sides and rear of the tank. The tank was of welded construction, with a circumferential weld seam being present between the manhole and the forward valve. (General Motors)

Chapter 5
Chevrolet CCKWs

With Europe firmly in the grips of all-out war, another War Department contract for 6x6 trucks could hardly be considered a surprise. Such an order was placed with Yellow Truck and Coach on 29 April 1941 for a further 18,990 CCKW vehicles. Of these, 1,200 were short-wheelbase trucks with winch for Lend Lease, covered under Defense Aid contract DA-W-398-QM-1. The remaining 17,790 trucks were on contract W-398-QM-10250, which was later reissued as 374-ORD-2724. Delivery on this order was to start in early October 1941, and to be complete by the end of the year. This order overwhelmed the 1,200-truck-per-week production capacity of Yellow Truck and Coach's Pontiac, Michigan, plant. The company was already struggling to maintain its truck and bus production for its normal commercial markets, while satisfying the demand for military trucks placed by the U.S. as well as overseas governments.

To overcome this problem, Yellow Truck and Coach again turned to Chevrolet, negotiating with Chevrolet Central Office for the assembly of 5,990 long-wheelbase no-winch cargo trucks in the Chevrolet – St. Louis plant. This arrangement, while approved by the government, was strictly between the GM divisions. In the eyes of the War Department, Yellow Truck and Coach was delivering the trucks – therefore, there are no CCKWs with Chevrolet nameplates. While the agreement in principle for this work was reached between Yellow Truck and Coach and Chevrolet in May, it would be 3 September 1941 before it was formalized via Yellow Truck and Coach purchase order A-59889, issued to Chevrolet.

The 17,790 U.S. government vehicles on W-398-QM-10250 were broken down as follows:

8,900 long-wheelbase trucks without winch
4,250 long-wheelbase trucks with winch
3,100 short-wheelbase trucks without winch
1,500 short-wheelbase trucks with winch
40 long-wheelbase tank trucks

In order to fulfill this plan, a new set of frame dies was created, used by the A. O. Smith Corporation in Milwaukee to manufacture frames for use in the Chevrolet – St. Louis plant. Midland Steel Products would continue to furnish frames to Yellow's Pontiac plant. Yellow Truck and Coach would issue all the purchase orders for the components used in Chevrolet production as well as its own production, and specify to the vendor what location to ship to. For example, Warner Gear would supply transmissions to Chevrolet from its works in Muncie, Indiana. Clark, however, would supply transmissions to Pontiac.

Adding the Chevrolet production facility was not without problems, a number of them unforeseen. Some of these difficulties were brought up in a 16 June 1941 meeting with Chevrolet representatives held in the office of R. A. Crist, Yellow Truck and Coach production manager. Notes from that meeting record the following:

"Several points were brought as to the differences in Chevrolet manufacturing practices and what understanding there was on this matter. Our management have simply told us that Chevrolet are expected to build our vehicle to our specifications. However, there are some minor deviations which can probably be worked out, such as the following – Chevrolet do not use Phillips head screws and do not have equipment to handle. Want to use their standard, same as they did in Oakland.

"(a)   Clutch Head Screws
"(b)   Cold Riveting vs. Hot Riveting (GMT)
"(c)   Breaking down of a crossmember into two assemblies."

A bit later the notation was made "In this connection, it should be pointed out that if we allow Chevrolet to use their slotted screws in place of our Phillips head screws a different screw driver is required for the tool kit."

The record of this meeting also includes a couple of other key points:

"(17) Serial Number Plates. GMT&C are to furnish fully stamped.

"(18) Stencils for Painting and Lettering. We (that is, Yellow Truck and Coach) assign a definite series of numbers for St. Louis and furnish

The CCKWs produced under contract W-398-QM-10250, also known as 374-ORD-2724, dated May 1941, were completed by March 1942. This example was CCKW-353 registration number 466030. (TACOM LCMC History Office)

the stencils to match these number assignments. There may be some problems in connection with painting and lettering which will have to be worked out."

The amount of material that would have to flow from Pontiac to St. Louis in order to execute this plan was staggering – and the method employed equally staggering. Once again, this is revealed in the 16 June meeting. "Material Shipments. It was agreed with Mr. Stallsmith (of Chevrolet Central Office) that we would try to ship one-half a month's shipments at one time. For the first month of October we will try and ship 750 sets by September 20th – the date we close for inventory – and the balance of 1100 sets for the first month starting October 6th and finishing October 10th."

Given the volume of material to be moved, it is not surprising that most of these shipments were made by rail. In terms of space occupied, the cargo body was the most bulky item to be moved. These bodies were build by Budd in Detroit, who supplied Yellow Truck and Coach and now also Chevrolet – St. Louis. Because of the limited storage space available in St. Louis, it was necessary to work out a day to day shipping schedule for Budd in order to neither overwhelm Chevrolet's storage nor create a shortage to occur, which would delay production.

In automotive manufacturing, what most people consider the construction of the vehicle is actually the assembly – but prior to assembly a great deal of manufacturing has to be done, engines, wiring harnesses, seats, bodies, etc., etc. All of material for these subassemblies must come together at the right time and place for production to begin, just as the subassemblies must then come together for the vehicle itself to be produced. Yellow Truck and Coach's Plant 3 in Pontiac was the Michigan CCKW assembly plant, as was Chevrolet St. Louis an assembly plant. Conversely, Yellow's Pontiac Plant 4 was an engine manufacturing plant.

In the 1940s, automobile assembly normally drew from a bank of materials stockpiled in advance of production. Period photos of the Pontiac assembly plant show acres of axles and vast warehouses filled with engines, wheels, and other subassemblies. Chevrolet St. Louis did not have the advantage of unlimited storage space, so it was determined that that plant would operate from a five-day supply, or bank, of material, including those items in transit to the plant. This of course required careful coordination not only between Chevrolet and Yellow Truck and Coach, but also between Yellow and the myriad of suppliers whose goods would be shipped directly to St. Louis.

It was planned that Chevrolet would begin CCKW production on 6 October 1941 with an average rate of 40 per day for the first week. Beginning Monday, 13 October this rate would increase to 110 per day, or 550 per week, through Christmas Eve 1941. Following this schedule, the entire lot of 18,990 trucks, including those to be built in St. Louis, would be delivered prior to 26 December 1941, at which time financial penalties of $5.00 per truck per day would be imposed by the government on that portion of the order which was unfulfilled.

The GMC 270 engine of CCKW-353-41224 from sales order number 200119, the first sales order of contract W-398-QM-10250, is viewed from the front. The light-colored fitting to the left was a holder for an oil can. The "SO 200119" scrawled on the firewall is the Yellow Truck and Coach sales order number, sometimes also listed as a TC number. From GM's point of view, this is the singularly important number, identifying all the features and equipment of the truck.(Jim Gilmore collection)

Numerous problems plagued the start of production in St. Louis, notably concerning the bills of materials, and exacerbated by the introduction of this new-type vehicle to the St. Louis workers. St. Louis fell behind from the outset, with the first truck not being completed until 10 October. A plan was floated to go to a six-day work week during November in order to catch up the deficit, but this plan ran afoul of the flow of material supply. In a 4 November letter to Chevrolet Central Office, Yellow Truck and Coach advised "...we had heard a rumor that you were going to work Saturdays and try to make up the lost week of 550 jobs. From our standpoint this is inadvisable and not necessary. There are critical shortages which might force a close-down in St. Louis if you tried to pick up those 550 jobs in November; notably, Midland frames, Budd bodies, Geometric radiator supports, our own engines, etc."

Accordingly, the St. Louis production schedule was revised so that production to fulfill contract W-398-QM-10250 would run into the week beginning 5 January 1942. Chevrolet's assembly record for this contract would stand as: 1,247 built in October 1941; 2,126 in November; 2,000 in December 1941; and 617 in January 1942. These trucks were given serial numbers CCKW-353-54224-A2 through CCKW-353-60213-A2, and registration numbers W-475306 through W-481295.

Whether assembled in Pontiac or St. Louis, all the trucks on contract W-398-QM-10250 were equipped with the type-1608 closed cab. Externally, this cab differed from the previously used 1574 only in the location of the rear-view mirror mounting, which moved from the door hinge to be affixed to the cowl itself. However, inside the cabs were much different. The 1574 cab had much the same appearance of the civilian truck cab from which it was derived, featuring an ashtray, locking glove box and doors, a civilian-pattern instrument array and Bedford cord seat coverings. The 1608 substituted more austere military-style instruments mounted in a stamped metal insert, faux leather seat covers, and dispensed with the locks and ash tray.

In May 1941 an additional small contract, number W-298-QM-10876, for CCKWs was awarded. This contract was for 1,210 trucks, 10 being CCKW-353 long-wheelbase cab and chassis without winch, built on sales order TC-200138 rolling on Timken axles. The remaining 1,200 CCKW-352 trucks were evenly divided between sales order TC-200135 for winch-equipped trucks and TC-200163 for CCKW-352 without winch, both groups equipped with Chevrolet axles.

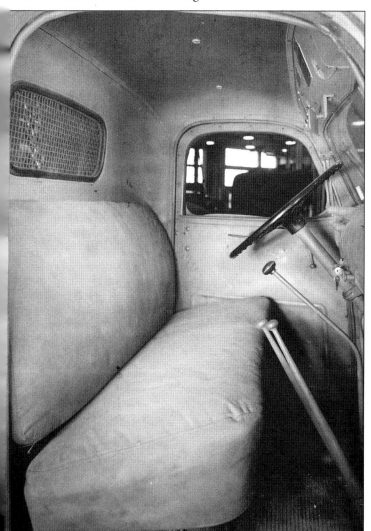

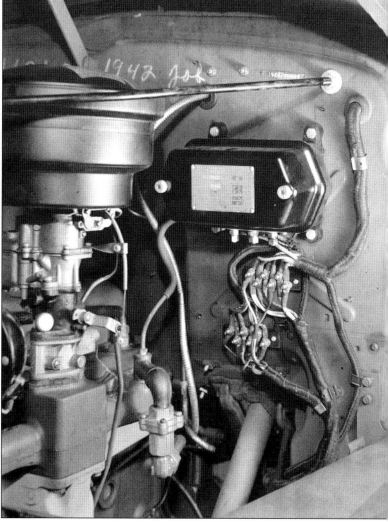

The CCKWs contracted for under W-398-QM-10250 retained the civilian-style dashboard and instrument panel. The steering wheel was the three-spoked rubber model used on early CCKWs with a horn button on the hub. (General Motors)

Mounted on the left firewall of cab serial number 1574-90003 is the Delco-Remy 6-volt, 25 amp, positive ground regulator, characteristic of the early electrical system. To the left are the air cleaner and carburetor of CCKW-353-41224. (General Motors)

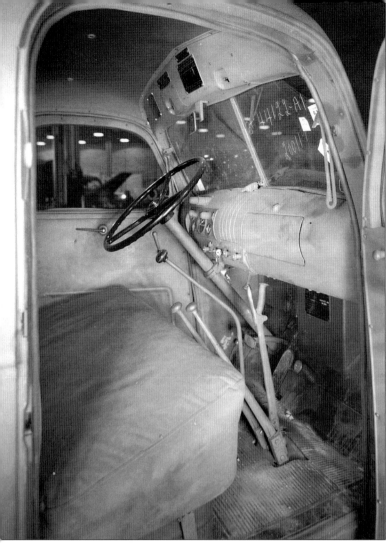

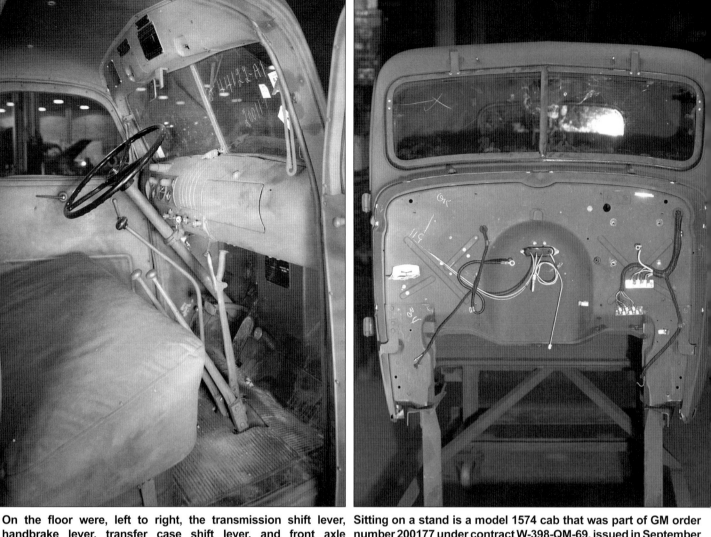

On the floor were, left to right, the transmission shift lever, handbrake lever, transfer case shift lever, and front axle engagement lever. Affixed below the center of the dashboard is the vehicle's nomenclature plate. (General Motors)

Sitting on a stand is a model 1574 cab that was part of GM order number 200177 under contract W-398-QM-69, issued in September 1941. Some of the wiring is installed, but the regulator is not yet mounted. (General Motors)

The rear tandem axle on this CCKW-353 from sales order 200119 of contract W-398-QM-10250 is the Chevrolet banjo or corporation type. The view is from the rear right of the vehicle. To the top left are the tow pintle and its coil spring. (General Motors)

The transmission, upper left, is viewed from a mechanic's pit, with a steel beam that is not part of the vehicle at the bottom. To the top right is the oil pan; also visible are the engine exhaust pipe, the steering gear, the left front spring, and, above the steel beam, the bottom of the running board and fender. Also visible is the brake master cylinder in its mount. (General Motors)

Right: CCKW-353 registration number 466455, produced under sales order 200216, was apparently a one-off concoction with a winch mounted on top of the chassis frame between the cab and the 106-inch-long cargo body. The Army ordered this truck on 3 November 1941 and it was delivered on 1 December 1941. Midship-mounted winches were typically mounted on prime movers. (General Motors)

Below: Immediately to the rear of the cab on the CCKW with the midsection-mounted winch were two spare-tire clamps. A special fuel tank was fitted below the winch and tire clamps extending from the rear of the cab to the front mud flap. (General Motors)

The Gar Wood winch mounted on the midsection of the CCKW-353 is observed from the left side, showing the chain drive of the winch, the gypsy head extending from the side of the winch in the foreground, and the left tire clamp. (General Motors)

The same CCKW-353 had the polarized cat's-eye-type marker lamps outboard of the headlights. The grille is the early model, wherein the bent tops and bottoms of the horizontal bars, which acted as flanges for welding to the grille frame, all pointed outward. (General Motors)

From the rear, the CCKW-353 with the midship winch resembled any other CCKW, except the winch wire rope protruded from above the rear crossmember and hooked to the left bumperette. These rear bumperettes are taller than those on a standard CCKW, presumably due to the winch installation. (General Motors)

The CCKW-353 with the unusual mid-mounted winch is viewed from the right rear. The purpose of placing a winch in that position was to perform winching operations to the rear, perhaps for use when emplacing artillery. (General Motors)

Long-wheelbase CCKW chassis are stored outdoors at Chevrolet's St. Louis plant. This plant completed its first CCKW on 10 October 1941. Although nearly identical, the St. Louis-produced trucks used Kelsey wheels, while on the CCKWs built in Pontiac those assemblies were made by the Motor Wheel Company. (National Archives)

Chapter 6

The CCW

As has already been seen, there existed in 1941 a critical shortage of powered front axles. Even with Chevrolet augmenting the production of Timken-Detroit Axle's Wisconsin Division, there were still too few axles available to meet the ever-growing demand for all-wheel drive vehicles. In the case of the CCKW, this situation was compounded by both International Harvester and Studebaker using the same Timken front axles in their military 6x6 programs.

It was learned that many of these 6x6 trucks were being used in rear-area logistic work where all-wheel drive was not required, this being particularly true with trucks being supplied for international aid. The decision was made to introduce 6x4 models with non-powered front axle on both the Studebaker and Yellow Truck and Coach (GMC) trucks.

The GMC would be almost identical to the 6x6 model then in production, hence the 6x4 was given the model designation "CCW" – losing the "K" that denoted powered front axle.

Yellow Truck and Coach's first effort along this line was a 6x4 with Timken axles built 24 June 1941 on sales order TC-200127. The manufacturer's serial number applied to this truck was CCW-350-A1-2001. Testing of this truck at Fort Holabird was not successful

and it was returned to the factory for credit – and a request made to construct a similar vehicle with Chevrolet axles. CCW-350-A1-2001 was not wasted however, as it was rebuilt into CCKW-353-23167-A1 on TC-200014 on 19 September 1941.

The second effort, which utilized Chevrolet axles, was more successful. Sales order TC-200152 saw the construction of CCW-350-A2 on 11 August 1941. The truck was built against contract W-298-QM-9095, with the result being that the contract was for 27,999 6x6 trucks, and one 6x4.

The second prototype passed Holabird's testing regimen, and a contract for 2,000 copies was awarded 25 August 1941. That contract, DA-W-398-QM-62, called for 1,996 of the trucks to be boxed for overseas shipment, with 15 of the trucks to have platform bodies in lieu of the standard cargo body. None of these trucks was to have winches, and all would be built in Pontiac. Production began 1 December 1941, and proceeded at a rate of 45 per day until 1 February 1942. With the Soviet Union and China pressing for these vehicles, the War Department approved these trucks to be built at the expense of delaying CCKW production as a result of utilizing common CCKW components to complete the 6x4 order.

In 1941, in response to a request for 6x4 trucks from the Soviet Union and China, 8,801 units were authorized of a version designated the CCW. Being destined for export, this run lacked U.S. Army registration numbers. (General Motors)

Beyond the standard straight axle replacing the powered front axle of the CCKW, and the obvious omission of the front drive shaft, the CCW was almost identical to its all-wheel-drive sibling. However, the transfer case was locked into the high-range position and lacked some of the internal components found in the CCKW unit. Because the U.S. Army truck capacity rating system of the day was that the load rating was to be that of "off road" capacity, which was half of on-road capacity, and because without the powered front axle, the CCW was not considered capable of off-road use, the new truck was rated as a five-ton 6x4.

The initial order for 2,000 CCW trucks was followed on 27 September 1941 with a new contract, DA-W-398-QM-78, for a further 2,100 examples to be built on sales order TC-200195. Once again, the sudden demand forced a revision in production schedules. In a memo dated 3 October 1941, R. A. Crist, Yellow Truck and Coach production control manager, records: "Another order has just been received for 2100 additional 6x4's for Lend-Lease program, making a total of 4100 of this type on order, all to be boxed.

"This new lot of 2100 will fall right behind the first lot of 2000, at the rate of 45 per day, and common materials will be taken from 6x6's to meet required delivery dates, thus setting back similar quantity of 6x6's, and making it necessary to increase the weekly schedule in February and March to meet the overall delivery dates."

Shipments of trucks on the initial order began in 1941 and were completed by 4 February 1942, while the second order production was finished on 10 April 1942.

Even while the first order was being assembled, yet a third order for the CCW was placed under contract DA-W-398-QM-203 for 4,700 trucks. Originally ordered for China, these trucks were later diverted to the Soviet Union. This order was completed on 8 June 1942.

The largest group of CCW vehicles, however, would be part of the massive contract initially dubbed W-398-QM-11595 and later designated W-374-ORD-2597. This contract, covering a vast array of GMC military trucks, initially was for 137,481 vehicles, including 14,700 CCWs. The total quantity of trucks on this contract was later upped to 240,250 6x6 and 6x4 vehicles. These 14,700 vehicles were built on sales order TC-200305 and were delivered in 1942.

These trucks were being built as production was shifting from steel bodies to wooden bodies. Few are aware that there were two types of steel body – the welded steel cargo body used on trucks that were delivered assembled, and a bolted steel body that was used on trucks that were shipped boxed. The bodies for these trucks were subject to considerable internal correspondence within General Motors. A memo of 9 July 1942 read in part "These sheets do not incorporate any information in respect to the 8000 6x4s on which we are to mount steel bodies, since this decision was only made late yesterday. As matters stand today and considering the number of 6x4's which have been built out of the 14,700 scheduled on 11595 contract (roughly 4400) it appears that we will be able to build a total of approximately 6000 6x4's before we run out of axles."

The memo went on: "....arrangements have been made with Budd to ship in to Pontiac a daily schedule of 200 steel bodies over and above our building schedule of trucks. These 200 bodies per day will be mounted on 6x4 trucks taken from storage lots and handled

When viewed from the side, the CCW had the same appearance as a CCKW. The cab was the model 1608 with the rear-view mirror mounted on the cowl instead of the top door hinge. (General Motors)

at Plant 3, in addition to the body mounting schedule for trucks produced daily."

That same day, Yellow Truck and Coach sales manager A. A. Dodd sent a memo to production control manager R. A. Crist concerning the steel bodies. It read, in part: "We were informed in telephone conversation with Colonel Van Ingram yesterday morning that 8000 2½ ton 6x4 trucks are required on wheels with welded type 12-ft steel cargo bodies for the U.S. Army, and were, therefore, requested to apply welded type bodies now lined up for 6x6 trucks for boxing, to the 8000 6x4 trucks: these bodies to be mounted by us at Pontiac and the 6x4 trucks shipped from there on wheels.

"It was determined by you that this could be accomplished on the following basis; the 2½ ton, 6x6 trucks, Item 1A and 1B, listed below could be shipped by us with a corresponding number of the 12-ft. steel knocked down bodies scheduled out of the Budd-Philadelphia Plant . . . ."

These knocked down steel bodies had been developed by Budd,

with the idea having been submitted to the Scheduling and Shipping Department of the Motor Transport Division, Quartermaster Corps, in September 1941. The knocked down bodies, which were intended to be used in trucks shipped to the USSR, saved 85 cubic feet per body in shipping space. In November 1941 the body was approved, and shipments of the all-steel knocked down body began in April 1942.

On 25 May 1942 an addition was made to contract W-398-QM-11595 calling for a further 107,069 vehicles, including 29,550 CCW 6x4 trucks for the Soviet Union. This group of trucks included for the first time ever CCW vehicles equipped with winch. Originally it was planned that production of these trucks would begin in January 1943, but in August 1942, the Army decided that it was preferable for Yellow Truck and Coach to focus its efforts on 6x6s for the U.S. Army and the final order for 29,550 CCWs was cancelled. The Soviets received Studebaker US-6 6x4s instead. The book thus closed on CCW production.

The CCW was produced in both long- and short-wheelbase versions. The rear tandem axle visible on this one is a Chevrolet banjo axle. With the exception of the CCW pilot produced in August 1941, all of the 1941 CCWs had Chevrolet axles. (General Motors)

The lack of a front powered axle is apparent in this frontal view of a 1941 CCW. The truck's nomenclature plate is wired to the grille below the GMC logo; this is an indication that the vehicle was being prepared for boxing for shipment overseas. (General Motors)

The rear of a 1941 CCW is viewed with the tarpaulin not installed. The CCWs intended for export were built to substantially the same standards as the 1941-model CCKWs. (General Motors)

A CCW being readied for shipment overseas is observed from the right with the tarpaulin and bows removed. With an unpowered front axle mounted, CCWs were intended for use on developed roads. (General Motors)

Compared to the seeming forest of shift levers in the CCKW to control the transmission, front-axle declutching, and the transfer case, the CCW had a very simple arrangement of a transmission shift lever and a hand-brake lever. (General Motors)

The 1941-model CCWs had the civilian-style dashboard, instrument panel, and fabric-covered bench seat. The wire grille on the rear window was a standard appointment on CCWs as well as CCKWs with hard-topped cabs. (General Motors)

Chapter 7
War Production Begins

In mid-1941 even more CCKWs were ordered, these being in three groups:

1,692 on an extension of contract W-398-QM-10250
700 Lend-Lease vehicles on DA-W-398-QM-69
15,600 trucks on contract W-398-QM-10890
17,992 Total

While the 1,692 and 700 trucks listed above would all be built by Yellow Truck and Coach, the 15,600 would again be divided between Yellow and Chevrolet. Chevrolet would assemble 4,950 of the vehicles, while the remaining 10,650 would be built in Pontiac.

Yellow Truck and Coach's Production Material Control purchased the material for all 17,992 of these trucks in one lot, making for little variation in the vehicles beyond the obvious wheelbase, with or without winch variations. However, there was an exception to this uniformity.

These additional truck orders would push Yellow Truck and Coach Plant 4 – the engine plant – beyond its capacity of 544 engines per day – which was to satisfy not only CCKW but all Yellow Truck and Coach demands. To overcome this problem, Yellow once again turned to Chevrolet. Whereas previously Yellow Truck and Coach had shipped engines to St. Louis for use there by Chevrolet, for the 4,950

trucks Chevrolet would assemble on this order, they would build GMC 270 themselves. These engines would be built in Chevrolet's Flint, Michigan, engine works, utilizing blocks furnished by Yellow Truck and Coach. The 270 blocks, whether used by Yellow Truck and Coach or Chevrolet, were actually cast by Pontiac Motor Company's foundry in Pontiac, Michigan. Like the trucks themselves, the engines would not carry any Chevrolet markings.

The assembly of the 10,650 trucks to be built in Pontiac dovetailed directly with the end of the production for the previous order. Chevrolet-St. Louis, however, had a gap in production between its original order and this new order for 4,950 vehicles, with no CCKWs being assembled from early January until the first of February. This gap may have been attributable to the start up of engine production. Notations from R. A. Crist record: "Mr. Livingston has today cleared with Mr. Wetherald of Chevrolet the fact that they will be in position to manufacture the engines for the 4950 trucks which they are to build and on which engines will be required approximately February 1st, 1942. Consequently, in the Chevrolet-St. Louis bill of materials for these 4950 trucks, Engineering Specifications will indicate that the engines are to be furnished by Chevrolet."

To provide 2½-ton trucks with a capability to defend themselves against aircraft attacks, in July 1942 tests were initiated at Aberdeen Proving Ground with machine-gun ring mounts M32 on a short-wheelbase CCKW and a long-wheelbase CCKW, seen here in a 28 July photo. (National Archives)

Once again, A. O. Smith would furnish the frames for the St. Louis trucks, which would also have Warner transmissions and Chevrolet axles. Once again, St. Louis was building only long-wheelbase, no-winch models.

The three orders discussed here were divided as follows:

Extension of Contract W-398-QM-10250

TC-200169 1,027 CCKW-353 wo/w 935 with Timken axles, 92 with Chevrolet

TC-200170   600 CCKW-353 w/w with Chevrolet axles

TC-200171   45 1e tank truck with Timken axles

TC-200194   20 1e tank truck with winch and Timken axles

The trucks built on contract W-398-QM-10250, like their predecessors, featured 6-volt positive ground electrical systems supplied by a 25-amp generator.

Contract DA-W-398-QM-69

TC-200177 330 type 1a CCKW-353 wo/w all to be boxed SUP

TC-200178 70 type 1b CCKW-353 w/w all to be boxed SUP

TC-200233 150 type 1a CCKW-353 wo/w all to be boxed SUP

TC-200234 150 type 1a CCKW-353 wo/w all to be boxed SUP

All of these trucks would have Chevrolet axles with standard differentials. The production of these 700 trucks was to be with the utmost urgency, so they were actually produced with materials ordered for contract W-398-QM-10250 so they could be shipped in November. The bumped 700 trucks on -10250 were then built using materials purchased on the later purchase order.

Contract W-398-QM-10890

TC-200184   1,350 type 1a CCKW-353 wo/w Chevrolet axles, standard differentials, St. Louis

TC-200185   3,600 type 1a CCKW-353 wo/w Chevrolet axles, high-traction, St. Louis

TC-200186   1,200 type 1a CCKW-353 wo/w Timken axles

TC-200187   850 type 1a CCKW-353 wo/w Chevrolet axles

TC-200188   3,300 type 1b CCKW-352 wo/w Timken axles

TC-200189   2,300 type 1c CCKW-353 with winch Timken axles

TC-200189   800 type 1c CCKW-353 with winch Chevrolet axles

TC-200191   2,100 type 1d CCKW-352 with winch Timken axles

TC-200192   100 type 1e tank truck Timken axles

Chevrolet axles would be found beneath 6,600 of these trucks, with Timken axles used on the other 9,000.

As Yellow Truck and Coach's front office was hard at work scheduling materials and production for these new orders, the assembly line workers in Pontiac and St. Louis were busy churning out trucks. By 6 October 1941 all 41,188 trucks on the original contract W-398-QM-10250 and preceding orders had been completed. There remained on order 39,541 6x6 and 4,100 6x4 trucks. To meet the demand, production in Pontiac was set at 240 per day from 13 October 1941 to 2 February 1942, when it would step up to 250 per day for the following week, before finally jumping to 300 per day from 9 February to 3 April 1942.

The long-wheelbase CCKW received a variation of ring mount M32 in which a machined ring produced by the Trackson Company of Milwaukee, Wisconsin, was supported by a cantilever frame consisting of two 3¼-inch-diameter vertical steel pipes with 6-inch channels for lateral supports. (National Archives)

Almost buried in this avalanche of orders was a small contract issued on 30 June 1941. This contract, numbered DA-W-398-QM-33, called for for 1,800 additional Lend-Lease trucks. These vehicles would be broken down into the following sales orders:

TC-200143 120 CCKW-353 no winch with Chevrolet axles

TC-200144 180 CCKW-353 with winch and Chevrolet axles

TC-200161 1,500 CCKW-353 no winch, 1,200 with Chevrolet axles, 300 with Timken axles.

The 300 vehicles on sales orders TC-200143 and TC-200144 were also given in production, and were produced immediately prior to the 700 priority trucks on DA-W-398-QM-69 mentioned above. These trucks had been built, torn down, boxed and were ready to ship by the end of November 1941.

Planning for Future orders

On 10 November 1941 Yellow Truck and Coach was queried by the Quartermaster Corps concerning what would be needed to increase production to 720 trucks of all types per day for the next 18 months. There were a number of factors to be considered, of course, and by 20 December some clarifications were issued in this query, key among which was the statement that Yellow Truck and Coach was to assume an 80% reduction in production for the civilian market.

Yellow Truck and Coach again looked to other General Motors Divisions for additional capacity, beyond what was already being sub-let to Chevrolet, St. Louis. Potential additional capacity could be found at the Pontiac Motor Division, estimated at 180 per day, the Fisher Body-Pontiac plant, and at Chevrolet-Baltimore, estimated at 50 per day. It was estimated that to set up Pontiac Motor Division for chassis assembly and Fisher for body assembly would cost $165,000 for tools, while converting Chevrolet-Baltimore would cost only $25,000.

Building the current orders

Not surprisingly, the Japanese attack on Pearl Harbor led to some revised thinking concerning tactical military vehicles. One such area was antiaircraft defense. Machine gun ring mounts were tested on CCKWs as early as July 1942, and on 24 November 1942 word was passed to Production Control to begin incorporating provisions for mounting such weaponry on CCKW-353 with steel cargo bodies. It was desired that 4,650 trucks so equipped be produced.

By that time troops in the field were receiving mounting kits along with instructions on how to cut a hole in the roof of the truck cab to facilitate operation of the weapon. The mounting, designated the M32 Gun Mount, was manufactured by the Trackson Company of Milwaukee, and was being issued to the Armored Force.

One of these kits was provided to Yellow Truck and Coach, whose personnel examined the kit and advised Budd of a slight change needed in steel body production to facilitate attaching the gun mount supports. This amounted to having 21/32 holes bored for mounting the supports, and slight changes to the front and side racks. These side rack changes were different than the ones called for in the field

Stability and strength for the frame of the ring mount M32 were enhanced by angled steel plates on each side. The closed cab was fitted with an opening with a raised, reinforced rim for the gunner, who stood on the seat to fire. (National Archives)

installation kit and made it easier to remove and install the sides.

A different cab, designated the Model 1609, would be required as well, with an opening to reach the ring. A Yellow Truck and Coach memo of 24 November 1942 addressed the issue of these cabs as follows:

"Messrs. Emmert and Maytag decided to rework required number of cabs with minimum tools from the instructions in the manual covering installation of equipment. Mr. Maytag has manual and template required, also guard ring and rivets." Four days later Sales Manager A.A. Dodd directed that 4,650 steel cargo bodies with provisions for gun mounting be purchased from Budd.

Dodd also threw a wrench in the works when he further directed that the following array of vehicles with provision for gun mounts be shipped in these time frames:

	Dec 1942	Jan 43	Feb 43
TC-200494 CCKW-353 no winch	546	1,278	610
TC-200495 CCKW-353 with winch	274	638	304
TC-200496 CCKW-352 no winch			666
TC-200497 CCKW-352 with winch			334

All of these trucks were to be boxed for export using two-unit packaging. Production of the cabs for these vehicles was to begin on Wednesday, 9 December 1942 and was to be completed at a rate of 70 per day. In order to meet this schedule, overtime was authorized on 5 and 6 December to set up the plant. The procedure to modify the 1608 cab into the 1609 cab was summarized by Mr. Maytag's memo of 1 December as follows:

"The tentative line up is to mark the cab roof, cut a starting hole, cut large opening in roof with unishear, flange on flanging form, place mount ring in place, drill or pierce rivet holes for attaching, squeeze or buck rivets and smooth down flange by hand or with air hammer. From here on the roof panel will follow present assembly set up."

While there had been some testing done with the gun mount and 12-foot steel body at the Yellow plant, that was not the case with the 9-foot body, which was cause for some concern. At a meeting held at the Budd Company in Detroit 2 December between Budd, Trackson and Yellow Truck and Coaches engineer, it was revealed that the nine-foot steel cargo body does not require any modifications to accommodate the CCKW-352-specific M37 mount. Thus, adding the cab opening and guard ring to these trucks was all that was required.

During the 1942 tests at Aberdeen, a short-wheelbase CCKW was fitted with a variation of the ring mount M32 with a ring supported by cantilever arms attached to vertical 6-inch steel channels. This mount was photographed on 28 July 1942. (National Archives)

The 1942 tests of ring mounts on CCKWs at Aberdeen Proving Ground disclosed weaknesses in the ring, which then was reinforced. A production ring mount M32 is viewed from the front in a 2 May 1945 photo. (National Archives)

Right: The same ring mount M32 seen in the preceding photo is viewed from overhead. The ring had three attachment points: to the end of each of the cantilever arms and to the lateral crossbar. (National Archives)

Below: Whereas the ring mount M32 on the long-wheelbase CCKW had an angled plate on each side for stability during the 1942 tests, the ring mount M32 on the short-wheelbase CCKW had an angled brace from the crossbar to the cargo body, partially hidden by the tarpaulin. (National Archives)

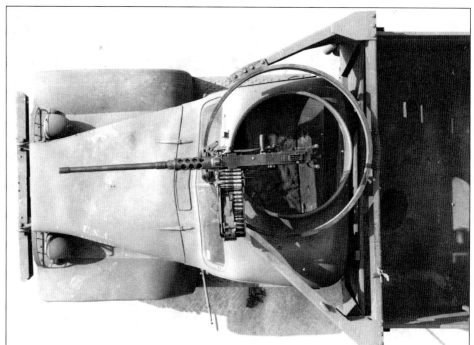

Although the variant of the ring mount on the short-wheelbase CCKW was designated M32 at the time of the July 1942 preliminary tests of the ring mounts on the CCKWs, it was standardized as the ring mount M37. (National Archives)

The ring mount M32 on a long-wheelbase CCKW during the early part of the ring-mount tests at Aberdeen Proving Ground is viewed from the front with a .50-caliber machine gun M2 installed. (National Archives)

With the tarpaulin pulled back, the brace on the right side of the ring mount M32 is visible. This variant of the mount, as opposed to the type with the brace plates, was appropriate for short-wheelbase CCKWs because of the ability of these braces to span the space between the crossbar and the cargo body. (National Archives)

During the 1942 ring-mount tests, several experiments were conducted with reinforcing the ring assembly. These ultimately resulted in a satisfactory ring. Behind the gunner is a rack for three ammunition boxes. (National Archives)

A soldier mans the .50-caliber machine gun on the short-wheelbase CCKW during the late-July 1942 phase of the ring-mount tests at Aberdeen. During these tests, problems with gun stoppages and dispersal of fire were traced to weaknesses in the ring assembly. (National Archives)

Chapter 8
The AFKWX

The cab over engine 6x6, or AFKWX, a concept that had lain dormant since the production of three trial vehicles in mid-1940, was revived with contract W-398-QM-11425, issued on 16 December 1941. This contract called for the production of 60 of the type, which Yellow Truck and Coach scheduled for production in May 1942.

These vehicles, and all subsequent AFKWX trucks, were mechanically similar to the CCKW and featured the same Chevrolet axles, but the 270 engines installed in these trucks were fitted with Zenith updraft carburetors rather than the downdraft carburetors used on the CCKW. None of the trucks was equipped with winches, but all had a welded all-steel cargo bed 15 feet long. The length of the bed – three feet greater than that of the long wheel base CCKW bed, was the AFKWX's asset. Additional length meant additional cargo capacity for high-volume, low-density cargos.

The cab for the initial production order was the Model 1615 closed cab. Unlike later-day civilian cab over engine trucks, the cab of the AFKWX did not tilt. The result was that rather than the relatively free access mechanics had to the CCKW engine, engine access on the AFKWX was problematic, and repairs of major problems often required the removal of the entire cab from the truck.

The 60 AFKWX-353 ordered on contract W-398-QM-11425 were built on sales order TC-200254, and were assigned registration numbers USA 492732 through 492791. While originally scheduled for May production, subsequent changes in scheduling resulted in only 18 of the trucks being built in that month, the balance of the order being produced in June along with the initial group of AFKWX trucks on the next order (which will be discussed in chapter 13).

A member of the same G-508 series of 2½-ton trucks as the CCKW, the GMC AFKWX-353 was a long-wheelbase cab-over design. The ACKWX-353 entered production in 1942, and production was limited to 7,235 units. This series of photos shows an example from the first order of 60 AFKWX-353s. (General Motors via Bryce Sunderlin)

Although the AFKWX-353's overall length was only 10 inches longer than that of the CCKW-353, it had room for a longer cargo body because of the cab-over design. The AFKWX-353 had a 15-foot cargo body, whereas the CCKW-353 had a 12-foot body. (General Motors)

Although barely discernible in this photograph, the GMC logo was lightly embossed to the top center of the radiator louvers. The grille and headlight brush guards were made of bar iron with a brace on each side. (General Motors)

From the rear, the AFKWX-353 appeared virtually identical to a hardtop-cab CCKW of that period, with the same style of tailgate and rear cross sill with recessed tail lights and tool box. (General Motors via Bryce Sunderlin)

In a photo of a first-order AFKWX-353 dated 29 May 1942, the position of the fuel tank under the frame below the cargo body is apparent. Owing to the high position of the cab, a step with a nonslip rubber tread was fitted above the small running board. (General Motors via Bryce Sunderlin)

Chapter 9
The Largest Truck Contract

New Year's Day 1942 found Yellow Truck and Coach president Irving Babcock, production control manager R. A. Crist, and W. B. Livingston huddled in Babcock's office planning for war production to meet the latest demands from the military of a nation now engaged in world war. The latest directives called for 4,700 trucks per week by May, rising to 6,000 per week in September. The then latest military program called for Yellow Truck and Coach to deliver 192,000 trucks. The possibility of CCKW production by Pontiac and/or Fisher had been eliminated, but now in addition to Chevrolet-Baltimore, Chevrolet-Oakland was also under consideration as CCKW assembly operations.

The strategy meeting resumed the next day, all in preparation for meetings in Washington on 3-4 January 1942. As had long been the case, axles were still a critically short item in meeting this ambitious production plan. In hopes of finding a solution, Irving Babcock called Timken Detroit Axle's Walter Rockwell on 2 January, encouraging Rockwell to reach out to the Ford Motor Company as a source for parts for the axles.

The timing of these meetings were not coincidental, because on 2 January 1942 the company was awarded the contract that had been rumored for weeks – contract W-398-QM-11595. This contract, for 136,812 trucks, would ultimately grow to encompass 240,250 vehicles – the largest vehicular contract ever issued by the U.S. Army. Other contracts issued concurrently with -11595 added 3,908 trucks and numerous spare parts to the total being faced by production planners in early January.

On 16 January 1942 R. A. Crist issued a memo to the staff outlining the critical need to adhere strictly to the production control schedules being issued that day. It read, in part, "The material schedule given therein are [sic] fixed and must be released as firm schedules on suppliers for the period from April through December 1942. The material schedule must be rigidly adhered to in every respect." The same memo also touched on the subject of subcontracting CCKW assembly work, "With respect to the 52,680 trucks which will be assembled by Chevrolet we cannot give you at this time the breakdown of assembly plants, but expect to have this information in a few days. It is probable that Chevrolet assembly will be all done in St. Louis and Oakland. Chevrolet truck assembly is limited to items 1-A and 1-B

CCKW-353 U.S.A. number 805588, produced under contract W-398-QM-11595, was fitted out as a 700-gallon water tanker. The tank was insulated and had two manholes with covers on top. Marked faintly on the side of the tank is "700 GALS. / WATER." (General Motors)

and Mr. Redford has already instituted steps to issue necessary bills of materials and parts lists."

Ultimately, it was decided that the CCKWs for this order would be assembled at three plants – Yellow Truck and Coach, Pontiac would be joined by Chevrolet – St. Louis Chevrolet – Baltimore.

St. Louis was to build 23,030 CCKW-353 cargo trucks without winch on sales order TC-200294 and 4,830 CCKW-353 cab and chassis only. Chevrolet – Baltimore would assemble 7,260 cargo trucks without winches on sales order TC-200421. Sales order TC-200295 would cover 17,560 CCKW-353 cargo trucks with winch to be built in St. Louis.

The 136,812 trucks initially ordered on contract W-398-QM-11595 encompassed 611 AFKW-350 series trucks, 14,700 CCW 6x4 trucks and 121,501 CCKW vehicles. But this total was increased on 25 May 1942 when Supplement 3 to the contract arrived. This extended production by a further 107,089 vehicles. This extension included 17,331 chassis trucks with varying equipment for the various service branches.

Production of CCKW trucks by Chevrolet-Baltimore began in June 1942, when 223 of the trucks were delivered.

As originally planned, the trucks on the initial order would be built between 18 May 1942 and 9 January 1943. To achieve this goal required the formidable production rate of 4,700 trucks per week, which is what Yellow Truck and Coach planned to produce. However, the nationwide steel shortage, caused by the huge demands placed be the armaments industry, soon wrecked the production schedule.

On 10 June 1942 came this letter from Col J. Van Ness Ingram in the Quartermaster General's office:

"Confirming conversation this date (Mr. Babcock – Colonel Ingram) the following agreement has been reached concerning the delivery of axles for the 2½ ton 6x6 trucks on the understanding that after July 1, 1942, Timken-Detroit Axle Company can manufacture 2500 sets of axles per week and that 1500 of these axles will be furnished the Yellow Truck & Coach Manufacturing Company and 1000 to the Studebaker Corporation, that if the Timken-Detroit Axle Company fails for any reason to deliver this number of axles per week any reduction below this number will be proportionately pro-rated between Yellow Truck and Coach Mfg. Company and the Studebaker Corporation.

"You are hereby requested to reduce your schedule of 2-1/2 ton 6x6 trucks using Timken axles from 2000 to 1500 per week effective July 1, 1942. It is agreed that Yellow Truck & Coach Manufacturing Company will furnish a new schedule of delivery based on the above number of axles from the Timken-Detroit Axle Company on Contract W-398-QM-11595. Such reduced schedule providing for 4200 vehicles per week, which will include 2700 sets of axles from General Motors Corporation, will be accepted."

The axle shortage resulted in a revision of the production schedule, with 50 per day to be built in Baltimore, 280 per day in St. Louis and the balance in Pontiac.

As can be seen, material shortages impacted all manufacturers, and not only in axle availability. Solder and welding rods were often in

At the rear of the tank was an equipment chest with two doors containing discharge hoses and tools for the operation and maintenance of the tank's controls. Normally, suction hoses would be stored on the side of the body, but they are not present here. (General Motors)

short supply. On 1 May 1942 the Studebaker Corporation shipped to Lt. Col. William Johnson at the Holabird Quartermaster Depot one of its closed cabs that lacked the detailed finishing that had been characteristic of both Studebaker and GMC cabs up to this point. The cover letter from Chief Engineer Jeffries indicated that omitting these steps would save two pounds of war-critical solder and a considerable amount of labor, and approval was sought to discontinue these finishing operations, if the Quartermaster would approve such changes. Johnson no doubt approved this change, as both Studebaker and Yellow Truck and Coach dropped these operations the next month.

On Friday, 26 June 1942, Yellow Truck and Coach's Pontiac plant was idled by a strike by plant workers protesting their lack of pay during a 20-minute blackout drill on the night of 24 June. While this would be the only strike at the plant during the war, strikes at various suppliers' plants at various times during the war also impacted production.

The steel shortage continued to hamper production, not only for Yellow Truck and Coach, but for all firms engaged in war production. While newsreels promoted scrap drives, the War Department sought ways to limit steel consumption in manufacturing. The Iron and Steel Limitation Order as amended on 13 July 1942 provided that 60 days after the governing date of 15 July the use of iron or steel would be prohibited for truck and trailer bodies on orders for Army, Navy, and Maritime Commission, except tank and dump bodies, as well as essential hardware, structural and bracing members for bodies essentially of wooden construction.

In order to comply with this stipulation, General Motors began producing wooden cargo bodies for CCWs and CCKWs in August 1942. Bodies would be built by three enterprises – Yellow Truck and Coach in Pontiac for use on the cargo trucks shipped "on wheels" from that facility, Chevrolet – St. Louis, for vehicles shipped on wheels from that plant, and Chevrolet – Atlanta, which would supply knocked down wooden bodies for use in conjunction with trucks shipped

knocked down from both Pontiac and St. Louis. The Atlanta-built bodies would be shipped not to the truck manufacturing plant, but rather, would meet the chassis at the point of export or export supply depot. Atlanta and St. Louis would build 9-foot and 12-foot bodies for use on CCKWs, while Pontiac would build those two lengths as well as a 15-foot body for use on the cab-over-engine AFKWX. No fewer than 11 firms in eight states were contracted to supply the dimensioned hardwood lumber for these body manufacturing operations.

However, the initiation of wooden body fabrication was only half of this equation. The other half was the manufacturing might of steel body fabricator Edward G. Budd, which supplied 80"x144" and 80"x108" steel cargo bodies not only to Yellow Truck and Coach but also Studebaker, Reo, and International Harvester.

On 12 September 1942, just before the mandated deadline, Yellow Truck and Coach's A. A. Dodd was advised by the Motor Transport Service concerning additional steel body usage in September and October, following a review of the in-process situation at Budd and an appeal to the War Production Board. As of 8 September Budd had in process the following all-steel bodies:

2,092 of the 80"x108" bodies
8,247 of the 80"x144" bodies

A letter to Yellow, identified as War Production Board Order 126, dated 15 September, was the final word on this subject. It read, in part, ".....your manufacturing divisions are granted exceptions as follows:"

"You are authorized to produce and deliver during September and October 1942, a total not to exceed 5025 cargo vehicles, equipped with steel bodies, for completion not later than October 31, 1942. This number represents completely fabricated steel bodies on hand at the Chevrolet plants, in transit, or at the Budd Manufacturing Company, Detroit, Michigan, as of the close of business, September 14, 1942."

The Motor Transport Service of Ordnance stipulated that the use of these bodies could not exceed the percentage laid down by Service of

The cabinet below the front left side of the 700-gallon water tanker contained a single-cylinder, four-stroke engine that powered a self-priming centrifugal water pump. The pump could be used to fill the tank or drain the tank, and water also could be removed from the tank by gravity. (General Motors)

Supply. Half of the steel bodies would be used in September, the other half in October, and all November production would use wooden bodies, as would any cargo trucks built in September and October beyond those specified above.

Of the 5,025 bodies covered by this letter, 120 were Government owned property held at Superior Body Company, where they had been removed from cargo trucks that were being converted to ordnance shop trucks. Furthermore, Budd fell 170 bodies short of its estimated delivery.

Of course, the 4,650 steel bodies utilized on the trucks with the 1609 cab discussed in chapter 7 were utilized on trucks built from December 1942 through February 1943, after the September 15 ban. Moreover, they were not included in the WPB exception letter of 15 September. Indeed, these 4,650 bodies were built new by Budd for that purpose – incredibly being assembled from parts already on hand. That Budd could do this seemed to wake up the Detroit Ordnance District, which directed that the District be supplied with "…a detailed inventory of remaining materials which are unusable for wood cargo bodies, together with a statement of any obsolescence charges you claim for tools, fixtures, etc., due to the conversion from steel to wood cargo bodies. All materials and tools considered as obsolescent shall be set aside and held for such disposal as the Government may make after settlement of the obsolescence charges. With the exception of the above mentioned 4650 steel bodies, all other cargo bodies will be constructed of wood."

Truck production took yet another blow owing to the steel shortage when the following telegram was received from the Purchasing and Contracting Officer of the Motor Transport Division of the Quartermaster Corps.:

"On the basis of available material you are hereby directed to immediately reduce production on two and one half ton six by six on all Quartermasters and Ordnance contracts to twelve thousand per month for balance of 1942 and all of 1943. You are directed to build out two and one half ton six by four now under contract. Existing contracts will be revised or cancelled. Confirm receipt of this directive."

This major reduction in production by 34% for 1942 and 41% for 1943 spelled the end of Chevrolet-Baltimore CCKW production. There simply was not enough material – or work – to keep three plants operating. St. Louis would build 200 trucks per day and Pontiac 360 per day. To effect these changes, Yellow Truck and Coach had to revise a number of sales orders. TC-200421, which originally called for Chevrolet-Baltimore to build 7260 CCKW-353 without winch, was revised to call for only 2,650 such trucks. TC-200470, which called for an additional 3,850 trucks of the same type to be built in Baltimore, was cancelled outright. TC-200294, for 23,030 CCKW-353 without winch to be built in St. Louis was revised upward to 27,640 trucks of the type.

Chevrolet – Baltimore CCKW production, which all happened in 1942, is summarized as follows – 223 in June, 931 in July, 546 in August, 871 in September, and the final 79 in October.

In the original plans, the 141,389 trucks for which Yellow Truck and Coach had authorized materials purchases in January 1942 would have been completed by 13 December of the same year. Now the new completion date was 1 May 1943.

To keep water in the tank from freezing, the tank was insulated and could be heated, either by a heater box inside the tank fed by an exhaust bypass, or, on some tank bodies, by a torch-type portable immersion heater that was inserted in the rear manhole. (General Motors)

This 700-gallon water tanker was equipped with corporation axles. A blackout lamp on the left fender was added beginning with serial number 192881, and asymmetrical brush guards were introduced to compensate for the new lamp. The GMC logo plate was eliminated from the grille (General Motors via Bryce Sunderlin)

Above: This CCKW-352 was one of the very early ones produced under contract W-398-QM-11595. Starting with that contract, the seams between the bottoms of the A-pillars and the cowl, previously filled and finished smooth, now were left unfilled. Absent is a screw above the rear louver of the side panel of the engine compartment, part of the radio-suppression system introduced around August 1942. (General Motors)

Right: Around the time the first CCKWs under contract W-398-QM-11595 began leaving the assembly lines in early July 1942, there developed a shortage of steel, and thus there were not enough supplies of it to meet the demand for steel cargo bodies for CCKWs. For a while, the factories installed a mix of steel bodies like this one and new, wooden bodies. (General Motors)

A CCKW-353 chassis, U.S. Army registration number 4159880, had a type 1609 closed cab with opening for a ring mount. The asymmetrical brush guard and lack of a GMC logo on the grille dates its production to after mid-March 1943. Although this chassis probably was destined to receive a cargo body, many CCKWs from serial number 150000 to 190000 were stored for some time as chassis before having special bodies or equipment installed prior to delivery in late 1943. (General Motors via Bryce Sunderlin)

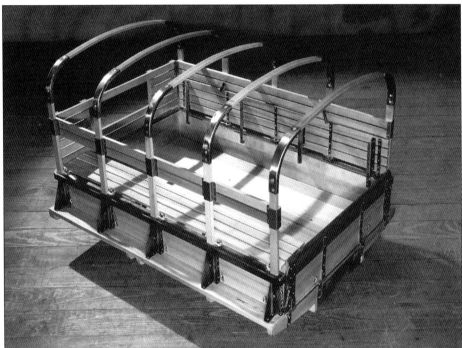

As the United States went into full wartime production in early 1942, a shortage of steel prompted the Army to order a shift from steel bodies for 6x6 2½-ton trucks to wooden bodies. This model of a wooden body, with the wooden parts being the light-colored ones and the metal parts the dark ones, was photographed on 10 February 1942, and the perspective is from the left rear. (National Archives)

A wooden cargo body, complete with paint finish, is observed from the right rear at the factory. In the absence of a steel rear cross sill, as found on steel bodies, now there were separate brackets for the tail lights and the trailer receptacle. There was still a storage box below the center of the tail gate. (National Archives via Jim Gilmore)

Above: Closed-cab, wooden-body CCKW-353-A2 U.S. Army registration number 4156293 was photographed at General Motors Proving Ground on 7 May 1943. It lacked a winch and had banjo axles and a Model 1608 cab. The vehicle was produced under contract W-374-ORD-2597, later redesignated W-398-QM-11595. (Fred Crismon collection)

Right: A closed-cab, wooden-body CCKW-353 is parked curbside in Detroit, Michigan, with several large crates in the cargo body. (Library of Congress)

What evidently was the same CCKW-353 in the preceding photo is viewed from the rear. (Library of Congress)

A short-wheelbase CCKW is driving up ramps into a railroad car for shipment. Its U.S. Army registration number, 4200048, identifies it as produced under contract W-374-ORD-2597 (W-398-QM-11595), and it had Timken axles and no winch. (General Motors)

On 9 March 1942 the Yellow Truck & Coach Manufacturing Co. of Pontiac, Michigan, began production of a new boxing procedure, the two-unit pack, in which two CCKW chassis were partially disassembled and packed into three boxes (four boxes for the CCKW-352) for shipment overseas. The following sequence of photos demonstrates that boxing method. Here, a cab is being removed from a chassis. (General Motors)

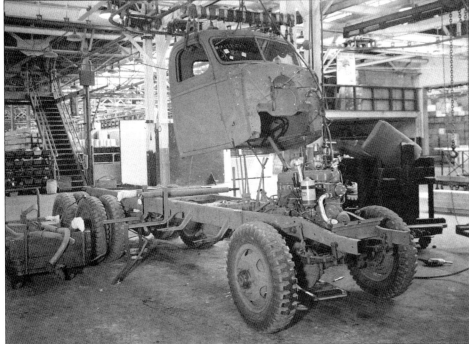

Unlike in the preceding boxing method, where a single chassis was boxed with the wheels and suspension intact, in the two-unit pack the wheels and suspension were removed prior to boxing. Engines and transmissions were left in place, but the transfer cases were removed. (General Motors)

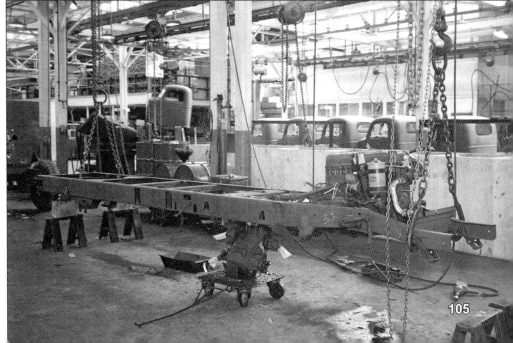

Above: A CCKW chassis frame is being lowered on top of another chassis frame on the chassis tear-down line in June 1942. The frames were situated in opposite directions, but both frames were right-side-up. A grille/brush guards and two exhaust pipes are lying atop the center of the lower frame. (General Motors)

Right: Various loose parts, some of which were in protective wrappers, were stowed in the bottom of the box before the pair of chassis frames was lowered onto the box bottom. This was an initial sample pack assembled at Yellow Truck & Coach on 16 June 1942, per engineering drawings. (General Motors)

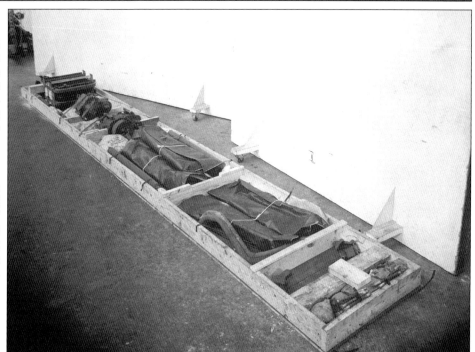

A single chassis frame has been placed on the bottom of the box, to demonstrate its positioning. Steel strapping is used to secure the frame to the box bottom. A grille and fenders are secured to the frame. (General Motors)

Above: The upper chassis frame now has been placed on top of the lower frame, and steel strapping secures the top frame in place. Fans, carburetors, air filters, and other fragile components have been removed from the engines. (General Motors)

Left: Ten wheels with tires are strapped to the top of the upper chassis frame during two-unit-pack assembly. Several cardboard boxes with loose parts are strapped to the front of the engine in the foreground. (General Motors)

At this point, with the contents of the chassis pack complete, the wooden frame has been built on top of the base of the box. Diagonal braces added to the rigidity and durability of the box. (General Motors)

The axle case is being packed. Two Timken tandem axles are on the lower tier, and on the top tier are two Timken front axles, situated at right angles to the lower axles. (General Motors)

An axle case is fully packed prior to installation of the side and top panels. In addition to six axles (for two CCKWs), leaf springs, and other parts, two wheels with tires are included. On the roller conveyor to the right is a box side ready for installation. (General Motors)

A closed-type cab has been prepared for two-unit-pack shipping. Five wheels with tires are stowed inside the cab. Thus, the 22 wheels and tires (including two spares) required for two CCKWs were distributed among the cab box, the axle box, and the chassis box. (General Motors)

With the driver's door open, it is demonstrated how the seat cushions and steering wheel and column were removed, and wooden bracing and steel strapping were installed to hold the wheels securely in place. (General Motors)

A two-cab pack is viewed from above, with a clear view of the positioning of the hoods on top of the cab roofs. To the right are side panels, ready to be nailed in place. The registration numbers are visible on the hoods. (General Motors)

A two-cab pack is shown before the sides and top are installed. The box bottom was the type in use effective 16 June 1942. Seat cushions with waterproof water wrappers were stowed in front of the windshields. Hoods were stowed atop the cabs; the one to the right bears U.S.A. number 4128831. (General Motors)

A cab box is complete except for the top. The paper liners, as seen here, were expensive, and government inspectors disagreed over the necessity of then, to GMC's distress. (General Motors)

Two-cab packs are loaded in gondola cars. Each car contained two chassis packs, two cab packs, and two axle packs: in all, the components for four CCKW-353 chassis. (The two-unit packs for the CCKW-352 added a fourth box, containing the spare-tire clamps and the fuel tank.) For a waterproof top covering for the boxes, Scutan paper was approved in March 1942, but Fibreen subsequently was used. (General Motors)

Cargo-body packs are loaded in a gondola car. The bodies were nestled in pairs; they were three pairs abreast, and there were three rows, for a total of 18 CCKW bodies. Special wooden bracing was installed in the foreground between the bodies and the rear of the gondola. (General Motors)

Chapter 10
The Open Cab

Work on a Universal Army Cab began on 25 March 1942. By Wednesday, 22 April 1942 this work was quite advanced and a meeting was held at the Budd Detroit plant body engineering department. Attending the meeting were Lt. Col. William B. Johnson of the Holabird Quartermaster Depot as well as numerous representatives of truck manufacturers, including Kramer of Ford, Haehl of Dodge, Frie of International Harvester, Jeffries and Sullivan of Studebaker, Schumaker of Chevrolet, Hall of General Motors Truck, and of course Budd representatives.

Budd's A. R. Lindsay fortunately documented this meeting in a memo, portions of which are quoted below.

"Colonel Johnson was well satisfied with the whole general plan as to size, shape, construction, etc.; from the Army point of view he felt that this design would meet their requirements.

"It was decided that General Motors Truck and Studebaker would proceed immediately with building a sample Cab and that they would work together on all details, especially the Flexible Rear Body Mounting as Studebaker felt that the body would have to be raised at this point to provide clearance of an existing chassis cross-member.

"There was further discussion regarding the method to be used

trimming the Top and Side Curtains. However, the design shown on our Top Layout and Back Curtain Sketches was generally agreed upon and Colonel Johnson expressed the desire that he would like to follow our regular Reconnaissance Front Curtain design, both in curtain details and curtain hardware – and, as agreed at this meeting, we will send samples of our Reconnaissance Front Curtain to both Mr. Hall at General Motors Truck and Mr. Sullivan at Studebaker.

"There was a great deal of discussion concerning the Machine Gun Mounting and there were various opinions as to the probable methods of supporting the Machine Gun Ring satisfactorily. However, the final out-come of this portion of the project seems to depend on the results that will be obtained on Mr. Jeffries' (of Studebaker) sample which he is building, to be tried at Camp Holabird."

Paralleling this effort was an initiative by the Armored Force to introduce an open cab. The Armored Force presented tentative specifications at a meeting of the Quartermaster Corps Motor Transport Sub-Committee held on 17 April 1942. This subject was revisited a week later, at which time Col. A. L. Campbell called attention to Budd's efforts. The Sub-Committee recommended that two examples of the Budd cab be procured for study.

In early 1942 the Army decided to develop a standard military open cab for its 2½-ton 6x6 trucks as a means to conserve steel and reduce the size of boxed trucks for shipment overseas. During the following months, GM and Studebaker built sample open cabs. The Army found Studebaker's prototype open cab, produced by Budd Manufacturing Co., satisfactory. Studebaker installed that cab on a few of its US6 trucks, as seen here. (National Archives)

Shortly thereafter, on 30 April 1942, representatives of Studebaker, Yellow Truck and Coach, the Budd Company and Lt. Col. Johnson held a conference at Studebaker's plant in South Bend, Indiana. At this conference Studebaker presented full-size drawings of a proposed open cab. After examining the drawings, the representatives concluded that attaching the machine gun mount to the frame as proposed would likely cause distortion. Instead it was suggested that the machine gun ring mount be supported from the cab assembly. Studebaker agreed to revise its drawings immediately and build an open cab to this design for study.

Thus the stage was set for two competing open-cab designs. This matter was settled in June, as documented in a memo from Col. W. A. Wood, Jr. Director, Requirements Division, to Headquarters, Services of Supply:

"1. At a meeting of the Quartermaster Corps Motor Transport Sub-Committee on June 5, 1942, it was the consensus of opinion of the members present that the standard 60" open type cab, as presented at that meeting, would be acceptable."

"2. The introduction of the Budd open type cab into the procurement program would unnecessarily complicate procurement and standardization."

On 20 June 1942, Colonel Amlong of the Quartermaster Corps sent Yellow Truck and Coach the following telegram:

"You are authorized to proceed with production of open cabs on 2½ ton 6x6 and 6x4 conventional trucks with the least practicable delay. Submit immediately final layout of cab confirming interchangeability with Studebaker open cab. Quote time in production at which open cab will be provided, quantity of vehicles under each contract, and costs involved."

Colonel Amlong's telegram dealt only with conventional cab trucks, not the cab-over-engine AFKWX, and because it was addressed to Yellow Truck and Coach, it did not raise the issue of the 1½-ton Chevrolet 4x4, which used the same cab stampings. Chevrolet, as previously noted, manufactured the cab stampings for its own 4x4 use

as well as for CCKW production.

Not surprisingly, Yellow Truck and Coach then asked Chevrolet to become involved. R. A. Crist's notes indicate "…due to Chevrolet entering into the situation because of their production of 4x4 and 4x2 trucks which used the same stampings as our trucks, there was considerable discussion over a period of 30 days regarding the point at which Chevrolet would be ready with their (cab) design. On 11 September 1942, Mr. Livingston advised the writer that a decision had been reached to buy open cab stampings from Chevrolet, and that Chevrolet would make their own dies for these stampings.

"Previously, on September 1st, Mr. Dodd had advised Engineering that Purchasing and Contracting Officer, under date of August 30, 1942, had authorized us to proceed immediately with the tools for open cabs for conventional type 2-1/2 ton 6x6 trucks."

With pressure continuing to be applied by the military, on 3 September 1942 Yellow Truck and Coach production made the following proposal to sales manager A. A. Dodd:

"From information available, it is now planned that the open cab for conventional type 2-1/2 ton 6x6 trucks will be put into production on the new buy of 78256 against Contract W-398-qm-11595 at plants indicated below:

"St. Louis – approximately February 1, 1943
"Baltimore – approximately February 10, 1943
"Pontiac – approximately February 15, 1943
"This is on the basis of no material cancellations, and that no further curtailments in production are necessary."

Obviously, as of late August 1942 it had been planned that Chevrolet-Baltimore would continue producing CCKWs into 1943, but as we have already seen, the axle shortage would cause Baltimore to be dropped in October 1942.

Perhaps adding another level of confusion to this change was the Army's reassignment of vehicle responsibility. Research, design, development, procurement, storage, distribution and maintenance of motor vehicles was transferred from the Motor Transport Service of

The same Studebaker US6 is viewed from the left side. On 23 November 1942, GMC was authorized to discontinue production of closed-top cabs and commence production of open cabs for conventional 2½-ton 6x6 and 6x4 trucks, but production did not go ahead until March 1943. GMC adopted the basic Studebaker design for its open cabs, designating it the Model 1619 cab.

A G.I. demonstrates the gunner's standing position on the folded-down back of the assistant driver's seat. The universal military cab was of all-steel construction and included three brackets for installing a ring mount for a machine gun, the most common type being the M36 ring mount. (National Archives via Jim Gilmore)

A standard military open cab is viewed from above from the right side. The canvas top is partially pulled back, exposing the raised passenger's seat. The side openings of the open cab were referred to as half-doors because they extended down only to a level about even with the seats. (National Archives via Jim Gilmore)

the Quartermaster Corps to the Ordnance Corps effective 1 August 1942.

On 19 August 1942 Lt. Col. R. G. Amlong dispatched a letter to Yellow Truck in conjunction with the adoption of the open cab. His letter, which primarily responded to Yellow's questions concerning details of the Studebaker open cab design, also included to following directive: "It is requested that you submit with the least practicable delay layout showing the manner in which gas can and Pioneer tool brackets can be mounted on vehicles equipped with open cab. In doing this you might confer with Studebaker Corporation with a view toward adopting standard mounting means."

As pointed out elsewhere in this volume, the mass production of vehicles requires considerable planning, and components and raw materials are ordered well in advance. Such was the case for the closed cab, doubly so as the same cab was used on both 4x4 and 6x6 trucks. To minimize scrap, reduce obsolescence charges, and speed production, in October 1942 an agreement was reached between the government and General Motors whereby the closed cab metal stampings in process would be used on Chevrolet trucks, and open cab stampings would thereby be introduced earlier on the GMC trucks.

On 23 November 1942 A. A. Dodd issued the following instructions to R. A. Crist:

"This is to confirm verbal instructions given to you by Mr. Livingston

to proceed with the cancellation of 19,000 Conventional type closed cabs under the original quantity of contract W-374-ORD-2597 (W-398-qm-11595) and the ordering of the Conventional type open cab material to replace the closed cab material.

"Material for Conventional type open cabs for the vehicle under the increased quantity of the contract is also to be ordered (Supplement No. 3 to Contract 2597 – 78,256 Conventional type trucks).

"We have informed the Ordnance Department that the Conventional type open cab will be started in production on March 15, 1943, and these figures are based on that starting date."

With the basic cab design settled, only a few details remained to be worked out. An Ordnance Department letter of 9 September 1942 spelled out many of the final details as they would apply to Contract W-398-QM-11595.

However, it would be 23 November 1942 before Yellow Truck and Coach's production department was finally authorized to replace the closed cab with open cab. In April 1943 the cab was specification TAC ES-No. 166.

While the documents relating to the cost of the conversion from closed cab to open cab have yet to be located, this saving was likely to be similar to that of Studebaker's, as found in their US6 production. In that case, the open cab was $2.66 less expensive than the closed cab that it replaced.

A universal military cab is mounted on a CCKW-353 chassis with a cargo-dump body. The cab had a rear-view mirror on the driver's side. (Fred Crismon collection)

Left: As seen on CCKW-353-A1 U.S. Army registration number 4139324, the early-type soft doors, also called hinged side curtains, of the universal military cab had two soft plastic windows of different sizes. (General Motors)

Below: The early-type soft top, also called the top deck, as seen on USA 4139324, was somewhat loose fitting, with an untidy appearance. The later soft top would be tighter fitting, and the doors would each have two windows of equal size. (General Motors)

Above: CCKW-353-A1 U.S.A. number 4139324 is observed from the front left. The cargo body was the all-wood type: a close examination of the photo reveals individual wood floor planks at the front of the body. (General Motors)

Left: GMC CCKW-353-A1 U.S.A. 4139324 was one of 2,227 open-cab 2½-ton 6x6 trucks produced under contract W-374-ORD-2597 (W-398-QM-11595), which also included 13,552 trucks with the Model 1608 closed cab. (General Motors)

The windshield assembly of the universal military cab consisted of two glass panes in a frame, hinged at the top to a tubular support frame. The tubular support frame pivoted on pins and brackets at the bottom. (General Motors)

Above: GMC CCKW-353-B1 U.S. Army number 4275705 was another early open-cab vehicle produced under contract W-374-ORD-2597. It was a 1942-model-year truck with a winch and Timken axles. (General Motors)

Right: Partially visible is the rear curtain of the cab. It lacked a window, and the canvas top deck overlapped it to make the rear curtain watertight. Details of the rear of the wooden cargo body also are visible. (General Motors)

An example of an early short-wheelbase 2½-ton 6x6 with the open cab was CCKW-352-A1 U.S. Army registration number 4286699. The letter S on the side of the cowl indicated that the truck had passed a radio-interference-suppression test. (General Motors)

Left: The same CCKW-352-A1 is viewed from the front left. On both sides of the fuel tank were enlarged and extended fuel fillers, a change instituted on CCKWs in March 1943. The filler caps on the CCKW-352 were now horizontally oriented, as opposed to their former angled configuration. (General Motors)

Below: In a left side view of CCKW-352-A1 U.S. Army registration number 4286699, the revised, elbow shape of the fuel filler on the front of the fuel tank is apparent. On the running board is a holder for a five-gallon liquid container. (General Motors)

The same CCKW-352-A1 is viewed from the left rear. The tires were U.S. Royal Master Grip 8-ply, size 7.50-20, with nondirectional treads. The tail lights and trailer receptacle were mounted on metal plates fastened to the rear of the body. (General Motors)

CCKW-352-A1 4286699 displays a late-type grille without a GMC logo plate, as well as the asymmetrical brush guards. The two windshield wipers were vacuum powered by means of a tube and hose connection to the engine manifold. (General Motors)

Left: The two spare tires are partially visible through the front rack on CCKW-352-A1 U.S. Army registration number 4286699. The tailgate had the typical complement of steps, reflectors, hold-open chains, and tie-down hooks. (General Motors)

Below: Front-winch-equipped CCKW-352-B1 U.S. Army registration number 4482698 lacked the five-gallon liquid container holders on the running boards but had the late-type, enlarged, elbow-shaped fillers on the fuel tank. (General Motors via Bryce Sunderlin)

A Timken axle is visible below the bumper and winch of this CCKW-352-B1. The top and bottom of each slat of the grille were bent at a 90-degree angle to form surfaces that were welded to the grille frame. In late-type grilles, as seen here, each pair of slats had their bends pointing to each other. On early grilles, the bends pointed away from each other on each pair of slats. (General Motors via Bryce Sunderlin)

Left: General Motors Corporation CCKW-352-B1 U.S. Army registration number 4482698 is observed from the right rear. Projecting from the cab to the front of the passenger's door is the front bracket for a ring mount. (General Motors via Bryce Sunderlin)

Below: Special-purpose vehicles based on CCKW chassis also were equipped with the open cab, such as this gasoline tanker, U.S. Army registration number 802044. Two 375-gallon gasoline tanks were mounted on the long-wheelbase chassis. (General Motors)

Right: The same gasoline tanker is viewed from the right side. Controls were included for manually discharging each 375-gallon tank independently of the other. The tanks were filled with gasoline through a manhole at the top of each tank. (General Motors)

Below: The locker at the rear of the gasoline tanker body contained selective controls and valves for the two tanks along with additional equipment. (General Motors)

Each gasoline tanker was provided with a chain to drag behind the body to discharge static electricity. That chain is visible below the tow pintle. (General Motors)

The rear of the gasoline tanker is displayed. Above and between the bumperettes was a discharge faucet. The locker on the left rear of the body contained a gauge, gasoline containers, and other equipment. (General Motors)

CCKW-352-A1 U.S. Army registration number 60100015 was photographed before its body was installed. Insofar as CCKWs were concerned, registration numbers starting with 60 were reserved for chassis with special technical and shop bodies. (General Motors)

The same CCKW-352-A1 shown in the preceding photo is viewed from the rear. With no body installed, an excellent view is available of the rear curtain and the rear of the cab, including the two rear brackets for a ring mount. (General Motors)

THIS IS HYDROVAC

By Bendix

The most advanced and best proved of all new power-braking units
Now available for trucks and busses

Hydrovac*—a hydraulic-vacuum power-braking unit developed by Bendix is everything you expect a genuine postwar product to be. Moreover, although it is entirely new in design and performance—the last word in advanced engineering—more than a million units have been built and it has been proved by billions of miles of service on the world's battlefronts.

Now available for civilian trucks and busses,

Hydrovac does the hard work of brake application, yet gives drivers the natural pedal action and feel needed for greatest safety and efficiency. This mighty *mechanical muscle* is easily connected into the vehicle's hydraulic system and needs no adjustment at installation or in service. Because of its compact, sealed design, it has no outside working parts to clog with rust and dirt. And it does not burden the engine because its power is

derived from the vacuum already existing in the intake manifold.

If you own, sell, buy or service trucks or busses, you will naturally want to know more about Hydrovac—the most advanced and best-proved new power-braking unit. For an interesting booklet giving full details, write direct to

**BENDIX PRODUCTS DIVISION
SOUTH BEND 20, INDIANA**

*Trade Mark
COPYRIGHT 1946 BENDIX AVIATION CORPORATION

Listen to "MEN OF VISION" Sundays 7 P.M. E.W.T. CBS.

First **IN CREATIVE ENGINEERING**
Builders of the INVISIBLE CREW

PRODUCT OF **Bendix** AVIATION CORPORATION
Precision Equipment

A vintage advertisement touts the advantages of the Bendix Hydrovac, a hydraulic-vacuum power-braking unit installed on CCKWs. In September 1941 the Hydrovac replaced the brake vacuum booster on CCKWs, and in May 1943 the second series Hydrovacs became standard in CCKWs.

Assembly-line workers at Chevrolet's St. Louis, Missouri, plant put the finishing touches on CCKW-353s. The presence of a winch and Chevrolet "banjo" axles on the first truck identifies it as a CCKW-353-B2. One worker can be seen standing on a small platform attached to a vehicle's wheel. These trucks have not had their final coat of paint applied as is apparent from all the unpainted fasteners dotting the body and primered fenders. (National Archives)

Completed open-cab chassis are parked outside of Chevrolet's St. Louis plant awaiting delivery. Open-cab CCKW production at the St. Louis plant commenced around 1 February 1943. (National Archives)

Chapter 11
CCKWs for the Navy

On 27 February 1943 Yellow Truck and Coach received a request to manufacture 15 special CCKW chassis for the Navy. These chassis, which would be used as the basis for vehicles designated Amphibious Craft Repair Units (ACRU), were divided into eight without winch, and seven with winch. All were to be furnished with 11.00-18 wheels and tires as found on the DUKW, single wheels being used on the rear, and a spare tire furnished as well. No spare tire carrier was to be provided, and the trucks were to be boxed, Twin Unit Pack, for export. It was specified that these trucks were to be shipped no later than 9 March 1943. The bodies for these trucks would be procured directly by the Navy's Bureau of Yards and Docks.

In order to supply the components for these trucks and meet the specified deadline, considerable shuffling of paperwork on the part of Production Control was required.

Fifteen trucks were cancelled from sales order TC-200297 which secured the Chevrolet axles required in order to utilize DUKW wheels. Sales order TC-200545 was issued to build the eight no-winch ACRU chassis, and TC-200546 was issued to create the seven chassis with winches. Seven trucks were cancelled from TC-200298

which secured the winches for the ACRU chassis, and were replaced by seven non-winch trucks that were added to TC-200296. The DUKW tires and wheels, which were in short supply, were robbed from DUKW production, and purchase orders were immediately issued for replacements.

The 15 ACRU chassis were built the week of 1 March. Because of the size of the tires, standard twin-unit boxing could not be used – plus conventional twin-unit boxing was for two identical chassis to be boxed as a pair, whereas for this order the Navy specified that one winch-equipped truck was to be paired with a non-winch truck in a pack. To create these special boxes, as well as the special single pack for the odd-numbered non-winch ACRU, and not interrupt the workflow of the boxing department, it was decided to work overtime on Sunday, 5 March 1943.

On 29 March there came a second order for more of the same vehicles, this time for 18 chassis. Two of the trucks without winch were to be delivered on wheels, along with a single example with winch. These were to be available for delivery to Fisher Body in Detroit on 2 April. The remaining 15 chassis, consisting of eight without winch and seven with winch, were to be boxed and ready for shipment on 4

From February 1943 to April 1944, GMC fulfilled several sales orders from the U.S. Navy for CCKW-353 chassis with Chevrolet axles and DUKW-type wheels and 11.00-18 desert-tread tires, two per axle. Some were equipped with front winches and some were not. The chassis with DUKW wheels and tires and a front winch depicted here was earmarked to receive a special-purpose body designated the amphibious craft repair unit. (General Motors)

April. Once again, it was authorized to rob 18 sets of wheels and tires from DUKW production to achieve these goals. These 18 trucks were a portion of an order for 150 of these chassis that had been scheduled for May production. The sales orders for the May production were TC-200547 for 72, now reduced to 62, without winch chassis, and TC-200548 for the winch models. Once again, the decision was made to work overtime on Sunday, 4 April in order to box these 18 trucks without disturbing the already scheduled boxing operations.

On 20 March 1944 the Detroit Ordnance District issued the following directive, "You are directed to divert sixty (60) chassis, 2-1/2 ton, 6x6, LWB, W/O/W, and sixty sets of Spare Parts for First Year only per List. No. TRK-741-R from regular production so as to supply thirty (30) of these jobs in March and thirty (30) in April for the Navy Department.

"Tires shall be 11:00 x 18 – 10 Ply, single front and Tandem single rear, Military Desert Sand tires.

"Frames to be drilled for body mounting in accordance with General Motors Overseas Operations Drawing No. X-4138."

It was realized shortly thereafter that this change order was incorrect, and on 29 March it was corrected to reflect 20 chassis with winch and 40 chassis without winch. The order, which originally specified that the vehicles were to be boxed, single-unit pack, was also changed to indicate the chassis were to be delivered on wheels. Change order P-223 to Contract W-374-ORD-6458 authorized these chassis.

The 40 trucks without winch were built on sales order TC-200617 and 20 chassis with winch on sales order TC-200618.

Another change order relating to Navy chassis and Contract W-374-ORD-6458 was issued 25 April 1944. In response to this change order, Sales Manager A. A. Dodd issued the following memo on 27 April: "Attached hereto is copy of Change Order P-263 under the subject contract, which directs that we proceed with the preparation of 276 additional chassis for the Navy Department as follows:

"204 – 2-1/2 Ton, 6x6, LWB chassis, WOW – Item No. 2

"72 – 2-1/2 Ton, 6x6, LWB chassis, WW – Item No. 5

"Each of the above vehicles to be equipped as follows:

"(a)   11.00/18 Single Front and Tandem Rear, 10 Ply, Military Desert Sand Tires.

"(b)   One (1) 11.00/18 spare tire and tube mounted on spare wheel

"(c)   Standard spare tire carrier for 7.50/20 size tire.

"(d)   Frames to be drilled for body mounting in accordance with General Motors Overseas Operations Drawing No. X-4138.

"(e)   Cab to be drilled for identification plates in accordance with General Motors Overseas Operations Drawing No. X-4182.

"(f)   All vehicles to be delivered on wheels.

"Please note that the Change Order included authority to divert necessary materials from Amphibian trucks and that delivery of these vehicles has been requested as follows:

"May – 1944 – 60 trucks

"June   90

"July   90

"August   36"

The same CCKW-353-B2 is viewed from the right side. A spare tire was stored on top of the chassis frame between the tandem wheels. The total number of these CCKWs with DUKW wheels and tires ordered was 444. (General Motors)

The following day GMC realized that all the winch-equipped chassis trucks, Item No. 5, on contract -6458, which they had been directed to divert to the Navy on this change order, had already been delivered. So, instead, they diverted winch-equipped cargo truck components to build the Navy chassis.

Even more of these special chassis were requested on 15 September, when 50 more of the type without winch and 25 more with winch were asked for. These chassis trucks were to be taken out of Contract W-20-018-ORD-1299. However, not only were none of the requisite item-2 and item-5 chassis scheduled until January 1945, there were no excess tires and wheels available in the DUKW program. To purchase the materials for these trucks would take 90 days, which then put the estimated delivery date at 120 days from receipt of the military change order.

This forecast delivery was not at all satisfactory to the Ordnance Department, which responded by requiring that the chassis be built in November. Change Order P-317 directing this timing was issued 20 October 1944.

As fulfilling this request would have required halting DUKW production – production which had a higher wartime priority rating than the creation of the atomic bomb – stopping amphibian production was not an option for GMC. For that reason, GMC requested the Ordnance Department secure the needed components from the suppliers. They were successful, and GMC's Blevins issued the following memo on 4 November 1944: "As directed in Change Order P-317, subject 75 vehicles for the Navy are scheduled for building and shipping in November. The scheduling of these vehicles in November is per Mr. R. A. Crist's instructions and is in advance of our original estimate. Therefore, every effort should be made to secure the materials so that they can be built the week of November 20, 1944. In Mr. Vinton's memo, which will be supplemented by a sales change, you will find that these vehicles will have special markings as were used on TC-200617 and TC-200623 for which we were given a drawing showing the location of the marks for each chassis. Only exception is that the 'ARU' numbers 93 through 117 are to be used and the same number will apply on two of TC-200649 and TC-200650."

The completion and shipment of these 75 trucks marked the end of Navy ACRU chassis production.

Above: The sample CCKW-353-B2 that GMC fitted with DUKW wheels and tires for the navy is viewed from another angle. The cab was fitted with the early-type soft cover, and brackets for a ring mount were present. (General Motors)

Right: The installation of 11.00-18 tires and wheels on the CCKW necessitated the use of special adapters on the axles, and the Chevrolet axles were selected because of their adaptability to these tires. (General Motors)

Some of the CCKWs with 11.00-18 desert-tread tires ordered by the navy received special shop bodies for use by amphibious craft repair units (ACRU). This example, U.S. Army registration number 0081152, bears markings on the bumper for the 464th Engineer Boat Maintenance Battalion of the 4th Engineer Special Brigade. (General Motors)

A more full view of the ACRU shop vehicle partially visible to the far right in the preceding photo, U.S.A. 0081147, is presented. Visible inside the body are various shop tools, including a drill press, bench grinder, and other machinery. (General Motors)

Chapter 12
Cargo-dump trucks

Engineer Board Report number 683, issued 20 May 1942 documented the early efforts of the Corps of Engineers to develop a dump truck version of the CCKW. This effort was made with the cooperation of the Daybrook Hydraulic Company of Bowling Green, Ohio. Two pilot trucks were procured for these tests. One was outfitted with a dump bed with inside dimensions of 70 inches x 147 inches and the other measuring 80 inches x 147 inches. Both bodies featured an overload spacer plate, which when in the raised position, prevented the front axle from being overloaded when hauling high-density material. The 70-inch wide body utilized a six-inch diameter lift cylinder, while the larger body used a seven-inch cylinder.

As the Engineers worked on their dump-truck design, the Quartermaster Corps adopted a dump truck based on the shorter CCKW-352 chassis. However, Report 683 noted, "It is understood that due to the lack of manufacturing facilities, it will be about 1-1/2 years before the Quartermaster 2-1/2 ton dump truck can be put into production." The Engineers objected to the smaller truck. While they recognized the risk of overloading the longer bed, its ability to transport longer timbers or a full squad of men outweighed the risk. The engineers also felt that the 2½-ton dump truck should be an across-the-board replacement for the 1½-ton 4x4 dump truck then in use.

Before the Quartermaster dump truck could enter production, the Engineers' position prevailed, and as previously mentioned, on 1 August 1942 Ordnance took over vehicle procurement from the

The Engineer Board began development of a combination cargo-dump body for the 2½-ton 6x6 chassis in December 1941, testing of which was conducted from January to May 1942. Intended for use by Army Engineers, the cargo-dump truck featured a 147-inch-long by 80-inch-wide (interior dimensions) tilting body on a long-wheelbase CCKW.

Quartermasters. By 16 January 1943 Ordnance had placed on order 18,138 dump trucks with winch.

The body for these trucks was to be 12 feet long, and configured for use as either a troop carrier or a dump truck. The body was to use the standard top bows and tarpaulin, although a cab protector was to be built into the front of the body. The hinged partition, as found in the Engineers pilot trucks, was to be featured. The resulting body had a 3.85-cubic-yard capacity with the partition lowered, reduced to 2.58 when the partition was raised. Rated cubic capacity is measured by the water level capacity of the body.

The demand for these trucks was immediate, and the Army requested that Yellow schedule 700 of these vehicles with winch for production the next month, March, and carrying forward into April they were to be delivered at a rate of 100 per day. Yellow Truck and Coach was unable to meet this request, owing to the difficulties in obtaining the needed materials. As a compromise, the Army agreed to take 1,300 dump trucks without winches in April.

Coincidental with the introduction of the cargo dump trucks was the introduction of the previously mentioned open cab. As a matter of fact, the third open cab truck produced (which was on sales order TC-200549) was sent to Streator, Illinois, for the pilot installation of the Anthony cargo-dump body, arriving there on 13 March 1943. Anthony was to build 99 more bodies and ship them to Pontiac for assembly on trucks the week of March 22, with the 100 vehicles to be shipped on wheels. A further 400 bodies were to built, boxed and shipped to meet with 400 additional chassis, boxed for export.

Additional production pilots were produced, with TC-200550 yielding a cargo dump chassis that was sent to Hercules Products bodies in Galion, Ohio, on 25 March. The Heil Company of Milwaukee was also sent a pilot on 25 March, that chassis being built on sales order TC-200551. All three of the pilot dump chassis, like the rest of the 1,300-truck order, had Timken axles. The dump truck production was divided, under the above listed sales orders, as 500 each for Anthony and Heil, and 300 for Hercules.

In order to aid in keeping the flow of chassis for these trucks straight in the factory, Mr. Blevins issued a memo on 16 March reading in part: "So there will be no confusion in the mounting of the bodies and hoists for the first one hundred (100) vehicles, wish to advise that we are marking the first one hundred (100) chassis tags 'Dump Body.' The balance of the twelve-hundred (1200) will be marked 'KD Dump.'"

Dump trucks, like cargo trucks, were scheduled for production with both Timken and Chevrolet axles. However, on 31 March 1943 a conference was held at the Tank & Automotive Center concerning standardizing axles under various types of trucks. Attending for the government were Colonel Van Deusen, Colonel Chormley, Mr. Robert Brown, and representing GMC were Dodd, Riggs, and Crist. Naturally the topic would impact the 18,138 dump trucks on order.

As a result of this conference the decision was made to switch

In keeping with its nature as a cargo as well as a dump truck, this example, U.S. A. number 4193732 based on an open-cab CCKW-353 chassis, exhibits racks with troop seats on the sides of the body. At the front of the body was a tall rack. The body was fabricated from welded hot-rolled steel plates with reinforcing channels on the sides. (General Motors)

5,510 dump trucks scheduled for Chevrolet axles in the upcoming production to Timken axles, in an effort to keep Timken axles beneath all the dump trucks. Unfortunately by 17 April this plan fell apart as a result of labor problems at the Timken axle plant, and 5,054 dump trucks with Chevrolet axles were back in the schedule.

There remained the matter of the winch-equipped cargo-dump trucks, a staggering 15,383 of them on sales order TC-200522. This reduction from the previously ordered 18,138 cargo-dump trucks was documented in a memo from R. A. Crist on 26 June 1943 reading as follows: "This will also serve to confirm your instructions that the cut back of item 1-B Dump Trucks, from 18138 to 15383 total, and the 448 trucks which are in the 1944 program – Contract W-374-ORD-6458 – are to be dealt with on a percentage basis; i.e., in making the cut-back it is to be spread equally over all body builders. We have, therefore, set up the following table which shows the percentage split of the body business as it now exists, and the number of bodies which are now to be allocated to each body builder on the basis of the new requirements."

18138 Dump Bodies

	Old Release	% Total	New 1943	1944	Total
Anthony	3000	16.5%	2611		2611
Galion	5000	27.6	3922	448	4370
Gar Wood	1000	5.5	870		870
Heil	1000	5.5	870		870
Hercules	4000	22.1	3500		3500
Perfection	4138	22.8	3610		3610
	18138	100.0%	15383	448	15831

Winches & Hoists

	Old Release	% Total	New 1943	1944	Total
Gar Wood	9069	50.0%	7692	224	7916
Heil	9069	50.0%	7691	224	7915
	18138	100.0%	15383	448	158931

By August of 1943 dump truck production was being jeopardized by delayed power take off shipments from Heil, to the point that GM sent people to Milwaukee in hopes of establishing a more consistent rate of production. The dual power take off would continue to be in critically short supply for some time, as well as the universal joints used in the dump body driveline.

By 7 September the Timken axle shortage seemed to be resolved, and the Dump Trucks with Chevrolet axles on sales order TC-200523, which by then had grown to 5327, were cancelled and replaced by a like number with Timken axles added to sales order TC-200522. Thus, it appeared that the Army's desire to standardize axles would work, at least with regard to the dump trucks.

That plan held until April 1944, when the ever-increasing demand for cargo dump trucks, and the ever-present axle shortage, combined to cause sales order TC-200607 to be written for 4,609 cargo dump trucks with Chevrolet axles. This would later be joined by TC-200683 for 9,860 more of the type, and in fact among the very last CCKWs built in St. Louis were 40 cargo dumps on sales order TC-200772.

The combined production of both Pontiac and St. Louis was 37,803 cargo dump trucks, including both thoese with Chevrolet and Timken axles. This does not include the pure dump trucks made specially for the Navy

The dump truck had the fuel tank and the battery box in the usual position for a long-wheelbase chassis, to the rear of the right side of the cab. The bottoms of the stake racks are exposed on the outside of the cargo-dump body. The front rack was fitted with an angled brace on each side. (General Motors)

The cargo-dump body is shown tilted. The power-hoist assembly featured a 7-inch hydraulic cylinder, visible here. The hoist assemblies were manufactured by the Heil Co. and by Gar Wood Industries. The body hinges were at the rear of the chassis frame. (General Motors)

Above: The spare tire was stored horizontally below the front left corner of the dump body. Bows could be installed in pockets on top of the racks for purposes of erecting a tarpaulin over the body, and tie-down hooks were attached to the sides of the body and on the tailgate for lashing-down the tarpaulin. (General Motors)

Right: Cargo-dump truck U.S.A. number 4139712 is viewed from the front. Protruding above the top of the cab is the top of the front rack. It was fabricated from wooden slats with metal-reinforced edges and two vertical stakes for supporting the rack. (General Motors)

The cargo-dump body is tilted in this view from the front. The two stakes on the front of the forward rack fitted through the top sill of the body and into two stake pockets mounted on the front of the body. Visible on the underside of the body is a tool box, located to the side, rather than the standard rear-mounted position on cargo trucks. (General Motors)

Because overloading the cargo-dump body with too much material toward the front of the body could place enormous stresses on the chassis frame and the front suspension, a folding partition was attached to the floor. Before a load to be dumped was placed in the body, the partition was raised, as here, and locked in place with bolts through the body sides. (General Motors)

The front rack of the cargo-dump body was equipped with a wooden cab protector with reinforced metal edges. This protector was hinged at the top and typically was folded upward and forward when the vehicle was used as a dump truck. (General Motors)

The cab protector is deployed; it was secured in this position by a turnbuckle on each side, attached to the front rack. At the lower front of the body is the tailgate lever. The dump hoist was operated by two levers in the cab: one to engage the power takeoff and start the pump running, and the other to control the pump in order to raise, hold, or lower the body. (General Motors)

The two structures protruding below the front of the cargo-dump body were designed to keep the body in alignment with the frame when the body was lowered. The left body hinge is visible above the rear tandem tires. (General Motors)

With the bed tilted, the 7-inch hydraulic cylinder and the lifting linkage are visible under the body. The hoist assembly had a total weight of 900 pounds. The body had an inside height of 14 inches. (General Motors)

The left side of a CCKW cargo-dump truck cab and the front of the body are viewed close-up. The operating lever for the tailgate is visible at the front of the body. The steel plate with the bent top at the top of the front rack acted as a support for the cab protector when deployed. (General Motors)

The right rear corner of the cargo-dump body and the right side of the tailgate are displayed. The tailgate was top- and bottom-hinged, with the tailgate lever designed to release the jaws at the bottom hinges, allowing the tailgate to swing on the top hinges. (General Motors)

Navy Dump Trucks

Early on, the allocation for 2½-ton 6x6 truck production had been laid down. The U.S. Army would use the GMC as its primary vehicle in this range, the Marine Corps would use International Harvester trucks, and Studebaker would be the preferred builder for foreign-aid vehicles. As we have already seen, there were some exceptions to this pattern, and the vehicles discussed in this chapter are among them.

Faced with an urgent need for dump trucks, and unable to secure enough Internationals to fill the immediate need, the Navy Department, at the behest of the Marines, approached the Detroit Ordnance District in early 1943 requesting 900 CCKW-352 trucks equipped with dump bodies manufactured by the Galion All-Steel Body Company, Galion, Ohio. This request was urgent.

On 8 February 1943 the Detroit Ordnance District contracting officer approached Yellow Truck and Coach to divert 900 short-wheelbase, non-winch trucks (item 1-C, in Yellow's terms) scheduled for the first quarter of 1943 to fill the Navy's needs. On 13 February this quantity was reduced to 860 trucks.

Yellow management instructed production to fill this request from Pontiac production in the following manner. Remove and place into storage cargo bodies already installed on 52 cargo trucks which had been built on sales order TC-200299. Not to mount the bodies on the 18 vehicles remaining on that same sales order. And, to omit the bodies from 790 of the trucks on sales order TC-200300. All 860 vehicles were to be shipped on government bills of lading to Galion, which would mount the bodies. Two of the trucks were to be expedited to serve as pilots.

New sales orders were generated to account for this work within Yellow, sales order TC-200542 was for the 70 vehicles taken from TC-200299, all of which had Chevrolet axles. The remaining 790 vehicles, which had Timken axles, would be covered by sales order TC-200300. On 25 February 1943 the Detroit Ordnance District changed its directive for the third and final time, reducing the total number of vehicles involved to 800. Therefore, 60 vehicles were cancelled from TC-200543 and put back on the TC-200300.

The first 52 vehicles, all with Chevrolet axles, were shipped from Pontiac in February, with 468 more following in March, and the final 280 shipping in April. Because of the time frame involved, the initial shipments were of closed-cab trucks, while the later shipments had open cabs.

A camouflage-painted short-wheelbase CCKW dump truck assigned to ACORN 7 releases a load during a construction project in the Pacific. ACORNs were naval units comprising a naval construction battalion (Seabees) and other elements. (National Archives)

A short-wheelbase CCKW dump truck assigned to ACORN 8 unloads a supply of pierced matting for airfield construction at Point Mugu, California. At this time, ACORN 8 was based with the ACORN Training Detachment at Port Hueneme, California. (National Archives)

In an excavating operation, a ¾-cubic-yard Buckeye power shovel is loading a Navy Special CCKW-352 dump truck with a Galion body at the center of the photograph. Two other Navy Special CCKW-352 dump trucks are partially visible toward the left. (U.S. Army Engineer School History Office)

Chapter 13
Mid-Production AFKWX

The initial production order for the cab-over-engine model discussed in Chapter 8 was followed almost immediately by an order for 612 more AFKWX trucks on contract W-374-ORD-QM-11595. As of 12 January 1942 these trucks were scheduled for deliveries of 100 trucks per month from June 1942 through November, with the final 12 to be built in December. The frames for these trucks would be made by Midland Steel.

On 25 May 1942 a new release of 962 Cab Over Engine trucks was requested to supercede the 612 already on order. In a memo dated 20 July 1942, which discussed the many diversions of CCKW materials from the prime contract to miscellaneous contracts in order to fill various government requests, there is an important mention of the AFKWX. The memo reads: "This accounts for 667 of the 668 diversions. The other one is the AFKW-353 (Cab-over-Engine) on

which you have already cut back the sales order from 612 to 611, to produce the sample DUKW."

As seen in this memo, beginning with these 611 trucks, built on sales order TC-200304, the internal GM documents refer to these vehicles as AFKW-353, the "X" being dropped from the model number.

During the production of these 611 trucks, the cargo body changed from all-steel to wooden. The first 250 trucks of this lot, serial numbers 3076 through 3325 (Registration numbers 4209047 through 4209297) would have steel cargo bodies. The remaining trucks, serial numbers 3325 through 3686, registration numbers 4209298 through 4209657, would have wooden bodies. While at the time General Motors built wooden cargo bodies for 6x6s in three locations – Yellow Truck and Coach in Pontiac, and Chevrolet in both St. Louis and in Atlanta – only Pontiac would build the 15-foot wooden body used on

A mid-production GMC AFKWX, U.S.A. number 4300150, as observed from the front right, was distinguished by an open cab with a canvas top and doors with the early-type mismatched clear-plastic windows, one horizontally oriented and the other vertically oriented. Another characteristic was the wooden body. (General Motors)

Above: Under the mammoth government contract W-398-QM-11595 (later redesignated W-374-Ord-2597), 2,172 AFKWX-353 cab-over-engine trucks such as U.S.A. number 4300150, depicted here, were delivered under two GMC sales orders: TC-200304, for 611 trucks (250 with steel bodies, 361 with wood), and TC-200471, for 1,561 trucks (wood bodies) built from May to November 1943. AFKWX-353s produced under those two sales orders are considered mid-production vehicles. Construction features of the wooden body are visible. Fastened to the sideboards were metal stake pockets, but the racks did not include troop seats. (General Motors)

Left: To the front of the passenger's door is the forward bracket for a ring mount for a machine gun. The windshield of the open cab was the same as that used on the open-cab CCKW, with a bottom-pivoting, tubular outer frame enclosing and holding the top-hinged windshield frame. (General Motors)

The same AFKWX shown in the preceding photograph, U.S.A. number 4300150, is viewed with the tarpaulin, bows, and cab top and curtains installed. The bodies, both steel and wood, of AFKWX-353s produced under contract W-398-QM-11595 were 15 feet long. (General Motors)

Mid-production AFKWX-353 4300150 is displayed with the windshield assembly lowered. Over the service headlights were marker lamps. A blackout headlight is peeking through the upper left brush guard. (General Motors)

the AFKW.

As 1 September neared, 310 of the cab-over trucks had been built (including the 60 on the first order). The Army was pressing for 27 more of the trucks on order, as well as 447 CCKW trucks. In memo of 22 August 1942, Yellow Truck and Coach's A. A. Dodd writes regarding these: "These trucks are all built and have not been warehoused before closing for inventory due to shortages cover radio shielding and repairs. As it is imperative that these all be shipped on or before September 5th, would ask that Mr. Hansel give these 474 trucks his personal attention and get them to the warehouse as quickly as possible to complete this shipment."

Despite this urgency of this request, 17 of the AFKWs would not ship until 9 September due to the company's annual inventory as well as the length of time required to make the necessary repairs to the trucks. However, by the end of 1942, all 671 of these trucks on the first two production orders had been completed. The vehicles were produced from May through December, with the monthly deliveries as follows: 18, 127, 115, 50, 65, 124, 130, and 42.

Sales order TC-200471 covered the production of another 351 AFKW with 15-foot wooden beds. This was increased to 970 of the trucks by Contract Supplement 13, and finally revised on 17 April 1943 to 1,561. But these trucks would be different; they would have open cabs.

The introduction of the open cab to the AFKW was the result of a requirement by the Purchasing and Contracting Officer of Ordnance on 20 July 1942. Yellow Truck and Coach objected to this, on the basis of the relatively small quantity of these trucks to be produced and the amount of engineering resources required to create such a cab design. Col. Van Deusen with Ordnance was insistent, however, and the design was proceeded with. A letter dated 8 January 1943 from A. A. Dodd stated: "We have just received notice of approval from D.O.D. of our Drawing No. MD-61527 dated 11-5-42 covering the

Open Type Cab for C.O.E. Trucks under the subject contract. This approval was received in a letter dated December 16, 1942, received here January 9, 1943 – a copy of which is attached.

"Please note that we are requested to start the C.O.E. Type Open Cab in production at the earliest possible date, and we are also requested to quote the cost change as promptly as possible."

Production of these 1,561 trucks, which had brought the total thus far on contract W-398-QM-11595 up to 2,172, began in May 1943. Demand for these trucks remained high, and in October R. A. Crist wrote

"During the months preceding October, 1943, there had been constant pressure to get every possible truck of the Cab-over-engine type. There were 2172 on contract W-374-ORD-2597 (11595). During October there was a big drive to clean up the contract on this items and many hand-springs were turn in an endeavor to meet Ordnance demand.

"Delivery of this type truck caused trouble throughout the war, due to Ordnance not forecasting their requirements first, then, because the difficulty securing parts peculiar to this type truck in the limited quantities required, and the limited special tooling provided."

More than once production of the trucks have to halted due to shortages of parts, notably radiator supports, spring shackles, brake pedals and left-hand cab support brackets. Compounding this was the use of sheetmetal originally allocated for the cabs on these trucks to produce DUKWs instead.

Ultimately, the 1,561 trucks were built from May through November 1943. The trucks were serial number 3687 through 5247. The registration numbers were 4209558; 4300109 though 4300458; 4484334 through 4484952; and 4549571 through 4550161, reflecting the various contract extensions. The monthly delivery figures beginning in May were 60, 324, 401, 226, 227, 220, and 103.

Chapter 14
CCKW Production Continues

The big changes to CCKW during 1942 had been the starting – and stopping – of CCKW production at Chevrolet-Baltimore, the introduction of the antiaircraft machine gun mount, the transition from an all-steel cargo body to one made primarily of wood, and the planning for the introduction of the open cab. But for the cessation of Baltimore production, all of these same issues would still be at play when the calendars were flipped to January 1943.

The wooden cargo body situation was the most chaotic of the above issues on New Year's Day 1943. On 11 December 1942 Colonel Tossy of the Detroit Ordnance District had sent Yellow Truck and Coach a letter that turned body production on its head. The letter read: "You are hereby directed to discontinue the assembling of wood cargo bodies at your plants after December 31, 1942; and you are also requested to hold to a minimum your commitments and releases to subcontractors supplying you with materials."

"The reason for the above is that, in the future the Government will do all contracting for your wood cargo bodies."

"It is apparent that the future program will give consideration to subcontractors, such as those who are presently supplying you with dimensional lumber, parts, and other material used in the assembly of the bodies, in that they will be utilized, as far as possible, as suppliers to the body manufacturers whom the government will select. Also, it is the intent of the Government that present commitments to the prime vehicle contractors will be recommitted to the body builders to the maximum extent, and that all subcontractors will be protected as far as possible. The exception to the above will be those subcontractors who will eventually be eliminated from the wood body program because they have other business."

Wooden bodies for the CCKW program at this point were being built in three locations: Yellow Truck and Coach, Pontiac; Chevrolet, St. Louis; and Chevrolet, Atlanta. The last location was building and boxing 12-foot bodies that were being used in conjunction with export boxed trucks. Those bodies were shipped directly to the same destinations as the boxed chassis, rather than being shipped to the truck assembly plants.

On 12 January, the Army issued a requirement that 2,950 long-wheelbase, no-winch trucks and 1,450 long-wheelbase with-winch trucks, all with closed cabs and with roof wells for machine gun

The CCKWs produced from late April 1943 to late January 1944 are considered the mid-production vehicles. These encompassed serial numbers 213652 to 321077 and were characterized by open cabs and wooden cargo bodies. Seen here in a 22 January 1944 photo is CCKW-353 U.S.A. number 4282420. (General Motors via Bryce Sunderlin)

mounts be delivered by 15 March. All were to be boxed for export.

To achieve this, sales orders TC-200297 and TC-200298 were revised downward, and new sales orders TC-200498 for the non-winch trucks and TC-200499 for the winch models were issued.

The Army, in the final month of 1942, had intimated its desire to change the delivery schedule considerably, and in some cases the quantities, of various specific truck types in 1943. On 6 January, after several meetings with government representatives, a so-called final schedule was arrived at and A. A. Dodd accordingly authorized production of the vehicles covered in Supplement 13 to Contract W-374-ORD-2597 (W-398-QM-11595). These trucks would enter production in May 1943.

The ripple effects of all of these changes often overlapped. St. Louis sales order TC-200294 serves as an example of this – and was mimicked by numerous sales orders. This sales order for CCKW-353 without winch featuring Chevrolet axles, to be delivered on wheels, was reduced from 27,640 trucks to 21,348 by a 15 January 1943 memo. The bodies on these trucks were to be as follows:

8,153 assembled steel bodies
2,268 knocked-down steel bodies later assembled in St. Louis
6,941 wooden bodies purchased by Yellow Truck and Coach
3,986 wooden bodies furnished by the government.

Later adjustments would raise the quantity of trucks on this sales order to 23,451, and added to this confusion was the whole closed-cab vs. open-cab matter, and this was just a single sales order out of the dozens on this contract.

This situation, complicated enough already, was compounded a week later. On 25 January Yellow Truck and Coach production received a memo sent three days earlier by A.A. Dodd, attached to which was a letter dated 19 January from the Detroit Ordnance District's Col. Tossy. Tossy's letter read, in part: "Attached are revised production schedules for 1943 on subject contracts. Will you please supply this office in writing confirmation of this schedule at your earliest convenience."

A responding memo to Dodd from Production Control Manager R. A. Crist addressed the many problems this letter caused. Crist wrote, "When your memo of the 22nd was received on the 25th, we assumed that the schedule sheet attached was a confirmation of the figures agreed upon in the early part of January, and which were incorporated in the January 16th schedule sheets issued with my letter of January 21st. You will recall that you handed Mr. Gunderson a revised production schedule sheet on December 30th, and the subsequent three weeks was spent in a complete revamping of the basic control schedules on paper, and we are now in the midst of completely rescheduling all material based on our January 16th Basic Control Schedule."

"Over the week-end I started checking the figures shown on the schedule attached to Colonel Tossy's letter, and much to my surprise I find a number of changes in schedules as well as a number of

CCKW-353 U.S. Army registration number 4501222 exhibits the late-type cab cover, with a tightly fitting top and canvas doors with two equal-sized soft-plastic windows. A metal stiffener on each side of the top created a straight, neat joint with the top of the door. (General Motors)

discrepancies. In short, this schedule does not agree with the program previously agreed upon. I have spent some completely rechecking these figures because it is a serious matter with us, if we have to go thru a complete rescheduling at this late date, and before we are finished with the job we started in January."

Crist summed up the issue further into his response – "Somehow or other, we must get across to Ordnance that changes in schedule present a major problem and cannot be dealt with lightly. It was my understanding that the purpose of getting together late in December was to reach mutual agreement on the schedule, so that all controversial issues could be ironed out before had and we would only have to through our paperwork once. Yet, before we can actually get our material rescheduling completed we are confronted with a revised schedule."

As a practical matter, much of the problem with the schedule changes requested by the military has to do with materials purchased by Yellow Truck and Coach. Yellow, who looked at the requested delivery dates issued early on, subsequently forecast its needs for materials and components for a given period of time and issued purchase orders accordingly – and also according to the specifications set forth in a given contract between Yellow and the Government. The Company's purchasing department was working with a January 1942 authorization for 141,389 trucks, a July 1942 authorization covering a further 78,607 trucks, a December 1942 authorization for 375 trucks, a 6 January 1943 authorization for 947 trucks and 20,026 trucks contracted for, but not yet scheduled for production.

On this matter, Crist further wrote in his response: "Material was purchased…to definite specifications at the time of authorization, with subsequent changes approved from time to time and bills of material were prepared and issued accordingly, with Sales Orders for each item in the Contract specifically tied up against each buy of material.

"Thus, the bills of material released against the 78607 trucks incorporated a number of changes; such as the HydroVac brake change, involving brackets, lines, fittings, cylinders, etc.; the new deep oil pan change in the engine, which also affected other related parts; new gas tanks with different fillers; new filters and parts in the radio suppression installation; and other minor changes.

"Consequently, in making the adjustments caused by advancing certain types of trucks from the 78607 buy (May to November inclusive) to the 141389 buy (Complete in April 1943), the paperwork is primary importance. The setting back of other types of jobs from the 141389 buy to the 78607 buy involves the same problem.

"Therefore, the break point between the 141389 buy and the 78607 buy is a major problem in any adjustment in schedule."

Several paragraphs later, Crist closed his response with:

"We are not taking action on this schedule, and will abide by the schedule of January 16th, except that we must have immediate decision on the Dump jobs to avoid a loss of 2700 trucks in production in March and April. In any event, aside from dropping the dump jobs and substituting 1-A Cargo's (long wheelbase, no winch trucks), we cannot make any changes in our present schedules before the Extension Contract comes into effect in May. I cannot spare the time to go down and argue with these people, but if necessary Gunderson can accompany you."

Mr. Dodd communicated Crist's concerns to the Detroit Ordnance District on 15 February. A representative of the Ordnance District responded on 24 February with a personally delivered proposed revision, requesting that Yellow Truck and Coach advise them what changes could be incorporated in Yellow's schedule without disrupting production.

Finally, on 5 March, a plan of production was informally agreed upon by Yellow Truck and Coach and the Detroit Ordnance District.

U.S. Army number 450122 is observed from the left side. The holders for five-gallon liquid containers on the running boards became a factory installation at approximately serial number 235000 in the early summer of 1943. (General Motors)

In a 6 March letter to the District summarizing the meeting, Dodd wrote to Col. Paul Tossy, "Your plan to discuss with the facility, proposed schedule changes and their effect on production prior to issuance of directives meets with our hearty approval, and we wish to assure you of our cooperation in endeavoring to effect such changes as necessary to make."

During this same time period the black-out driving lamp began to appear on the left front fender of the truck, and the brush guard was revised to protect it. Almost immediately thereafter the GMC logo was deleted from the grille in response to a mandate that all manufacturers of military vehicles cease including their emblems on the vehicles.

The deep oil pan mentioned in Crist's communication was a characteristic of the 3020 engine, the model that began to be used on the trucks built under Extension 3 of Contract 11595 (the buy of 78,607 trucks).

In November 1942, Yellow Truck and Coach had advised Ordnance that in March 1943 CCKW production would begin to feature open cabs. On 11 February Yellow Truck and Coach contacted Chevrolet-Central Office concerning these cabs on trucks produced by Chevrolet-St. Louis. That letter revealed: "It is planned, that you should start production of Open Cabs on vehicles approximately March 16th, or on 2300 of your March schedule and full production from then onward. As now planned regular production material should be available at St. Louis to meet the above program the latter part of February or the first week of March."

However, on 9 March, Ordnance demanded 1,300 dump trucks with closed cabs and Timken axles, a demand that changed production scheules at plants in both St. Louis and Pontiac. Ultimately, the open cabs were introduced to St. Louis production in the following manner:

	Feb	March	April	May	Totals
TC-200294	-	-	1,016	950	1,966
TC-200501	-	600	1,200	-	1,800
TC-200504	-	-	35	-	35
TC-200506	-	162	156	-	318
TC-200507	-	-	30	-	30
TC-200508	-	204	396	-	600
TC-200295	-	1,202	1,203	-	2,505
Total		2,300	4,400	950	7,650

Pontiac production was impacted as follows, largely due to the 1300 dump trucks using Timken axles, which thus far had not been used in St. Louis production.

	Feb	March	April	May	Totals
TC-200549	-	-	500	-	500*
TC-200550	-	-	300	-	300**
TC-200551	-	-	500	-	500***
TC-200296	-	916	1,303	-	2,219
TC-200297	197	547	0	-	744
TC-200502	-	750	0	-	750
TC-200503	-	150	218	-	368
TC-200298	-	1,266	1,787	-	3,053
TC-200500	-	-	1,000	-	1,000
TC-200512	-	0	1,379	-	1,379
TC-200543	-	330	0	-	330
TC-200513	-	37	0	-	37
TC-200511	-	70	100	-	170
Totals	197	4,066	7,087	-	11,350

*With Anthony dump body
** With Hercules dump body *** With Heil dump body

The tarpaulin on CCKW-353 U.S. Army registration number 4234797 is folded up, revealing the wooden cargo body and the racks. The troop seats on each side are in the deployed positions. U.S. Royal Master Grip 8-ply, 7.50-20 tires with nondirectional treads are mounted. (General Motors)

By the end of March, Ordnance had run into trouble getting adequate quantities of Ordnance Mobile Shop and Air Corps Oil Service bodies, and requested that Yellow Truck and Coach delay production of the chassis for these types by one month, with long-wheelbase cargo trucks without winch being constructed instead. This impacted 264 Oil Service trucks and 1,200 Van trucks that were being built in St. Louis. Shortages of dump bodies as well as the dual power take off revealed on 30 March resulted in 1,000 of the winch-equipped cargo dump trucks that had been scheduled for April production to be pushed back, and winch-equipped long-wheelbase cargo trucks to be produced instead.

On 22 March an improved, heavy duty, steering gear box began to be used, starting with serial number 201680.

On 5 April 1943 Yellow Truck and Coach accepted Letter Purchase Order, Supplement No. 19, Contract W-398-QM-11595 (W-374-ORD-2597), which adjusted the quantities of various trucks and chassis on that contract. To achieve the new goals, production, effective 1 July, was to be scheduled at 3,225 trucks per week. In addition, Yellow was behind schedule already, so in order to catch up, the April through June 30 production had to be sped up to a daily rate of 603 trucks per day on a five-day per week basis. To make this level of output somewhat more manageable, a six-day per week schedule was opted for, a change that resulted in a daily goal of 509, vehicles with the Pontiac facility producing 321 of these, and St. Louis the remaining 188 per day.

Yellow Truck and Coach walked a tight wire, balancing the ever-changing needs of Ordnance with the materials flowing into the plant, in-plant storage, and scheduling production so as to keep assembly-line workers steadily employed. Sometimes, despite all this planning, something went wrong. Such a case occurred in the first week of April 1943, when labor trouble at Timken Roller Bearing Company impacted production of axles at Timken Detroit Axle Company, with the result that about a week's production was lost. As a result, Yellow had to close its truck and engine assembly lines on Saturday, 17 April.

Thus far, Yellow Truck and Coach, in addition to building cargo trucks, cargo dump trucks, water tankers and fuel tankers, also built a bewildering array of special chassis. Each type truck, be it an air compressor truck, ordnance shop truck, Signal Corps van or any of the dozens of others, had a unique type chassis, with unique specifications. Some included fuel tanks, some did not, some included trailer electrical connections, others did not – the detail differences were many, which of course compounded any rescheduling issues. On 21 April this situation improved dramatically upon receipt of a letter from the Detroit Ordnance District. It stated: "It is proposed that as quickly as practicable all #2 chassis and all #5 chassis for various branches of the Services shall be standardized as long wheelbase without winch and long wheelbase with winch respectively.

"Customary deletions to be dispensed with and all material ordinarily furnished on the chassis upon which cargo bodies are mounted will be the accepted #2 and #5 chassis.

"You are requested to advise this office at the earliest possible moment of the cut-off quantities for the chassis furnished to various branches of service, approximate date on which the cut-offs will be accomplished, schedule for subsequent production on the standardized chassis models and such price changes as may be involved."

In implementing this new program, A. A. Dodd's memo of 23 April 1943 advised that the new program would be in place when production was initiated on the revised contract, forecast to begin in Pontiac about 4 May and in St. Louis approximately 11 May. The trailer couplings and tail lamps on the new chassis trucks would be furnished loose.

While this change did streamline production considerably, there remained some problems, and the government contracts did contain deadlines. Contract W-398-ORD-11595 called for completion by the end of 1943, with the exception of 5,327 cargo dump trucks Ordnance had asked to be delayed into 1944. This was brought up by Yellow Truck and Coach President Irving Babcock in July 1943. Production Control Manager Crist's response indicated that the production schedules were planned so as to meet this goal, although he did elaborate: "However, from a purely practical standpoint and looking at the actual production situation as it stands today, with respect to materials and manpower, it looks like a hopeless task. We are operating hand to mouth on the Albion malleable castings, due to lack of manpower at Albion. Timken is around 3000 sets of axles behind schedule and Mr. Livingston hasn't any assurance from them or Ordnance that they will pick up this shortage as well as meet future schedule, which is necessary to meet production as scheduled. Winches and power take-offs continue to plague us. Chevrolet axle steel is tight. And there are dozens of items on which we are working hand to mouth."

While still struggling to meet the 1943 production goals, by mid-July Yellow Truck and Coach had to begin issuing purchase orders for the materials needed to produce the 82,205 trucks scheduled for the first six months of 1944 production. On 12 July an agreement was reached with Chevrolet pertaining to their role in this production. Chevrolet-St. Louis would assemble 40,140 of the trucks, and Chevrolet-Flint would build 40,140 engines for them.

By August 1943 the war effort was stretching American production capacity to the limits, and beyond. The draft was increasingly depleting the skilled labor force, and the demand on raw materials exceeded availability. Many items were rationed and allocated – a good thing in the overall picture – with the War Production Board (WPB) directing materials to those projects most urgently needed in the big picture, independent of the strength of will of manufacturer or military service.

In the case of Yellow Truck and Coach, this situation was very much a double-edged sword. The DUKW enjoyed the highest WPB priority rating, and materials for the amphibians flowed freely. The CCKW, however, had a lower-priority rating, and its production paid the price, as exemplified in the following memo dated 14 August 1943, which came on the heels of a 3,144-truck shortfall registered in July that year:

"In view of the increasing number of shortages of material, which situation is growing more critical by the hour, the lack of Timken axles due to DOD directive diverting them elsewhere, and the shortage of manpower and absenteeism, I doubt if we will produce 11,000 trucks this month. Our daily schedules are actually set up on a basis of 300 per day for YT&C and 200 per day for St. Louis, or a total of 500 per day, which at 26 days, would produce 13,000 trucks. However, we have lost three Saturdays this month due to shortages, which would reduce the figure to 11,500, and we will probably lose more. Consequently, we will go into September behind schedule between 6000 and 7000 trucks."

This projection proved a bit pessimistic, with the actual shortfall as of 1 September being 5066 trucks, still a substantial number. That month additional manpower was needed in the Pontiac plant in order to increase DUKW production, so CCKW production there was reduced while being increased in St. Louis. Over a three month period time, November through 1 January, it was planned to taper Pontiac production to 220 trucks per day, while at the same time St. Louis was raised to 300 per day. Further, the cumulative shortfalls in CCKW production would be caught up in January 1944, rather than over the balance of 1943. Through careful planning it was established that this could be done while still using solely Chevrolet axles in St. Louis, with Pontiac using both types.

On 7 September 1943 the military began to specify the source of supply for the winches used on the CCKW. Previously, Yellow Truck and Coach (which would formally become GMC Truck and Coach Division on 20 September) used both Gar Wood and Heil winches, based on price and availability. That changed with a letter from the Detroit Ordnance District 7 September which read "You are directed to place your purchase order for 13,200 type 2U winches with The Heil Company, 3000 West Montana Street, Milwaukee, Wisconsin at once.

"It is the understanding of this office that the above amount of 2U winches together with the 10,038 now on order with the Heil Company will complete your 1944 ASF requirements."

Bearings were and are critical to the operation of virtually all war material, and the Army Air Force's targeting of Germany's bearing factories is well known. Less well known is that the United States itself was faced with a severe bearing shortage, a situation that became critical for GMC in late September 1943. At that time the WPB placed bearings under strict production control and allocation, which had the effect of dramatically reducing Chevrolet transfer cases and axles, as well as Timken axles. The impact on CCKW production was immediate and severe, forcing the issuing of new Basic Control Schedule Sheets on 24 September. The cover letter for these sheets summed up the situation:

"(2) Effective Monday, September 27th, the current production schedules are changed as follows:

"(a) Pontiac. Daily rate changed from 320 to 200 per day, necessitating the elimination of the second shift on truck assembly.

"(b) St. Louis. Daily rate changed from 200 to 150 per day."

These changes, added to the previous shortfall, meant that GMC was now planning to enter 1944 19,002 trucks behind, which they hoped to catch up 12,500 in January and 6,502 in February. The need to complete these contracts would delay beginning production of the 79,935 trucks then ordered on Contract W-374-ORD-6458 until sometime in February 1944.

In an effort to enforce the steady supply of components to its plants, when in November 1943 the Army negotiated for more trucks, GMC returned a conditional offer: "This completion date for 76,657 vehicles is agreed to, subject to their being made available to our subcontractor, Chevrolet-Gear & Axle Division, General Motors Corporation, Government-Owned Facilities for an increase in production of 900 sets of Chevrolet axles per week, starting no later than 1 July 1944, and is also subject to there being made available to our subcontractor, Warner Gear Division, Borg-Warner Corporation, Muncie, Indiana, additional facilities for increased production of transmissions for 2½ ton, 6x6 trucks, which we understand is being handled direct with the Warner Gear Division by Cincinnati Ordnance District."

The transmission and transfer case situation became so critical due to bearing shortages that in November and December of that year, no Chevrolet axle-equipped trucks could be built in Pontiac. Compounding an already bad situation was a request from the Detroit Ordnance District, received 17 November, for 1,335 long-wheelbase chassis trucks in January 1944, 1,300 in February and 1,355 in March. The problem with this request was succinctly put by R.A. Crist on 22 November: "This was in addition to 420 for November and 800 for December which been provided in our latest schedules at D.O.D.'s request without prior notice – all of which indicates an utter lack of planning at D.O.D. since there are none of these in the current contract.

"If anyone has the time, in the peacetime of the future, to read all these lurid details of production and can peer back into the hour-glass of the past, they would be apt to remark – "I wonder how in the h--- they built anything" – i.e., if they understand anything about mass production in the manner of the automotive industry."

Late in 1943 General Campbell posed the question to the Chief of Ordnance: "Why are not wooden bodies replaced with steel now that steel is available?" To this matter, on 3 December 1943, the Assistant Chief, Tank-Automotive Center, John K. Christmas, sent a memo to the Chief of Ordnance – Washington that would have a very visual impact on the CCKW. This memo introduced what is commonly referred to as the "composite" cargo body, a body with a wooden floor and steel sides. Beyond introducing the composite body, the memo also offered insights into wooden cargo body production, and is quoted here.

"1. At the outset of the present war effort our cargo bodies for trucks were of all-steel construction. We were directed by A.S.F. on 31 May 42, QM-451.21 to change over to wood cargo bodies at the earliest possible date and no later than 1 Sept 42 because of the shortage of carbon steel sheets. It was originally planned to have the vehicle manufacturers supply the wood cargo bodies as part of their vehicle contract. However, it was ultimately decided to place prime contracts for wood cargo bodies with small manufacturers according to a plan proffered by the Smaller War Plants Corporation."

The memo continued;

"3. Experience with the present wood cargo bodies, in which there are a minimum of steel reinforcing members, indicates the advisability of returning to the all-steel construction. However, this would adversely affect the smaller companies now producing the wood cargo bodies and consequently we propose effecting an engineering change at the earliest possible date to utilize a larger percentage of steel and secure a more rugged and durable body. The Tank-Automotive Center, working with industry, has prepared working sketches….and tentative bills of material for a composite cargo body. This body uses steel for the front panel, side panels, tail gate, bolsters and floor skid strips. Wood is used for the floor, longitudinal side sills and tool box floor.

"4. The change will bring about an increased requirement of approximately 2000 tons per month of carbon steel sheets."

"6. The Tank-Automotive Center is preparing an O.C.M. item to be read for the record. They are also arranging for the early completion of working drawings and detailed bills of material for the following body sizes: 80" x 144", 70" x 108", and 88" x 132". It is believed that this engineering change can be placed in production by approximately 1 July 1944 if we can receive prompt authorization."

When 1943 closed, GMC's annual production of CCKW and AFKW had totaled 131,708 trucks. Pontiac had built 79,993 of them, with St. Louis completing 51,715 of them.

U.S. Army registration number 44548846 was an example of a mid-production short-wheelbase CCKW-352 with a front winch. The late-type fuel filler is clearly visible below the spare tire. It was elbow shaped and 3¾ inches in diameter. (General Motors)

Above: CCKW-352 U.S.A. number 4807201, equipped with a winch, is displayed. The flap on the door below the rear side window allowed the driver to reach out from the cab to operate the latches at the bottom and the rear of the door. (General Motors)

Right: The same CCKW-352 shown in the preceding photo is observed from the left rear. This vehicle was part of GMC sales order TC-200639, part of contract QW-20-018-ORD-6052, which the Army awarded to General Motors on 8 September 1944. (General Motors)

In a rear view of the same CCKW-352, U.S.A. number 4807201, the design of the rear of the wooden body typical of mid-production CCKWs is exhibited. Visible below the bumperettes is the Timken rear tandem axle. (General Motors)

Left: A mid-production CCKW-353 with a winch is viewed from the front. This vehicle was U.S. Army registration number 4548846 and was fitted with Timken or split axles. The photograph was dated 24 January 1944. (General Motors)

Below: CCKW-352 U.S.A. number 4807201 is observed from the right side. Beginning with serial number 321670 in late February 1944, CCKWs were equipped with reinforced frames and the brake system was revamped. (General Motors)

149

CCKW-362 U.S. Army registration number 4548846 is seen from the right rear. A five-gallon container holder is located on the front of the running board, and on the inboard side of the running board are an axe and a mattock handle, secured with brackets and straps. (General Motors)

Above: This official photograph of a 2½-ton 6x6 long-wheelbase cargo-dump truck was taken by the Ordnance Operation, Engineering Standards Vehicle Laboratory, Detroit, Michigan, on 24 November 1944. The vehicle was serial number 395376H1. The number 187 was marked on the bumper. (TACOM LCMC History Office)

Left: The same cargo-dump truck is viewed from the front. Instead of the wide piece of shaped steel at the top of the forward rack that served as a support for the cab protector, as seen in earlier photos, now there were two small supports, one on each side, projecting from the top of the rack. (TACOM LCMC History Office)

Cargo-dump truck serial number 395376H1 is viewed from the left rear. A wheel without a tire is mounted on the spare-tire carrier below the front of the body. (TACOM LCMC History Office)

Left: The same cargo-dump truck is observed from the right side with the cab protector deployed. Turnbuckles were still used to secure the cab protector in place when deployed. (TACOM LCMC History Office)

Below: The floor of the dump body was a single sheet of 12 gauge (.1046) steel, without a filler or a sub-floor sheet. The partition to restrict the amount of load when the vehicle was used as a dump truck was 35 inches from the front of the body and was fitted with a piano hinge. (TACOM LCMC History Office)

This CCKW-352 chassis without a body bears U.S. Army registration number 4549114 on the hood. The small letter S on the cowl certifies that this vehicle has been tested for its radio-interference shielding. (General Motors)

Above: The same CCKW-352 chassis is viewed from the right side. Jutting above the left side of the chassis frame between the spare tires and the front tandem tires is the exhaust tail pipe. (General Motors)

Left: CCKW-352 4549114 is observed from the left front. The top and the cap of the late-type 3 ½-inch filler tube were at the same height as, and level with, the top of the sheet-metal sleeve enclosing the fuel tank. (General Motors)

With the body not present on this mid-production CCKW-352 chassis, the rear of the sheet-metal sleeve that enclosed the fuel tank is fully visible, including three large and one small holes in it. Details of the spare-tire clamps also are visible. (General Motors)

Left: A 700-gallon water tank truck based on a mid-production CCKW-353 chassis was photographed at the Ordnance Operation, Engineering Standards Vehicle Laboratory in Detroit, Michigan, on 1 February 1944. This vehicle was serial number 283457. (TACOM LCMC History Office)

Below: The 700-gallon water tank truck is observed from the right side with the cab top and curtains removed. Two large manholes and hinged covers were atop the tank; located between them, front to rear, were a vent and a fill hatch. (TACOM LCMC History Office)

The top and curtains have been removed from the cab in this view. At the rear of the water tank are doors for an equipment locker. A section of suction hose is strapped to the rear fender. (TACOM LCMC History Office)

The 700-gallon water tank truck based on a mid-production CCKW-353 chassis is viewed from the right rear with the top and curtains on the cab. (TACOM LCMC History Office)

The equipment locker contained water hoses and tools for the operation of the water tank. A step was attached to the bottom of each of the rear mud flaps and a grab handle was on each side of the tank. (TACOM LCMC History Office)

The 700-gallon water tank truck was photographed from above at the Ordnance Operation, Engineering Standards Vehicle Laboratory in Detroit, Michigan, on 1 February 1944. A single spare tire was stored vertically at the front of the tank. (TACOM LCMC History Office)

The compartment below the front left of the water tank contained a single-cylinder, four-cycle, air-cooled gasoline engine that powered a self-priming centrifugal pumping unit. Also in the compartment were related valves and controls. (TACOM LCMC History Office)

Above: On top of the forward half of the rear fender is a pioneer-tool rack, with a shovel and a mattock handle visible. Strapped to the rear of the fender is a section of suction hose. When the spare tire was removed, it was retrieved from this side of the chassis. (TACOM LCMC History Office)

Right: A 700-gallon water tank truck with a .50-caliber machine gun on a ring mount and the top removed from the cab was photographed at the Ordnance Operation, Engineering Standards Vehicle Laboratory, Detroit, on 3 May 1944. This example had Chevrolet axles. (TACOM LCMC History Office)

The GMC 270 engine and accessories are viewed in the engine compartment of a 700-gallon tank truck on 1 February 1944. Most mid-production CCKWs had the 3020 version of the 270 engine. (TACOM LCMC History Office)

Chapter 15
Composite Bed Introduction

As 1944 dawned, GMC held two contracts, known internally as the "1944 Group of authorizations for production in 1944, and the early part of 1945." The vehicles to be assembled on these contracts consisted of:

73,496 CCKWs on Contract W-20-018-ORD-6548
4,000 AFKWs on Contract W-20-018-ORD-6548
75,791 CCKWs on Contract W-20-018-ORD-1299

These trucks were to enter production immediately behind the final extension of contract 11595, and, as with previous contracts, a number of these trucks were to be boxed for overseas shipment. The number to be boxed varied, according to the government specifications outlined in the army supply program. From January to June the number ranged from 7,606 per month to 11,660. Boxing the vehicles demanded not only a great deal of lumber, but a considerable amount floor space as well as manpower.

Despite the considerable demand for the CCKW, another other big project that GMC was tackling in early 1944 – the DUKW – actually had a far higher war priority rating, and thus an even greater demand. To free up floor space and manpower in the GMC plant in order to achieve DUKW production goals, the decision was made to discontinue, at least temporarily, boxing operations at the GMC plant.

A 22 January 1944 memo to A. A. Dodd addressed the subject in this manner: "We will, therefore, close down our boxing operation at GMC Truck Plant during the latter part of January, February, March, April and until approximately the middle of May, but will retain all of the equipment so that we can resume operations again about the middle of May. During this period all export boxing of vehicles will be done at the Pontiac Motor Division Plant and the Chevrolet-St. Louis plant. This, of necessity, eliminates some of the flexibility previously available for changes in the export boxing schedule and it is, therefore, important that the boxing schedule shall not be increased during the above period."

This move released 38,800 square feet of GMC plant space. And, while it was planned that GMC would begin boxing again in mid-May, in fact, no production boxing of CCKWs was done again at the GMC plant. A small shop remained, however, where experimental and sample pack boxing operations were performed.

The production schedules established previously called for 450 CCKWs per day to be built in January 1944. Of these, 210 would be built in Pontiac and 240 in St. Louis, with total production for the month forecast at 11,250 trucks. However, only 10,423 were actually

The composite steel/wood body for the CCKW entered production in February 1944. Two key identifying features of that body are visible, albeit faintly, here: the hex head bolts positioned at intervals on top of the side sill, and the three hex-screw bolts on the body below and outboard of the ends of the tailgate hinge pins. (TACOM LCMC History Office)

built, due to a number of reasons, indicative of the trouble GMC faced meeting production goals.

On the first day of production in the new year, Pontiac only turned out 100 trucks due to absenteeism, a problem that, despite improvements, kept production from ever reaching the goal of 210 per day. Material shortages also entered the picture, with only 107 trucks being built on the 22nd due to a shortage of transmissions.

St. Louis too was plagued with the same problem, albeit to a lesser extent. Absenteeism on the first meant that only 96 trucks were built, but the goal of 240 was reached by the 7th. Output dropped, however, to a mere 44 on the 12th due to part number 2146449 shackles failing to arrive. These incidents serve to illustrate but a few of the issues that would confound planners both within General Motors as well as within the government throughout the remainder of the war.

The transmission problem became so severe that in the last week of January and first week of February a series of meetings were held between various divisions of General Motors, Ordnance, Clark, who was supplying transmission to the Pontiac plant, and Warner, who was supplying the St. Louis plant. Upon ascertaining realistic transmission forecasts, the Pontiac and St. Louis production schedules were revised downward to 184 per day at each plant, working six days per week, until June, when the earlier targets would be reinstated. This schedule was agreed upon on Saturday, 5 February 1944 and issued on Monday the 7th. These changes meant that the production of the vehicles called for in contract 2597 would not be completed in Pontiac until late February and in St. Louis during early March. In the bigger scheme of things, the transmission shortage resulted in a cut of 22,000 trucks from the 1944 production plans.

This cut in planned production set off an avalanche of paperwork within the Army and GMC. An 11 February memo from R. A. Crist outlined the issue and is quoted here in part.

"(3) Our analysis of Ordnance's requirements of types of vehicles revealed another crisis, insofar as materials and schedules are concerned. It was found that the combination of the reduced schedules and the changes in requirements of specific types of vehicles by months, brought about a condition where Contract 6458 would have carried over into year 1945 and we would have been forced to requisition, order, schedule and allot materials against the new contract 1299 for delivery of vehicles starting in May.

"The resulting complications in cancelling out existing commitments for material and re-ordering against the new contract 1299 would have resulted in chaos, both in Production and Service. It would have been an impossible situation to deal with from a spare parts standpoint and, certainly, from a Production standpoint it is doubtful if we could have handled the problem.

"(4) Consequently, as a result of our discussion with Mr. Babcock on Monday, the 7th, you arranged a conference with Colonel Whitworth the same day which was attended by Messrs. Dodd, Riggs and Crist. It was Mr. Babcock's request that, since the vehicle specifications were the same for the two contracts, arrangements might be made for Change Order Supplements to the contracts which would permit the "lifting" of certain quantities and types of vehicles out of Contract 1299 and placing them in Contract 6458, and then "lifting" the same quantities of other types out of Contract 6458, placing them in Contract 1299, so that Contract 6458 could be completed substantially as of the end of September before starting on Contract 1299.

"Further, this procedure (while involving considerable paper work) would permit present purchase orders to stand on material common to all types of trucks, necessitating only the purchase of parts peculiar to the types of vehicles scheduled for May through September delivery, at this time."

Of course, part of the "considerable paperwork" mentioned above involved the Sales Orders, which Crist addressed as point six of his memo, saying:

"(6) A complete revision of Sales Orders is involved. To facilitate the handling of this paper and in order to understand what has happened, we are submitting herewith a set of four sheets which outline the exact changes in Sales Orders which must be made at once to permit Production to deal with these revisions. It is important that this be done immediately. We believe you will want to carry suitable notations on the Sales Order Supplements to indicate the number of vehicles which will carry the 6458 contract price and the number which will carry the 1299 contract price."

This revision of schedule and reduction of production had the side effect of causing the introduction of a new variation of the CCKW, which Crist refers to in paragraph 10: "Engineering must immediately recheck and advise any changes in bills of material, with respect to the following items:

"(a)   Item #9 – Cab-Over-Engine. 4000 now lifted from contract 1299 and placed in Contract 6548.

"(b)   Item #8 – Cargo Dumps.   9609 now lifted from Contract 1299 and placed in Contract 6458. Of this total, 4609 will now have to take Chevrolet axles and the only bill (author note – bill of materials) issued to date is for Timken. THIS IS URGENT.

"(c)   Item 1-E Gas Tanks   1400 now lifted from Contract 1299 and placed in Contract 6458."

Despite the fact that the exhaustive work listed above was outlined on the 11th, three days later the Detroit Ordnance District phoned GMC, and in essence, wanted to add 6,000 trucks back into the program.

The frustration that this request caused the production control and purchasing departments is readily apparent in Crist's 15 February memo to R.J. Emmert. It reads, in part, "Just about the time I finished the Basic Control Schedules last Saturday, after working out the revised schedule for the previous 8 days and nights, Mr. Dodd came down and advised that D.O.D. wanted to add back into the schedules 5066 item 1-A Cargos for the last half of the year; also 65 item #2.

The same CCKW-353 portrayed in the preceding photograph is viewed from the right in a photograph taken at the Ordnance Operation, Engineering Standards Vehicle Laboratory, Detroit, on 22 November 1944. This vehicle was serial number 346561. The U.S.A. number, 4480143, is visible under high magnification on the hood. (TACOM LCMC History Office)

Later, there were some other adjustments requested, bringing the total up to around 6000 units that they wanted put back into the 1944 program.

"That just about topped everything, because of the extreme changes previously requested and the effort that had been made to reach an agreement and freeze the figures. I told Mr. Dodd that I would not change the schedules at this time again under any conditions, as it was necessary that we get our detail revisions under way and issue new shipping releases to suppliers so as to stop the excess flow of material between now and June 1st. Further, I stated that I could not possibly see any way to put this many trucks back into the last six months in view of the already high program, lack of manpower, inability to handle, etc., I also had in mind the engine situation, and the fact that we are already gambling on transmission and axle facilities being made available to meet the program currently laid out.

"Mr. Dodd presented the picture to Mr. Babcock and I was called to his office yesterday, in your absence, and Mr. Babcock stated what he would like done. Briefly, he wants the trucks projected into the program and he offered several suggestions as to how it should be done, but since I was unwilling to commit myself to this program he asked that I go over the situation with you and we would then get together later this week."

March 1944 brought even more requests for changes to truck production through a number of directives issued by the Detroit Ordnance District. Among these were letters on 18 March, 20 March and a teletype on 27 March requiring that the delivery dates for gas tankers be advanced. Similar letters on 7 March and 30 March requested that the delivery schedule for Cargo-Dump trucks be improved. A 28 March letter revised the schedule for the boxing of trucks. Also requested was the diversion of 60 trucks to produce special vehicles for the Navy, described elsewhere in this book.

Perhaps most interesting, however, was the requirement that GMC mount used, reconditioned, government furnished bodies on chassis as required by Change Order P-227. All these changes resulted in a new schedule on 8 April 1944.

Perhaps in anticipation of the coming European invasion, Ordnance was pushing hard for the gas trucks. On Saturday, 18 March 1944, Colonel Whitworth, Contracting Officer, DOD sent GMC via a messenger a letter concerning this. It contained the following information:

"Authorization is herewith given to cover additional costs if it is necessary to secure delivery of 200, 750 gallon Gasoline Tank jobs in March and April. It is suggested that the Columbian Steel Tank Company, Kansas City, Missouri, has 71 sets of tanks that can be made available for Gasoline Tank Trucks. The person to contact at this company is Mr. W. M. Godberry, Kansas City, Missouri, telephone – Long Distance 266. These tanks can be purchased from the Columbian Steel Tank Company. The are being held by Columbian Steel Tank Company at this time pending termination of contract, and are available for purchase. The schedule here following is suggested as minimum requirements:

"Units   Month – 1944
"200   April
"500   May
"500   June
"500   July
"386   August

"Accomplishment in excess of this schedule, if possible of attainment, is requested.

"It is desired to emphasize the urgency of this production as these items are now classified as critical and shall carry a priority next to that of the Amphibian.

"You are authorized to divert Item 1a, LWB, Cargo Chassis and Cab, w/o/w, as may be necessary for the accomplishment of above schedule."

The 71 tanks referred to by Colonel Whitworth had been made to Chemical Warfare specifications, and in order to use them for gas tanks, it would be necessary to remove pumps from 50 of the tanks, revise the plumbing of the tank and add provisions for camouflage.

Whereas previously Butler had been manufacturing the gasoline tanker bodies for GMC, in order to meet the increased demand, an additional source of supply had to be located. It was found in Fruehauf, which indicated it could produce the 329 tanks that were required that were beyond Butler's capacity. Each Fruehauf tank would cost $111.07 more than the Butler tanks, and specific authorization for the additional cost had to be sought from Ordnance.

The same Colonel Whitworth who dispatched the messenger with the request for faster gasoline tanker delivery also issued the directive regarding reusing used cargo bodies on 28 March 1944. Colonel Whitworth's letter on this matter stated:

"In accordance with the provisions of the "Changes" Article of said contract (W-374-ORD-6458) you are hereby directed to make the following change in the specifications of the supplies purchased under this contract.

"You are directed to mount Government furnished, used, reconditioned Wood Cargo Bodies on all 2 ½ Ton, 6x6 Chassis with and without winch beginning 1 April 1944 and until further notice."

"This Change Order excepts the sixty (60) Chassis ordered for the Navy Department under Change Order P-223 of subject contract.

"No work, with the exception of the mounting of the bodies, is to be done by General Motors Corporation (GMC Truck and Coach Division) inasmuch as the bodies will be properly reconditioned for shipment. If bodies arrive improperly reconditioned, it is requested that that this office be advised immediately.

"The contractor will be reasonable in notifying the Production Section, Motor Vehicle Branch, in advance, the date this Change will go into effect, and will also notify the Resident Inspector of the vehicle serial number (or quantities of parts when applicable) on which this Change will be initiated so that the Resident Inspector may properly accomplish receiving reports."

On the same day that Col. Whitworth sent his letter, Lt. Col. F. R. Mead sent a letter to GMC on the same matter, providing additional details. "For the month of April, 1980 of these reconditioned bodies are to be shipped. At present, 733 are scheduled to be shipped from the Sixth Service Command, Chicago, Illinois and 292 from the Fifth Service Command, Cincinnati, Ohio. The source of the balance of these bodies will be conveyed to you as soon as information is available to this office.

"It is not intended that this program will interfere, in any way, with present or future body mounting schedules on A1 Cargo's, it is simply intended that whatever is scheduled to be delivered as chassis will now have reconditioned bodies mounted. The information contained in Mr. P. T. Garland's letter of 17th March has been conveyed to the Control Branch of the Office, Chief of Ordnance, Detroit, to cover the required number of new SUFM bodies for the regular cargo schedule."

The same late-model CCKW-353 is viewed from above. The steel rub strips bolted between the wooden floor planks of the cargo body are clearly visible. The rack stakes were metal, while the rack and troop-seat slats were wood. (TACOM LCMC History Office)

As a result this directive, GMC stopped shipment on the chassis trucks on sales orders 200581 and 200592 after March shipments and begin shipping instead cargo trucks with the reconditioned bodies. In addition, a number of chassis trucks that had been previously OK'd were returned to the final conditioning and body mount department and had reconditioned bodies mounted on them. This work required the issuance of "Rework Warehouse Cards" which were then attached to the shipping copies of sales orders.

Despite all these changes, finally on 28 March 1944 the last truck on the massive contract W-398-QM--11595, also known as W-375-ORD-2597, was shipped. As part of this, on 22 February, the D.O.D. approved the shipping of 300 trucks on wheels by Chevrolet, St. Louis. These trucks, on sales order TC-200563, were originally scheduled to be shipped in crates as part of a group of 580 such vehicles. However, Chevrolet could not obtain enough shooks – the lumber from which the crates for the trucks were made. This is the type of lumber shortage that had spurred the development of the composite bed in late 1943, which were scheduled to enter production in the near future.

Production begins on contract W-20-018-ORD-1299

In early 1944, General Motors corporate policy was such that its divisions were only permitted to order materials six to seven months in advance of the need for the parts in assembly. Also at this time, the War Production Board policy changed such that requirements for 3rd and 4th quarter materials had to be submitted to by 15 April. To satisfy both of these requirements, a paperwork scramble began on 5 April. A portion of an April memo from R. A. Crist addresses this subject, reading: "For the information of all concerned, this means we are placing orders for 40634 trucks on contract W-20-018-ORD-1299, including the adjustments shown in these revised schedules submitted herewith. This is the number of trucks we are going to build in this contract through December to meet the authorized 1944 WPB production program. Up to this time we had only placed orders for axles, transfer cases and transmissions for this number of vehicles."

It was hoped the previously laid out plan to mount reconditioned cargo bodies would save the government money, reduce the demand on the overtaxed lumber industry, and perhaps even speed production. In reality, it complicated production considerably. As a result GMC's R. J. Emmert called a meeting with representatives of the Detroit Ordnance District on 6 April 1944. In a memo documenting this meeting, Emmert wrote, "Our schedule this month calls for the mounting of used cargo bodies on new chassis. Our attention has been called to difficulties with this program, which originate because bodies shipped to us are short many parts and, in addition, many of the parts on the bodies are in poor condition.

"Captain Messersmith, Mr. Anderson, Mr. Norton, and Mr. Judd called at the plant to determine what should be done inasmuch as it is impossible for us to mount these bodies. Lt. Kadie and Mr. Chenault, as well as Mr. Moody and Mr. Brinkman, were called into the meeting to discuss the problem. The following program was outlined:

"1. Ordnance will stop the further shipment of used bodies until the Depots can be supplied with a bill of material and instructed that no additional bodies can be shipped to us unless they are complete and in good condition. However, Mr. Norton estimated that 200 bodies have already been shipped.

"2. Captain Messersmith will arrange to have a supply of all mounting parts shipped to us. This supply will be Government property received in our plant on a consignment basis. We will be given instructions to withdraw parts from this stock to make up for parts that are missing from the bodies shipped to us. The arrangement applies to the mounting parts of the bodies and the rear tail lamp only.

"3. In order to permit us to ship trucks, Mr. Judd will order some 500 new bodies shipped to us to mount in place of used bodies.

"4. Lt. Kadie and Mr. Chenault agreed to take trucks with bodies 'as is'. Our own Inspection Department and Mr. Chenault will keep a record of the trucks by chassis number to show which are shipped with new bodies and which with old.

"5. Mr. Judd will see that Ordnance issues a work order to us to which can be charged extra labor involved in straightening up mounting brackets for the bodies, tail lamps, mud guards, etc. Where labor is performed in straightening and reforming parts, the amount of labor should be noted on a work order or traveler card and the card is to be signed by the workman, but the Government Inspector, and by the foreman of this department."

On 20 April 1944, Change Order P-227A was issued by Ordnance, which modified the previously-issued change order and instructions. The pertinent part of the change order read: "This Change Order amends and supplements Change Order No. P-227 on subject contract to the extent that you may mount new bodies on the trucks set forth in Change Order No. P-227 where used, reconditioned bodies are not available in order to keep production at full capacity."

In fact, new bodies were used to keep production moving, those bodies being supplied by Saginaw Furniture on Order 4G-111083, who shipped bodies at the rate of 45 per day. However, even this plan ran into obstacles due the transportation crisis which gripped the nation due to wartime traffic demands. The general situation was reported by R. V. Blevins, with GMC's material control department, on 20 April. He wrote "TC-200592, item #5, has the Saginaw cargo bodies mounted and they are now in the warehouse ready for shipment. This completes this sales order for 119, of which 70 are less bodies and 49 with Saginaw cargo bodies. An additional quantity of 516 new bodies has been released from Saginaw Furniture which will be mounted on TC-200581, item #2, making a total of 1016 bodies released for both sales orders.

In late 1943, a plan to replace the wooden bodies of CCKWs with all-steel ones was shelved in part because of the adverse effect it would have on manufacturers of wooden bodies. As a compromise, a composite cargo body with a steel vertical structure and a wooden floor was developed, and this became a key feature of the late-production CCKWs. (TACOM LCMC History Office)

"In checking our shipping schedule on TC-200581 with Mr. Garland, have found that we will be short 248 chassis with bodies on our April shipping schedule of 1144. Permission has been secured whereby we can ship 224 vehicles out of our April shipping schedule without cargo bodies. To do this we have assigned chassis serial numbers CCKW-353-37253-1 to 356476, incl. Balance of 24 chassis will have to have new cargos mounted."

A 6 May 1944 memo issued by Mr. Blevins advised of a change in plan, as well as providing production details. The pertinent parts advise "D.O.D. has directed us to ship, less cargos, 800 vehicles on TC-200581, item #2, out of May's production. This means that we will have to stop mounting reconditioned or new cargo bodies after 1371 have been mounted on this sales order." Further, it revealed "The cumulative mounting figure for May on TC-200581, Item #2, and TC-200592, item #5, is 1420 for which Saginaw bodies have been released to a total of 1167, leaving a balance of 253 that are to have reconditioned bodies from Covered Wagon."

Saginaw Body Manufacturing Company was supplied components for their bodies by Budd. On approximately 21 April 1944 contract W-20-018-ORD-1744 was issued whereby Budd would supply Saginaw components for 3999 of the new composite bodies. This was followed on 18 August by contract W-20-018-ORD-6558, for the materials for a further 16,200 bodies. Orders for composite body components for use by Covered Wagon were placed first on 14 April, when contract W-20-018-ORD-302 for 2469 bodies was issued, and followed on 26 August with components for 8816 more on contract W-20-018-ORD-6559.

However, these contracts were not the first issued for the new composite body. Contract W-11-022-ORD-1698 for Budd components for 2700 bodies to be supplied to Batavia Body Company had been issued on 3 February 1944 and contract W-01-009-ORD-43 for 974 sets of composite body components to be supplied to National Woodworks had been issued 18 February. Both of these companies supplied CCKW bodies to Chevrolet-St. Louis. However, it should be noted that at least 18 different firms from Vermont to California supplied the composite body for the CCKW.

The 800 chassis referenced in Blevin's memo were covered by Change Order P-227D. However, Change Order P-227C, of 8 May, reveals information that has caused confusion among historian's for years. That change order revised Change Order P-227 by deleting the word "wood" from the direction. This was done in order to authorize the mounting of reconditioned steel cargo bodies. The mounting of reconditioned bodies continued at least through June.

As if the new concepts referred to above were not enough, in May GMC was directed to change from a two-unit pack of export boxing to a single unit pack. While at first blush, this does not seem to be that much of a change. However, R. A. Crist reveals the significance of this change in these words "Single unit pack necessitated the mounting of a body on every vehicle scheduled for export boxing, as compared with the practice under two-unit packing whereby two-unit body packs were shipped direct from sources." Pontiac Motor Division began boxing CCKWs in the new single unit pack on 5 June, with St. Louis doing the same ten days later. Change order P-289, 9 June 1944, dictated that from 1 July moving forward 70% of the cargo trucks were to be boxed, as were 80% of the cargo dump trucks. By 21 August change order P-355 had been issued, which reduced the number of cargo dumps to be boxed to 60%.

Yet another change in the boxing program came on 5 June 1944 when Detroit Ordnance District dispatched a letter requesting that 500 CCKWs be shipped as chassis only, with dry charged batteries, be shipped to Harris Manufacturing Company in Stockton, California. These trucks were shipped with wooden cargo bodies installed. Ultimately, change orders P-290 and P-290A were issued, directed that 250 each chassis trucks with winch and without winch, all with dry charged batteries, were to be shipped to Harris. Harris would assemble the composite cargo bodies, using components supplied by Budd, and would mount the bodies as well as crate the trucks.

The flow of material into the plant, in particular truck bodies, was leading GMC's Pontiac plant to burst at the seams. Partial relief of this problem is reflected in the text of a May memo from Crist stating "All cargo, dump and stake bodies are to be painted when delivered from the suppliers. Any bodies now on hand in prime are to be painted on or before May 23rd as after this date the paint booths will be removed to make additional storage space. This space will accommodate approximately 300 cargo, dump and stake bodies. Incoming bodies will have to be watched very closely as our June schedule averages 158 per day – which means that we could have approximately two days bank."

The rapid advance in Europe following the D-Day landings brought about increased demand for trucks, as discussed on page 428. To meet this demand, the Army requested that production of trucks be stepped up, adding 3000 trucks to the 1944 program.

The army's requirements continued to change, and by mid-1944 GMC was forecasting 1945 production and had begun the scheduling process. A 29 July 1944 memo addressed some of the pitfalls of the coming program. "In Mr. Gray's submission of figures from D.O.D. they asked for trucks starting January of types which are not included in the purchase of 35427 now being placed on order under Contract 1299; in other words, the scheduled dump trucks, gas tanks and short wheelbase jobs in January and February and March which part of the proposed contract for 21811 units. I discussed this matter with Mr. Babcock and it was agreed that I should set up our schedules to call for completion of contract 1299 before any trucks were built against the new proposed contract.

"We began requisitioning of the 35427 trucks to complete Contract1299 on June 17th, and this buy is only now being completed and we are having some difficulty in getting steel placed in fourth quarter 1944 for this requirement. Consequently, at this late date we cannot schedule production for January and February for types of trucks which have not yet been placed on order.

"Consequently, we have made our schedule projection entirely on the basis of cleaning up the 35427 trucks first, and then following with the 21811 units which are included in the new contract under negotiation, which is in accordance with my discussion with Mr. Babcock. Therefore, our schedules will not match with D.O.D's. expressed requirements as submitted by Mr. Gray, and there is no way we can meet their requirements at this late date."

The memo concluded with this request: "You will note from the schedule herewith that we will be required to build 2823 trucks in March out of this new contract for 21811, which means that raw materials must be made available in January for February fabrication and March production. Would you please give us formal authority to proceed with this rescheduling at earliest possible moment?"

In August 1944 the labor situation in the Pontiac area was strained – too many industries were vying for the available labor pool, and within GMC the DUKW program had a clear priority in production, meaning that the DUKW assembly line had priority in securing labor. In an effort to maintain production within the limits of available labor, increasing amounts of CCKW production was shifted to St. Louis. In fact, ultimately it was decided that St. Louis solely would produce the CCKW, with Pontiac exclusively building the DUKW (which like the CCKW, was being built in both plants).

But, in August 1944, the immediate objective was to relieve Pontiac labor by shifting some production to St. Louis. A total of 5,605 cargo and chassis trucks with Chevrolet axles originally scheduled for the Pontiac during the last quarter of 1944 and 5,227 trucks scheduled for early 1945 were moved to St. Louis as a result of a 10 August revision of production schedules. The related paperwork noted "Inasmuch as the engine material for this combined 1944 and 1945 program on Contract 1299 has already been ordered, and a great deal of confusion would be caused by attempting to balance Flint engines with St. Louis production and because it is now too late to cancel and have Flint reorder to cover 4th quarter and early first quarter production, and also because of many frozen schedules in engine components, it was agreed with Mr. Babcock with the engines for the total of 10832 trucks diverted to St. Louis will be shipped from Plant 4-Pontiac."

With all the changes, the originally planned date of completion for contract 6458 of the end of September had been pushed back to 10 November 1944. Even that was unattainable, due to a delinquency of 14 of the cab over trucks discussed elsewhere in this volume, and three CCKW fuel tankers, the bodies for which had been damaged in a train wreck while in transit to GMC.

As production began on the next contract, W-20-018-ORD-1299, almost immediately it fell behind schedule. Ice and snow storms gripped much of the nation, and movement of components ground to an icy halt. Particularly impacted was the shipment of dump bodies, which the army was urgently requesting. Adding to these considerable weather delays were the ongoing problems with Albion Malleable Iron. These culminated with the replacement of five of these castings with stampings from Fisher Body Company. On 19 December, GMC placed orders with Fisher for stamped versions of the both front spring rear brackets as well as frame support bracket, gusset and stud assembly. These parts were scheduled to begin shipping by Fisher on 15th February, and would begin to be used in production in the following month, after the supply of castings had been consumed. While these dates were slightly missed, the stamped parts did free foundry capacity, and the end result was an improvement in CCKW production.

It is worthwhile to point out that as a result of the early 1944 efforts, during the year CCKW-353s were shipped with new wooden bodies, reconditioned wooden bodies, reconditioned steel bodies and new composite bodies.

1945

On New Year's Day 1945 change order P-397 was issued, which deleted the spare tire from all vehicles delivered on wheels, and from boxed trucks to the extent that tires are available. This was a result of an shortage of tires, as consumption by the forces in Europe had exceeded all forecasts. In Michigan the situation became so desperate that 110 trucks were being built with six wheels rather than ten, and tire and wheel assemblies were being rotated between GMC and Pontiac Motor Division who was boxing the truck. However, no truck was shipped with less than ten tires, as the additional four tires for those trucks built with only six arrived prior to the trucks being crated.

On 8 January 1945 the Detroit Ordnance District asked for expedited delivery of 150 chassis trucks with winch to replace trucks lost during the Battle of the Bulge. These trucks were shipped from St. Louis.

By February 1945 a new contract, 20-018-ORD-6052 had begun to replace contract 20-018-ORD-1299 on the CCKW assembly lines. These trucks had a rotary light switch, rather than the push-pull type, as well as an improved, larger, voltage regulator, as well as improved fuel pumps.

On 2 February the Office of Defense Transportation and Interstate Commerce Commission issued Embargo #47, which would go into effect at 12:01 AM 3 February. This embargo directed that no railroad could place cars for loading or sign or issue bills of lading for freight moving on any railroad through the states of Ohio, Pennsylvania, New York, New Jersey, Maryland, Delaware, District of Columbia and certain other areas, with few exceptions.

A series of events contributed to a shortage of natural gas in the winter of 1944-1945, an explosion leveled a Cleveland liquefied natural gas storage facility (and a square mile of Cleveland on 20 October 1944; the Columbia natural gas pipeline near Pittsburgh blew out 4 January; and 2 February the Conservation Department of the War Production Board, which had previously directed Panhandle Eastern pipeline to curtail its interruptible industrial customers, told Michigan Consolidated Gas to cut off gas to its industrial service area.

The impact of this was felt by GMC, who on 6 February 1945 sent a letter to the Detroit Ordnance District on this subject. This letter read in part: "We directed you attention to the fact that the shortage of gas in Ohio and bordering states was curtailing operations in many of our subcontractor plants and included in the partial list of our subcontractors affected, the Newport Rolling Mills, Newport, Kentucky.

"As a result of the gas shortage, our subcontractor, Newport Rolling Mills, has operated only five days since December 20, 1944. Due to the resultant shortage of steel, it now appears we will be unable to maintain our Amphibian Truck schedule for the month of February unless we can secure material from warehouses or other sources. The Newport Rolling Mills have a priority rating of No. 6 for gas, which is apparently not high enough, although there are only seven ratings."

The combined impact of the freight embargo and gas shortage cannot be understated, tire chains, which were required to be supplied with the vehicles by contract terms, could not be delivered because the freight embargo prevented steel reaching American Chain, their manufacturer. Oil pan production stopped in Salem, Ohio at Mullins Steel due to the gas being turned off. Heat treating of engine connecting rods, done by Harbrand Corporation, stopped due to no gas, and steel for more connected rods was unavailable due to the gas plant explosion. Akerman Manufacturing in Wheeling, West Virginia, maker of the cab mounting channels, was without gas, as were their steel supplier, Wheeling Steel. Clutch shipments stopped from Inland Manufacturing in Dayton, after their gas was turned off on 29 January.

An example of how desperate the position became is revealed in a telegram sent to Colonel Whitworth, Contracting Officer, on 5 February. The message contained in the telegram: "Due to shortage of pintle hooks resulting from shortage of steel at both Clifford Jacobs Company, Champaign, Illinois and American Forging, Chicago, Illinois, manufacturers of forgings for Holland Hitch, our subcontractor, serious consequences will be suffered in our production of 2 ½ ton 6x6 trucks. Stop. We intend to continue building vehicles minus the pintle hooks until our storage area is filled which will probably be about

Left: Scores of late-production GMC CCKW long-wheelbase cargo trucks are parked in a holding area. At the bottom right, the left rear corner of a composite cargo body is visible, with wooden floor planks and steel rub strips, side board, and tailgate. Several U.S. Army registration numbers are visible, including 4683605, 4669576, and 4706604. (General Motors)

Below: CCKW-353 serial number 346561 is viewed from the left side on 22 November 1944. The five bows for the cargo compartment are stored over the front end of the left side rack. A shovel is secured to the running board below the cab. (TACOM LCMC History Office)

This 750-gallon gasoline tank truck, serial number 394556, was photographed at the Ordnance Operation, Engineering Standards Vehicle Laboratory, Detroit, on 22 November 1944. The vehicle was based on a late-production long-wheelbase CCKW. Since fuel trucks were easily identifiable and highly desirable targets for enemy gunners and aircraft, the gasoline tank truck was equipped with bows to support a tarpaulin to camouflage the truck as a cargo vehicle. (TACOM LCMC History Office)

Wednesday February 7th. Stop. We cannot, however, mount bodies nor box for export without pintle hooks. Stop. Chevrolet-St. Louis boxing line goes down at noon today and Pontiac Motor Division boxing line will go down Wednesday morning, February 7th. Stop. It will be necessary that you shut off delivery of government furnished cargo bodies as we have no space for storage of same."

The pintle hook shortage was resolved in only a couple of days, but the tire chain shortage lingered much longer. On 9 February Brigadier General A. B. Quinton, Jr. directed that CCKWs shipped on wheels could be shipped without tire chains until 20 March 1945. This was formalized in Change Orders P-425 and P-132.

In mid-February 1945 reinstated the previously discontinued short wheelbase winch-equipped truck. This required the development of a single unit pack for this model, as none of the type had been produced since the single unit pack was introduced, and this work was done quickly.

GMC's Blevins issued a memo 14 February reading: "Instructions have been received whereby we are to start boxing Item 1-D's, short wheelbase, with winch, in the near future (TC-200639). Mr. Crist has instructed us to build a chassis for a sample pack as soon as possible. In checking the materials with Messers. Adams and Elliontt, find that we have the side rails, tire carrier and gas tank. Mr. White advises that he has one gas tank and tire assembly. Therefore, we can start to assemble the material today so that this vehicle can come off the chassis line tomorrow, February 15th.

"The writer has contacted Messrs. Schweitzer and Burke (D.O.D.) and has requested that they deliver to use one 9' GI cargo body today or tomorrow. Mr. Burke contacted the proper authorities and advised that the first of the 9' bodies available would be of wood construction and would come from Ordnance depots. The body we required immediately will be shipped from Rossford and he will endeavor to have it delivered to us this week."

Change order P-436 for contract 1299 and change order P-148 on contract 6052 were issued on 21 February 1945, which directed GMC to supply to Consolidated Shipbuilding Corporation, Morris Heights New York, CCKW-353 chassis, with dry charged batteries at the rate of 500 per month. Consolidated would then mount government furnished bodies and crate the trucks for overseas shipments.

April brought with it even more changes, as a gas main break in St. Louis cut the supply to the Chevrolet plant, causing a 2 ½-day loss in production. Further losses in production were the result of strikes at Timken and Kelsey-Hayes. Wire rope for winches was in short supply, and at one point in the month GMC lots held 900 trucks that could not be shipped due to the lack of wire rope.

R.A. Crist circulated a memo on 23 April 1945, and the passages excerpted from it below give insight to the situation:

"It was found that Timken would "short" us an additional 1000 sets of axles in April due to the Timken and Kelsey-Hayes strikes; further that this would mean that we could only provide a service requirement of 2000 sets in the second quarter instead of the 3000 as requested. Therefore, in order to comply with the April 20th directive it would be necessary to drop 4000 trucks out of the building schedule in order to obtain 3000 sets of Timken axles for service. In our telephone conversation with Mr. Tom Chancellor of D.O.D. on Saturday the 21st (our dual call) we advised him that this would mean taking 1000 #8 Dump Trucks out of the combined April and May schedule. He talked with Colonel Icks of O.C.O.D. and called back and advised that they would give us a deadline of May 15th to get out the April Service requirements of 1000 Timken axles, but that the axles had to be shipped regardless of trucks affected."

In April 1945 plans were in place for GMC to deliver 153,668 6x6 military trucks in calendar year 1945. In early May, following the victory in Europe, the order was reduced to 145,293 trucks. By mid-May this had dropped to 139,368. At the same time, a 1946 Ordnance Program existed for 45061 trucks to be built from January through October 1946. By June 1945 that year's program had been

Below: The 750-callon gasoline tank truck is viewed from overhead, showing the manhole covers on top of the tanks. On each side of the tanks were a stowage rack for five-gallon liquid containers with wooden slats on the floors, and an equipment compartment. The right compartment contained selective operator-valve controls, and the left compartment contained a gauge, fuel cans, and other gear. (TACOM LCMC History Office)

further reduced to 114,882.

By 5 June 1945 on of the most radical changes in the CCKW program since early 1941. A memo issued on that date summarized the new plan like this: "In accordance with an agreement reached between Mr. Douglas and Mr. Coyle of Chevrolet, we are taking over all Duck (sic) production as of the end of August 1945 which will clear their passenger car line at St. Louis, and all of the 6x6 truck production is being shifted from Pontiac to St. Louis of August 1st, which will clear our #1 truck chassis line for WPB Civilian truck production."

In order to achieve this goal, Pontiac immediately began to step up CCKW production in order to clear component inventory. Also, new bills of material had to be generated for Chevrolet St. Louis, which up to this point had not built trucks with Timken axles, nor the cab over engine trucks.

Also, the Ordnance Department directed that the boxing operations at Harris Manufacturing and Consolidated Shipbuilding be halted at the end of July, and General Motors absorb those quantities in their boxing operations.

Sales orders TC-200765, TC-200766, TC-200767 and TC-200768 were issued covering the production of Timken axle-equipped cargo and dump trucks in St. Louis. However, by the time the war ended and CCKW production halted, only 1119 trucks with Timken axles had been produced by Chevrolet – St. Louis. Of those, 36 were winch equipped CCKW-353 chassis; 90 were winch-equipped CCKW-353 cargo trucks built in August. The remaining 993 trucks were cargo-dump trucks, with 192 of them delivered in July and 801 in August. The plan to wind down production in Pontiac succeeded, with the last CCKWs being built in Michigan being 625 assorted models in June 1945 and 202 bomb service trucks in July.

When military production stopped, according to R.A. Crist, Production Control Manager, GMC had delivered 528,829 6x6; 24,910 6x4 and 21,147 DUKWs. Of these, 331,675, or 62.7% of the 6x6s were equipped with open cabs. The average value of the CCKWs produced was about $2,500.00.

Above: A single spare tire is stowed on the 750-gallon gasoline fuel truck, on a clamp-style carrier between the cab and the front gasoline tank. Whereas earlier CCKW gasoline fuel trucks had steel frames to retain the liquid containers along the gasoline tanks, the late-type trucks had retainers fashioned from steel frames with wooden fillers. (TACOM LCMC History Office)

Right: The equipment compartment doors each have a T-shaped latch handle in a recess. The wooden board at the rear of the body was fitted between an angle-iron retainer on each side; each retainer was fastened to an equipment compartment with four hex screws. (TACOM LCMC History Office)

Chapter 16

The End of the AFKWX

As 1944 began, GMC, as Yellow Truck and Coach formally became on 20 September 1943, had in hand contract W-20-18-ORD-6548, which at that time called for 77,496 6x6 trucks, 4,000 of which were to be AFKW cab-over-engine models. These trucks had originally been ordered on contract W-20-018-ORD-1299, but were transferred between contracts so that in this manner contract 6548 would be substantially completed by the end of September when work on contract 1299 would begin.

When assigned to contract 1299, the 4,000 trucks were on sales order TC-200604, once moved to contract 6548, there were put on sales order TC-200608. Regardless of the sales order, these trucks would differ from their predecessors. Instead of the GM-produced 15-foot wooden cargo bodies, these trucks would feature 17-foot stake bodies. Such a body had been rendered by GMC in proposal drawings in October 1943. The wooden bed would feature structural steel cross-sills, but would use standard troop seats components. After production of a sample, GMC body design was modified to include a swinging tailgate rather than the stake enclosure used on

the prototype and shown in the accompanying photos. To support the additional bed, the length of truck frame rails was extended to the rear. The revised trucks were designated by the Army Cargo, Special Body, COE, M427.

The newly-designed bed, in keeping the government's desire to source bodies to outside vendors, would be built by the Montpelier Body Company, Montpelier, Ohio. The bodies were purchased directly by the government and shipped to GMC for installation.

The large number of cab-over-engine trucks in this release brought with it an engine-manifold problem. The COE used a three-piece manifold that heretofore was produced by using temporary fixtures. The setup and teardown time installing these tools delayed production of standard (CCKW) 270 manifolds. With the large order in hand, GMC opted to create new tooling for these manifolds, so as to minimize disruption in standard manifold production. By November, it was apparent that once again materials shortages would prevent GMC from meeting Detroit Ordnance District's delivery schedule on these vehicles. Shortages in castings, traceable to ongoing labor problems at

Four thousand late-model AFKWXs were produced under contract W-374-ORD-6458, sales order TC-200608, from May to November 1944. These were assigned registration numbers 4738470 through 4742469. From March to May 1945, 1,000 more late-model AFKWXs were built pursuant to two 500-truck sales orders, TC-200643 and TC-200685, with registration numbers 4838518 to 4839017. The chief visual difference between the late-model AFKWX and the mid-production model was the late model's extended wooden body, which was 17 feet long: 2 feet longer than the mid-production body. (General Motors via Bryce Sunderlin)

Left: From the front, the late-model AFKWXs were virtually indistinguishable from the mid-production vehicles. The 4,000 AFKWXs of contract W-374-ORD-6458 had Chevrolet "banjo" axles. (General Motors via Bryce Sunderlin)

Below: This late AFKWX was detailed to the Ordnance Operation, Studebaker Proving Ground, where it was photographed on 6 September 1944. This truck was designated Studebaker Proving Ground vehicle number 1-318 (F-2-78), and marked on the side of the cab is F-2-78. (TACOM LCMC History Office)

The cab top on this late AFKWX is the late type, which was tight fitting and had metal stiffeners along the sides above the doors. Similarly, the side curtains are the late type with the equal sized soft plastic windows. (General Motors)

Albion Malleable Iron Company, were the root cause, but the situation was worsened by a shortage of fenders. GMC requested a seven-day extension in the delivery of 14 vehicles. Ultimately, Ordnance granted an extension until 10 December, but GMC managed to get the last of these trucks out in November. The 4,000 trucks on sales order TC-200608 were built from May through November, with monthly deliveries of 575, 854, 811, 525, 806, 370, and 59. The trucks were assigned serial numbers 5248 through 9247, and bore registration numbers 473870 through 4742469.

TC-200643 for 500 of the trucks were completed as follows: 123 in March, 285 in April, and the last 92 by 8 May 1945. A second sales order, TC-200685 for a second 500 were completed as follows: 132 in May, 335 in June and the final 33 by 7 July 1945. All the cab-over-engine AFKW trucks, regardless of contract, were built in Pontiac and were shipped on wheels, with non being crated.

Open-cab AFKWXs are under construction. GMC logos are faintly visible at the top of the opening for the radiator grille on the first cab in line. The rear curtains have been installed on the first several cabs and are dangling from the rear of the cabs. (General Motors)

The extended chassis frame and body are visible from this angle. When the chassis was extended, the tandem wheels were not correspondingly moved to the rear, so, to avoid a weight-distribution problem, it was necessary not to place too heavy a load to the rear of the body. The side racks of the late AFXWXs were in three sections. The front and rear sections had three stakes, while the center section had two stakes. The stakes, as well as the sideboards, the troop seats, and the rack slats, were wooden. (General Motors)

Chapter 17
Building the CCKW

The efficient mass production of any type of vehicle requires the careful coordination of many things: space, parts, material and manpower. Many hours of planning go into such operations. The CCKW was no different. While Yellow Truck and Coach (GMC) did manufacture some of the truck, the vast majority was produced elsewhere, with GMC performing the assembly. Tires, axles, body, lights, electrical components, and cab sheet metal were but a few of the items made elsewhere, and brought together on the CCKW assembly lines in Pontiac, St. Louis, and Baltimore. Each of these items, as well as every nut, bolt, washer, and gallon of paint, was bought with a specific truck in mind. Granted, they were not labeled as such, but the company certainly did not turn to a vendor and say "send me a boxcar full of spring hangers, we'll figure out some place to use them" – no, the components were ordered to build the trucks for specific contracts, and parts that were to become military spares, though often ordered concurrently, were bought on separate purchase orders. Rare was the case and desperate was the situation when parts allocated for spares were used in production, and vice-versa.

While everyone involved knew the urgency of production, particularly after Pearl Harbor, the company could not simply produce "as many as you can, as fast as you can." Rather, there had to be careful planning so that all the components appeared at the assembly line at the same time. Labor was often the critical component. If the rate of production was set too fast, eventually final assembly operations would outstrip the supply of a component, be that an axle, tires, master cylinder, etc., which would in turn bring about a stoppage of assembly line operations, and the laying off, even if for only a few days, of the assembly line workers. Workers who feel their jobs are unstable soon look for work elsewhere, and in wartime Pontiac, St. Louis, and Baltimore there was plenty of stable work to be found. Hence, every effort was made to prevent such layoffs, although a few were inevitable, some of it a result of a shortage of the natural gas needed to make certain iron components.

Because of the meticulous planning that went into the purchase of components and scheduling of assembly, great chaos could ensue whenever the military suddenly changed the game plan, either because of the sudden need for a specific type of vehicle, the equally sudden discontinuance of certain vehicle, or a change in priorities such that GMC no longer could get the needed amounts of components or steel. There were times when the ink was scarcely dry on one set of production schedules when they had to be discarded and new ones drafted, and new sets of purchase orders issued, because of the continuing number of changes. And it should be remembered that these developments took place in an age before computers, when all such work had to be done by men and women, who sometimes worked around the clock to achieve these goals.

The relationship between GMC and the Detroit Ordnance District became at times contentious, with DOD feeling GMC was not being cooperative, and GMC believing DOD to be indecisive, and lacking in understanding of automotive production. Ultimately the right personnel came to be in place in both institutions, and the relationship remained harmonious, but GMC never achieved the maximum CCKW production rate they were geared up for due to shortages of materials and the changing priorities of the War Department.

One corner of the Pontiac, Michigan, facility is awash in a sea of CCKW, AFKW, and DUKW vehicles in August 1943. Parked neatly in a 10-by-10 truck square in the center are 100 new CCKWs, a quantity that represents about one-third of a day's scheduled output in Pontiac at this time, with the St. Louis plant adding another 200 daily. To produce the half-million-plus trucks that GMC shipped during WWII required a virtual army of men and women working in the plants of GMC, Chevrolet, and their suppliers. The flow of material into the plants, and the stream of trucks leaving, were constant. (General Motors)

The following sequence of photographs documents assembly-line work at GMC Truck & Coach Plant 2, Pontiac, Michigan, on 2 May 1945. Here, a worker heats a rivet. To the left is a blackboard listing chassis numbers and models currently on line. (General Motors)

Near the start of the frame assembly line, a worker fits the rear cross member into an assembly jig. To the left is a V-brace that will be fastened to the cross member. The large holes in the brace and the cross member will accept the tow pintle assembly. (General Motors)

With a fixture holding the V-brace in position against the rear crossmember, an autoworker uses a heavy-duty rivet press to join the parts together permanently. The assembly fixture has been inserted through the hole through which will pass the pintle hook spring. (General Motors)

The subassembly seen under construction in the preceding photo, the rear cross member of the chassis frame and a V-brace, is viewed upon completion. The V-brace reinforced an area that otherwise could suffer much stress when a trailer was hitched to the tow pintle. (General Motors)

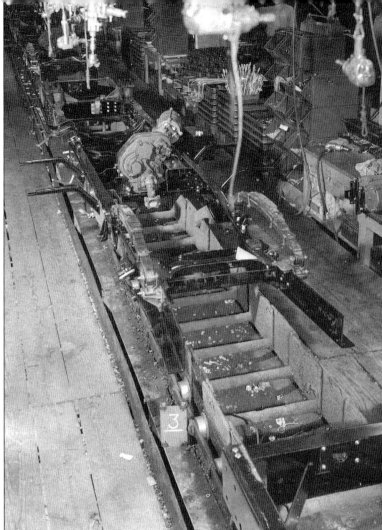

Work has just begun on this chassis frame at GMC Truck & Coach, Plant 2, on 2 May 1945. The running board supports are attached, but the springs and transfer case are yet to be installed. (General Motors)

On this part of the chassis assembly line, springs and transfer cases were installed on the frames. To the lower right is the rear of a chassis frame, showing the rear cross member and the V-brace. (General Motors)

GMC 270 engines are suspended from the engine-station conveyor. The nearest engine is equipped with a late-type dual power takeoff, used on CCKW-353s with winches and dump bodies with power hoists. (General Motors)

 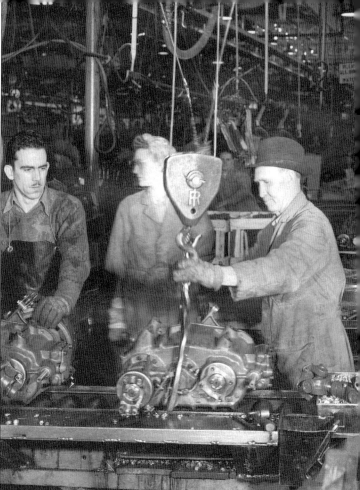

On the transfer-case-station line at GMC Truck & Coach on 2 May 1945, a transfer case has been lowered using a chain hoist and lifting tongs onto a CCKW-353 chassis frame. Extending from the front (nearest) end of the transfer case is the short driveshaft, also known as a propeller shaft, that would join transfer case to the transmission. (General Motors)

At the transfer-case station at GMC Truck & Coach, the man to the right is removing the lifting tongs from a transfer case just delivered to the bench. This type of transfer case was the one used with Timken, or split, axles. An entirely different design of transfer case was used with Chevrolet, or banjo, axles. (General Motors)

Assembly-line workers, including two women, make adjustments to transfer cases that are almost ready to be installed on CCKW chassis. Transmission-to-transfer-case drive shafts have been installed on the transfer cases to the left. (General Motors)

Above: A chassis frame has been fitted with springs and transfer case. Protruding from the sides of the frame are supports for running boards. Below the frame is the conveyor. (General Motors)

Top right: In this view of the chassis-frame assembly section, the view is from the fronts of the frames to the rears. On the nearest frame, the battery box and the fuel tank supports are installed. (General Motors)

Right: An assembly-line worker secures a canvas pad to the fuel tank bracket prior to the bracket being attached to the frame, or even being painted olive drab. This pad would buffer the fuel tank, preventing the subtle vibrations incidental to operating the truck from wearing a hole in the fuel tank. (General Motors)

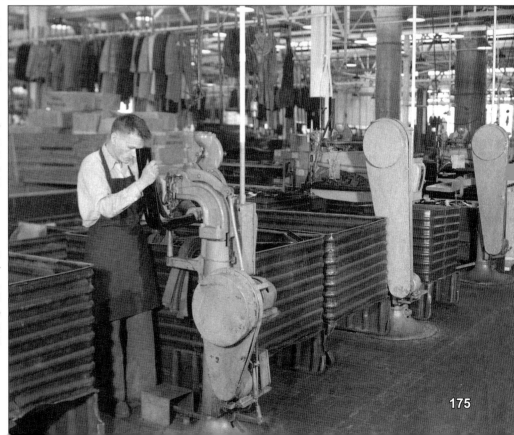

175

Left: A machinist watches a gauge as he balances a drive shaft for a GMC 2½-ton 6x6 truck. Balancing drive shafts was an operation essential to the smooth operation of the vehicles. (General Motors)

Bottom left: This photo conveys an idea of the extent and complexity of Line 1, looking north. At this stage of the chassis assembly line, springs were installed on frames. Above is a jungle of hoses and cables for various hand-held power tools. (General Motors)

Bottom right: Here, chassis frames were fitted with transfer cases: in this case, the type used with Chevrolet, axles. Also installed are the front springs and parts of the rear suspensions, including the springs, spring seats, and cross shafts. (General Motors)

In this sector of Line 1, Chevrolet axles are being fitted on the chassis frames. A front axle and two tandem axles are suspended over the frame in the foreground, ready for installation. The Hydrovac has been installed to the rear of the transfer case. (General Motors)

In an outdoor storage area at GMC Truck & Coach Division's Pontiac, Michigan, factory, hundreds upon hundreds of Timken axles are stacked tall, awaiting installation on 2½-ton 6x6 trucks. Both front axles with tie rods and steering mechanisms and tandem axles are visible. (General Motors)

Chevrolet axles are stored in this area at GMC Truck & Coach in Pontiac. Rectangular wooden frames were used to stack the units. Piles of unused frames are in the background. (General Motors)

Inside the Pontiac plant, Timken split axles are being prepared for installation on chassis frames. The two axles on the conveyor in the foreground are front ones; the ones in the background are tandem units. (General Motors)

Workers prepare Timken axles for installation on chassis frames. These are tandem axles, and the bolt-together joints on the differential cases that gave the Timken axles the alternate name "split axles" are visible. (General Motors)

This part of the assembly line was where drive shafts, or propeller shafts, were installed. On the closest chassis frame, the shafts for the tandem axles are to the rear of the transfer case, and the front shaft is lying crosswise. (General Motors)

A complement of one front axle and two tandem axles is shackled to a sling suspended from a hoist, ready to be placed on a chassis frame. These are Chevrolet axles, also called corporation axles. (General Motors)

Timken axles have been mounted on several chassis frames on the GMC Truck & Coach assembly line at Pontiac, Michigan, in a July 1945 photograph. On the closest frame, the drive shafts and muffler are installed. (General Motors)

Chevrolet axles are installed on these 2½-ton 6x6 long-wheelbase chassis frames on Line 1, looking south. The difference in shapes of the transfer cases used with Chevrolet axles, as shown here, and the transfer cases used with Timken axles, shown in the preceding photo, is apparent. (General Motors)

At this point in the chassis assembly line at GMC Truck & Coach Division's Plant 2, Pontiac, Michigan, the frames have been turned right-side-up. In this July 1945 photo, the closest frame includes a front winch, complete with cable, leader chain, and hook, while the next frame in line lacks a winch. (General Motors)

To the left, 2½-ton 6x6 chassis frames with Chevrolet axles are nearing completion on Line 1. Bumperettes and the tow pintle are installed on the second frame in line. To the right, engine assemblies are being delivered on conveyor tracks from the first floor. Painted on the front cross member of the chassis in the foreground is the manufacturing date, 7/14/43. (General Motors)

Long-wheelbase chassis frames pass through a spray booth while being conveyed down Line 1. The frames, which arrived from the manufacturer with a black finish, now have been painted olive drab. The fuel tanks have been installed on several of the frames in view. (General Motors)

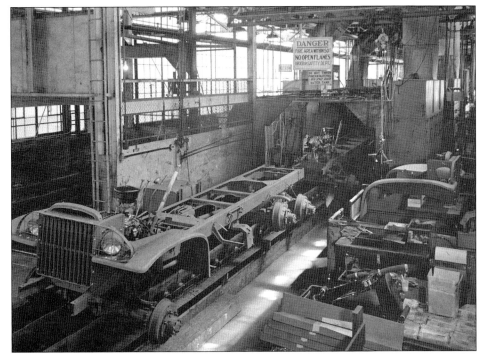

As the next step in the assembly process after chassis frames emerged from the paint booth, the radiator, grille and brush-guard assembly, fenders, and lights were installed. To the right adjacent to the booth is a fender/radiator subassembly awaiting installation. (General Motors)

In the third-floor warehouse of GMC Truck & Coach Division in Pontiac, wheels for 2½-ton 6x6 trucks were handled and stored. In the center are conveyor tracks and hooks. Some wheels with tires mounted are in the background. (General Motors)

Wheels move along a conveyor track in the third-floor warehouse. Just beyond the conveyor are stacked hundreds of fuel tanks for short-wheelbase CCKWs. (General Motors)

Right: Nondirectional-tread tires and wheels make their ways along curved, overhead conveyor tracks in the third-floor warehouse. On a trolley in the left foreground is a large stack of locking rings for the wheels. (General Motors)

Below: To the left in this view in the third-floor warehouse at GMC Truck & Coach is a conveyor track for wheels. In the right foreground are wheels mounted with tires, and to the rear are stacks of wheels. (General Motors)

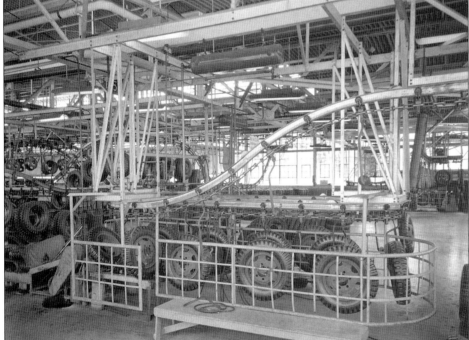

Above: In the third-floor warehouse, an overhead conveyor carries wheels with tires mounted. Distinguishable on the nearest tire are markings for U.S. Royal Master Grip. (General Motors)

Left: This appears to have been a tire-inflation station, as an air hose with a valve fitting is lying on the bench in the foreground. (General Motors)

Tires are mounted on these CCKW-353 chassis. Running boards and the front bumpers have been installed on at least the first two chassis in the line. Overhead are many wheels with tires on conveyors. (General Motors)

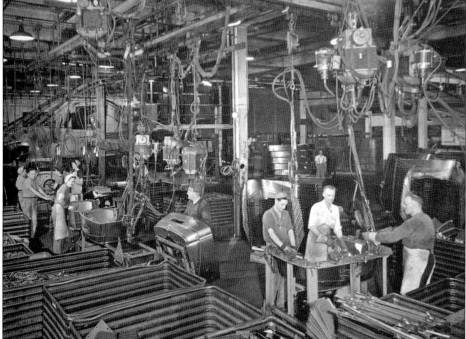

Above: This is part of the truck-cab and cowl subassembly area on the first floor. Open-cab side panels are attached to the conveyor and ready to be sent to the open-cab assembly line. (General Motors)

Left: In the truck-cab and cowl subassembly sector, to the right, three workers are assembling a cowl; it is oriented with the top of the cowl to the right. To the center and the left, assembled cowls are being placed on a conveyor. (General Motors)

In the 2½-ton 6x6 open-cab and cowl assembly line on the first floor of the GMC Truck & Coach Division factory, workers, most of whom are women, continue the assembly of cowls. They wore scarves or hair nets to keep their hair from getting in the way or becoming caught in machinery. (General Motors)

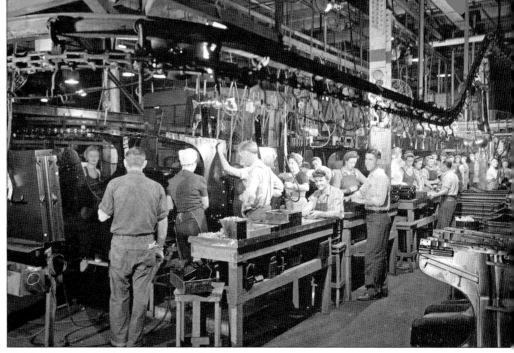

Open cabs are undergoing assembly on the truck-cab subassembly line on the first floor. To the right are some side panels, with the curves of the door openings visible. To the far left is an open cab with the right rear corner showing, including a bracket for a ring mount. (General Motors)

Two cab-over-engine cab assemblies with their rears facing the camera are on trolleys on tracks on the first floor of GMC Truck & Coach. The assemblies are a dark color except for the bare-metal fasteners and the U-bolts on the two rear brackets for a machine-gun ring mount. (General Motors)

Windshield assemblies for open-cab CCKWs are under construction at this sector of the assembly line. The glass panels are installed in the frame the two women in the foreground are working on. In the left background are subassemblies of fuel tanks, spare tires, and spare-tire clamps for short-wheelbase CCKWs. (General Motors)

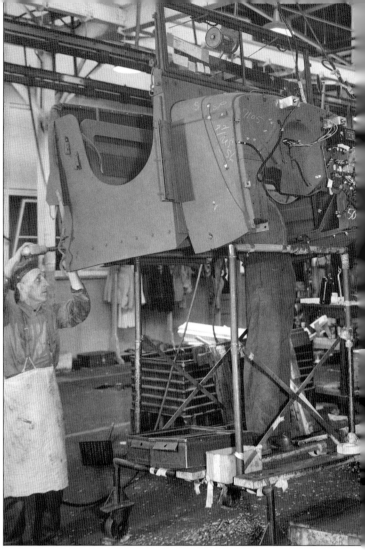

Cowls have been installed on the fronts of these open cabs for cab-over-engine AFKWX-353 trucks on the first floor of the GMC Truck & Coach plant. (General Motors)

Electrical components, terminals, the regulator, and wiring are visible on the firewall. The folded bottom of the assistant driver's seat is visible inside the door. (General Motors)

Open cabs for 2½-ton 6x6 CCKWs are under construction on the open-cab assembly line, located on the first floor of GMC Truck & Coach. Windshields are installed, as are voltage regulators, wiring harnesses, and universal rifle brackets. The bow, rear curtain, and safety strap are present on the closest cab. (General Motors)

On the line to the left are open cabs, complete with fenders, headlights, and engine enclosures, for AFKWX-353s, while in the foreground and to the right are cab-and-cowl assemblies for CCKWs. (General Motors)

On the 2½-ton 6x6 open-cab conveyor line on the first floor of GMC Truck & Coach, the worker to the right of center is hoisting a cab assembly. On the conveyor to the left are more open-cab assemblies. Several hoods are on overhead conveyors. (General Motors)

Cabs are being installed on this part of Line 1. The chassis in the foreground is soon to receive its cab, probably the one on the stand to the left. The next chassis in line have had their cabs mounted. (General Motors)

Cabs have been installed on these long-wheelbase CCKW chassis. The first full chassis in view is positioned over a pit and has its top and rear curtain in place. The hoods have not yet been installed over the engine compartments. (General Motors)

Seamstresses fabricate canvas seat cushion covers for trucks at GMC Truck & Coach Division. The items under assembly in the foreground may have been seat-cushion covers. Other canvas components included tarpaulins and cab tops, curtains, and doors. (General Motors)

GMC workers put the final touches on a late-model long-wheelbase CCKW chassis. A woman is making adjustments to the right door, while the man in the foreground works on an engine component. Suspended in the background are hoods. (General Motors)

All of the CCKW-353 cabs in this view of the front end of Line 1, Department 11, have their cab covers and top hoods, but the side panels of the hoods, each of which comprised a front panel and a rear panel, are not yet installed. (General Motors)

A painter uses a spray gun to touch-up a wooden bodied CCKW. The wooden cargo bodies were part of a solution to the shortage of sheet steel in 1942. Wooden bodies were heavy, consumed a lot of parts, and were expensive to build. (General Motors)

At GMC Truck & Coach Division, construction of AFKWX trucks took place alongside the construction of CCKWs. To the right, AFKWXs proceed along an assembly line, while to the left are an open-cab, long-wheelbase CCKW chassis and, suspended from overhead conveyors, hoods and seat cushions for CCKWs. (General Motors)

Right: Mixed in with CCKWs toward the front end of the assembly line are two AFKWXs to the right. All of these trucks are fitted with late-type cab covers and doors: note the equal-sized clear plastic windows on the doors. (General Motors)

Below: Scores of 2½-ton 6x6 military trucks are lined up inside the GMC Truck & Coach Division plant. Most of them are CCKWs, with several displaying long-wheelbase-type fuel tanks, but several AFKWXs are visible in the left background. (General Motors)

A CCKW-353 is next to a storage area for Type 270 engines. Although these engines remained a constant throughout CCKW production, various submodels of the 270 engine were used. The introduction of the 3020 submodel in May 1943 marked the transition from early-type to late-type 270 engines. (General Motors)

Wooden cargo bodies for GMC 2½-ton 6x6 trucks are being loaded onto a flatbed trailer. Although most of the components appear to be present on the bodies, the left tail light and the trailer electrical receptacle are not installed on the holder on the body in the foreground. (General Motors)

Above: Wooden cargo bodies are stored four high on the factory floor. Originally, General Motors Corporation manufactured the wooden cargo bodies used on CCKWs, but then a conglomeration of woodworking companies, approximately fifty of them, contracted to produce the bodies. (General Motors)

Left: Short-wheelbase CCKWs fitted with Timken axles make their way down the assembly line. On the closest truck, a pusher attached to the conveyor is snugged-up to the rear differential case to shuttle the truck along the line. On the second truck in line, a wooden cargo body is visible. (General Motors)

The worker to the left operates an overhead crane as a wooden cargo body is being lowered onto the frame of a CCKW-352. Specifications for the wooden bodies authorized the use of oak, maple, spruce, and plywood, but the longitudinal side sills were to be made of straight-grained white oak. (General Motors)

Several General Motors AFKWX 2½-ton 6x6 cargo trucks with wooden cargo bodies approach the end of the assembly line at GMC Truck & Coach Division. They are fitted with open cabs and have the same type of canvas cab tops and doors as the open-cab CCKWs. (General Motors)

A CCKW is undergoing testing for the integrity of its radio-suppression system. Radio suppression, which became standard on CCKWs at around serial number 100000, involved adjustments to the vehicle's electrical system along with other modifications to suppress noise disturbances in the electrical system that could interfere with reception of radio signals or permit detection of the vehicle's location by enemy radio receivers. (General Motors)

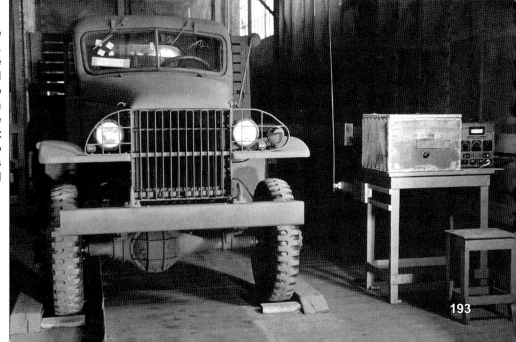

GMC workers are passing bags containing Weed tire chains into the cab of a CCKW on the assembly line. The CCKW's on-vehicle equipment included one pair of single tire chains and two pairs of dual tire chains, to be stored under the driver's seat. (General Motors)

As a tribute to GMC Truck & Coach's manufacturing prowess, hundreds upon hundreds of CCKWs are parked in neat rows and columns outside the plant. The vehicles are open-cab models and lack bodies. Resting on the frames are temporary fuel tanks of the type used when chassis trucks were driven to body manufacturers who installed specialized bodies and fuel tanks. (General Motors)

Chapter 18
The Airborne CCKW

One of the keys to the successful prosecution of WWII by the Allies was rapid projection of power. Motorized transport was more common within the U.S. armed forces during this time than in the armies of any other nation. Although millions of GIs walked every foot of the way to combat, or so it seems, Dodges, Jeeps, and GMCs seemed to be everywhere, transporting weapons and supplies, if not the troops themselves.

Rapid advancement by airborne and seaborne forces, as well as ground forces, made finding a way to rapidly bring motor transport to the front highly desirable. The obvious answer was to fly it there in a cargo aircraft. Unfortunately, the Army's standard WWII cargo truck, the GMC CCKW, was simply too large for the Army's standard transport aircraft of the time, the Douglas C-47 Skytrain, known unofficially as the Gooney Bird.

After various failed attempts at slinging trucks under the aircraft – a practice found, not surprisingly, to be very disruptive to the aircraft's handling characteristics – another method was sought. The relatively small size of the C-47, itself a problem, was compounded by the small size of its cargo door, and its placement in the side of the aircraft. The challenge for the engineers and technicians was to break the CCKW down into a few large subassemblies, each small enough to be loaded into a C-47. Using this method, it was found that a single CCKW could be transported in two C-47 aircraft.

GMC began research on this possibility in September 1943, with initial experiments conducted at Aberdeen Proving Ground in February 1944. The test unit was a CCKW-352, short-wheelbase closed-cab unit. Early on, GMC was directed to create a means of modifying not only the chassis, but also the cargo-dump body. Later the program was expanded to include the cargo body as well. Ultimately, a system for breaking trucks down was developed, and it worked for both long- and short-wheelbase vehicles. The success of these tests proved the validity of the concept and a multifold approach to implementing it was begun.

On 12 September 1944, the Detroit Ordnance District advised GMC that deliveries of 1,200 of the modified vehicles were requested beginning 1 November 1944, with all 1,200 to be delivered within

General Motors' CCKWs had established their reputation as dependable, rugged trucks in a number of campaigns by early 1944, but they did not lend themselves well to airborne operations because of their size. Thus, air-transportable 2½-ton 6x6 cargo and dump trucks based on CCKW chassis, such as the dumper version shown here, were developed with split chassis and bodies so they could be knocked down for air transport and reassembled upon landing. (Patton Museum)

60 days. The quantity to be modified was subsequently increased to 2,429, the vehicles being covered by Change Orders P-315 and P-315A to contract W-20-018-ORD-1299. These change orders specified 1,145 CCKW-353 cargo trucks without winch, 805 long-wheelbase cargo trucks with winch, and 479 CCKW-353 cargo dump trucks with winch, all air-transportable, were to be created, all boxed for export, in single-unit packs.

The 1,145 airborne cargo trucks without winches and with Chevrolet axles were scheduled for production in St. Louis on sales order TC-200651. The 805 airborne cargo trucks with winches and Chevrolet axles were also scheduled for St. Louis on sales order TC-200652. The 479 airborne cargo-dump trucks, which would have Timken axles, were to be built in Pontiac, on sales order TC-200653.

By 29 December 1944 additional quantities of the airborne CCKWs had been requested by the Army. The additional trucks consisted of 3,880 more CCKW-353 without winch, 2,497 more with winch, and 731 more CCKW-353 cargo-dump trucks with winch. Whereas on the initial order for 2,429 trucks the government was to furnish the dolly, for these 7,108 trucks the dollies were to be furnished by GMC. Once again, GMC would build all the cargo-dump trucks in Pontiac with Timken axles, under sales order TC-200696. The Pontiac plant would also build 900 of the no-winch airborne cargo trucks with Chevrolet axles on sales order TC-200697 and 500 of the winch-equipped airborne cargo trucks on sales order TC-200698, also with Chevrolet axles.

Chevrolet-St. Louis was to build 1,000 of the no-winch trucks with Chevrolet axles on TC-200699 and 1,000 with winch on sales order TC-200700. All of this production by both plants was completed by the end of June 1945.

While the GMC factory converted many vehicles, others were converted by Divco as well as by Ford at the latter's Richmond, California, facility. Modifications at Richmond began during the first week of April 1944 and continued through 10 May 1944.

Also, conversion kits were supplied for installation by third-echelon repair shops. It was estimated that it would take 45 man-hours to convert a cargo truck by the 3rd Echelon Shops (compared to the 20 man-hours allocated at the GMC plant); dump trucks were estimated to take an additional 10 man-hours. It was estimated that an experienced crew could load or unload one of these vehicles in five man-hours, and reassemble it in 10 man-hours; again, dump trucks took longer.

The various methods of achieving the conversions make it difficult to pinpoint the total number of vehicles ultimately equipped as "Airborne" CCKWs.

In addition to the prototype, there were 407 short-wheelbase CCKW-352 trucks of the airborne type. These trucks were converted by Divco of Detroit, Michigan, over the following period; April 1944, 232 vehicles, May 1944 174 units, and the final single conversion being completed in June. In addition to these rare short-wheelbase airborne trucks, Divco also converted 44 dump trucks in April and a single additional dump in June. Divco's contract was valued at $80,000.00.

The frames of the airborne trucks were cut to the rear of the cab and fishplates welded on with which it would later be bolted together. The beds of the trucks were cut into as well, with smaller fishplates provided to rejoin their halves.

A special valve and coupling unit was installed that allowed the brake system to be separated without the introduction of air, or undue loss of brake fluid. Also provided in the kit was a Weaver single-wheel dolly and various bits of tubing.

Operationally, the bed was removed in two sections, the rear driveshafts separated at their universal joints, the brake and fuel lines separated and outer rear wheels were removed. The windshield, fenders, and running boards were removed from the front section.

The frame halves were unbolted, with the rear of the front section supported on jacks, and the Weaver dolly installed. The right front spring was compressed (to provide clearance while passing through the C-47's cargo door) using a kit-supplied tool.

The tubing in the kit was used to plumb fuel from a Jerry can to the engine, and the front half of the truck was started and driven into the aircraft, the dolly supporting the rear and providing additional means of steering. The front half of the bed, running boards, fenders, body sills, bows, tarpaulin, windshield, and tools were manually loaded around the front section of the truck. The weight of the components in the first aircraft was 5,360 lbs.

The rear half of the chassis, with the bed removed, was then rolled in a second C-47. Without the bed or drive train components it is not terribly heavy, and it was manually pushed up the ramp and into the cargo area. The rear half of the bed, remaining tires, fuel tank, muffler, body racks, and frame splicing, were loaded in the aircraft behind the chassis. The second planes load totaled 5,211 lbs.

Counter to latter-day myth, these trucks were not designed to be air-dropped, or to be transported in gliders, rather flown into a prepared landing field. The aircraft with the truck cab could be unloaded in half an hour, the rear section unloaded in 20 minutes, and a team of five experienced mechanics with the proper tools could reassemble the truck in about two hours. This allowed the trucks to get the trucks to forward areas faster than possible by sea, rail or driving. For perspective, the famed high-speed Red Ball Express had a speed LIMIT, not average, of 25 MPH, the C-47 a cruising speed of 175 MPH.

To meet the need for air-transportable cargo trucks, experiments were underway by early 1944 to develop a means of splitting the chassis and the body to form two elements that could be loaded aboard aircraft. The cover for the vertical splice near the center of the dump body is visible on this example that was photographed at General Motors-Hoden's Ltd. in Australia. The cab has a distinctive top.

On the 5 February 1944 a short-wheelbase 2½-ton 6x6 airborne truck is shown assembled, with a tarpaulin in place, at Aberdeen Proving Ground. The flanged joint where the two chassis-frame sections were spliced together is visible below the spare tire and fuel tank. (National Archives via Jim Gilmore)

A short-wheelbase airborne CCKW is in the process of being disassembled at Aberdeen Proving Ground on 5 February 1944. The tarpaulin, the spare tires, and the outboard tandem wheels and tires have been removed, and the splice joining the cargo body halves is being disassembled. (National Archives via Jim Gilmore)

The rear section of the airborne CCKW has been removed, revealing the surfaces on the floor and sides of the body where the two halves of the body were spliced. (National Archives via Jim Gilmore)

Left: The front half of the body has now been detached from the chassis of the airborne CCKW. Also removed are the windshield and the assembly containing the spare-tire clamps and the gasoline tanks. (National Archives via Jim Gilmore)

Below: A 2½-ton 6x6 airborne truck has been separated in this view taken at Aberdeen Proving Ground on 5 February 1944. Next, a single-wheeled dolly would be fastened to the chassis frame to the rear of the cab. The rear section of chassis with the tandem wheels did not require a dolly. (National Archives via Jim Gilmore)

Above: In order to make the windshield removable to reduce shipping height, the pillars on either side, which normally also served as the upper front door jam, were cut. No cutting was required beneath the windshield, which swung up for ventilation on closed cab CCKWs and was not attached to the cowl except at the pillars. (National Archives via Jim Gilmore).

Right: This view of the airborne CCKW tested at Aberdeen provides a unique perspective of a closed cab with the top removed. The top of the steering wheel has been cut off to reduce the wheel's height. On the left windshield pane is a detachable defroster, held fast with suction cups. (National Archives via Jim Gilmore)

The rear half of the airborne CCKW chassis is viewed from the front, showing the tie plates by which that part of the chassis frame was spliced to the forward half of the frame. The drive shafts are secured with ropes. (National Archives via Jim Gilmore)

The front half of an airborne CCKW is being prepared for loading into a C-47 cargo plane at Aberdeen Proving Ground on 5 February 1944. The fenders and running boards had been removed from the vehicle. Above the dolly is a first-series Hydrovac. (National Archives via Jim Gilmore)

Right: Military personnel and a civilian look on as the front half of the airborne CCKW is being prepared for loading into the C-47 in the background. The brush guard has been modified per a Modification Work Order (MWO) for fitting a BO driving light to an early CCKW. The kit for this modification included a light and grille guard that was to be bolted to the original grill. (National Archives via Jim Gilmore)

Below: Using a wooden ramp, personnel are pushing the front half of an airborne CCKW to the cargo door of a C-47 at Aberdeen Proving Ground. This was part of a series of trials to assess the feasibility and relative ease or difficulty of loading the front section into a cargo plane. (National Archives via Jim Gilmore)

The following sequence of photos taken by or for the GMC Truck & Coach Division document the conversion of a long-wheelbase CCKW cargo-dump truck to an airborne truck. The right side of the body is shown before the cutting began. (General Motors via Jim Gilmore)

The cargo-dump body has been raised and is supported by a chain hoist as conversion work for an airborne truck begins. (General Motors via Jim Gilmore)

The front rack of the cargo-dump body has been removed. This is the rear face of the rack, with the hinged cab protector secured in the closed position with turnbuckles. (General Motors via Jim Gilmore)

201

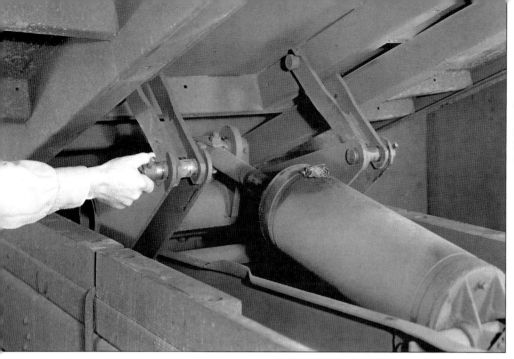

A worker removes a pin from the right lifting linkage of the hoist assembly. It was necessary to disconnect the lifting linkages before removing the cargo-dump body. (General Motors via Jim Gilmore)

Preparatory to removing the cargo-dump body from the chassis frame of the CCKW-353 undergoing conversion to an airborne truck, workmen remove the hinge pins. (General Motors via Jim Gilmore)

The dump body has been disconnected from the hinges and the hoist assembly and is suspended above the chassis frame. Running along the bottom of the side of the body is the right linkage rod for the tailgate control. (General Motors via Jim Gilmore)

The area where the chassis frame will be cut for conversion to an airborne truck is displayed, showing the fuel tank and the battery box in the foreground and the spare tire on the opposite side. (General Motors via Jim Gilmore)

Workers have unfastened the retainer straps and are about to remove the fuel tank from the chassis frame. (General Motors via Jim Gilmore)

The long-wheelbase-type spare-tire carrier has been removed from the chassis frame and is resting on the floor. Two dark, rectangular spots on the frame represent where the carrier and the latch retainer were removed. (General Motors via Jim Gilmore)

During conversion of a long-wheelbase CCKW to an airborne truck, the fuel tank and the battery have been removed and are sitting on the floor, along with the battery-box cover. (General Motors via Jim Gilmore)

With the cargo-dump body removed, details of the drive shafts and, to the right of them, the second-series Hydrovac are visible. At the top is the lower rear of the cab. (General Motors via Jim Gilmore)

With cutting operations about to take place on the chassis frame during conversion to an airborne truck, the rear drive shafts have been disconnected and wooden blocks have been positioned to support the frame. The view is from the right side. (General Motors via Jim Gilmore)

As viewed from the right rear corner of the cab, markings have been applied to the frame to indicate the locations of the cuts, giving precise measurements in inches from two lateral hat-section cross-members. The tailpipe has been detached from the muffler below the driveshaft. (General Motors via Jim Gilmore)

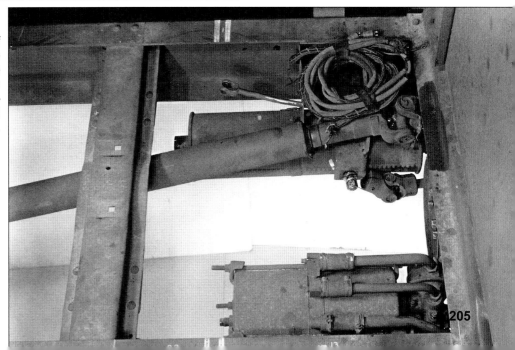

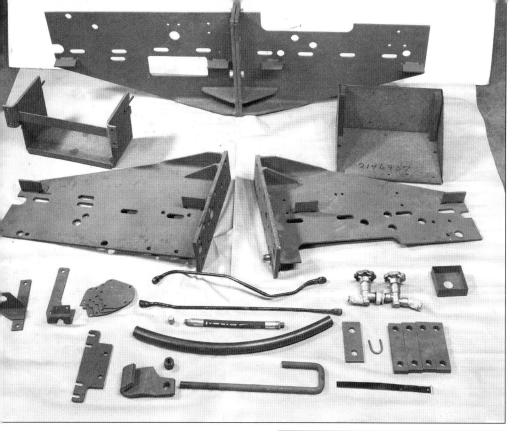

These parts were provided to fabricate the airborne-truck modification. A pair of tie plates was to be attached to each outboard side of the chassis frame, with the plates to meet at the point where the frame was split. Then, screws and nuts through the tie plates secured the spliced frame together. Other parts and fittings also were supplied for making the modification. (General Motors via Jim Gilmore)

The tie plates are in place and secured to the separated frame with bolts and nuts. Markings indicate where further holes are to be drilled to accept bolts and nuts. The downward sloping design of the bottoms of the plates added structural strength to this potentially weak portion of the frame and added more surface area for fastening together the two flanges per side. (General Motors via Jim Gilmore)

The tie plates on the left side of the frame are viewed. The drive shafts have been disconnected from the tandem axles and are hanging on the floor. A framing square is set on top of the rear section of the chassis frame to verify the trueness of the flange's positioning. (General Motors via Jim Gilmore)

A steel cargo-dump body that has been converted for use on an airborne truck is viewed upside down. The body was cut in half laterally, and the dark-colored strips were flanges that served to splice the two halves together. The hinged partition for limiting the load of the dump truck is in the stowed position. (General Motors via Jim Gilmore)

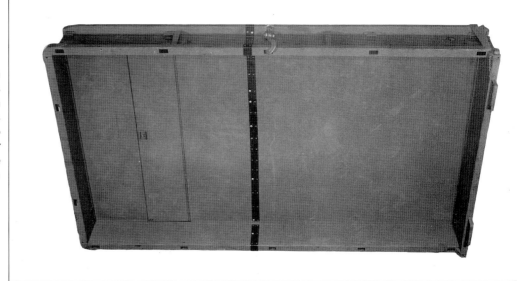

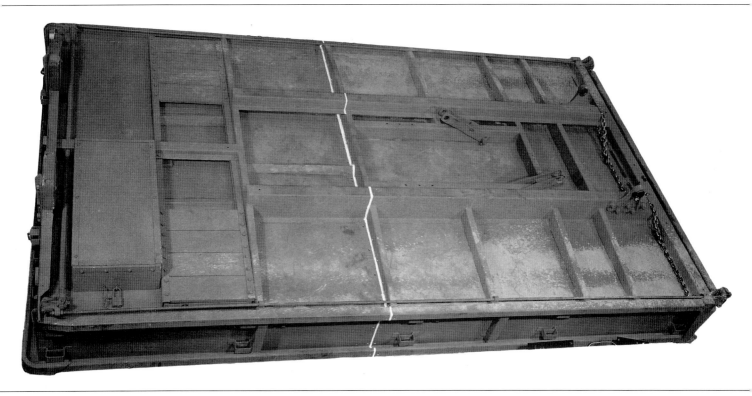

Above: A cargo-dump body is viewed upside-down before it has been cut in half for conversion for use on an airborne truck. Lines have been marked in where the cuts will be made. The front of the bed is to the left. (General Motors via Jim Gilmore)

Right: The flanges for fastening the cargo-dump body sections together have been attached with Phillips-head screws and nuts to the body section to the left. Holes have been drilled near the cut edges on the body to the right to accept screws that will hold the two body sections together. (General Motors via Jim Gilmore)

The two halves of the airborne cargo-dump body have been joined together and secured with the flanges. The several flanges on the frame under the body were welded to the frame and attached to each other with nuts and screws. (General Motors via Jim Gilmore)

The tie plates, previously held in place with bolts, have now been welded securely in place, with welds being apparent on the top edges of the plates and in the oval holes that were in line a little above the bottom of the chassis frame. The rectangular slot in the rear flange plate accommodated the spare-tire carrier. (General Motors via Jim Gilmore)

The inside of the right chassis-frame joint of an airborne truck is viewed. Five hex bolts and locking hex nuts are secured to the inner side of the flange. To the left is the Hydrovac assembly. (General Motors via Jim Gilmore)

The same frame joint seen in the preceding photo is viewed from the outboard side, with the rear of the cab to the top right. The fuel-tank brackets and the battery box have been installed on the tie plates. (General Motors via Jim Gilmore)

209

As viewed from the left side of the chassis frame, the drive shafts for the tandem axles have been reconnected, and the plumbing has been connected to the Hydrovac. The two valves to the right of center, part of the conversion kit for the airborne truck, were for shutting off the brake lines when the two sections of the truck were disconnected. (General Motors via Jim Gilmore)

Right: The cargo-dump body has been reinstalled and the hoist assembly reconnected on the CCKW-353 chassis being converted to an airborne truck. The flanges that connect the two halves of the body together are visible on the side and the bottom of the body. (General Motors via Jim Gilmore)

Below: An open-cab CCKW-353 with winch has been converted to an airborne truck. The tie plates that serve to identify this as an airborne truck are highly visible below the spare tire. The flange that marks the joint between the body halves is less prominent to the front of the center stake of the rack. (Fred Crismon collection)

The front of a CCKW airborne truck is being readied for loading into a C-46 cargo plane during an airborne show at National Airport, Washington, D.C., in early November 1944. The dolly consisted of a castering wheel mounted on a crossbar that was bolted to the flange plates. (National Museum of the United States Air Force)

Left: To the left of the front of the CCKW airborne truck seen in the preceding photo is the rear of that truck. The front faces of the tie plates are in the foreground. The tie plate to the left had five screw holes on the inboard side, whereas the plate to the right had only three screw holes. (National Museum of the United States Air Force)

Below: This photograph of a CCKW-353 airborne truck at Aberdeen Proving Ground is dated 19 December 1946. The open-cab vehicle was fitted with a winch and Timken axles. The manner in which the spare-tire carrier fit in the rectangular opening in the rear tie plate is apparent. (Ordnance Museum)

The front section of an airborne truck supported by a dolly is displayed in a 1 December 1944 photograph. The fenders, headlights, windshield, and running boards have been removed for shipment. (General Motors)

The same front section of a CCKW airborne truck is observed from the right rear. The battery box remained in place for shipment. Three brackets for the stanchions of a machine-gun ring mount are on the cab: on the rear, the right rear corner, and the front of the door. (General Motors)

The rear section of an airborne truck that corresponds to the front section in the two preceding photographs is shown, with the tie plates toward the right and the cargo-dump body removed. (General Motors)

From this angle and in this lighting, this CCKW-353 airborne cargo truck, GMC ordnance serial number 414077 and U.S. Army registration number 4708819 is indistinguishable from a stock CCKW-353. The photo was taken by the Ordnance Operation, Engineering Standards Vehicle Laboratory, Detroit, on 22 March 1945. (TACOM LCMC History Office)

Left: The same CCKW-353 airborne cargo truck seen in the preceding photo is shown with the cab top and the tarpaulin and bows removed, exposing to view the wooden body. The top of a universal rifle bracket is visible in the right rear corner of the cab. (TACOM LCMC History Office)

Below: The splice between the front and the rear halves of the wooden cargo body of the CCKW-353 airborne truck was immediately to the rear of the center stake of the rack. The reinforcing plate on the side of the body is visible in that location. (TACOM LCMC History Office)

Above: As seen in an overhead view of GMC ordnance serial number 414077 and U.S. Army registration number 4708819, the lateral splice line of the two halves of the wooden body is faintly visible at the center of the bed. Lying on the bed is the dolly and drawbar. (TACOM LCMC History Office)

Right: The same CCKW-353 airborne truck is viewed from the rear with the tailgate lowered in the horizontal position. The troop seats are deployed, and a safety strap is attached to the rears of the side racks. (TACOM LCMC History Office)

A 22 March 1945 photo depicts GMC ordnance serial number 414077 and U.S. Army registration number 4708819 from the front, showing details of the Gar Wood winch, the asymmetrical brush guards, the grille, and the service headlights, the blackout headlight, and the marker lamps. (TACOM LCMC History Office)

A look under the hood of the same CCKW-353 airborne truck taken on 22 March 1945 shows a typical late-production CCKW engine compartment. (TACOM LCMC History Office)

Left: Similarly, the cab of that CCKW-353 airborne truck was a standard late-production type, complete with a wooden steering wheel and vacuum-operated windshield wipers. To the lower left is an M1 rifle in a universal rifle bracket. These brackets were removed when the truck was being prepared for air shipment. (TACOM LCMC History Office)

Below: A CCKW-353 airborne truck has been disassembled for air shipment, and detached components are scattered about. To the left is the forward section of the wooden cargo bed, with the edges where the bed was spliced with the rear section of the bed appearing in the foreground. (Fred Crismon collection)

A short-wheelbase CCKW airborne truck is the subject of this 19 December 1946 Aberdeen Proving Ground photo. Although the short-wheelbase CCKW used spare-tire clamps instead of the chassis-frame-mounted spare-tire carrier of the long-wheelbase version, the rectangular opening for that carrier is visible on the right rear flange plate. (Ordnance Museum)

Corporal Al Yribia uses an acetylene torch to cut the top off a closed cab CCKW during work to make the vehicle transportable by air from Port Moresby, Papua, to Nadzab, Northeast New Guinea, on 11 October 1943. The conversion work was performed by Headquarters Company, 440th Signal Battalion. (National Archives)

Corporal Yribia performs cutting work on the steel body of a CCKW to modify it for transportation by air. The rear half of the body is in the background. Two cargo planes were to be used to transport the sections of this truck. (National Archives)

In the case of closed-top CCKWs, another way to transport these vehicles by air was to remove the entire cab. One such instance is seen inside a Curtiss C-46 cargo plane at Chabua Airfield in Assam Province, India, on 1 December 1944. The truck was to be flown over "the Hump" to China. Also visible are the fuel tank, racks, bows, tarpaulin, ammunition boxes, and a tire. (National Archives)

A closed-top CCKW cab inside a C-46 cargo bay is being moved by Clark forklift. Marked on the window backwards (i.e., readable from inside the cab) is "Chaubua" [sic], an approximate spelling the town of Chabua, in the Indian state of Assam. This was the tough way to transport a CCKW, but, given the exigencies of the China-Burma-India Theater, a necessary one. (National Archives)

Chapter 19
Low-Silhouette Trucks

oncealment of military assets is always of considerable interest. While many think of this in terms of camouflage, for military engineers most often the first thing to come to mind is silhouette. A lower silhouette not only means better concealment, it also means a smaller target for the enemy if spotted.

This concept was brought to transport vehicles at a meeting between the Army and various truck manufacturers held at Camp Holabird on 20-21 August 1941. At that time the development of low-profile trucks by the manufacturers was requested. Initially, these were to be 4x4 designs, but soon 6x6 trucks were involved as well.

Various proposals were submitted by GMC and other manufacturers in response to this. However, the Japanese attack on Pearl Harbor caused the military's emphasis to shift to the models already in production, and the low-profile project was shelved until 21 February 1942. At that time GMC was awarded a contract to build five each prototypes of four different models, a mixture of 4x4 and 6x6 types. On 27 May a further award for five modified 6x6 vehicles was given to Yellow Truck and Coach, making for a total of 25 low-silhouette trucks the firm was to build.

Production of the prototypes, which was done in Yellow Truck and Coach's experimental shop, was hampered by the low-priority rating given the project by the War Department. Such a rating was an impediment in getting the needed materials. A year after the award, on 1 February 1943, five of the trucks were being tested by the Army, 10 were still being assembled, and 10 were in the final stages of design work.

On 5-6 February 1943 examples of the low-profile trucks produced by various manufacturers were exhibited at Fort Holabird, where they were not generally received favorably. There were objections that the compact design would make maintenance difficult, and the unconventional arrangement of the vehicles was uncomfortable. It was suggested that the bodies could be lowered on current production vehicles and thereby meet many of the project goals.

Among the vehicles exhibited and tested over those two days were 3-ton 6x6 models produced by International Harvester and Studebaker. The GMC 3-ton models, the DAKW and DCKW, were not yet ready, and GMC president Irving Babcock sent a letter protesting what he saw as premature testing to the Chief of Ordnance on 19 February. The letter said that Col. Van Deusen at Detroit Ordnance District had stated that the consideration of the low-profile trucks was being deferred and "was no longer a rush item for either late 1943 or early 1944 purchasing."

Mr. Babcock's letter also introduced the CCKW with convertible low-profile body. This vehicle was outlined in these two paragraphs:

"During our discussion, we asked what the 1944 requirements would be on the Infantry Troop Carrier stating that we had no knowledge that the Army was even considering a single purpose vehicle of this nature until we learned an order had been placed with Dodge for 45,000 of their 3/4-ton truck modified into a six-wheeler but still retaining the same power plant and axles. When we inquired about this vehicle last fall, we were advised it was only to be used to carry infantry troops also that the Army realized that the power was

As part of experiments to lower the silhouette of the CCKW and provide it with an option for built-in troop seats, GMC developed a convertible body. This multiple-use body could be configured as a troop carrier or, by folding the troop seats over a longitudinal well along the center of the body, a flatbed cargo carrier. (Fred Crismon collection)

low and flotation questionable but that the load being a live one could get out and push the vehicle uphill or over bad terrain. As a cargo carrier it is limited not only in respect to maximum load capacity but also performance on grades and poor roadways.

"We believe that we can provide in the present 2½-ton GMC 6x6 a combined troop and cargo carrier by having a depressed aisle in the body so that troops can sit on the normal floor level of the body with their feet in a well, thereby giving in effect a lower silhouette. At the same time maintaining the good acceleration, flotation and gradeability. Further, when not used to carry troops, our proposed truck would carry its full rated load of ammunition or other cargo either by placing load on seats and in center aisle or on a flat floor which could

be quickly provided by dropping seat sections into depressed center aisle. Alternately, the forward part of the body could carry cargo and the rear half troops, or vice versa. At the request of Colonel Robins, Services of Supply, we are providing four sample vehicles with this arrangement."

Yellow Truck and Coach completed all of its low-silhouette trucks, including the DAKW, DOKW, and DCKW 6x6 models, by mid-1943. The vehicles were then delivered to the Army for testing at various posts, including Fort Holabird, Aberdeen Proving Ground, Fort Knox, and Fort Benning.

Although many of these vehicles were retained as late as 1949, no further production of the low-profile trucks was undertaken.

Right: The CCKW with a convertible body shown in this and the preceding photo was U.S.A. number 4482697. By 19 February 1943, GMC had delivered four sample CCKWs with convertible bodies to the U.S. Army. For this vehicle, the spare tires were mounted on each side of the cab. (Fred Crismon collection)

Below: The fuel tank of the CCKW with convertible body had a capacity of 60 gallons and was mounted above the chassis frame to the rear of the cab. This necessitated the mounting of the spare tires on the sides of the cab. The left filler is visible to the upper rear of the spare tire. Atop the fuel tank was a toolbox. (Fred Crismon collection)

The convertible body is viewed from the rear, showing it deployed for seating troops. Racks formed the seat backs, and a narrow tailgate with a single step attached to it was used. A rack is installed on the front of the body. (Fred Crismon collection)

In this photo, the front left and right troop seats have been folded inward to form a flat bed across the forward half of the convertible body. The front rack has been removed, showing the top of the fuel tank with a filler on each side and a toolbox on top. (Fred Crismon collection)

All troop seats are folded inward, to form a flat bed throughout the convertible body. Although the tailgate was of steel construction, the side panels of the rear of the body were of wooden construction with steel corners. (Fred Crismon collection)

Eight G.I.s are seated in the rear of U.S.A. 4482697, to which an artillery piece is hitched. The convertible body was designed to hold up to 18 troops. By the time this photo was taken, an accident had befallen the fender, the rear half of which is crumpled. (Fred Crismon collection)

Right: In early 1943, in response to a field artillery requirement for a 2½-ton low-silhouette prime mover, General Motors delivered five DCKW low-silhouette derivatives of the CCKW to the Army. Several different designs were furnished. This one featured a dome on top of the hood to provide clearance for the air cleaner. Open cabs were common to all of the DCKWs. (Fred Crismon collection)

Below: A low-silhouette DCKW was photographed during trials at Holabird Ordnance Depot, Baltimore, Maryland, on 3 February 1943. The objects on top of the winch drum were cable rollers and their housing. Because the spare tires were in the ways of the cab doors, a step was provided below the rear on each side of the cab. (Fred Crismon collection)

Right: In a frontal view of the DCKW at Holabird, the dome that provided clearance for the air cleaner is offset to the left of the centerline of the hood. The axles were the Chevrolet "banjo" type. The vertical and horizontal cable rollers are visible above the winch drum. (Fred Crismon collection)

Below: The body of the DCKW was constructed of wood and had an interior length of 144 inches and in interior width of 80 inches. The engine was the GMC 270, the transmission was the Clark 204-VO-217, and the transfer case was by GMC. (Fred Crismon collection)

The DCKW tested at Holabird is shown with the tarpaulin and cab top and doors installed. The half-door openings on the side of the cab had metal covers, and the canvas doors were of a revised, shortened design. (Fred Crismon collection)

GMC also produced several 3-ton 6x6 low-silhouette trucks, designated the DAKW. It was powered by a GMC 360 six-cylinder engine. bore U.S. Army registration number 4344713 on the hood. Two spare tires were stored side-by-side on the right side of the cab. The tires were size 8.25-20. (Fred Crismon collection)

Right: This DAKW was tested by the Armored Force Board at Fort Knox, Kentucky. The DAKW's winch had a cable-roller assembly similar to the type fitted on the DCKW low-profile truck. The winch had a capacity of 5,000 pounds. The DAKW had a maximum road speed of 51 miles per hour and a cruising range on paved roads of 310 miles. (Fred Crismon collection)

Below: The DAKW had a single, long fuel tank below the right rear of the cab and the front of the body. This example bears U.S. Army registration number 4344710. The cab was fitted with the early-style canvas top and doors. (Fred Crismon collection)

Above: The DAKW had an overall height of 93 inches, but this was reducible to 76 inches by removing the cab top, lowering the windshield, and taking down the bows and tarpaulin. The tailgate was narrower than the full-width types used on CCKW cargo bodies. (Fred Crismon collection)

Right: General Motors also produced an experimental low-silhouette 3-ton, 6x6 truck designated the DOKW. On this truck, the driver was positioned in an extension of the cab outboard of the right side of the chassis frame. Otherwise, it was virtually identical to the DAKW. (National Archives via Jim Gilmore)

The DOKW's U.S. Army registration number, 4344718, was painted on the hood. The brush guards were asymmetrical, with the right one protecting a service headlight and a marker lamp and the wider brush guard on the left protecting a service headlight, marker lamp, and blackout headlight. (Fred Crismon collection)

The cross sills under the cargo body were shaped to fit the stepped cross section of the bottom of the cargo body. The body was of steel construction, with wood-slatted troop seats. A toolbox was under the front of the body on each side. (Fred Crismon collection)

The extended left side of the cab is viewed from the side. Although General Motors representatives reported that they were confident in the company's ability to produce a low-silhouette 3-ton 6x6 cargo and troop-carrier truck in large quantities, with a concurrent capacity to produce sufficient GMC 360 engines, the project did not go into production. (Fred Crismon collection)

Chapter 20
Charcoal-Gas Converter

Americans at home during World War II faced fuel rationing and shortages since the bulk of the Nation's production was being sent to U.S. and Allied forces overseas. Yet even these vast resources were not enough to feed the advancing armies. On more than one occasion, Allied troops had to slow or stop their offensive against the Axis due to fuel shortages. This situation was particularly acute in China, whose representatives sought gas producers that could be used to power the GMC trucks being supplied to their nation.

In June 1942 a meeting was held in Washington to discuss the potential for the U.S. to develop gas conversion equipment for use by vehicles overseas, in order to lessen gasoline consumption. The gas production equipment would convert solid fuels into a gaseous form that conventional engines could burn. These gases are created through the partial burning of high grade coal, dry wood, or charcoal. Of those, charcoal gas has the best BTU value.

These systems encompass four principal components: the generator itself, in which the gas is made; the cooling system, which lowers the temperature of the gas leaving the generator and separates large particles of ash and dust; the filters, which remove smaller particles; and the controls, or gas regulator, which mix the supplied gas and air and feed it to the engine.

The Army tested gas converters made by four organizations – M&R Products Company; the Tennessee Valley Authority in conjunction with Georgia Tech; the War Products Company; and Yellow Truck and Coach. Regardless of manufacturer, no abnormal wear on the engine or contamination of the oil was found by the testing personnel at Aberdeen Proving Ground. Those tests also indicated that 12 to 14 pounds of charcoal was equivalent to one gallon of gasoline when fueling the engines.

Contract W-2425-QM-205, later W-364-ORD-2800, was issued to Yellow Truck and Coach for the production of a CCKW equipped with a gas converter. Material to construct the basic truck was diverted from contract 11595 – a move that necessitated replacing that material on a December 1942 sales order. The engine installed on this truck had a special, enlarged intake manifold. The other manufacturers were supplied stock CCKWs for their test installations.

The Aberdeen testing concluded that the M&R Products convertor was the most adaptable, easiest to operate and maintain, and observed: "This model, as tested, is already in production and obtainable in quantity." The TVA version was noted as having the sturdiest construction, but both the War Products and Yellow Truck versions were unacceptable in the forms tested.

While the Aberdeen report recommended that the M & R Products converter be considered for acceptance by Ordnance, it noted that finding suitable supplies of charcoal overseas could be a problem, and that operators of converter-equipped trucks would need additional training. The Chinese, operating outside of the normal procedures, went directly to M&R with an order for 5,000 of its convertors. Upon learning of this, the U.S. Army stopped pursuing the project.

In mid-1942 the U.S. Army arranged for four companies to develop charcoal gas converters for fueling 2½-ton 6x6 trucks. Gas converters generated gas for internal-combustion engines by the partial combustion of coal, charcoal, or wood. The Army conceived a need for such vehicles in areas where gasoline could not be obtained. This truck was equipped with GMC Yellow Coach & Truck Division's submission of a gas converter. (National Archives via Jim Gilmore)

Left: The gas-converter equipment on the side of GMC's submission is observed from a closer perspective. From the expansion chamber, hot gases passed up a pipe to a cooler on top of the cab roof. From there, they passed down to a cloth filter on the left front fender. (Fred Crismon collection)

Center Left: Each of the four pilot 2½-ton 6x6 trucks with gas converters had different configurations and locations for the converters. GMC's version had the generator on the right running board. Above the generator was a tank for water that was used to inject dry steam into the fire zone and for cooling. To the front of the generator was an expansion chamber. (National Archives via Jim Gilmore)

Center Right: The left side of GMC's submission for a gas-converter truck is shown. The cooler mounted on top of the cab, the gas pipe running downward from the front of the cooler, and the cloth filter, which removed particulates from the gas, are in view. (National Archives via Jim Gilmore)

Right: Further details of the gas pipes, the cooler, and the cloth filter are in view. The cooler, in addition to cooling the hot gas produced by the generator, also served to remove large particulates of ash and dust from the gas. (Fred Crismon collection)

227

Inside the engine compartment of GMC's submission of a gas-converter 2½-ton 6x6 truck were mixing valves and a security filter through which the gas flowed before entering the carburetor. (National Archives via Jim Gilmore)

Another firm that submitted a gas-conversion vehicle for the Army's consideration was M&R Products, Inc. Their entry, seen in a photo dated 28 July 1943, featured a square-shaped generator on the left side of the truck to the rear of the cab, two cyclone filters to the rear of the truck, a charcoal dryer and filter, a main cloth filter, and a security filter. (Fred Crismon collection)

The M&R Products gas converter is viewed from the left side. On the ground below the cab, the security filter has been released from the housing above. The charcoal dryer and filter is lying on the ground to the right below its housing. (National Archives via Jim Gilmore)

Inside the engine compartment of the M&R Products gas converter was a carbo-charger. This unit assisted in propelling gases to the engine intake manifold, and it also regulated the proper air-gas mixture. (National Archives via Jim Gilmore)

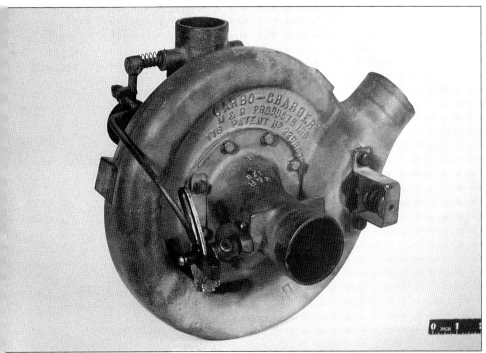

The carbo-charger of the M&R Products gas converter is displayed. This mechanism was manufactured by M&R products, and it is viewed from its rear side as installed in the engine compartment. (National Archives via Jim Gilmore)

At the rear of the M&R Products gas-converter truck were two cyclone-type filters. They are lying on the ground below their respective housings. A gas pipe is routed between the two housings. (National Archives via Jim Gilmore)

Another participant in the gas-converter tests was TVA-Georgia Tech, which submitted a cylindrical gas generator to the right rear of the cab. Below the generator was an expansion tank. Fastened to the front of the generator was a water tank, and to the rear of the center of the cab was an auxiliary water tank. This vehicle is seen in an Aberdeen Proving Ground photo dated 11 October 1943. (Fred Crismon collection)

Above: The TVA-Georgia Tech gas-converter truck, based on a short-wheelbase CCKW, is viewed from the left side, showing the routing of the gas pipes from behind the cab to the engine compartment. (Fred Crismon collection)

Right: The War Products Co. was one of the four submitters of gas-converter trucks for trials by the Army. Their vehicle had a cylindrical generator to the left rear of the cab. To the rear of the generator and below the front of the body were coolers, which also acted as filters. (National Archives via Jim Gilmore)

The gas pipes and cloth filter and security filter inside the engine compartment of the TVA-Georgia Tech gas-converter truck are viewed from the left side looking to the rear. (National Archives via Jim Gilmore)

A mechanic is lifting the filter element from the cloth-filter casing on the War Products gas converter. Two round covers for the openings at the bottom of the casing have been removed. (National Archives via Jim Gilmore)

On the right side of the War Products Co. gas converter, to the rear of the cab was a large, cylindrical, cloth-filtering unit. Mounted on the fender to the side of the engine compartment was an electrical blower. Gas entered this filter after leaving the coolers. (National Archives via Jim Gilmore)

The electrical blower on the front right fender is viewed close-up. The blower was used for starting the engine. The gas pipe from the cloth filter proceeds above the running board and up through the fender to the blower. (National Archives via Jim Gilmore)

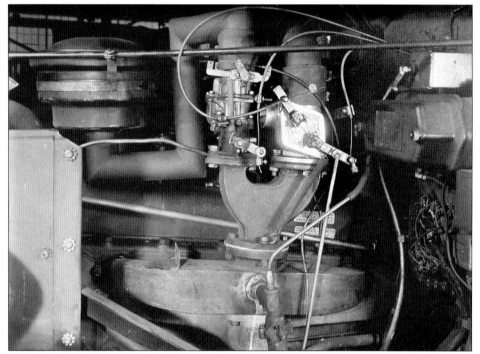

With the right side panels of the engine compartment removed, the original mixing valve and oversized intake manifold of the War Products gas converter are visible. The oversized intake manifold later was replaced by a standard-sized one. (National Archives via Jim Gilmore)

In a detail view of the War Products gas converter on the left side of the vehicle, the fire box is to the lower left, and the cylindrical objects to the center and the right are the coolers. (National Archives via Jim Gilmore)

Chapter 21
Accessory Kits

Although the Yellow Truck and Coach/GMC did produce some specialized trucks, such as cargo/dump trucks and tankers, as well as trucks with specialized equipment (airborne trucks, for example), most trucks were rather routine.

In order to meet the varying needs of the Army, a variety of accessory kits were developed. Among these were kits to permit permanent equipment for fording of deep water, kits to provide a heated crew compartment, and a host of other special equipment. However the most common kit was one to permit the mounting of an M49 antiaircraft machine gun on the truck. For those times when one M2 heavy machine gun was not enough, another kit permitted the mounting of the formidable power-operated M55 quad machine gun in the cargo bed.

A number of these kits were not fully developed until near the end of WWII, such as the A-frame mount and the previously mentioned mounting of the quad machine gun. However, these kits, as well as some developed after VJ-Day, were used during the Korean War, as well as during peacetime.

The quad mount tests, for example, were not initiated until December 1944. The A-frame, while initiated in February 1944, was not recommended for standardization until OCM 27511 was issued on 3 May 1945. Testing of the permanent deep water fording kit began in March 1944, but the report was not completed until 3 October 1945. Not all efforts at developing accessories were successful. Various attempts at creating traction aids that essentially made the CCKW a half-track universally were rejected as being too time consuming, cumbersome and resulting in excess wear on the truck tires.

The Ordnance Department authorized the development of a universal A-frame kit for mounting on the front ends of winch-equipped trucks, including the 2½-ton 6x6 CCKW, in February 1944. Guy cables with a spreader bar between them to the rear of the cab served to reinforce the boom. (National Archives)

In a photo taken at Aberdeen Proving Ground on the same date as the preceding photo, 11 June 1946, a closed-cab CCKW-353 is rigged with a universal A-frame kit supported by a single guy cable. To the rear of the bumper on each side of the chassis frame was a folding jack to support the front end when engaged in very heavy lifting operations. (National Archives)

The jacks have been lowered in their support position on a CCKW fitted with a universal A-frame kit. The ruler to the side provides a scale reference. The brackets to which the heels of the boom were pinned were bolted to the chassis frame. (National Archives)

Because of the lengthy time it took to install a deep-fording kit on a CCKW and to remove it, in early 1943 GMC Truck & Coach Division began developing a permanent fording kit for these trucks. Tests proved that the kit was suitable for operational use in repeated fordings of short duration in water up to four feet deep. CCKW-353 4806279 is shown with the exhaust extension and heat shield to the front of the left front tandem tires. (General Motors)

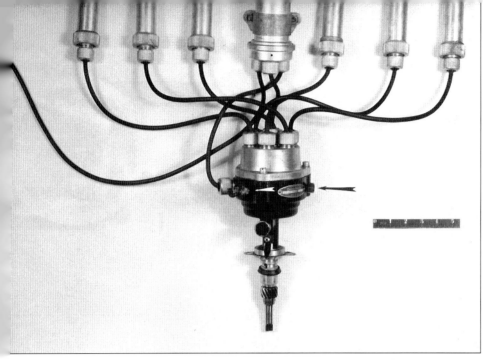

To devise an effective permanent fording kit, it was necessary to waterproof many of the vehicle's mechanisms and systems. One of these was the ignition system. Shown here in a December 1944 photo are the waterproofed ignition components, including the distributor, coil, and spark plugs. A watertight carburetor and air cleaner were part of the permanent fording kit. (National Archives via Jim Gilmore)

Right: During early tests of the permanent fording kit, considerable water was able to enter the crankcase, forcing oil and water emulsion out through the crankcase oil-filler cap. To fix this problem, a shutoff valve was installed on the crankcase ventilation tube, to the upper left of the photo. Closing the valve during operation in water solved the flooding problem. (National Archives via Jim Gilmore)

Below: CCKW-352 U.S.A. number 4289453 crosses a body of water using a permanent fording kit. The object to the front of the grille appears to have been a device to register the draft of the vehicle or the depth of the water. The water, of course, would flow freely into the cab when the truck reached a certain depth. (National Archives via Jim Gilmore)

235

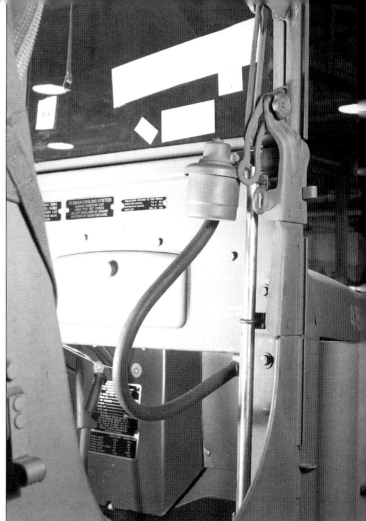

In the permanent fording kit as originally tested, the crankcase vent and the distributor vent were connected to a common line that terminated with an oil-bath air filter on the right side of the cab. (General Motors)

Another open-cab CCKW, Army number 4852939, is seen without the air cleaner and pipe but with a flexible hose with an Hydrovac air cleaner at the end. Visible is one of the many arrangements of data plates used in the CCKW. (General Motors)

CCKW 4289453 is viewed from the left side, showing the flexible hose that formed the air-cleaner intake in the permanent fording kit. An extension is not present on the engine exhaust to the front of the tandem tires. (National Archives via Jim Gilmore)

Several submodels of the M37 ring mount were used on the closed-cab CCKW-352. The ring itself was designated the M49. Shown here is the ring with the skate or trolley, ammunition-box tray, pintle mount, and .50-caliber machine gun installed. The trolley was a carriage that could be positioned and locked at any given position around the ring. (Rock Island Arsenal Museum)

The M2 .50-caliber machine gun has been removed from the M49 ring of an M37A1 ring mount. The M37A1 ring mount was used on closed-cab CCKW-352s with wood cargo bodies. The M37 ring mount was employed on steel-body closed-cab CCKWs. The M37A2 was used on closed-cab CCKW-352s with wood cargo bodies, and the M37A3 was used on 700-gallon water tank trucks and 750-gallon gasoline tank trucks with camouflaged tops. (Rock Island Arsenal Museum)

A trolley, also called a skate, for a ring mount is viewed from above. At the top is the socket into which the base of the pintle fit. Below the socket is the locking handle for the skate. On top of the body of the trolley are two rollers; similar rollers were on the bottom of the trolley, and these facilitated the movement of the trolley on the ring. (National Archives)

A D40733 cradle-and-pintle assembly is seen from the left. Several different models of this assembly were used, and they varied in such regards as the shape of the cradle, the number of pin holes, and whether a holder for an ammunition tray was present or not. The pintle allowed the gun to be elevated and rotated, while the trolley allowed it to be swung fully around. (National Archives)

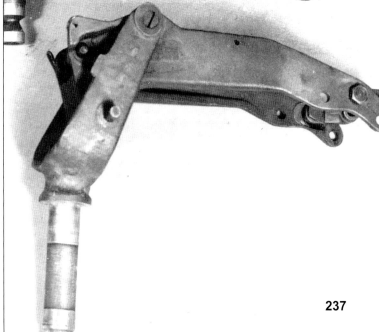

Above: The cab of a CCKW, even an open model, can be sweltering in summer. During the winter the engine provides a minimal amount of heat for the occupants. As we shall see, a heater kit was developed that would enhance the driver's comfort. For soldiers riding on the troop seats in the rear, there was no such luxury. Hence, during the late 1940s this so-called arctic enclosure, featuring a heavy insulated cargo cover, was developed. This example, from the 229th Signal Operations Company, is seen in Montana *en route* to Whitehorse, Canada, during exercise "Sweetbriar" on 8 January 1950. (U.S. Army Engineer School History Office)

Right: The arctic enclosure features solid ends with a hinged door *en lieu* of the canvas end curtains used with the standard cargo cover. A compact gasoline-burning heater was mounted inside, near the front of the cargo bed. (TACOM LCMC History Office)

To provide light antiaircraft protection to installations, the Army developed the Multiple .50-Caliber Machine Gun Trailer Mount T81E1. It comprised of the mount, trailer, T45E1 and the multiple .50-caliber machine gun mount M45E1. The M45E1 was deployed in a firing position on the ground. Each gun was equipped with an ammunition chest to the side. (Patton Museum)

To provide better mobility for light antiaircraft batteries, in early 1944 the Antiaircraft Artillery Board commenced tests of the installation of the Trailer Mount M55 with Multiple Caliber .50 Machine Gun Mount M45 on a 6x6 2½-ton truck. (Rock Island Arsenal Museum)

Left: A Gun Trailer Mount T81E1 is viewed from behind. At the upper center is the gun sight, with a gap between the plates of the armored shield for sighting through. Behind the gunner's seat was the power plant. (Patton Museum)

Right: One of the problems encountered early in the testing of the multiple .50-caliber machine gun mount, as shown here, was that the tow bar and lunette interfered with the winch as originally positioned, prohibiting the towing arm to rest, as intended, on the floor. The Antiaircraft Artillery Board designed a new winch mount that solved the problem. (National Archives via Jim Gilmore)

239

Above: The Antiaircraft Artillery Board designed this raised mount for the winch to to keep the gun-mount trailer's tow bar from interfering with it. (National Archives via Jim Gilmore)

Right: An M55 trailer mount with M45 multiple gun mount is rolled up ramps to the cargo body of a CCKW. The two men at left are drawing the trailer mount using the improved, raised winch mount designed by the Antiaircraft Artillery Board. (National Archives via Jim Gilmore)

Below: Secured on the body of a CCKW is an M45 multiple .50-caliber machine gun mount. The trailer's tow bar no longer interfered with the new, raised winch. (National Archives via Jim Gilmore)

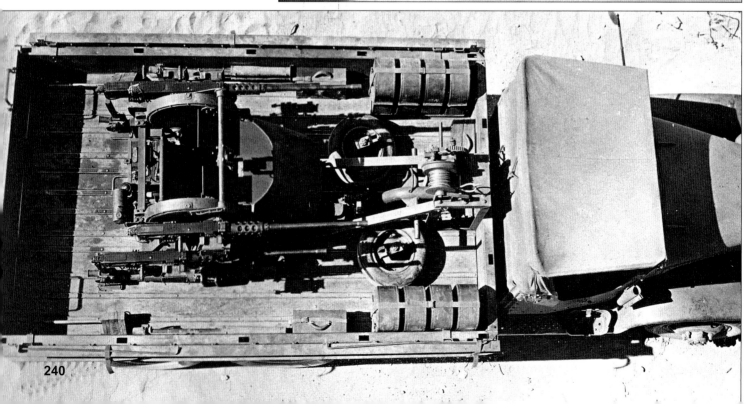

The improved winch mount designed by the Antiaircraft Artillery Board is viewed from the left side. Manufactured by the American Coach & Body Co., the winch was hand operated and rated at two tons. The pedestal it was mounted on was fitted with two diagonal angle-iron braces. The CCKW used in the testing the M45 multiple gun-mount had a composite body: steel sides, front, tailgate and a bed of wooden planks and steel rub strips. (National Archives via Jim Gilmore)

Left: In this view of an open-top CCKW-353 with the M45 multiple gun mount positioned in the cargo body, the original winch mount at the front of the body is in view. Eight .50-caliber ammunition chests were stowed in two racks at the front of the body. (National Archives via Bryce Sunderlin)

Below: Similar to the field-modified rail conversions for CCKW and AFKWX, was this factory-produced conversion. This apparatus would enable the CCKW to act as a light industrial locomotive, moving a few cars at a time. This example was photographed stateside on 27 January 1945. The two front flanged steel wheels are visible below the front bumper. (Fred Crismon collection)

241

Above: A long-wheelbase, open-cab CCKW has been converted to a road-rail vehicle in a photo taken at Aberdeen Proving Ground on 1 August 1945. This conversion was designated Project No. 6209/8-9-6. (National Archives via Jim Gilmore)

Right: The CCKW-353 road-rail vehicle seen above is viewed from the front left, portraying some details of the front suspension. When the vehicle was centered over tracks, the flanged wheels were lowered to rest on the tracks. (National Archives via Jim Gilmore)

Another view taken at Aberdeen Proving Ground on 1 August 1945 shows the rear suspension of the rail-conversion kit. Mounted on the rear of the chassis frame was a standard knuckle-type Janney railway coupler. (National Archives via Jim Gilmore)

Above: CCKWs were often called on to operate in Arctic and wintry conditions. In an effort to improve the trucks' mobility on snow and ice, experiments were conducted with dual front wheels to improve flotation. Metal treads also were developed that encircled the front and tandem tires to assist in traction. (National Archives via Jim Gilmore)

Left: The CCKW-353 towing a 40mm Bofors gun tests its metal treads on what appears to be ice. The treads for the tandem wheels fit around both sets on each side of the vehicle rather than around the individual paired wheels, as on the front wheels. (National Archives via Jim Gilmore)

A CCKW-353 with dual front wheels and metal treads tows a 40mm Bofors gun in the snow. It is not clear to what extent this arrangement of wheels and metal treads was used operationally. (Military History Institute)

Left: To improve the effectiveness of trucks in Arctic conditions, the Army developed equipment to winterize these vehicles, including an engine heater to enable drivers to immediately start their engines at temperatures of -40 degrees Fahrenheit. Seen here is the exhaust stack of an engine heater and a radiator cover. (National Archives via Jim Gilmore)

Below: Components of the Arctic engine heater kit included a gas-fired heater and retractable exhaust stack (right), a fuel tank for the burner (center), and a canvas radiator cover (top left). This heater facilitated engine starting in extreme cold temperatures by heating the coolant in the engine block. (National Archives via Jim Gilmore)

Chapter 22

Army Air Corps

The U.S. Army Air Corps, renamed the U.S. Army Air Forces 20 June 1941, and finally the U.S. Air Force on 18 September 1947, used, in addition to the standard cargo trucks, some specialized chassis. In spite of that official name change, throughout GM's documents these chassis continued to be designated "Air Corps" chassis. Accordingly, references to the "Air Corps" will continue well after the establishment of the USAAF. Among the speicalized chassis were high-lift trucks, bomb service trucks, and airfield service trucks. Each of these was engineered to meet specific needs of the using branch. All three of these types were developed and produced during WWII, although only the airfield service trucks saw widespread use before the hostilities ended. All variants, however, did see extensive use after WWII, including service during the Korean War.

High Lift Trucks

The development or adoption of a new weapon or military hardware often entails the need for new support equipment – the very reason new items are referred to as "weapons systems." The Douglas DC-4, developed in the 1938 and adopted by the U.S. Army Air Forces in February 1942 as the C-54 "Skymaster," was one such case. The C-54 rested on a tricycle landing gear, unlike the tail-dragging C-46 and C-47. The C-54's level cargo floor made cargo handling easier than in its sloped-floor contemporaries, but presented the new problem of having the cargo door several feet above runway level.

It was therefore decided to equip a number of CCKW trucks with vertical lift bodies. In a letter dated 16 November 1942, H. C. Hatch, Sales Engineer with Gar Wood Industries, wrote to Lt. R. H. Burke

of the AAF Material Center, Equipment Laboratory that "…as nearly as we can determine, it will be approximately six weeks before we will be able to deliver the special Hi-Lift bodies which the Hoist and Body Division are working out for you and also before we will be able to deliver the special bomber handling crane." Pressure from the Army Air Forces on Gar Wood to expedite delivery is evident in the closing paragraph of the letter: "We assure you that we are doing all possible to rush these units to you and sincerely hope that we will be able to better the above delivery promise."

The Air Forces' sense of urgency was not shared by all. Regarding a request for 100 cargo trucks, Brigadier General R. A. Wood, Jr., Director, Requirements Division, wrote the following on 31 July 1943: "The requirement for the Truck, 2½ Ton 6x6 Cargo necessary to the production of the Truck, High Lift, will be included in the forthcoming revision of Section I of the Army Supply Program, 1 August 1943."

In approving this purchase, M. G. Lutes, Army Service Forces, notes "Diversion from present contracts is not authorized due to the critical status of supply of trucks, 2½ ton, 6x6."

Contract 2119-AC-227 for $75,000 was issued to Gar Wood Industries in May 1943 for lift truck conversions. It was followed the next month by 2119-AC-342 calling for more conversions.

Ultimately, in addition to Gar Wood Industries, the Heil Company was also contracted to modify trucks to High Lift configuration. Contract 2119-AC-264 was issued in May 1943 for such work, and was followed by Contract 33038-AC-11418 in June 1945.

In April 1943 the Army released specifications for a CCKW with a mechanical high-lift body. The purpose of this truck was to lift the body to various heights to facilitate loading and unloading cargo aircraft. It was to have a rated load of 5,000 pounds and a proof load of 8,000 pounds. (General Motors)

The Hi-lift employed a dual-scissors mechanism powered by twin hydraulic cylinders to raise and lower the cargo body. The cargo body was wooden, equipped with racks and bows for a tarpaulin. (Fred Crismon collection)

The utility of these trucks, which were dubbed the Hi-lift, is obvious in this photo of one of them, bed raised and holding a radial engine, at the same level as the floor of a Curtiss C-46 Commando. With the Hi-lift, it was a simple matter of rolling heavy cargo to or from the body and the plane. (National Archives via Jim Gilmore)

The tailgate of the CCKW Hi-lift truck was T-shaped, presumably to enable it to fit inside aircraft cargo doors, acting as a ramp between the aircraft and the cargo body. A spotlight was on a flexible mount at the left rear of the body. (Fred Crismon collection)

At the top of the pedestal to the right of the tailgate was a lever with a round knob, presumably the control lever for the lift mechanism. (Fred Crismon collection)

The Hi-lift body could be raised to any height from 54 inches above ground level to 120 inches. The frame of the Hi-lift apparatus, which was attached to the top of the chassis frame of the truck, was of heavy-duty steel construction. (Fred Crismon collection)

Once the racks were removed from the sides of the Hi-lift body, the sides, mounted on hinges, could be lowered to form extension platforms, as seen here. The lever on the right side of the rear of the lift body, seen lowered in the preceding photo, is now in a raised position. (Fred Crismon collection)

Above: A Hi-lift truck based on an open-cab CCKW-353 is displayed. The spare tire of the Hi-lift was stowed vertically under the front left of the lift body. This example has different, heavier-duty racks and rack pockets than the earlier vehicles in the preceding photos. (Fred Crismon collection)

Right: GMC CCKW Hi-lift truck U.S.A. number 4238906 poses with the body raised. The forward arms of the lift on this model were of a straight design, contrasting with the bent design of the arms on the earlier version, and the aft arms lacked lightening holes. (Fred Crismon collection)

A CCKW-353 Hi-lift truck is fitted with a tarpaulin, and the troop seats are deployed. The tailgate had a diamond-tread pattern on the inside and a beveled rear edge. Timken axles were present. An operating cable and pulleys for the tailgate are visible at the rear corner of the body. (Fred Crismon collection)

The body is extended in this rear view of an open-cab Hi-lift truck. Numerous differences are visible between this vehicle and the earlier, closed-cab version. For example, a spotlight is on each side of the rear of the body. The exterior of the tailgate was wooden planks with steel corners and hinge straps. (Fred Crismon collection)

Airfield Service Trucks

That aircraft consume great amounts of fuel is a concept widely recognized. Less well known is the fact that aircraft, particularly those with radial engines, consume large amounts of oil. To address these needs, the Army procured two near-identical vehicles, the F3 fuel tanker and the L2 lubricant truck. Both types of vehicle were assembled by the Heil Company of Milwaukee, using cab and chassis supplied by Yellow Truck and Coach/GMC. Sales order TC-200437 called for 350 of these trucks to be built in Pontiac, while later sales order TC-200452 called for a further 740 to be assembled in St. Louis. Sales order TC-200509 added another 460 St. Louis-built trucks.

On 30 March 1943, in a meeting in Col. Van Deusen's office, it was agreed that all Air Corps tanker chassis would be built with Chevrolet axles. Of these, 2,520 would be built in St. Louis on sales order TC-200554. In 1943 4,616 chassis were scheduled for production for Airfield Service use. Prior to 17 May 1943, these,

and many other chassis, were especially produced for various specific bodies installed ex-works. However, on that date, it was decided that moving forward a common cab and chassis would be used for most specialized trucks, including the Air Corps airfield service trucks, Chemical Warfare Service trucks, and Signal Corps trucks, among others. This practice considerably smoothed production and distribution, and provided greater flexibility in meeting various urgent requirements.

The F3 fuel tanker's capacity of 750 gallons limited it to refueling small observation aircraft and fighters. Bombers were refueled with larger semitrailer refueling units that did not involve the CCKW. The L2 lubricant truck had a capacity of 660 gallons. Both units came with an array of dispensing equipment, housed in the compartments alongside the truck body. The compartment directly behind the passenger's side of the cab held hose reels. A manhole was provided in the top of the tank through which the tank was refilled.

The CCKW-based Truck, Fuel or Oil Servicing, 750-gallon, 2½-ton, 6x6, L2 was developed for delivering fuel and oil to the aircraft of the U.S. Army Air Forces. This example was U.S. Army registration number 482040. The servicing equipment was produced by Heil. (Fred Crismon collection)

The L2 featured a 750-gallon tank with platfoms with toe rails to the sides. A manhole and a spotlight were on top of the tank. Between the tank and the cab was a separator, for removing any water from the fuel. Two steps were on each side of the rear of the vehicle. General Motors delivered the chassis for these without fuel tanks, spare tire carriers or exhaust tail pipes. (Fred Crismon collection)

In the compartment with two doors to the front of the body were valves for controlling the various fuel/oil lines and components. Another door with a handle and two clamp latches at the bottom and a piano hinge at the top is on the side of the upper part of the body. (Fred Crismon collection)

The lockers on the front right side of the body were taller than those on the left side and held hose reels and nozzles. Above the tandem tires were lockers for storing fuel hoses and fittings. (Fred Crismon collection)

Bomb Service Trucks M27 and M27B1

The Allied bombing campaigns in both Europe and the Pacific consumed vast numbers of bombs – 1,613,000 tons in Europe alone – and with most bombs weighing a half ton or less, the sheer number of bombs is simply staggering. Given that each one of these bombs was largely man-handled into position in the aircraft, the need for an efficient means of transporting and dispersing this ordnance is readily apparent.

In December 1942 the Army Air Forces requested that a power operated hoist for installation in a 2½ ton truck be developed. Such a truck could be used to load and unload bomb trailers at both bomb dumps and at the aircraft, as well as transporting the bombs between those points. It was envisioned that this truck would replace or supplement Bomb Trailer M5.

The Gar Wood firm of Detroit built a pilot model of such a truck. The firm took its name from that of its founder, Garfield Arthur Wood, who was widely recognized as the father of the power-operated dump truck. The prototype bomb service truck was delivered to Patterson Field, near Dayton, Ohio, for testing by the Air Service Command in April 1943. Starting with a GMC CCKW, Gar Wood had crafted from I-beams a steel superstructure consisting of two A-shaped frames mounted to the truck bed. These frames supported yet another I-beam which projected beyond the rear of the truck and supported a four-wheel trolley riding on the lower flange of the beam. Also included with the truck was a dolly and two nine-foot sections of what was in essence a miniature railroad track. This equipment was to be used to push the bombs directly to the bomb bay of the waiting aircraft.

After testing and evaluating the equipment, in May 1943 the Air Service Command recommended that the equipment be adopted, after a few modifications. These changes included: reducing the weight of the hoist, track and support; redesigning the lifting hook to conserve space; reducing the weight of the dolly and track set; increasing the composition of the outfit to include two dollies and four sections of track, with both dollies and track being stowed outside the truck body; and the addition of an automatic dead-man device on the winch.

Two pilot vehicles were built in an effort to meet the refined criteria outlined above. The overall height was reduced from 143 to 126 inches by redesigning the A-frame structure. The trolley now rode on top of a track made from two pieces of channel, rather than beneath an I-beam. The hook passed between the two channels, which were separated by 8¾ inches. The addition of an overload slip clutch satisfied the requirement for a dead-man device.

The crane trolley was operated by a double-drum winch mounted behind the truck cab. The winch was comprised of two drums, two gear cases, two control levers and associated sprockets, shafts and linkages. The winch was chain-driven from the truck's power take off, an arrangement that required that any reversing of the winch operation had to be achieved using gears in the winch gearbox. A narrow winch drum was wrapped with wire rope that was used to raise and lower the hook while the wider winch drum moved the trolley, and thus the hook, fore and after along the boom beam. A flag attached to the left boom channel marked the normal rearward position of the trolley when a 4,000 pound bomb was being lifted. "Normal" in this instance meant a position that just permitted adequate clearance between the bomb and the truck's tailgate. In the event the trolley went beyond

Based on the CCKW, the M27 and M27B1 bomb-service trucks were specialized vehicles with a boom and hoist for delivering bombs to aircraft. An open-cab example is shown with a two-ton dolly and track set for moving heavy bombs from the vehicle to beneath a bomber. (National Archives)

the normal position a semaphore extended horizontally, signaling the operator as to what had occurred. The reason for this precaution is that with that size bomb there existed the possibility of tipping the truck or damaging the boom were the weight to be too far to the rear.

With the previously mentioned modifications in place, the truck was classified Standard in October 1943 as the "2½-ton, 6x6 (4dt) Bomb Service Truck M27." In March 1944, however, the specifications were modified to include the addition of a curved section of track for the bomb dolly. In May of the same year the Ordnance Committee set up the characteristics for converting a cargo truck to a bomb truck in the field. That recommendation was approved in June, and included a provision for a field service modification work order to provide instructions for this work.

The winch used on the M27 was made by Gar Wood, and used many of the same parts as the wrecker winch on the Ward LaFrance M1A1 Heavy Wrecker, and were accordingly in high demand. Hence, Ordnance wanted to utilize a different winch. Ultimately it was decided to use a winch nearly identical to that used as the wrecker winch on the Diamond T wrecker. While in demand, this winch was more readily available than the one previously used, and like the former winch, parts were already existent in the Army supply system. In June 1945 the Ordnance Committee classified the vehicle using the Diamond T-style winch as Standard, designating it M27B1, and the M27 was reclassified as Substitute Standard. The conversion kit for field use mentioned earlier was reclassified as Limited Standard at the same time.

Concurrent with these developments of the truck itself, work was under way concerning the dolly and its miniature railroad track. The dolly furnished with the original Gar Wood prototype was fabricated from steel pipe with wooden chocks to hold bombs in place. It rode on track made from standard 12-lb ASCE rail, spaced with a 31-inch gauge. Each track section was nine-feet long.

During testing at Patterson Field, three additional dolly and track sets of different designs were also evaluated. Dolly number 2 was constructed of welded sheet metal and featured a concave top to fit the shape of the bomb. The track furnished with this was made of pressed steel, and was gauged at 19¾-inches between rails. Dolly number 3 was also pressed steel, riding on pressed steel track with a 20-inch gauge, but it had a unique feature. The wheels on this dolly were exposed above its concave top, as well as below, enabling the user to flip the dolly over, using its flat "bottom" as the top to carry loads that were also flat. Dolly number 4 was fabricated from sheet steel and had a shallow v-shape at the top to stabilize bombs. It rode on solid T-rail track with a 21-inch gauge.

These three additional sets, as well as the set originally furnished by Gar Wood, were tested and evaluated, and a fifth set then designed encompassing the best features of all. This set used a modified version of the number 2 dolly, which incorporated cast steel wheels with a pressed steel carbody, and track sections lengthened to 11 feet. A curved section of track was also included, allowing greater flexibility in the positioning of the truck relative to the bomber. The stowage brackets for the straight track sections were provided on the outside of the truck.

This dolly set, known as Dolly and Track Set Pilot Model No. 5, along with one of the improved pilots for the Bomb Service Truck M27 were sent to the Army Air Forces Board, Orlando, Florida, for testing. After those tests, the Board recommended that one dolly, four 11-foot straight track sections, and one curved track section be included with each M27. The Board also developed an adapter, or removable bomb rack, that would permit the dolly to carry simultaneously a number of 500-pound or smaller bombs, making more efficient use of the equipment. This too was Standardized along with the track and dolly in September 1944. GMC began shipping chassis for these trucks in January, 1945.

While 3713 M27 and M27B1 trucks were ordered in 1944, with production not beginning until so late, the M27 and M27B1 saw relatively limited use during WWII, but were widely used in the postwar era, including the bombing campaigns of the Korean War.

The first pilot of the bomb-service vehicle, constructed by Gar Wood, featured a bomb-hoist beam made of I-beam, and it resulted in an unacceptably tall overall vehicular height. On the A-frame toward the front of the I-beam was a leveling screw operated by a hand wheel. (National Archives)

On the first pilot, the hoist rode on the lower flange of the I-beam. The truck is shown here with a bomb poised above the dolly and track supplied with the truck. (National Archives)

On the second pilot of the bomb-service vehicle, the operator has his right hand on the hoist control lever and his left hand on the trolley control. In the background is the cab of the open-topped CCKW. (National Archives)

The adjustable, automatic overload slip clutch in the PTO shaft, seen in the preceding photograph, is viewed close-up. This was part of an automatic "dead man" device on the winch drive shaft to prevent damage to the cables. (National Archives via Jim Gilmore)

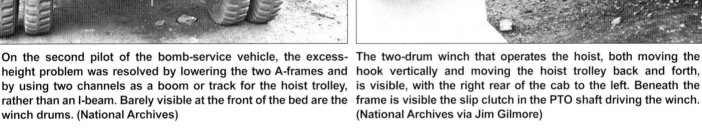

On the second pilot of the bomb-service vehicle, the excess-height problem was resolved by lowering the two A-frames and by using two channels as a boom or track for the hoist trolley, rather than an I-beam. Barely visible at the front of the bed are the winch drums. (National Archives)

The two-drum winch that operates the hoist, both moving the hook vertically and moving the hoist trolley back and forth, is visible, with the right rear of the cab to the left. Beneath the frame is visible the slip clutch in the PTO shaft driving the winch. (National Archives via Jim Gilmore)

To test the soundness of the dolly and track set, experiments were conducted with the second pilot vehicle lowering a 4,000-pound bomb on the trolley and checking the performance of the trolley on the tracks. The corporal is holding a measuring stick marked off in feet and half-feet. (National Archives via Jim Gilmore)

The dolly and track used in the tests with the second pilot bomb-service truck are viewed close-up. The dolly and the tracks were intentionally built as light as possible for ease of handling. (National Archives via Jim Gilmore)

The dolly is turned upside-down to expose the four wheels. The construction of the tracks and the dolly was steel. (National Archives via Jim Gilmore)

A stop has been installed on one side of the track to keep the dolly from rolling off. The stop was secured in place with one or more pins fitted with a retainer chain. (National Archives via Jim Gilmore)

During the track and dolly tests, a 4,000-pound bomb has been placed on the dolly. (National Archives via Jim Gilmore)

Above: The tracks failed during the test. Their lightweight construction, although convenient for handling purposes, proved to be too flimsy to bear the weight of a 4,000-pound bomb over soft ground. (National Archives via Jim Gilmore)

Right: A plumb bob was suspended from the nose of the bomb to indicate vertical; the bomb and dolly were tilted precariously by this point in the tests. (National Archives via Jim Gilmore)

The tracks did better on hard surfaces. Here, a 2,000-pound bomb on the dolly has been delivered to below the bomb bay of a B-25. The rear of the bomb-service truck is to the right. (National Archives via Jim Gilmore)

Above: The 2,000-pound bomb on the dolly and track below the B-25 is viewed from the left side. A nomenclature plate is affixed to the side rail of the dolly. (National Archives via Jim Gilmore)

Left: In October 1943 the vehicle designated Truck, 2½-ton, 6x6 (4DT), Bomb Service, M27 was classified as standard. This example bore U.S. Army registration number 4711674. Partially visible in the body to the rear of the cab is a bomb dolly. (General Motors)

Each M-27 bomb-service truck was furnished with four sections of straight track for the dolly and were stored on the outside of the body. This production vehicle exhibits the hoist arrangement that had become standard. (General Motors)

Right: A photograph dated 7 November 1944 shows an M27 bomb-service truck from the right rear. The tubular bracing from the rear of the boom to the rear A-frame, and from the rear A-frame forward, provided rigidity to the extended rear of the boom. (TACOM LCMC History Office)

Below: This overhead photograph dated 6 November 1944 provides a view of the winch to the rear of the cab, which operated the bomb hoist and trolley. Lying on the floor of the body are a curved track section and two bomb dollies. (TACOM LCMC History Office)

Viewed from the front, the tops of the A-frames and the horizontal boom were prominent above the top of the M27 bomb-service truck's cab. Attached to the left front support is a flexible work spotlight. Jutting out from the sides of the body are the dolly track sections. (TACOM LCMC History Office)

From the rear of the M27, the A-frames supporting the dual-track horizontal boom are in view. The body was fitted with a steel tailgate, below which was a recessed toolbox. A toolbox was mounted on the right rack, and a spotlight was on the left side of the forward A-frame. (TACOM LCMC History Office)

An M27 bomb-service truck is viewed from the right in a 7 November 1944 photo. On the horizontal boom, in line with the forward A-frame supporting the boom, is the trolley, the part of the hoisting mechanism that moved the bomb forward or to the rear. (TACOM LCMC History Office)

M27 bomb-service trucks also were issued without the front winch, such as this example, U.S. Army registration number M4139503. This shows the manner in which the tarpaulin was erected over the body, with the rear of the horizontal boom being exposed. (National Archives via Jim Gilmore)

Left: This photograph illustrates the results of improperly loading 1,000-pound bombs in the body of an M27 bomb-service truck, coupled with an abrupt stop at ten miles per hour. The bomb at the front apparently was tossed, coming to rest in a precarious position. (National Archives via Jim Gilmore)

Below: Shortages in the supply of the prescribed hoist winch for the M27 led to the development of the M27B1 bomb-service truck, which used a different model of behind-the-cab winch. Ultimately, this vehicle became the preferred model, with the M27 being reclassified as Substitute Standard. Seen in a 5 July 1944 photo is M27B1 GMC serial number 461948-1. (TACOM LCMC History Office)

In a demonstration similar to the one depicted in the preceding photograph, a 4,000-pound bomb has been loaded improperly and has shifted about 90 degrees from its original, stowed position on the bed of an M27. Improperly loading bombs on the bed could have very damaging results. (National Archives via Jim Gilmore)

To lift bombs, a spreader bar with a hook on each end was connected to the hook on the bottom of the hoist block. The hooks on the spreader bar engaged lugs on the bomb. This photo shows damage caused when a hook caught the tailgate hinge rod. (National Archives via Jim Gilmore)

On the M27B1, gone were the racks on the side of the body, but the track sections still were stored on the side. The body was of a different, taller design than that of the M27, and it was produced by the Ernest Holmes Company. (TACOM LCMC History Office)

Above: The tarpaulin for the M27B1 did not extend to the top of the body, leaving a gap of almost a foot. Cleats were not provided on the sides of tbe body for lashing the bottom of the tarpaulin; rather, the tarpaulin was lashed to horizontal rods above the top of the body. (Fred Crismon collection)

Right: M27B1 bomb-service truck U.S. Army registration number 00102811S exhibits the canvas cover and doors for the open-cab CCKW. The front closure of the tarpaulin over the body extended to the bottom of the body. (Fred Crismon collection)

An M27B1 is observed from the rear with the tailgate lowered. Stowed on the left side of the body are a bomb dolly and a curved section of track. (Fred Crismon collection)

263

The rear of an M27B1 is viewed. A bomb dolly was stowed on each side toward the rear of the body; their bottoms are in view, including the four wheels on each one. The diagonal braces for the horizontal boom were anchored at the bases of the forward A-frame. (Fred Crismon collection)

The twin-tracked horizontal boom of the M27B1 is observed from the ground. The hoist hook, at the bottom of the trolley, is visible at the front of the horizontal boom. Below the hook is a transverse bulkhead built of plywood. (Fred Crismon collection)

The M27B1 is viewed from above, with the rear of the horizontal boom at the bottom. A good view is provided of the twin-track design of the boom. The trolley of the boom is in the background at the front of the boom. (Fred Crismon collection)

Above: As seen in an overhead view of an M27B1 bomb-service truck, the floor of the body consisted of wooden planks with steel rub strips between each plank. The trolley is to the rear of the horizontal boom, with the four wheels of the trolley being visible. (TACOM LCMC History Office)

Left: In a photo dated 5 July 1945, the left interior of the body of M27B1 bomb-service truck GM serial number 461948-1 is observed. Stowage for the curved track section and a bomb dolly was provided on the sidewall. (TACOM LCMC History Office)

Another dolly and a tool chest are secured to the inside wall on the right side of the M27B12's body. This bed is of composite construction, as one would expect given the photo's 5 July 5 1945 date. (TACOM LCMC History Office)

The engine compartment of the same M27B1 shown in the preceding photo is viewed. The air cleaner is the late-type SAE/Military Standard flange-mounted design, which from CCKW chassis 321078 on was affixed to the top of the late-type, cast-iron Zenith Model 30B11 carburetor. (TACOM LCMC History Office)

The canvas cargo cover of the bomb service trucks serves not only to protect the vehicle's hoisting mechanism, but also conceals the truck's true purpose. (TACOM LCMC History Office)

M27B1 bomb-service truck U.S. Army registration number 00102370S and GM serial number 46-1948-1 is viewed from the front in a photo dated 5 July 1945. Compared with a preceding photo of an M27 from the front, the –B1 version had a horizontal arm with cable sheaves below the front end of the horizontal boom. (TACOM LCMC History Office)

The cab of the same M27B1 shown in the preceding photograph features the military-type dashboard and instrument panel. On the floor are the two bar-like levers that control the dual-output PTO used on these trucks. The bar-shaped lever on the left controls the rear (hoist) winch, and the right bar lever controls the front winch. (TACOM LCMC History Office)

In a view of hundreds of newly manufactured CCKWs, in the left background are several rows of bomb-service trucks. These were M27B1s, as indicated by the long, horizontal arms below the fronts of the horizontal booms. (Fred Crismon Collection)

Chapter 23
Chemical Warfare Service

The Chemical Warfare Service was charged with maintaining the U.S. chemical warfare arsenal. Besides the poisonous gases that fortunately were not used during WWII, this arsenal also included such material as smoke generators, flamethrowers, and even 4.2-inch mortars. It also was charged with the defensive measures against enemy chemical attack. Handling this material required specialized equipment, including trucks.

M1 Chemical Service Truck

This truck, very similar the M27 bomb truck, was used to handle 55-gallon drums, 1-ton chemical containers, smoke tanks, field filling equipment and other large, bulky objects. On the bed of the M1 Chemical Service Truck was mounted a monorail frame with a 1½-ton capacity chain hoist, equipment compartments attached to the body side boards, and a chock. The chock was a steel frame bolted to the floor of the bed, fitted with 12 blocks shaped and spaced to cradle a 1-ton container placed lengthwise, or five 55-gallon drums positioned crosswise. The chain hoist trolley, positioned 58 inches above the floor of the truck, or 99 inches above the ground, extended 57 inches beyond the rear of the bed.

In the compartments were stowed rubber aprons, chemical protective suits, rubber gloves, rubber boots, funnels, decontamination

Right: The Truck, Chemical Service, M1, was designed to transport materials for chemical warfare. Based on the long-wheelbase CCKW-353, the M1 featured a steel I-beam superstructure rail with a 1½-ton trolley hoist. The cargo body included removable tool and equipment boxes and had provisions for holding a one-ton container and 55-gallon drums.

Below: Truck, Chemical Service, M1 U.S. Army registration number 4135056 was based on a closed-cab CCKW-353 chassis. The box hooked to the inside of the left sideboard of the body contained, among other things, a half-ton chain hoist, pioneer tools, and other implements necessary for chemical warfare operations.

The chock, track, and chain hoist are shown in a 9 February 1943 photograph. Below the chock is the wooden floor with steel rub strips. The tall box to the right front of the body held six one-piece impermeable protective suits, six rubber aprons, eight pairs of rubber gloves, three three-gallon M1 decontaminating apparatus, three M2 funnels, and thee paddles. (Air Force Historical Research Agency)

An M1 chemical service truck is seen from the rear with the tailgate lowered. The low box on the right side contained six pairs of rubber boots, two tool kits, white cotton waste, and two pails.

This photo demonstrates a one-ton container secured in the chock. It was stored on the chock lengthwise, whereas 55-gallon drums were stored on the chock sideways.

Two men at a depot wrestle a one-ton container into place using the chain hoist. The hoist bar attached to the container was a standard piece of equipment for the M1 chemical service truck.

A cable sling is attached to a one-ton container for a hoisting operation. As is evident in the photo, the container could not be hoisted high enough to clear the bed when the cable sling was employed.

apparatus, and a variety of tools. The Chemical Warfare Service (CWS) purchased over three thousand of these trucks during WWII.

Decontamination trucks

Arguably the most important task of the CWS was to provide decontamination services and equipment to U.S. troops. For decontamination of equipment contaminated with mustard gas, the CWS used a compound known as DANC – decontaminating agent, non-corrosive. Decontamination of vehicles, aircraft, and other large equipment would require a great deal of agent and time with small decontamination gear, so in June 1941 the CWS purchased six power-driven decontaminators from F. E. Myers and Brothers, who adapted their orchard sprayers for this task.

Myers was contracted to produce decontamination apparatus on a production basis, and was joined in March 1942 by Friend Manufacturing and John Bean. Later A.B. Farquhar of York, Pennsylvania. These firms produced the M3 and M3A1 decontamination apparatus. Because of the difficulty in obtaining built-to-order PTO-equipped CCKW chassis, in the spring of 1943 the CWS standardized the M4. A skid-mounted apparatus powered by a 22-horsepower engine, the M4 could be mounted on any CCKW. The M4, however, was almost universally unpopular with the troops.

Although fortunately never confronting a chemical attack, this equipment was used extensively for a variety of purposes ranging from improvised firefighting equipment to field showers – where the hot water generated by the apparatus was welcomed by war-weary troops. With considerable use comes the need for maintenance, and thus arose complaints from the field in 1943 regarding the lack of part interchangeability among the various manufacturers' models. Responding to this, the Service opted to standardize on the John Bean M3A2, which it considered to be the most satisfactory. Late in the war Chemical companies and their decontamination trucks were called into service to spray insecticide. The CWS procured 4,561 power-driven decontamination apparatus from January 1942 through December 1945.

Flamethrower service trucks

As flamethrower-equipped tanks began to be used in the Pacific, the need arose to provide the hundreds of gallons of thickened fuel and vast amounts of compressed air required by the tanks. To accomplish this task, the Service Unit, Mechanized Flame Thrower, -E8, was devised. This vehicle was standardized as the M4 Service Unit, Mechanized Flame Thrower on 4 October 1945.

As seen on an open-cab CCKW-353, a soldier lifts the hinged hood covering the pumping equipment of a power-driven decontaminating apparatus. On the deck are shutoff valves and a pressure gauge. For decontaminating vehicles, planes, weapons, and anything with metal surfaces, DANC (decontaminating agent, noncorrosive) was used. (Chemical Corps Museum)

Left: A CCKW-353 with a powered decontaminating apparatus is viewed from the left rear. This vehicle had the prototype rubber-lined 400-gallon tank. A platform with safety rail on each side was provided for the convenience of the decontamination crew. The Chemical Warfare Service contracted for the first six power-driven decontamination apparatuses in the spring of 1941 with F. E. Myers & Brothers, Ashland, Ohio. (Chemical Corps Museum)

Right: Unit markings are on the bumperettes of this CCKW-353 with a cylindrical tank on the decontaminating apparatus. Ladders with two rungs were attached to the mud flaps. On top of the 400-gallon tank is a manhole and cover. Several shutoff valves are below the tank. (Chemical Corps Museum)

Left: Since bleach is highly corrosive to metal, experiments were undertaken to determine the best materials for the chemical tanks. This unlined example, fashioned from wooden strips, fared no better than metal when filled with bleach; Mathieson bleach caused it to leak and pit after 92 hours of use. (Chemical Corps Museum)

Above: The CCKW-mounted decontaminating apparatus was standardized as the Apparatus, Decontaminating, Power-driven, M3A1. This M3A1 decontaminating apparatus was installed on CCKW-353 U.S. Army registration number 4165790. (Chemical Corps Museum)

Left: This photograph was taken to document the new, modified plumbing added to the rear end of the discharge piping of a Meyers-produced Apparatus, Decontaminating, Power-driven, M3A1. Labels indicate the part numbers of the new pipes and pipe fittings. (National Archives via Jim Gilmore)

A close-up view shows the modified piping to the lower left rear of a Meyers M3A1 decontaminating apparatus. Also present in the view are the trailer receptacle, left tail light and reflector, tow pintle, and the wooden construction of the chemical tank and the platforms. (National Archives via Jim Gilmore)

Crewmen are filling the 400-gallon chemical tank of an M3A1 decontaminating apparatus with creek water by means of the apparatus's pump and a hose. Lined up on the platform and on top of the apparatus are chemical containers. (National Archives via Jim Gilmore)

Right: Three men wearing protective masks and gloves are pouring bleach into the tank of an M3A2 power-driven decontaminating apparatus. The U.S. Army registration number on the hood of the CCKW-353 is 432295. Marked on the door is "1st Chem. Co. Decon," or 1st Chemical Company Decontamination. (Chemical Corps Museum)

Below: Another type of decontaminating apparatus mounted on CCKWs was the Apparatus, Decontaminating, Power-driven, M4. On this model, which was mounted on a skid, the chemical tank was to the front and the power unit was to the rear. Side platforms are not present on this example, mounted on CCKW-353 registration number 464241. (Chemical Corps Museum)

Right: A M4 decontamination apparatus is mounted on an open-cab CCKW353 equipped with a winch. Platforms are present alongside the decontamination apparatus, and a pioneer-tool rack is fastened to the safety rail. (Chemical Corps Museum)

Below: A line of closed-cab CCKW-353s is at the A.B. Farquhar plant, a manufacturer of agricultural equipment in York, Pennsylvania, to have M4 power-driven decontamination apparatuses installed. Almost 40 vehicles are in view. (Chemical Corps Museum)

One of the CCKW-353s sent to the A.B. Farquhar plant in April 1944 is viewed from the rear prior to the installation of an M4 power-driven decontamination apparatus on the chassis. Farquhar was a relative latecomer to producing power-driven decon apparatuses, as F. E. Meyers, Friend Manufacturing Co., Gasport, New York, and John Bean Manufacturing Co., Lansing, Michigan already had produced the apparatuses. (Chemical Corps Museum)

Crates containing M4 power-driven decontamination apparatuses are in the foreground in this view at the A. B. Farquhar plant in April 1944. In the middle background is a line of CCKW-353s with the M4 apparatuses mounted. Farther in the background are quantities of CCKWs that have yet to have the M4 apparatuses installed. (Chemical Corps Museum)

Right: M4 power-driven decontamination apparatuses are lined up inside the A. B. Farquhar plant. The skids they were mounted on allowed them to be carried on CCKWs or dismounted and placed on other types of vehicles. Since they were dismountable, the pump and slurry agitator were operated by an onboard engine instead of from the vehicle's power takeoff, as the M3A1 had been. (Chemical Corps Museum)

Below: Workers at A. B. Farquhar prepare to hoist an M4 power-driven decontamination apparatus onto the chassis frame of a CCKW. Farquhar experienced great difficulties in procuring sufficient quantities of the gasoline-powered 22-horsepower engines for these units. (Chemical Corps Museum)

CCKW-353 chassis are being prepared for installation of M4 power-driven decontamination apparatuses at the A. B. Farquhar plant in York, Pennsylvania in April 1944. Wooden crossbeams have been mounted on the chassis frames to support the apparatus. (Chemical Corps Museum)

Workers open a crate containing an M4 power-driven decontamination apparatus at the A. B. Farquhar plant in April 1944. In the background are an open-top CCKW and a closed-top CCKW, both of which have received their M4 power-driven decontamination apparatuses. (Chemical Corps Museum)

A welder is at work on the safety railing of an M4 power-driven decontamination apparatus on a CCKW at the A. B. Farquhar factory in York, Pennsylvania, in April 1944. In the foreground is a stack of mud guards, and the man at the center appears to be installing a mud guard. (Chemical Corps Museum)

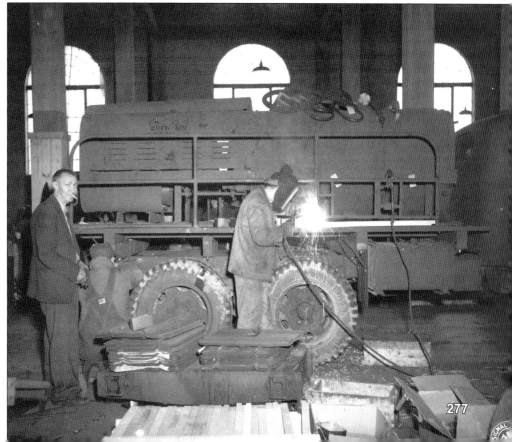

Workmen at A. B. Farquhar manhandle a stowage box up to the platform on the right side of the M4 power-driven decontamination apparatus. At the rear of the apparatus is a manual starting crank. On the rear of the platform is a spare-tire clamp as used on the CCKW-352. (Chemical Corps Museum)

Right: Assembled at the A. B. Farquhar plant is a mix of long-wheelbase CCKWs, some with closed cabs, some with open cabs, and some with the M4 power-driven decontamination apparatus installed, some with the apparatus yet to be mounted. When completed, the decontamination trucks were driven in convoys to ports of embarkation. (Chemical Corps Museum)

Below: This power-driven decontamination apparatus, which appears to be the M4 model, is mounted on a long-wheelbase CCKW with the power unit to the front; note the hand crank. A storage locker is in the usual position for the spare tire, and the spare tire is mounted behind the cab. (Chemical Corps Museum)

Above: The same vehicle is viewed from the right side, showing the position of the spare tire behind the right side of the cab. The tire appears to have been secured to a bolt-on bracket instead of in a tire clamp of the type used on short-wheelbase CCKWs. (Chemical Corps Museum)

Left: The rear end of an M4 power-driven decontamination apparatus produced by A.B. Farquhar. York, Pennsylvania, is shown. In Army jargon and manuals, these CCKW-based decontamination units were sometimes referred to as the "decon-PD."

Right: An M4 power-driven decontamination apparatus of the type produced by the Bean Manufacturing Co. of Lansing, Michigan, is viewed from the right side. The chemical tank is to the front (right), and a sprayer and hose are stowed on top of the tank.

Standard Oil Development Co. developed under contract with the National Defense Research Committee the E8 mobile service unit for replenishing M4A1 and M4A3 medium tanks armed with the Flame Thrower, Mechanized, E12-7R1. This truck was intended to reduce the time it took to recharge the flamethrower system, which required 275 gallons of main fuel, 12 gallons of secondary fuel, 2 gallons of igniter fuel, and main-propellant and auxiliary air. Now, this procedure could be performed near the front lines. Major equipment in the body of the E8 included a large mixing tank and an air compressor. (Chemical Corps Museum)

Another type of CCKW-based mobile flamethrower service unit included two large tanks for manufacturing flamethrower fuel. At the front of the body was an air compressor. At the right rear corner of the body was a gasoline-pumping unit. On the left side of the body were six high-pressure storage cylinders, above which were a high-pressure manifold and valves. (National Archives via Steve Zaloga)

A CCKW-based flamethrower-service truck replenishes the fuel and compressed air of a T66, a mobile flamethrower based on the M47 medium tank that did not advance beyond the prototype stage. (Chemical Corps Museum)

Chapter 24

Corps of Engineers

The Corps of Engineers with its broad range of responsibilities requires a myriad of specialized equipment. Hence, it is not surprising that the CCKW was adapted to be the basis for an extensive array of motorized equipment. From the outset of CCKW development, the Corps began utilizing the chassis. In fact, some of the first CCKWX were used as the basis for Corps-operated water purification trucks.

This usage was soon followed by the installation of air compressor beds, a modification that was introduced in response to complaints from troops using the vehicle that the then-standard 4x4 GMC AFK-352 was not powerful enough to transport the 105-cubic-feet per minute LeRoi compressor being mounted on it.

The Engineer Board therefore adapted the 6x6 chassis for this use. The Engineer Board at Fort Belvoir also initiated some other developments, such as the pipeline and the line construction trucks. But troops in the field who were using the vehicles continued to provide the impetus for some of these developments, such as the 6x6-based fire truck, the first of which was created in the field by troops who desired more water than their Chevrolet 4x4 pumper could transport.

Some of the specialized equipment had just begun to be delivered when the war ended, such as the bolster trucks. These trucks, converted by Oneida Ltd. In Canastota, New York, were not delivered until early 1945.

As with all the branches, for the Engineers the end of WWII did not mean the end of work to improve the CCKW. Various crane trucks did not begin to appear in numbers until after the end of WWII hostilities. Such postwar advances not only were a staple during the post-WWII years, but also formed the basis for many of the trucks that would be built on the forthcoming Reo-designed G-742 series chassis.

Air Compressors

The U.S. Army Office, Chief of Engineers, began evaluating portable air compressors for use by Engineer troops in the field in the early 1930s. By 1937 it had been decided to adopt a gasoline-engine driven truck mounted 105-cubic-feet-per-minute unit for issue to troops. In conjunction with this effort studies were made of a variety of pneumatic tools to determine which tools, style, and brand, should be supplied with the compressor. In February 1940, a quantity of 79 105-CFM compressors were ordered from the Sullivan Machinery Company to be mounted on 1½ - 3 ton cab-over-engine GMC 4 x 4 truck chassis. An additional 819 similar compressors manufactured by LeRoi and mounted on similar chassis were subsequently purchased

Throughout the 1930s and continuing in World War II, the U.S. Army Engineers investigated methods of supplying its troops with mobile, truck-mounted air compressors to power hand tools for construction and demolition work. This AFK-352 1½–3-ton 4x4 Type C.O.E. [Corps of Engineers] compressor truck with a LeRoi compressor represented one type developed. (National Archives via Jim Gilmore)

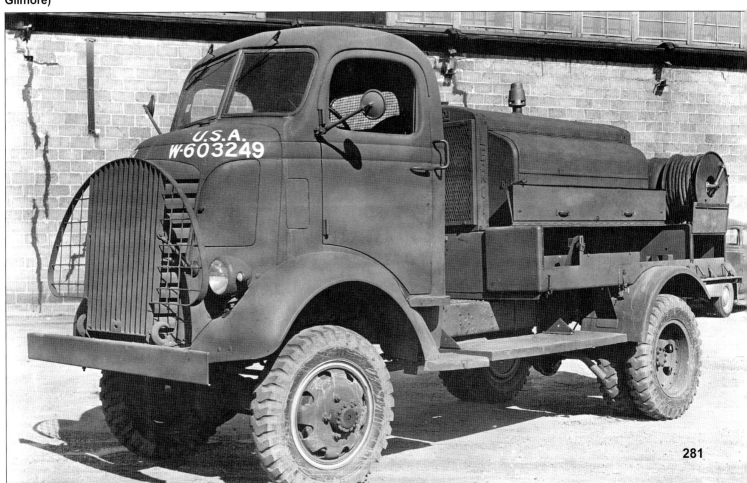

from July 1940 through May 1941.

However, the 4x4 was soon determined to be top-heavy, and underpowered, resulting in poor off-road performance. From July 1941, mounting the compressor on a half-track chassis for use by armored units was considered, but this idea was discarded in September 1941.

In late 1941 the Engineers removed a LeRoi compressor from its 4x4 chassis and placed it experimentally on the chassis of a GMC 6x6, making the necessary modifications to both compressor body and truck chassis to accomplish this. The resultant vehicle, weighing 13,175 pounds fully equipped, was subsequently tested and found to exceed the capabilities of its predecessor in every area save reduced maneuverability due to its wider turning radius.

Fifteen days after Pearl Harbor, plans were drawn up for a factory-produced pilot model of the new vehicle to be assembled by LeRoi. On 24 February 1942 an order was placed with LeRoi for 1,038 units, the first of several orders.

The model designation for this compressor was the LeRoi Model 105GA. The compressor was driven by its own four-cylinder, 318-cubic-inch engine, also built by LeRoi (in fact, at this time LeRoi was a noted builder of industrial engines in addition to its compressor work). The engine was joined to the compressor itself by a clutch. The compressor is a three-cylinder, two-stage, air-cooled unit with intercooler. It can deliver 105-CFM at 100 PSI. As adopted, the compressor and truck assembly, serviced and ready to work, weighed 14,300 lbs.

The initial design proved so trouble free that only minor changes were made to the compressor, including increasing the size of the exhaust valves and in 1943 beginning to use the standard Military

Senior oil filter on the compressor engine in lieu of the smaller, previously used Purolator unit.

In December 1943 an investigation was made regarding the desirability of equipping the compressor trucks with winches. Completed in February 1944, the conclusion of this report was that a front-mounted PTO-driven winch was desirable. In part this was due to the pioneering nature of Engineers work; often far ahead of improved roads, and also the utility of the winch in general Engineer operations. Subsequently, winches were standardized on future procurements of these compressor trucks; in fact even to this day most trucks in Engineer units are equipped with winches.

The other obvious change to the trucks was the substitution of the Studebaker-developed military standard open cab on the truck chassis beginning in 1942. The closed-cabbed compressor trucks were built on chassis using the Timken, or split-type axle, while trucks with open cabs can be found with either the Timken, or GM Corporation (banjo-style) axles. The basic chassis was similar to that used on the cargo, with a relocated spare tire carrier and modifications to the bed mounting brackets.

Beyond the initial order for 1,038 of these compressor trucks, a further 7225 were ordered through May 1944, at a cost of $27,538,556.39 including spares. On the final day of 1943, 2,020 of these were available in overseas theaters. During the following two years, an additional 1,310 were dispatched to the European and Mediterranean Theater, and 1,077 to the combined Pacific Theaters.

The wartime basis of issue for the 105-CFM LeRoi mounted on GMC chassis was as follows:

Engineer Regiment, Combat (Corps)	19
Engineer Regiment, Combat (Sq. Div.)	13

To provide mobile compressors with improved off-road capability, a standard LeRoi compressor was removed from a 4x4 truck and mounted on 6x6 chassis. This experiment proved successful, and the arrangement was standardized as the Truck, 2½-ton, 6x6, Motorized Compressor. (U.S. Army Quartermaster Museum)

Engineer Regiment, General Service	20
Engineer Battalion, Combat (Triangular Div.)	9
Engineer Battalion, Separate	9
Engineer Squadron	6
Engineer Troop, Mechanized	2
Engineer Regiment, Aviation	29

Most of these numbers are about 50% greater than those used in peacetime.

Tools

Development work on suitable tools for use with the compressor was concurrent with that of the compressor itself. Due to the harsh environment most such tools must work in, it was found that by and large commercially available tools were suitable for military use with only minor changes.

Those tools deemed essential in 1939 for inclusion in the truck-borne tool set included rock drills, paving breakers (jack hammers to laymen), clay diggers, saws, wood boring machines and tire inflation equipment. As time passed this list was changed, with the "normal" tool load consisting of the following:

1 Thor Model 25 Paving Breaker, with sheeting driver attachment, two tamper pads and rods, two chisel and three moil point bits.

2 Thor Model 412 Clay Digger with two each moil point, flat pick and clay spades.

1 Thor Model 62 wood boring machine, with four different size augers each in 12 and 36-inch lengths.

1 Thor Model 75 sinker rock drill, with two-each 2, 4, 6, and 8-foot drill steels

1 Skilsaw model 2127 Circular Saw

1 Reed-Prentice "Timberhog" 24-inch pneumatic chain saw

1 Ingersoll-Rand nail driver

1 Graco PK-100 grease gun kit

From the outset, the first four tools were considered an integral part of the compressor truck, and are included in the compressor operator's manual. The balance of the tools listed above were adopted subsequently, but were nevertheless supplied with almost every compressor truck built. These tools were issued as sets through January 1944, after which time they were issued individually. This practice avoided needless issuance of tools (chainsaws to Aviation units, for example).

This 6x6 motorized compressor, U.S.A. number 498476, was based on a long-wheelbase CCKW and featured a model 1608 cab. The left cover of the compressor and engine enclosure is open, revealing the compressor engine (front), the 105-cubic-foot-per-minute (cfm) compressor (rear), as well as the instrument panel and air cleaners. One spare tire was provided, mounted on the left side above a running board. (U.S. Army Engineer School History Office)

Running across the chassis to the rear of the cab was a transverse toolbox. A safety strap is connected to the rear of the cab and the front of the compressor and engine enclosure. A tool compartment with a top-hinged cover was above the tandem wheels on each side of the vehicle. (U.S. Army Engineer School History Office)

283

The cover of the tool compartment on the right side is open, showing an air hose and a Thor 75 Sinker pneumatic rock drill inside. A smaller tool compartment is to the rear of the large compartment. To the rear of the compressor and engine enclosure is the air receiver, on each side of which is a reel with 50 feet of ¾-inch I.D. air hose. (U.S. Army Engineer School History Office)

Air-powered tools and related equipment are arrayed next to motorized compressor U.S.A. number 498476. The box to the far left is a grease-gun kit. Next to the front tire is a Skilsaw, to the right of which is a wood-boring machine. Leaning against the running board by the driver's door are two pneumatic clay diggers. By the rear tandem tire is a chain saw. (U.S. Army Engineer School History Office)

This motorized compressor was based on an open-cab CCKW-353 with a front-mounted winch, U.S. Army registration number 60108150. On the front of the engine and compressor enclosure was a radiator with "LEROI" in raised letters on the top and the sides. (U.S. Army Engineer School History Office)

As seen on U.S. Army registration number 4819712, the object on top of the engine and compressor enclosure was the engine exhaust. (U.S. Army Engineer School History Office)

Visible above the tank-like air receiver at the rear of motorized compressor registration number 4819725, is the LeRoi logo prominently displayed on the rear of the compressor and engine enclosure. Flanking the air receiver are the air-hose reels. Below the air receiver is the 50-gallon fuel tank, which provided fuel to the vehicle engine and the compressor engine. On the tool box to the right is a stencil giving data dated December 1955. (U.S. Army Engineer School History Office)

The same motorized compressor shown in the photograph at left is viewed here from the front. The top of the radiator of the compressor engine with the LeRoi logo is visible through the windshield. Stenciled in small figures on the front of the hood is information about an antifreeze treatment that was administered in December 1955. Chalked on the front bumper by Granite City Engineer Depot personnel is the Federal Stock Number (FSN) for the complete vehicle. (U.S. Army Engineer School History Office)

An instructor is giving lessons on the operation of a LeRoi air compressor. To the right is the air receiver, with a capacity of eight cubic feet. Proceeding from the right of the receiver are the compressor intercooler, the compressor, the instrument panel, the compressor engine, and the engine radiator. (U.S. Army Engineer School History Office)

Above: A standard tool included with the motorized compressor was the Reed-Prentice Timberhog 24-inch pneumatic chainsaw. After considering several other pneumatic chainsaws made by Henry Disston and Sons, Mall, the Army classified the Reed-Prentice Timberhog as Standard on 21 June 1943. Later that year, the Army began to procure in quantities a sharpener as an accessory for the Timberhog. (U.S. Army Engineer School History Office)

Right: The U.S. Army Engineer Board began preliminary investigations into developing a pneumatic circular saw in August 1940. An ensuing test of four brands of circular saws culminated in an order for 987 12-inch pneumatic circular saws with rotary motors to Skilsaw, Inc., on 1 April 1942. This model was judged lighter, easier to handle and maintain, and more versatile and powerful than its competitors. This saw was standardized on 21 June 1943. (U.S. Army Engineer School History Office)

After Army Engineer units began experiencing freezing air lines on its compressors during cold weather, in February 1941 work was begun investigating means of keeping those lines clear by either vaporizers or air-line lubricators in February 1941. Following several months of tests, the air-line lubricator was found to be superior, and a contract was tendered to Ingersoll-Rand for 2,000 units of an air-line oiler that was standardized as a component of Pneumatic Tool Set No. 1 on 21 June 1943. (U.S. Army Engineer School History Office)

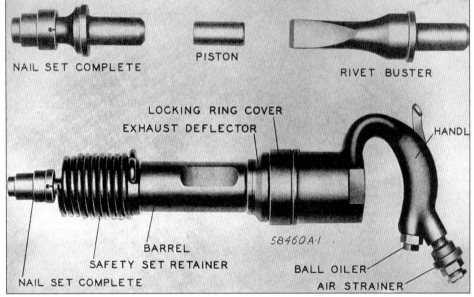

NAIL SET COMPLETE

PISTON

RIVET BUSTER

LOCKING RING COVER
EXHAUST DEFLECTOR

HANDL

BARREL
SAFETY SET RETAINER
NAIL SET COMPLETE

58460A·1

BALL OILER
AIR STRAINER

Also part of the standard Pneumatic Tool Set No. 1 for use with U.S. Army Engineers motorized compressors was the Ingersoll-Rand pneumatic nail driver. The Engineers began selection trials for a pneumatic nail driver in October 1939, the object being to acquire an air tool that could drive large spikes into green lumber and perform related tasks that claw hammers were unsuited for. As seen here, the nail driver had a curved handle and was equipped with a several attachments for driving and countersinking nails up to 60-penny in size. Also included was a rivet buster. (U.S. Army Engineer School History Office)

The Army initiated investigations into acquiring pneumatic grease guns in January 1941, culminating with an order for 1,000 pneumatic grease-gun kits from Gray Company, Inc. (Graco), in November 1941. The kit was designed for general-purpose greasing of trucks, trailers, tractors, compressors, and command cars. The unit used a one-pound grease charge, and with the pneumatic grease gun, a mechanic could completely grease a 1½-ton truck in 15 minutes. Shown here is a pneumatic grease-gun kit with a Graco model and serial-number plate on the inside of the lid. (U.S. Army Engineer School History Office)

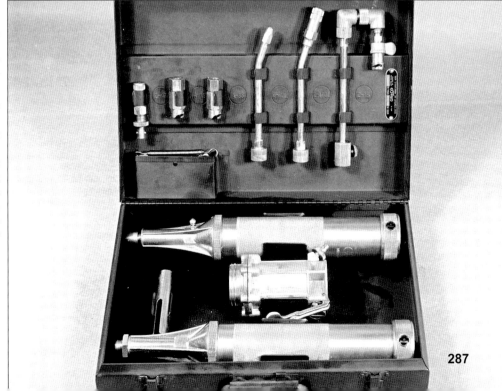

With a motorized compressor based on an open-cab CCKW in the background, an engineer uses an Ingersoll-Rand pneumatic nail driver to drive a spike into a timber while the soldier kneeling to the left bucks-up the timber. The pneumatic nail driver was a great time-saving tool, with its ability to drive home a large spike or drift pin much faster than could a man swinging a hammer. (U.S. Army Engineer School History Office)

A student bores a hole in a boulder with a Thor No. 75 Sinker pneumatic rock drill in preparation for blasting. The Sinker was used for hard, deep-hole drilling, quarrying, and shaft-sinking. Next to one of the grips was a throttle lever, for varying the speed of the drill. Various extension rods and drill bits were available for use with the rock drill. (U.S. Army Engineer School History Office)

At the Engineer School, Fort Belvoir, Virginia, students in the air-compressor course use pneumatic clay diggers to excavate. Part of the tool set of the motorized compressor, the pneumatic clay digger was used for trimming, overhead cutting, and side-wall trimming in excavation work. It loosened clay, which can be very difficult to dig, so it could be removed with a shovel. (U.S. Army Engineer School History Office)

In April 1944 a master sergeant operates a Thor Model 25 paving breaker, with a motorized compressor in the background. The paving breaker was designed to tackle the toughest demolition jobs, from busting concrete and pavement of all types to taking down columns and walls. An accessory for the paving breaker was a sheet-driver head, for driving sheet pilings into the ground. (U.S. Army Engineer School History Office)

Above: This vehicle, apparently a one-off model of which very little is known, was a CCKW fitted with a large air compressor behind the closed cab. The chassis was a long-wheelbase made even longer—perhaps up to 175 inches—by extending the tandem suspension to the rear. The vehicle bore U.S. Army registration number 422656. The entire project smacked of improvisation: note for example how the air tank is secured with wire to wooden blocks. (Fred Crismon collection)

Left: The compressor truck is viewed from overhead. On the sides of the rear half of the bed were racks and large toolboxes; the lid of the left one is open. (Fred Crismon collection)

To transport pontoons for constructing temporary bridges, the U.S. Army Corps of Engineers acquired pontoon bolster trucks. The bodies were made by the Casastota Division of Oneida. Above the tandem tires is the bolster. (U.S. Army Engineer School History Office)

A CCKW bolster truck is viewed from the rear. The tires were big 12.00 x 18s; some bolster trucks had dual tandem wheels. The bolster trailer used with these trucks to transport M4 floating bridge was a slip-pole design manufactured by several companies: Converto, Hobbs, and Highway Products, Inc. (U.S. Army Engineer School History Office)

Fire Trucks

At the outset of WWII, the U.S. Army's fire apparatus tended to be simply standard commercial fire trucks. Of course, the major problem in theater of operations was the limited off-road mobility, and limited water capacity. Designed for urban areas with fire hydrants available, the water tanks were small, and the 4x2 chassis of these trucks were not suited for the poor or non-existent road conditions in combat areas.

Class 335

In typical Army fashion, the GI Fire Fighters took the matter of correcting these deficiencies into their own hands in Algeria during the summer of 1943. At that time the 469th Engineer Maintenance Company transferred the pump and other equipment from their issued standard commercial chassis-based Ford Class 325 pumper onto an LWB closed cab CCKW. They also added a captured German 850-gallon water tank to the truck, which belonged to the 1208 Engineer Fire Fighting Platoon. The conversion was so successful that the Chief of Engineers ordered the Engineer Board to develop a similar piece of equipment.

A conversion kit was developed to combine a CCKW and a 325 pumper to yield a pumper on a tactical chassis. Initially this kit was to have used a new larger 500-GPM pump and to have been designated Class 535. However, in September 1944 the decision was made to retain the 300-GPM pump of the Class 325. Because of this the designation of the conversion equipment was changed from Class 535 to Class 335 before procurement began. The final specifications for the class 335 conversion kit were issued on 3 November 1944 as Engineer Board Specification 795. An initial order was placed on 22 March 1945 with General Fire Truck Corporation for 50 conversion kits, which were classified as standard on 16 June 1945. With a front-mounted pump that could discharge up to 250 pounds per square inch water pressure coupled to the all-wheel-drive chassis, this formed a formidable piece of fire fighting apparatus.

Class 530

While the 335 conversion kit was being developed, so too was an entirely new fire truck. Again, the name Class 535 was assigned. Among the desired changes were a midships-mounted pump (instead of the front-mounted pump of the trucks listed above) to protect the pump in the event of a collision. There was much difficulty developing a power take off capable of delivering the full engine power to the fire pump. Solving this hurdle proved to be such a challenge that even by the time of the Japanese surrender the problem had not been resolved. The Class 535 again was renamed, becoming the Class 530. An initial order for 24 trucks was placed on 16 March 1945 with the McCabe-Powers Auto Body Company of St. Louis. The $46,141.20 order was the subject of Engineer Board Contract W-109-ENG-310.

The first CCKW-based fire truck appears to have been concocted in Algeria in the summer of 1943 when the 469th Engineer Maintenance Company transferred the pump and other equipment from their standard commercial chassis-based Class 325 pumper, along with a captured German 850-gallon water tank, to this CCKW-353 of the1208th Engineer Fire Fighting Platoon. The truck photographed in Sicily in November 1943. (National Archives)

The Class 535 fire-truck conversion equipment was the subject of U.S. Army Corps of Engineers Project ME490, authorized on 19 April 1944, to produce a standardized fire truck based on a 2½-ton 6x6 chassis, with a 500-gallon-per-minute pump. McCabe-Powers Auto Body Company of St. Louis was the successful bidder, submitting a prototype for testing by mid-June 1944. However, three months later it was decided to substitute the 300-gallon-per-minute of the Class 325 equipment, so the Class 535 was redesignated Class 335, as seen here. Fifty units of the conversion equipment were ordered from General Fire Truck Corporation in March 1945. (U.S. Army Engineer School History Office)

The Army placed an order for 24 Class 530 fire trucks with McCabe-Powers Auto Body Company in March 1945. It was equipped with a 500-gallon-per-minute pump and combined an off-road capability with the ability to fight all types of fires. Principal features were a tank for water or premixed foam, hose, pump, and portable fire extinguishers. (U.S. Army Engineer School History Office)

Class 530 fire truck U.S. Army registration number 4678299, based on an open-cab CCKW-353, lacks much of the standard on-vehicle equipment, such as fire hoses on the reels, and the ladders and suction hoses that normally were stored on the right side of the body. (U.S. Army Engineer School History Office)

Mounted on the front of the Class 530 fire truck was a direct-driven 500-gallon-per-minute centrifugal pump. These vehicles were equipped with 11.00-18 low-pressure tires to enhance off-road capability. A combination siren/flashing light was on the left fender, and two spotlights were on the front of the cab. (U.S. Army Engineer School History Office)

The pump assembly's main components were the Barton-American Type F pump, vacuum-type primer, and power takeoff assembly. The pump was driven by a floating shaft that engaged the crankshaft, and it discharged 500 gallons per minute at 120 psi at approximately 2,400 rpm. (U.S. Army Engineer School History Office)

Stenciled on the plate toward the rear of the body of U.S.A. number 00477942 is a variety of valuable information, including that this was a Class 530 fire truck, CCKW-353 serial number 416470-B2, with GMC 270 engine serial 270681573, and was equipped with a Darley Model F pump, serial number 26, certified in January 1947. (U.S. Army Engineer School History Office)

This Class 530 fire truck bears U.S. Army registration number 4678299. It is shorn of its fire-fighting accessories, such as hoses and ladders, but the hose reels are present to the rear of the open cab. Solid brace plates replaced the earlier support rods for the platform below and to the rear of the body. (U.S. Army Engineer School History Office)

The rear of Class 530 fire truck U.S.A. number 00477942 is viewed. A small spotlight is on a stanchion on each side of the rear of the body. In the rear of the body, with wooden pallets on the floor, was the hose bed, where 1,000 feet of 2½-inch hose and 300 feet of 1½-inch double-jacket hose were stored. (U.S. Army Engineer School History Office)

Crane trucks

Various branches of the Army had requirements for cranes during WWII. The Quartermaster Corps needed cranes for material handling, as did the Navy and Marines, while the Engineers needed cranes not only for material handling, but also construction. The hydraulic crane shown on these pages however owes much of its development to the Army Air Forces.

A December 1946 letter from the HQ, Air Forces to the Chief of Ordnance outlined the various reasons why the 1½-ton M6 and 2½-ton M27 and M27B1 were unsatisfactory under the conditions of what at that time was termed "modern warfare." The October 1946 Conference on Bomb Handling and Loading Equipment established a requirement for an improved bomb service truck with full revolving crane, telescopic boom, and full power operation.

The 16 December 1948 Ordnance Committee Item 32526 took up this project, reading in part:

"Preliminary design studies have considered general requirements of all arms and services for a truck-mounted crane of 2-ton capacity, as well as bomb handling service. Tentative military characteristics have been coordinated with Army Field Forces, the Ordnance Department Board and various technical services. The Chemical Corps has a requirement for such an item to replace the Truck, 2½-Ton, 6x6, Chemical Service, M1 and the Truck, 4-ton, 6x6, Crane, Swinging Boom, M1. The Corps of Engineers and Navy Bureau of Ordnance have requirements for a similar crane mounted on a special chassis. Investigation of various commercial designs has determined that one crane, with minor modifications, will be suitable for mounting on standard or special chassis, and will meet the requirements of all interested arms and services."

While the overall goal was to develop a crane that could be mounted on the forthcoming T55E1 and M35 chassis, in the interim the decision was made to acquire two hydraulic crane units from Austin-Western and mount them on CCKW chassis. These two trucks would serve as pilots for the newer vehicles. In time, the concept was developed into the M108, which utilized the M35-style Reo-designed chassis.

The two CCKW-based trucks, designated T62, were to be used for testing, with one being dispatched to Aberdeen Proving Ground, and the other evaluated by the Air Force. The projected cost of the project, beyond the truck chassis, was $25,000, and it was estimated that the pilots would be completed by 1 June 1949, and the Aberdeen evaluation would be completed by 1 July.

To improve the mobility of cranes, efforts were made to equip CCKWs as crane carriers. This example had a Sehield Bantam M49 crane mounted on the rear of the chassis of U.S. Army registration number 4799072. Mounted on the front of the chassis frame was a rest for the crane boom. (Jim Gilmore collection)

A Truck, 2½-ton, 6x6, Crane, T62, is viewed from the right side with the crane in the travel position. The vehicle's fuel tank is below the body to the rear of the cab. Two spotlights were mounted at the upper rear of the cab. (TACOM LCMC History Office)

As viewed from the rear of a Truck, 2½-ton, 6x6, Crane, T62, the crane is traversed to the left side of the vehicle and the boom extended. Outriggers are in place at four points on the body. (TACOM LCMC History Office)

The Truck, 2½-ton, 6x6, Crane, T62, as depicted in a Detroit Arsenal photo dated 11 April 1950, represented an early effort by the Army to field a hydraulic wrecker. The crane is in the traveling position, facing to the rear, with the telescoping boom retracted. The operator's booth was on the right side of the boom. Bows were supplied for installing a tarpaulin over the crane. (TACOM LCMC History Office)

A Truck, 2½-ton, 6x6, Crane, T62, is viewed from the right rear in an April 1950 photo. A single spare tire was stowed to the rear of the cab. A spotlight was mounted on the left frame of the crane below the boom. (TACOM LCMC History Office)

Pipeline Trucks

Adequate supplies of fuel are critical to the waging of war on the modern battlefield. As recorded elsewhere in this volume, at some points in the European campaign, as much as 30% of the available fuel was being expended trucking the remaining 70% to the front. That pipelines would provide a more efficient means of transporting bulk fuel was well-known prior to WWII, and in 1942 the Engineer Board was testing portable pipeline equipment. During the summer of 1942 tests of portable pipelines and pumping gear were being conducted at Camp Young, California, and in the Shenandoah National Park, Virginia. These tests pointed out the inadequacy of standard military vehicles for this task – with some of the specific major problems being the loading, unloading, and shifting of the heavy materials often requiring the use of a crane and a great deal of manual labor.

Contemporary training of the first two Petroleum Distribution units at Camp Claiborne, Louisiana, indicated the same problem. These units had been supplied with ten CCKW-353 cargo trucks as part of the organizational equipment, and the Engineer Unit Training Center Heavy Shops at Camp Claiborne set out to modify these trucks to better suite petroleum construction operations. Some of these modifications were later deemed objectionable, but nevertheless the trucks were used as intended.

To improve upon this effort, in December 1942 the Engineer Board began addressing the matter. This work was done under the authority of Project BR 370 "Transportation for Portable Pipeline." However, in granting approval, Services of Supply limited the scope of this work to "determining means of best adapting and employing existing types of standard vehicles."

Accordingly, the Board set to work designing an experimental bed and boaster arrangement for a two-wheel pole-type trailer. By January 1943 the design was complete, and the Spencer Trailer Company of Augusta, Kansas, was asked to build an example, utilizing a Gar Wood winch. The truck and trailer were shipped to Camp Claiborne in early April 1943, which forwarded them on to Fort Belvoir for evaluation.

Tests there of the truck, which utilized gin poles for lifting and maneuvering pumping equipment, proved highly satisfactory. The accompanying trailer, however, was not, its draft pole being far too weak. The Barrage Balloon Board in Tennessee also tested the trucks with the M-1, A-9 and Mark IV Barrage Balloon Winches, where it performed satisfactorily.

Ultimately, a pipeline truck conversion set was fabricated. This consisted of a wooden truck bed 11 feet 5½ inches long and 8 feet 2 inches wide, with roller tailboard and tubular front sill. Behind the cab, protected by a tubular headache rack, was a Gar Wood N. 3 M.B.S. 10,000-pound capacity, PTO-driven single-drum winch. Two spotlights were attached to the headache rack, and a tool box mounted beneath the bed. The A frame used to lift equipment was stowed alongside the bed when not in use. Also included in the 3,300-pound kit were pipe bars, load binders and snatch blocks. It was estimated that personnel in the field could remove the cargo bed from a CCKW-353 and mount the pipeline conversion kit in 25 man-hours, without welding.

The conversion kits were recommended for Standardization on 18 October 1943, and was approved on 6 November as Required Type, Adopted Type, Standard Article and Current Supply, Critical Essential Item. Six sets were to be issued to each Petroleum Distribution Company. A total of 540 sets were procured, with 18 coming from Hyde Manufacturing Company, Fort Worth, Texas; 131 from the Roehlk Spring and Body Company in St. Louis, Missouri – all the preceding having each been issued a single contract. The Camp Claibourn shops fabricated 90 of the conversion kits. The balance of 301 kits were produced under three contracts by the McCabe-Powers Auto Body Company of St. Louis.

Many of these sets were sent to the field, with six sent to the Southwest Pacific, 12 to North Africa, 54 to the United Kingdom, and 142 sets sent to the China-Burma-India Theater, where they were used to build a pipeline alongside the Ledo Road.

A 5 March 1946 report on these vehicles noted "The 2½-ton pipeline truck accomplished everything that the project was established to do. It provided a versatile, dependable and highly satisfactory means of handling pipe and other pipe-line equipment. It was used extensively in the field and contributed immeasurably to the success of several construction projects which were vital to the winning of the war."

The Engineer Board developed this pipeline truck as a result of field experiments with portable pipelines and pumping equipment during 1942. The need for an efficient means of not only transporting joints of pipe and pumping stations, but also a means of putting this equipment in place, led to the development of the truck. (U.S. Army Engineer History Office)

The roller-tailboard at the rear of the bed aids in loading and unloading heavy gear, such as that burdening the truck here. The pipeline bed, A-frame, rear winch and PTO were furnished as a kit, which was then used to convert a cargo truck or chassis truck into pipeline configuration, rather than the trucks being shipped complete from the manufacturer's facility. (U.S. Army Engineer History Office)

The A-frame, shown here erected, was normally stowed alongside the special pipeline bed when not in use. A rear-mounted winch, mounted beneath the headache rack just behind the cab, supplied the lifting power for the A-frame, which was used when loading and unloading the cargo, and placing gear. (U.S. Army Engineer History Office)

Because of inadequacies with the trailer that was developed in conjunction with the truck, tests were conducted utilizing the trailer as a semi-trailer, with a bolster positioned on the pipeline truck bed. This effort was not successful, and most units resorted to transporting pipe sections in cargo trucks. However, the pipeline truck itself was wholeheartedly considered a success by all who used it, which directly resulted in similar trucks, built on later-style chassis, being used by the Engineers into the 1980s. (U.S. Army Engineer History Office)

Mobile Map-making Trucks

The value of an accurate map to military operations is obvious. Less obvious is the daunting logistical problem of getting an adequate number of maps to the front. The Army Map Service, with a printing plant on the outskirts of Washington, D.C., would be unable to supply the myriad of maps that would be needed world wide should the United States become involved in the war that was sweeping around the globe.

Accordingly, in the late 1930s the Army chose to address this problem by moving the map making and printing operation closer to the front lines. The size and weight of mapmaking and printing equipment meant the earliest form of mobile topographic map-making equipment required the development of special printing presses, weighing half of comparable conventional models.

During 1937 a Mobile Reproduction Plant for use at the Corps level had been developed, one that could be housed in a tractor-trailer, with an accompanying 1½-ton truck transporting the required generator and other equipment. By 1941 the design had evolved to the point everything was housed in a single semi-trailer. As the unit was considered for classification as limited standard, it was requested that this be redesigned for truck, rather than semi-trailer mounting.

On 5 June 1940, work began on a larger program, Project SP319, Mobile Map Reproduction Train, Topographic Battalion. This complex processing and printing plant was housed in eight semi trailers, and was delivered to Fort Belvoir for testing in April 1941.

By November 1941 it was apparent that the size of the semi trailers made their maneuverability as well as concealment problematic. The Engineer Board then decided to explore using van-type trucks rather than the trailers. Mounting the equipment in CCKWs was a success. A second, more refined prototype was ordered in December 1941, and was delivered in March 1942. While largely satisfied with the equipment from the production standpoint, the maneuverability was questionable due to the semi-trailer mounting. Almost immediately the Engineer Board proposed to redesign the eight-van train to utilize seven different types of van trucks instead. The 10-unit truck train, constituting a Company, would consist of four four-ton press trucks, one four-ton camera truck, and five 2½-ton trucks, each individually outfitted as follows: one plate process truck, one plate grainer truck, one laboratory truck, one photographic truck, and one map layout truck.

Peter Wendel and Sons, Inc., of Irvington, New Jersey, delivered the first complete truck-train of the redesigned type in January 1943. Upon this equipment were based the trucks that would equip the Army's mobile map-making units during WWII. Before the war was over, a dozen Army Topographic Engineer Battalions, four GHQ Topographic Battalions, 27 Corps Topographic Companies, and 33 Engineer Air Force Companies were in existence, and churning out millions of maps.

The mapmaking sections of the U.S. Army Corps of Engineers fielded mobile labs for making and reproducing maps. These were based on the CCKW chassis and featured van-type bodies manufactured by McCabe Powers Autobody Co. and Peter Wendell and Sons. This example carried map reproduction equipment. (U.S. Army Engineer School History Office)

This mapmaking van bears markings for the Map Reproduction Layout Section. Under the front of the body is a spare-tire carrier with a wheel on it. Under the rear of the body are leveling jacks. (U.S. Army Engineer School History Office)

A mobile map-reproduction lab truck based on a closed-cab CCKW is viewed from the front. To the rear of the bumper were two screw-type jacks, designed to stabilize and immobilize the vehicle to limit vibrations during map-reproducing operations. (U.S. Army Engineer School History Office)

The rear of the map-reproduction lab is viewed. The lower half of the rear of the body formed a tailgate, hinged at the bottom, and the top half of the rear of the body also was hinged or removable, judging from the weather-strip flap at the top. (U.S. Army Engineer School History Office)

A closed-cab CCKW has a van body marked "MAP REPRO. TRUCK / PHOTO. SECTION," indicating it was used for reproducing maps. Outwardly, the mapmaking trucks were similar in appearance, but they had different sets of equipment for various purposes inside. (U.S. Army Engineer School History Office)

"MAP REPRODUCTION TRAIN / PLATE GRAINER" is stenciled on the side of the body of this mapmaking truck. The plate-graining process involved roughing by machine the face of a flexible sheet of zinc or aluminum for use in the offset-photolithographic printing of maps. (U.S. Army Engineer School History Office)

The plate-grainer truck is viewed here from the front. At the top corner, an opening, possibly for a ventilator, is covered. Stenciled on the front of the hood is information about a servicing of the cooling system conducted in March 1946. (U.S. Army Engineer School History Office)

The same mapping truck is viewed from the front. Two data plates are visible on the front right of the body. The purpose of the rack on the upper front of the body is unclear but probably was intended to hold specific equipment. Not all mapping trucks had this rack. (U.S. Army Engineer School History Office)

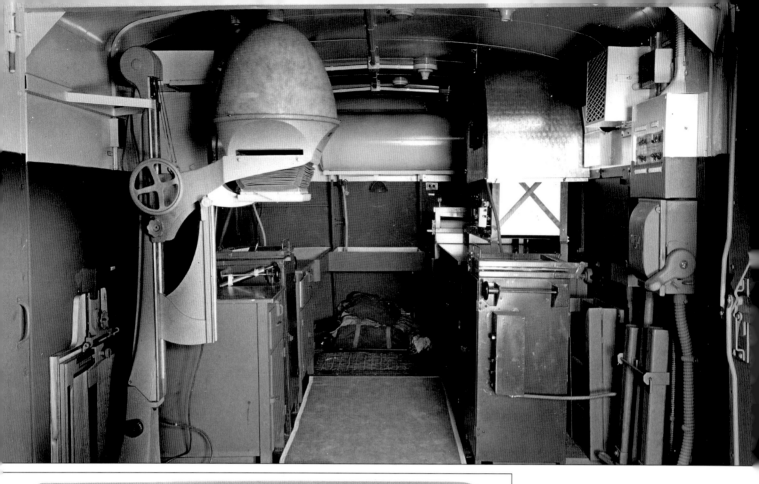

Above: The interior of each van in the mapmaking section was different. This is the interior of the Reproduction Equipment van. (Office of History, U.S. Army Corps of Engineers)

Left: A rear view of the same mapping truck shows the large tailgate, fitted with several brackets and a webbing strap at the center. Next to the tow pintle is an electrical receptacle for a trailer. The rear stabilizing jacks are visible below the tail lights. (U.S. Army Engineer School History Office)

Shop, Motorized, General Purpose

In the broadest of terms, during WWII the United States Army fielded two types of shop van based on the GMC CCKW. The well-known series were the ordnance maintenance shops, typified by the ST-5 and ST-6 shop van, with its hard metal enclosure. These were provided in a variety of internal configurations, as well as utilizing two types of body enclosures. The focus of this segment, however, is the less-known motorized shop utilized by Engineer Maintenance Companies, known precisely as the Shop, Motorized, General Purpose.

It would be impossible to discuss this versatile vehicle without invoking the name Kibbey Couse. Mr. Couse, son of famed artist Eanger Irving Couse (1866-1936), was an inventor and engineer. In the 1930s Couse had developed a motorized machine shop. Couse saw a potential market for his invention as in essence a mobile airfield service facility. To capitalize on this, Couse moved his operation from Taos, New Mexico, to Newark, New Jersey. Interest in the mobile machine shop continued to rise, perhaps culminating in a five-page article in the December 1938 issue of *Popular Science* magazine.

As the clouds of war drew near for the United States, considerable preparatory work was done toward preparing for the nation's mobilization. In September 1940 the decision was made by the Corps of Engineers to transform the Engineer Shop Company into a highly mobile unit. On 1 November the Table of Organization and Equipment for the Shop Company included several as-yet non-existent mobile shops. In an effort to fill this void, the Engineer Board at Ft.

Belvoir, Virginia, began preparing lists of tools and equipment to be housed within various mobile shops. By mid-April 1941 a list of eight shop types had been compiled. While this list was still being compiled, the Engineer Board had ordered five shop truck bodies and three semi-trailer shop bodies from Peter Wendel and Sons, Inc., of Irvington, New Jersey. The truck bodies would be mounted on government-furnished standard GMC 2½-ton 6x6 truck chassis, while the trailer bodies would be mounted on Fruehauf 2DF trailer chassis furnished by Wendel.

Even before these bodies had been completed, the decision was made to issue a similar contract to a firm which specialized in this type of body – and for this the obvious choice was Couse. Thus, on 19 April 1941 Corps of Engineers Specification T-1150 was issued, which encompassed the Couse design. Two weeks later a contract was issued for four of these bodies – one of these bodies was to be fully equipped. In October the contract was modified such that the three remaining bodies were to be finished as welding; machine shop and a tool and bench vehicle, all three equipped with tools furnished by the Engineer Board.

In June 1941 the work of the Engineer Board's program grew to include maintenance equipment of the Engineer Aviation Battalion. The next month the Board recommended the use of two types of motorized shops by these battalions. One was to be a mobile welding shop, the other a mobile machine shop. The specifications for these shops were enumerated in Engineer Board Specification EBP29, 17 July 1941. These trucks were designed for operation either in pairs, or individually, as dictated by operational requirements. The bodies,

The first U.S. Army mobile shop units to reach the field were the Couse Type A and Type B models, the Type A being a welding shop and the Type B a machine shop, shown here. The trial vehicles were built on 1941 Ford 19W81 cab over engine truck chassis, while the production model was based on 1942 Ford 29W81 1½-ton 4x2 chassis. The Types A and B were handicapped by there non-standard 4x2 chassis, but despite this were utilized in forward areas. (U.S. Army Engineer School History Office)

which were approximately 7'9" long and 7'7" wide and 6'10" high, were mounted on 134-inch wheelbase, 1½-ton cab over engine Ford 19W81 4x2 chassis. The vehicles tipped the scales at 15,500 pound each.

The welding truck, designated Type A, featured a special-design Couse dynometer-welder suitable for use as welder, or as a generator supply power to lights and hand tools. It also included a 5-ton rear mounted hoist, a ten-ton hydraulic lift, a ten-ton capacity Porto-power, and electric drill, an acetylene generator as well as an oxy-acetylene torch set and a host of hand tools.

The machine shop, designated Type B, was in a virtually identical body, mounted on the same type of Ford chassis. This truck featured a three-ton capacity hoist, a 14 to 28-inch lathe with 6-foot extension bed, an air compressor, a generator with battery charger, a heavy pneumatic drill press, valve and valve-seat grinders, three electric drills, grinders, pneumatic chipping hammers and a wide variety of hand tools.

The pilot models of both of these trucks were issued to the 21st Engineer Regiment (Aviation) at Langley Field, Virginia in March 1942. Ultimately, both of these trucks were found deficient by the using unit, in large part due to there non-military standard chassis. However, even before the Engineer Board had received these reports from the field, orders had been placed for additional units – 32 pairs on 25 November 1941 and 112 pair on 24 March 1942. The latter were built on 1942 Model Ford 29W81 chassis and bore registration numbers 0014860 through 0015083. The price per pair of these vehicles varied from contract to contract, ranging from a high of $41,000 to a low of $38,565.52.

At the same time that the initial Type A and Type B trucks were ordered in June 1941, the larger shop truck program was further expanded when the Davey Compressor Company of Kent Ohio was awarded contract WB145-eng-210 to install a power take off, air compressor, welder and generator in a Couse-supplied body, the entire assembly to be mounted on a 2½ 6x6 chassis.

Concerns about weight and other factors resulted in a new specification being issued on 9 August 1941. The new specification, EB Spec EBP 31, was for a mobile repair shop for combat units. This specification, while similar to the Couse units mentioned earlier, featured a canvas top and sides on the machine shop. It was felt that this was an improvement from an operational standpoint, due to lighter weight, and from a tactical standpoint, as the vehicle now more closely resembled a routine cargo truck, rather than being a special truck and inherently a high priority target. A contract was issued to Couse for two test articles conforming to the new specification, designated model C-1, to be mounted on government-furnished 2½-ton 6x6 chassis.

In November of 1941 sixteen of the various mobile shops, representing 6 of the 7 types of shop bodies contracted for (Beyond the scope of this text was ¾-ton truck-based shop) were assigned to the 56th Engineer Ship Company for service testing during the First Army maneuvers in North Carolina. The general assessment of the concept was very favorable, with 235 out of 250 pieces of equipment being repaired by the mobile shop force at an average cost of less than $5.00 per repair. Of the remaining fifteen, parts were unavailable for two, while the final thirteen exceeded the limitations of the mobile shop force.

The tests concluded that the Wendel trailer-based shops were too heavy and lacked manuvaribility, the Couse heavy panel-type trucks were also too heavy, and the Wendel van-type trucks housed a minimum of the required equipment. The Couse type C body, with canvas top and sides, was shown to be clearly superior to the other shops.

Field tests by the 36th Engineer Regiment (Combat), the 16th Engineer Regiment (Armored) and the 121st Engineer Regiment (Combat) produced the same results.

It was determined to proceed with the development of four types of shops housed in Couse Type C bodies. These were the Electrical repair shop, General Purpose repair shop, Small-tool repair shop and the tool and bench shop. Based on the lessons learned during the Carolina Maneuvers some changes were made in the shop design. The refined bodies would feature an all-steel welded bed, folding steps, built-in benches and stowage compartments, fold-up work plates and an aisle running from the back of the cab to the rear axle. The new specifications were set forth on 13 December 1941 as EB Spec EBP 111, Body for Motorized Engineer Maintenance Shop. On the same day a contract was issued to Couse for a sample article to the new spec, followed later in the day for a further contract for six more units. The first of these was completed in February 1942, and the Army shipped the tools and equipment for the trucks to Couse for installation. Concurrently,

Initial development work on larger Army mobile shops included both truck and trailer mounted units using bodies produced by Peter Wendel and Sons. These bodies were similar to those used on CCKW-based water purification trucks. (U.S. Army Engineer School History Office)

under the authority of the Chief of Engineers, the Engineer Board contracted for eight move bodies in order to expedite the outfitting of the 470th Engineer Shop Company. Couse was awarded two more contracts, totaling 24 units (at $3,000 each) in March 1942.

In November 1942 the Board shipped a fully-equipped pilot model of the electrical repair shop to the Columbus General Depot. In April 1942 it had been determined that all motorized shops were to equipped at the Columbus Depot. This shop, originally intended for repair of searchlights, featured a generator, air compressor, battery charger, grinder, welding and cutting equipment and a variety of tools and repair kits.

Virtually concurrently the pilot model of the General Purpose shop was also delivered to Columbus. This truck was furnished with a 3KW generator, 9-inch swing lathe with 3 ½ foot bed, bench grinder, hydraulic press, a drill press, oxyacetylene cutting and welding equipment, portable electric drills and grinders and a staggering array of hand tools. The General Purpose shop was also supplied with a 1-ton cargo trailer laden with a gasoline-powered arc welder and associated equipment.

Columbus also received pilot models of the small-tool repair shop, which featured primarily pneumatically-operated equipment, and the tool and bench shop, which was laden primarily with hand tools and small hydraulic presses. The small tool repair truck was not furnished with a winch, whereas in production all three of the other types were winch-equipped, and furnished with a 5-ton capacity A-frame hoist. The creation of the General Purpose shop was announced to using troops via a 6-page article, with cover feature, in the October 1942 edition of The Maintenance Engineer, a publication of the Chief of Engineers.

Despite the considerable advancement made to this point in body design, the Engineers were still not entirely satisfied. On 9 June 1942 the Engineer Board issued a purchase order to the St. Louis-based McCabe Powers Body Company for $365 for modifications to a Couse body, which the government shipped to McCabe-Powers. The ensuing modifications reduced the size of the canvas, altered the bows, reconfigured some work benches and improved the blackout lighting. The Engineer Board recommended these changes beginning with the 1944 production, and the change in specification was so approved.

However, in the interim demand for mobile shops had become so great that a $363,000 contract for 212 bodies had been issued to Cleveland-based American Coach and Body Company in February 1943. American completed the order in August 1943. Demand had simply outstripped Couse capacity.

Further orders required body production by McCabe-Powers, Hicks Body Company, Perley A. Thomas Car Works, Superior Coach and Krieger Steel Sections. Ultimately the mobile shop sets were deployed in every Theater, ranging from the Aleutians to New Guinea, Guadalcanal and throughout Europe. The type C beds were also mounted on the Studebaker US6 while rigid-side Couse L bodies, similar to their early army prototype, were supplied to the U.S. Navy on International M5H6 chassis. Post-WWII similar shop sets were developed by Couse utilizing first the G-742 Reo 2½-ton chassis and later the G-744 5-ton chassis. The CCKW-based trucks remained in the U.S. Army inventory into the 1950s, and many were supplied to allied nations through the U.S. Military Assistance Program (MAP).

The Couse firm was contracted to build two pilot models of shop truck as well. These pilots featured rigid sides much like those of the Couse Mobile Airport. This example is built on a 1941 CCKW-353 that had originally been produced as a cargo truck. (U.S. Army Engineer School History Office)

The rigid sides of the initial prototypes gave way to canvas sides on subsequent Couse experimental models, designated Type C. Here is one of first prototypes of this style, which was built on a 1940 CCKWX-353 chassis, originally produced as a cargo truck. The roof-mounted crane was a feature that did not make it into mass-production. (U.S. Army Engineer School History Office)

Left: The Couse Type C design was further refined by McCabe-Powers Auto Body Company of St. Louis. Also, the roof-mounted hoist gave way to a front bumper mounted A-frame. This General Purpose shop is representative of the configuration of the type. The gasoline-engine driven generator is visible at the left rear of the bed. (U.S. Army Engineer School History Office)

Below: The layout of the Tool and Bench truck was similar to the General Purpose shop. However, it lacked the 3KW generator found in the latter. (U.S. Army Engineer School History Office)

The General Purpose Shop was announced to the personnel of the Corps of Engineers via this cover story in the October 1942 of the Engineer's publication The Maintenance Engineer. (U.S. Army Engineer School History Office)

The Small Tool Repair truck was created to primarily repair pneumatic tools in the field. Such pneumatic tools were commonly found as accessories supplied with air compressor trucks. This type of truck lacked the front-mounted winch found on the other three styles of Engineer mobile shop trucks. (U.S. Army Engineer School History Office)

The Shop, Motorized, General Purpose was developed for the combat engineers as a means of supplying them with a fully equipped, mobile conveyance for all of the machinery and tools necessary for performing repair and maintenance work in the field. The vehicle was based on the CCKW chassis. Unlike the CCKW-based ST-5 and ST-6 shop bodies, the Shop, Motorized, General Purpose utilized a canvas tarpaulin on a steel frame to conserve weight. Shown here is Shop, Motorized, General Purpose U.S.A. number 4704176. (U.S. Army Engineer School History Office)

Even with the tarpaulin installed over the body, the Shop, Motorized, General Purpose was recognizable by the three bows and two removable horizontal frame members visible in outline through the tarpaulin. Also part of the mobile shop, not shown here, was a gasoline-powered 300-amp arc-welding suite mounted on a 1-ton trailer. (U.S. Army Engineer School History Office)

Shop, Motorized, General Purpose U.S. Army registration number 4799057 is shown with the tarpaulin removed, revealing the design of the frame that supported the tarpaulin. On the sides of the body were gates that could be lowered to provide platforms. (U.S. Army Engineer School History Office)

The same vehicle shown in the preceding photo is viewed from the front. At the bends of the bows of the frame supporting the tarpaulin were hinged struts which could be swung outward to support the sides of the tarpaulin in the fashion of an awning. A bumper-mounted A-frame boom powered by the winch also was supplied. (U.S. Army Engineer School History Office)

A Shop, Motorized, General Purpose is viewed from the rear with the tarpaulin removed. These vehicles were based on the Couse Type C body, and all-steel, welded structure with built-in work benches and storage compartments. The need for a tarpaulin to protect the metal tools and equipment in the truck is obvious. (U.S. Army Engineer School History Office)

A rear view of a Shop, Motorized, General Purpose shows the tarpaulin lashed in place. Standard equipment for these vehicles included a 3-kilowatt generator, gas-welding equipment, a 9-inch swing lathe with 3 ½ foot bed, a bench grinder, hydraulic press, drill press, portable electric drills and grinders, and an impressive supply of hand tools. (U.S. Army Engineer School History Office)

Shop, Motorized, General Purpose 00122044 is displayed with the cab top removed and the tarpaulin lashed to the body. A Chevrolet front axle is visible. When the A-frame boom was deployed, it was mounted on brackets on the front of the chassis. (U.S. Army Engineer School History Office)

Mounted under the front of the chassis frame of Shop, Motorized, General Purpose 60108118 is a pivoting jack, to stabilize and support the front end of the vehicle during lifting operations with the A-frame boom. The left boom bracket is faintly visible above the jack on top of the frame next to the winch. (U.S. Army Engineer School History Office)

Line Trucks

War is hard on infrastructure. Telephone and power lines are often among the first things destroyed, either deliberately by the aggressors, or deliberately by retreating troops, or merely as collateral damage through bombing or ground campaigns. Yet telephone and power service is considered a necessity, not only for the civilian populace, but also the advancing armies. During WWII, the U.S. Army used the K-43 telephone line maintenance truck, built on the 1½-ton Chevrolet 4x4 chassis and featuring a commercial line maintenance body.

However, this body was considered too small, and the truck to light, to be ideal for this work. Accordingly, in April 1944 work began to develop a new vehicle that addressed these concerns. The decision was made that the new truck should be based upon the standard GMC CCKW chassis, and furnished as a kit, so that the using troops in the field could perform the conversion of a standard cargo truck into a specialized line maintenance truck.

During the initial phase of development, this conversion was intended for use by the Corps of Engineers for power line maintenance. However, after the initial pilot model was under construction, the Chief Signal Officer directed that the Signal Corps Board cooperate with the Engineer Board in developing a body useful to both service arms.

The first pilot model was constructed by the McCabe-Powers Auto Body Company of St. Louis, Missouri. Per army requirements, the body was designed as a kit. This kit was divided into five main parts; two sides, the floor and front; a rear-mounted winch with derrick and power take off; and a line tool set. All this was to be furnished in large crates – as one would imagine given the size of a truck body.

On the initial pilot, the rear winch used was the same as that used on Engineer pipe line trucks; while the standard SAE power take off, commonly used the power a CCKW front winch, was used.

The first pilot had been completed by 29 July 1944 and was tested by the Engineers at Fort Belvoir. Its performance was found satisfactory, and it was then was shipped to the Signal Corps for testing at Fort Monmouth. The Signal Corps found a number of deficiencies,

among them – there tools would not fit – not surprising given that they became involved after fabrication had begun, and further the Signal Corps preferred to use their standard winch and hoist as found on the K-43, rather than the winch and hoist used on the pipeline construction truck. Signal Corps testing concluded in September 1944.

Because of the extensive changes needed in order for the body kit to satisfy the Signal Corps requirements, a second pilot was produced rather than modifying the existing pilot. The second pilot, also produced by McCabe-Powers (a firm specializing in line equipment bodies) was built incorporating the changes requested by the Signal Corps. The Engineers were agreeable to all the changes to the body recommended by the Corps of Engineers. However, the use of the Signal Corps standard winch required the use of a full-torque PTO. The Engineers preferred the Ohio-National Model 31, which was not a standard Ordnance item, but which permitted the retention of the truck's front winch. More significantly, this PTO required no changes to the truck chassis, and could be installed in the field in a couple of hours on any CCKW.

The Signal Corps preferred the use of the DUKW transfer case, due to its extensive testing, and it being a standard Ordnance item. The Engineers objected to this, because such use would also require changing a cross-member and propeller shafts, which were in short supply, as well as necessitating installation only on trucks with Corporation axles. The extensive modifications also would require that conversion from cargo truck to line maintenance truck be done at the depot level, rather than by the using unit.

Ultimately, the Engineer's point of view prevailed, and on 25 June 1945 it was recommended that the kits be adopted as standard, procurement of the conversion kits begin. Trucks equipped with the line maintenance bodies were designated V-17.

The companion vehicle for the V-17 was the V-18 earth boring machine truck. The V-18 featured a large, rear-mounted auger with variable sized bits. The V-17 and V-18 operating in tandem could erect, dismantle, or repair overhead power and telephone lines. In later years, responsibility for both the V-17 and V-18 were transferred to the Signal Corps.

CCKWs like this one were used for rigging electric and telephone lines in World War II. Although the CCKW could easily haul cable reels and line-construction equipment and tools, there was a need for a more fully equipped line-construction truck. (National Archives via Jim Gilmore)

Above: In the summer of 1945, the Engineer Board developed and tested a CCKW-based body that could transport all tools and rigging equipment necessary to build, rebuild, maintain, and service electric transmission and distribution systems. After two prototypes were built, and the usage of the vehicle expanded to include telephone lines, the vehicle was standardized as the Truck, V-17/MTQ (2½-ton, 6x6, Telephone Line Construction and Maintenance). (National Archives)

Right: A ladder and the hoist boom are stowed in the bin to the upper left of the rear body of the 2½-ton, 6x6 line-construction truck. A pole jack, for extracting line poles, is stowed in a rack on the left rear floorboard, while on the inside right rear of the compartment is stowed the collapsible line reel. In the center bottom of the rear opening is a sheave for use with the winch, with additional sheaves mounted on shafts crossing the front and rear of the bed. To the front of the spare tire is a cover over the winch that powers the rear-mounted A-frame. Stabilizing jacks are hung beneath the rear of the bed. These are lowered when using the A-frame. The canvas top provided for the body has been folded forward for this photo of the interior. (U.S. Army Engineer School History Office)

313

The V-17/MTQ included a pole-setting boom and hoist on the rear. On top of the body was what appears to be a stowage rack. Bins built into the exterior sides of the body contained tools, parts, and supplies. (U.S. Marine Corps Museum)

The platform atop the truck pivots near the front. It can be manually rotated and swung to the side to provide on-level access to the lines atop power or telephone poles. The small compartment just above the forward body reflector and behind the beverage cooler houses a side output shaft for the winch, on which could be installed the collapsible cable reel which is stowed in the bed. This V17/MTQ, based on an open-cab CCKW chassis, bears USMC markings. (U.S. Marine Corps Museum)

The companion vehicle for the V17 is the V18 earth boring and pole setting truck, an example of which is seen here on 20 March 1946. Though it is similar to the 1½-ton 4x4 Chevrolet K44, the Chevy's lack of needed mobility led to the creation of the 6x6 model. Like the V17, the V18 was fitted with large single tires rather than the CCKW-normal duals at rear in order to further improve mobility. (National Archives)

By January 1945, an earth augur for boring holes for telephone and electrical poles had entered operational service with the U.S. Army Engineers. The augur, which in this example was mounted on a CCKW, also was capable of general-purpose digging: for example, it could excavate foxholes in frozen ground at a rate of about six per hour. (Fred Crismon collection)

An earth borer is erected on the rear end of a closed-cab CCKW and has just begun to bore a hole in frozen ground. The man standing on the body to the left has his hands on the borer controls, while the man on the ground clears snow. (Fred Crismon collection)

Two members of the 634th Light Equipment Company, 327th Combat Engineers, Ninth Army, Pfc. Dominic B. Cassena, left, and Cpl. William Singer, operate an earth augur in frozen soil near Ederen, Germany, on 9 January 1945. (National Archives)

Water Purification Trucks

It is doubtful that any commodity is more valuable to any army than is pure drinking water. This seemingly simple statement has huge implications. While Hollywood has oft left the impression that troops in the field eagerly refill their canteens from convenient streams, or that somehow remarkably the water-supply system in bomb-shattered villages still work, these scenarios do not always play out in real life.

While the U.S. Army did procure mobile water purification equipment during WWI, very little of this equipment reached Europe, the U.S. instead relying upon equipment supplied by Allies, primarily Great Britain.

The lesson taught – that the U.S. military needed the organic ability to supply large quantities of troops in the field with potable water – was not lost. Soon efforts were underway to improve the wartime units produced by the Wallace and Tiernan Company. The result was an improved offering from that company, suitable for mounting in a 3½-ton truck, and featuring a 100 gallon per minute centrifugal pump, pressure sand filter, chlorinator and testing equipment.

This equipment was tested by the Army during 1922 and by the Marine Corps in 1923, and on 10 June 1924 was recommended for Standardization. Procurement of the gear was contemplated for fiscal year 1929. Prior to procurement, some changes were made, most notably mounting the gear on a 4x4 truck with pneumatic tires rather than a solid-tired 4x4 truck. Also, the purification equipment would be driven via PTO off the truck engine, rather than via its own powerplant. The new unit incorporating these as well as a few other changes was designated Water Purification Unit, Mobile, M-II on 12 April 1929.

Once fielded, using units began to encounter some difficulties, chief of these involving the chlorinator unit. Upon investigation, it was revealed that the operators were not following proper procedures, and further training was recommended. However, despite this admonition and modifications directed for the vehicles in the field, the M-II did not live up to expectations. Thus, in 1934 a new development project was initiated.

For this iteration of the mobile water purification system, the Engineers, who bore the responsibility for this and the preceding vehicles, reverted to a pump driven by its own engine. Also the contact tank used on earlier models was eliminated. The contact tank had functioned as a holding tank, allowing the chlorine additional time to act. Also the amount of water analysis equipment carried was reduced even further. It was decided that all of this gear would be mounted in a van-type body with a steel top and featuring large openings in the sides and rear. Those openings were to be covered by canvas with glassine windows.

The new equipment was first installed on a 2½-ton 4x2 cab over engine chassis. But this combination was found to lack suitable mobility. Accordingly, the outfit was mounted on the then-new 2½ ton 6x6 chassis coming into production. This combination tipped the scales at 15,400 pounds versus the 13,800 pound weight of the 4x2, although the all-wheel drive and increased number of tires more than made up for the gain in weight when it came to mobility.

With the design now established, three additional units were procured, which joined the prototype in field testing. These new units were dubbed Water Purification Unit, Mobile, M-III, Model 1938.

The field testing indicated that the design was basically sound, however a few minor modifications were indicated. With those changes made, the revised unit was designated Water Purification Unit,

This Water Purification Unit, Mobile, M3, Model 1940, was mounted on a GMC CCKWX. This particular truck was one of a batch of ten delivered in 1941. A total of 89 of the water purification trucks ordered that year. (National Archives)

Mobile, M-III, Model 1940. This unit could produce 75 gallons of potable water per minute, and utilized a Wisconsin model AB gasoline engine to drive the pump.

So refined, the M-III, or Mark 3, entered production. Twenty-four units were ordered on 24 July 1940, at a cost of $3,666 each, and were to be mounted on CCKW chassis furnished by the government, and thus not included in the cost amount stated. This order was followed by one for 25 units, placed on 21 July 1941, by which time the cost had risen to $4,182 each. Two days after Pearl Harbor an order was place for 44 further units, and before the end of the year another 20 had been placed on order. Wallace and Tiernan received orders for a further 442 during 1942, which were followed by 144 more in 1943. During 1944 a further 105 were placed on order, but contract terminations reduced the quantity actually produced to only 32.

While the equipment housed in these trucks changed little during the course of production, such was not the case for the bodies. The Army maneuvers of 1941 had pointed to the need for several changes in the body, which were implemented. This included, sliding windows with blackout curtains replacing the canvas windows; light-tight rear doors rather than canvas; the addition of a ventilation system; eliminating the skirting on the underside of the van body; and relocation of the suction inlet to the rear of the body.

With these changes in place, and full-scale production under way, there remained room for improvement. Some were relatively minor, such as refinements in the chlorine-metering assembly to reduce its vulnerability to bomb concussion. More drastic was the reinforcement of the truck frame. The Automotive Inspection Service at the New York Port of Embarkation reported that the chassis of the CCKW was too weak to allow the water purification trucks to be loaded and unloaded by means of slings. Also, the 80th Engineer Water Supply Battalion had found the frames to be too weak for off-road operation during maneuvers in 1942. The Engineer Board's Desert

Test Section developed three alternative methods of reinforcing the frame, all of which were approved by the Ordnance Department as field modifications.

Perhaps an even larger problem was reported by troops in the field. The specialized body of the Mark 3 was readily apparent to everyone around, including the enemy, whether they be on the ground or in the air. The mere fact that it was different made these vehicles priority targets, and some method of camouflage, even when in motion, was desired. One response to this request was to actually mount the purification equipment inside a standard long wheel base cargo truck, utilizing a skid.

Technicians at the Engineer Board's Desert Test Branch stripped the gear from a Mark 3 and set about creating a skid-mounted version of the water purification unit. Without the body of the truck, the Engineers had to development alternate means of bracing various components of the equipment. That said, no fundamental changes in the equipment were required, although some relocation of components was required, as were some changes in the plumbing. Once complete, the 107-inch long, 46 ¼" wide, 58 ¾ inch tall unit worked exactly as expected, and fit neatly into the back of a CCKW. The truck-unit combination also weighed 1,000 pounds less than did the conventional Mark 3 truck. Approval was given to obtain a pilot model of the skid-mounted unit from Wallace and Tiernan. C.B. Schumacher of that firm designed a pilot unit, very much following the lines of the experimental built by the Engineers. Tests of this unit indicated that it worked even better than the normal Mark 3. However, there was still some concern about the equipment being more exposed to the elements in a canvas-covered cargo truck as opposed to the enclosed body of the conventional unit. Further, by this time the Engineers had begun testing water purification equipment featuring diatomaceous silica as a filter medium, and elected not to pursue further development or procurement of the skid-mounted sand-filtered purification unit.

The water connections in these early trucks were on the side, and one is visible here just forward of and slightly above the rear side reflector. Later trucks had these connections in the rear. The large windows not only allowed light in (and, unfortunately, out) but also provided ventilation, important given that the crew was working with chlorine. (National Archives)

The heavy water purification equipment and body led to the chassis of the GMC being overloaded. The Engineer's Desert Test Center developed and approved three methods of reinforcing the frames in the field, including the technique shown here. (U.S. Army Engineer School History Office)

Water Purification Unit, Mobile, M3, Model 1940, U.S. Army registration number 605472, is an example of an early-type M3. A small, indistinguishable insignia is on the cab door. Purifying equipment is visible through the large windows. (Office of History, U.S. Army Corps of Engineers)

An engineer tends to the apparatus inside the body of a M3 mobile purification unit. This unit could purify 75 gallons of water per minute, or one gallon in a little over a second: a real boon to an army on campaign, dependent on a reliable supply of drinking water. (Office of History, U.S. Army Corps of Engineers)

Chapter 25
Army Medical Corps

While the Army Medical Department's use of ¾-ton Dodge ambulances during WWII is well known, less well known that the Department also used the versatile CCKW in many ways. The trucks were an integral part of field hospitals and laboratories, and even pushed across Europe as mobile service clubs, bring a touch of "back home" to soldiers weary of combat far from stateside comforts.

Clubmobiles

While the Army Medical Department fielded various types of CCKW through the years, arguably the most interesting of these were the Clubmobiles. Clubmobiles, the brain child of Commissioner of American Red Cross in Great Britain Harvey Gibson, had been in existence since late 1942. The mobile coffee and doughnut shops, staffed by women of the American Red Cross bore names of familiar U.S. cities. The earliest models were converted from a variety of vehicle types, British Fords, buses, etc., and provided an uplift to spirits of service men stationed in or passing through Great Britain.

As plans began to be made to invade continental Europe, General Eisenhower requested Commissioner Gibson provide Clubmobile service as soon as tactically possible after the landing. The Army believed that this service could reach more men if the Clubmobiles operated from Army and Corps Headquarters. To achieve this goal, it was planned that 10 Clubmobile Groups, each with eight Clubmobiles, one cinemobile, two cargo trucks, and three small support vehicles, be formed.

Field operations would require very different Clubmobiles than were being used in England. A more rugged vehicle, capable of operating in off-road conditions, would be required, along with portable electric generating facilities. The obvious choice for the chassis for new Clubmobile was the Army's jack of all trades, the CCKW – which unfortunately were in chronic short supply. Finally, an agreement was reached such that if the Red Cross would convert the Army-furnished CCKWs into ambulances, they could then be further converted into Clubmobiles, with the stipulation that should an emergency develop they could revert to ambulance configuration. The Army further would furnish two generator trailers and one 100-gallon water trailer to each Clubmobile group, along with two maintenance men. The

During preparations for the June 1944 invasion of Normandy, the U.S. Army requested that the American Red Cross organize a fleet of Clubmobiles to accompany the Army in the coming campaign to liberate Europe. Although there already had been Clubmobiles in England, converted from Green Line buses, these were big, unwieldy affairs, and the CCKW was selected as the chassis for a new type of Clubmobile because of its ability to navigate a variety of road conditions. The Army stipulated to the Red Cross that in order to use Army-supplied chassis the vehicles first had to be set up to use as ambulances, and then could be outfitted as Clubmobiles, so long as they could quickly revert to ambulance should the need arise. Clubmobiles served beverages and snacks and dispensed convenience items to the troops, provided a little entertainment and good cheer, and were a tremendous morale booster. These three Clubmobiles were with the Third Army in Germany. (General Motors)

American Red Cross Clubmobile girls would also serve as the truck's drivers, as well as performing first echelon maintenance.

By the end of March 1944 the new Clubmobiles had entered service. Their bodies, which were produced in Great Britain, held a complete kitchen with a doughnut machine, doughnut racks, six six-gallon coffee urns, a public address system and record player, and an assortment of records. Five 35-gallon water tanks near the ceiling and below the body supplied water to the stainless steel sink for use in making the pastries and coffee. A fifteen gallon water heater was provided. It was expected that a single such Clubmobile could furnish 150 men per hour with two doughnuts and coffee each.

The loading plan for the vehicles was such that each tipped the scales at 17,464 pounds, including truck, fuel, flour, coffee, sugar, soap, cigarettes and playing cards. Just as Eisenhower had wanted, the Clubmobiles arrived in France not long after the combat troops, the heavily-laden CCKWs driving across the Normandy beaches in July and August 1944, and moving with U.S. troops across Europe into Germany.

Surgical Trucks

More grim was the task of surgical trucks. In the fall of 1941 the Armored Force took it upon itself to develop a surgical truck for use as a mobile clearing station. During the first week of January 1942, the Surgeon General's Office was authorized to begin a research project in that field: Development Project F-15.03. Coordinated with these efforts was the development work of the Medical Department Equipment Laboratory. The pilot model was delivered to the Laboratory in July 1942, and was dubbed "Truck, Surgical." It was designed such that the truck body was to be the site of treatment, with the attached tent serving as a staging area for up to 20 litter-bound patients. When not in use the tent was stowed atop the truck cab. Inside the heater-equipped body was a 50-gallon water tank, a sink with hot and cold outlets, cabinets for supplies and equipment and two dome lights and one surgical operating light. These trucks were planned to be delivered

at a rate of six per division to all armored divisions in the United States during late 1942 and early 1943.

During the second half of 1943 a different type of surgical truck was developed for use by auxiliary surgical groups. It differed from the Armored Division model primarily in that treatment from this truck would be performed in the attached tent, with the truck itself carrying only the material – specifically enough equipment and instruments to perform 100 operations. These trucks would be utilized in extreme forward areas, and 207 of them had been delivered by the end of October 1945. The Medical Department also utilized mobile dental operating trucks and mobile dental and medical laboratory trucks, which used the same "Body, Medical Department Van, 2 ½ ton" as the surgical trucks.

Mobile Optical Truck

The U.S. Army's basis for planning during WWII (and for a couple of decades thereafter) was that they should plan for, and be equipped to, take everything for modern society with them. It was along those lines that in 1938 Alfred Turner Wells suggested that there be developed Mobile Optical Shops. In May 1942 the American Optical Company, a firm founded by Wells' grandfather, delivered the first of these trucks. The type was intended to serve the estimated 15% of U.S. servicemen who wore glasses. The first model was built on a cargo truck, and in addition to the equipment, was provisioned with 18,000 pairs of single vision lenses, 8,400 frames, 600 pairs of extra temples and 1,200 spectacle cases. No equipment was carried for examining eyes, the unit was solely to repair or replace damaged, previously prescribed lenses The crew and equipment could edge and mount 120 lenses per day, which was estimated to be adequate for a field army of 300,000 men. Later versions of the truck featured a van body rather than utilizing a cargo body as a basis. Not only was Wells presented a Legion of Merit for his design, he also was commissioned a Major and served in the Pacific as supervisory chief of the Army's optical repair and supply detachments.

Clubmobiles served in various theaters and assumed different guises. This improvised Clubmobile, featuring a roughly constructed screened-in club body with a gable roof, is prepared to dispense coffee and doughnuts to aviation engineer troops at Munda, New Georgia, in June 1944. (National Archives)

Red Cross worker Barbara Ridgway pours a cup of coffee for Cpl. Ben Baden in Luxembourg on 9 October 1944. Clubmobiles often were dubbed with nicknames, and this one was the "General Lee." On the average, one Clubmobile could furnish 150 men with two doughnuts each per hour. A Clubmobile fully loaded with flour, sugar, water, coffee, lard, cigarettes, soap, playing cards, and other typical supplies weighed 17,464 pounds. (National Archives)

Betty Holmes slogs through mud to pass a tray of fresh doughnuts up to Dee Kurtz in a Red Cross Clubmobile in France on 1 October 1944. The vehicle's nickname, "Topeka," is painted faintly on the body. Each CCKW-based Red Cross Clubmobile had a doughnut fryer, doughnut racks, six six-gallon coffee urns, a sink with running water, a 15-gallon water boiler, a portable M1937 cooking range, a record player with an exterior speaker, and a collection of records. (National Archives)

At a town in Luxembourg on 9 October 1944, G.I.s line up to enjoy coffee and doughnuts dispensed from the "General Lee." Clubmobiles constructed for the 1944–45 campaign in northwestern Europe were based on both closed-cab and, as seen here, open-cab CCKWs. Below the vent near the rear of the body is an access door for the cooking range. (National Archives)

A Red Cross Clubmobile is doing business in a village between Übach-Palenberg and Baesweiler, North Rhine-Westphalia, Germany, in January 1945. What appears to be a poster displaying insignia or symbols is visible on the inside of the door at the rear of the Clubmobile body. (National Archives)

Troopers of the 101st Airborne Division gather around an open-cab CCKW Clubmobile to enjoy hot coffee and fresh doughnuts in Fenetrange, France, while moving up to the front on 21 January 1945. Ten Clubmobile groups, designated by letters, were organized for the campaign in northwest Europe, each of which had eight Clubmobiles, one Cinemobile for showing movies, seven cargo trucks, two small Hillman pickup trucks, and one Jeep, as well as two generators on trailers and one 100-gallon water trailer. (National Archives)

American Red Cross Clubmobiles served not only U.S. servicemen, but also military personnel of other Allied nations. Here, "Green Devils" of No. 46 (Royal Marine) Commando, 1st Commando Brigade, wait their turns for coffee and doughnuts at a Clubmobile. The surname of the American Red Cross worker inside the Clubmobile was Swanson, from Fort Wayne, Indiana. (National Archives)

Troops of the 71st Infantry Regiment enjoy the comforts of an American Red Cross Clubmobile in the vicinity of Achen, Lorraine, France, on 12 March 1945. Written in faint block letters on the front of the body over the cab is "AMERICAN / RED CROSS / CLUBMOBILE." Each Clubmobile had five 35-gallon water tanks, at the top of the body and underneath the body. (National Archives)

German children are not getting much attention from members of the 35th Infantry Division, XIII Corps, Ninth Army, lined up for service at a Clubmobile in Sandbeindorf, Germany, in April 1945. Numerous markings are present on the side of the vehicle, including an insignia marked "UP FRONT / 1ST BN 405TH" and several place names in the States. (National Archives)

At an undisclosed location, combat troops wait for the serving to begin at a Clubmobile of Group C. Coffee urns are visible on the counter inside. Women who volunteered for Clubmobile service were mostly from the middle and upper classes and had to be strong and possess a good reserve of stamina and fearlessness, for they served near the battle fronts and had to endure many of the same privations and discomforts as the troops. (Fred Crismon collection)

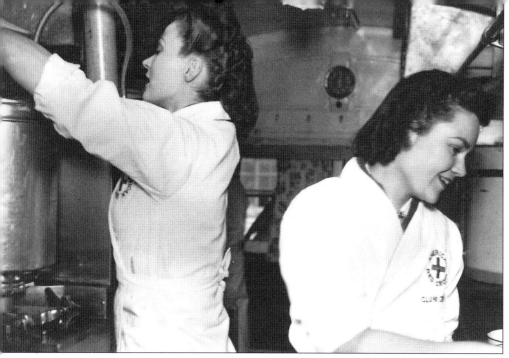

Two Clubmobile "Doughgirls" prepare coffee somewhere in Great Britain. The Red Cross volunteers of the CCKW-based Clubmobiles drove, maintained, and performed basic repairs on their vehicles. Before departing for the Continent, they underwent a training course in England wherein they learned how to drive and maintain these vehicles.

In the fall of 1941, the Armored Force began developing a surgical truck, and in August 1942, that force conducted trials at Fort Knox, Kentucky, to investigate the suitability of a CCKW-based surgical truck and tent for operational use. Here, mechanics work on the wheels of one such truck. (Patton Museum)

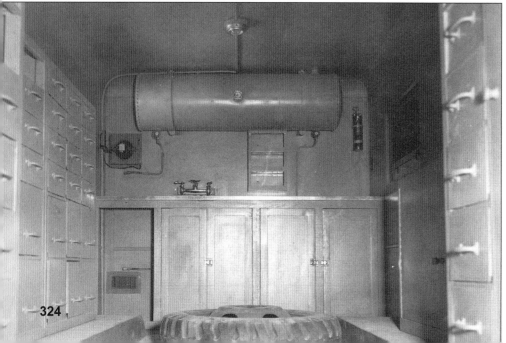

The interior of the surgical truck, viewed through the rear door, included a 50-gallon water tank, a sink with hot and cold water taps, cabinets and drawers for medical supplies and equipment, and lights powered by a 6-volt system. The spare tire was not normally stored inside. (National Archives via Jim Gilmore)

This was the surgical tent used in conjunction with the CCKW surgical truck during the August 1942 suitability tests at Fort Knox. The view is of the rear of the tent, showing the rear entrance, equipped with a blackout fly. (National Archives via Jim Gilmore)

Above: The CCKW surgical truck is backed into the surgical tent; the tent side wall has been rolled up to show the position of the truck. Marked on the driver's door of the CCKW is "MEDICAL DEPARTMENT / U.S. ARMY." (National Archives via Jim Gilmore)

Right: Protruding from the front of the surgical body above the cab was a combination heater that heated both the interior of the surgical body and water for the sink. Ventilation flaps on the tent are held open with lines. (National Archives via Jim Gilmore)

The 1st Armored Division was instrumental in early efforts to develop a surgical truck. The division produced this one-off, improvised example in 1942. It featured a windowless body mounted on a long-wheelbase CCKW with an enclosed cab. (National Archives via Jim Gilmore)

The Surgeon General of the United States provided the design for the standardized surgical truck. Based on the CCKW chassis, it featured a body with side windows, curved cutouts for the tandem wheels, and an air/water heater. (National Archives via Jim Gilmore)

The surgical truck improvised by the 1st Armored Division is viewed from the rear with a tent attached to the side. Inside, a surgeon is working on a "patient." Markings for the 47th Medical Battalion are on the left bumperette, and the insignia of the 1st Armored Division is on the right bumperette. (National Archives via Jim Gilmore)

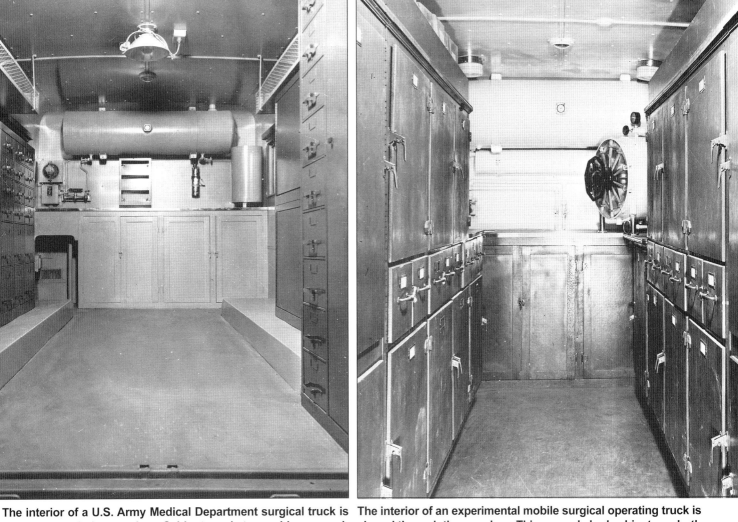

The interior of a U.S. Army Medical Department surgical truck is viewed through the rear door. Cabinets and storage bins on each side held medical equipment and supplies. At the upper front of the compartment was a water tank. At the center of the ceiling was an operating lamp. (National Archives via Jim Gilmore)

The interior of an experimental mobile surgical operating truck is viewed through the rear door. This example had cabinets on both sides extending almost to the ceiling. An electric fan rests on the counter at the front of the compartment. (National Archives via Jim Gilmore)

Elements of a mobile surgical operating unit are deployed. These included a CCKW surgical truck, a trailer, and a tent. Marked on the truck are red crosses and "MEDICAL DEPARTMENT / U.S. ARMY." Mounted in the front of the trailer is a generator. (National Archives via Jim Gilmore)

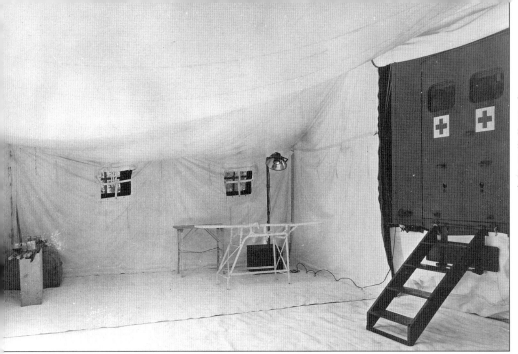

The interior of the surgical tent was a very light color and was fitted with a floor and small windows. To the right is the rear of a surgical truck with steps attached. Set up in the corner is a portable operating lamp and an operating table. (National Archives via Jim Gilmore)

A U.S. Army Medical Department surgical truck is observed from the rear. At the lower center of the body is a folding step with a diamond-tread pattern. The rear doors were hung on piano hinges and had small windows. (National Archives via Jim Gilmore)

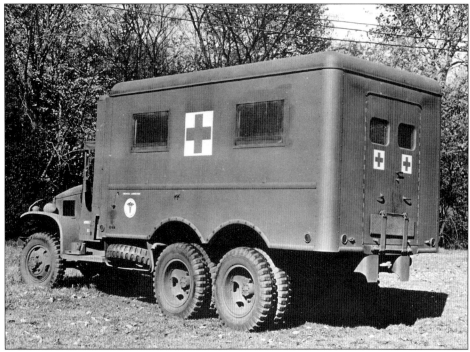

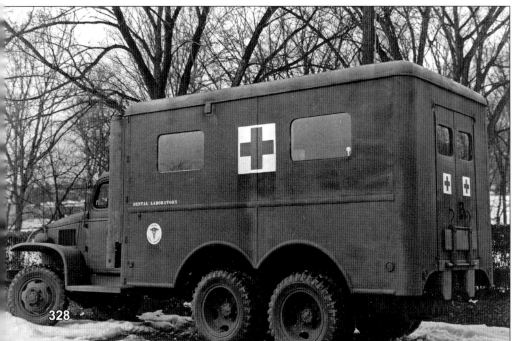

The Army was slow in developing dental operating trucks, but it finally let a contract for 107 dental lab trucks, such as the one shown here, in December 1943. Staffed by an officer and four men, these units delivered dental prosthetic services to troops in isolated and forward areas. (National Archives via Jim Gilmore)

There were variations in the interiors of thee surgical trucks. This one was equipped as a medical laboratory. Lockers and filing cabinets with a counter on top are on each side. To the front of the compartment, water faucets are visible atop the counter, and a water tank is above. (National Archives via Jim Gilmore)

The inside of a mobile dental laboratory is shown. These vehicles made it possible to fit or repair dental replacements in the field: a procedure that formerly required sending the patient to a dental facility in a rear area for a week or more at a time. (National Archives via Jim Gilmore)

This vehicle, U.S. Army registration number 4165275, was designated a dental operating truck and was equipped for performing dental operations and surgeries. Development of these units came late, with the first purchase order, for 35 units, being placed in June 1944. (National Archives via Jim Gilmore)

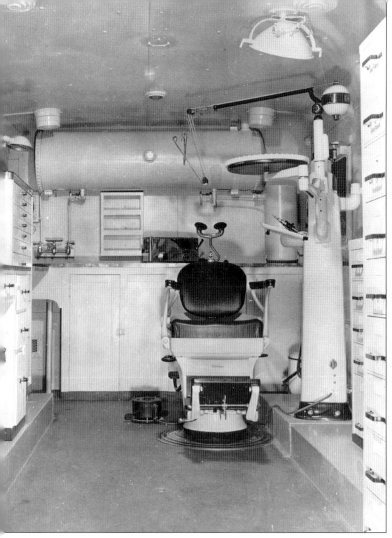

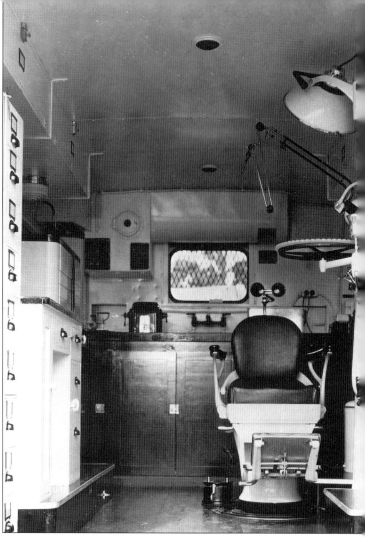

Equipment found inside the body of the dental operating truck included a dental chair, overhead operating lamp, sterilizer, and dental appliance stand with drills mounted on flex arms, along with the typical sink, water tank, cabinets, and drawers. (National Archives via Jim Gilmore)

The interior of the USAAF dental operating truck was similar to the one shown at left except for a few details, such as the lack of a water tank at the upper front of the compartment and the presence of storage lockers to each side of the ceiling. (National Archives via Jim Gilmore)

The U.S. Army Air Forces used this type of dental operating truck to bring dental services to its frontline personnel. The body lacked some of the accessories that were present on the preceding photo of a dental operating truck, such as the external heater, and had more windows. (National Archives via Jim Gilmore)

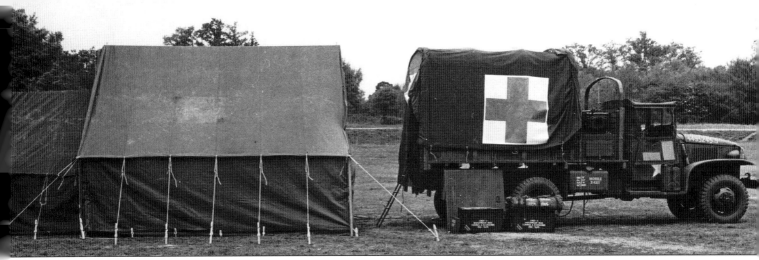

Above: The U.S. Army Medical Department fielded mobile x-ray laboratories based on the long-wheelbase CCKW chassis. It featured a tarpaulin-enclosed body, to the front of which was mounted a generator unit. A large tent and other equipment were part of the unit.

Right: This view is through a tent set up to the rear of a mobile x-ray laboratory, with the rear of the mobile lab in the background. In World War II, the main use of x-ray equipment in forward areas was to disclose fractures and localize foreign bodies such as bullets and splinters.

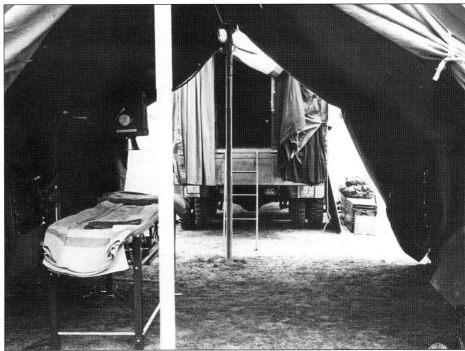

The generator unit to the rear of the cab of a mobile x-ray unit is observed from the right side. It supplied electrical power for the x-ray apparatus and film-processing accessories and was mounted on top of a wooden locker with a door on the side.

Part of the equipment of a mobile x-ray unit was a field x-ray film drier, here. Other accessories for developing film included a stainless steel processing tank and a water-conditioning unit to maintain the film-developing solutions at a constant temperature.

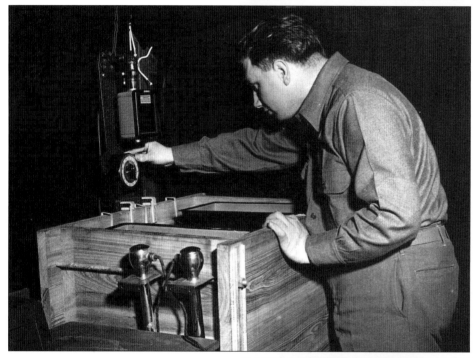

A technician of a field x-ray unit demonstrates the development of the transparencies.

An officer confers with members of a field x-ray unit. The crates on the ground contained shockproof x-ray head controls and accessories.

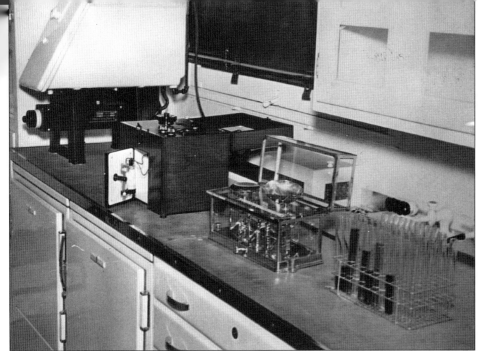

Items and equipment on top of a counter in the interior of a mobile laboratory are viewed. In the foreground is a test-tube rack.

Equipment in the Cleaver-Brooks mobile chemical and bacteriological lab is shown. It is not clear if this was the one-off mobile chemical-bacteriological lab the Quartermaster Corps ordered to do testing at over 100 canning plants around the United States in 1944.

A technician handles specimen jars in the Cleaver-Brooks mobile chemical and bacteriological laboratory. The plate at the top identifies the unit by purpose and manufacturer.

Because approximately 15 percent of U.S. servicemen wore corrective eyeglasses, mobile optical units were developed to supply eyeglasses and optometric services to troops in the field. Various vehicles, including CCKWs, were fitted out as mobile optical shops, such as this one photographed in Massachusetts in April 1942. (General Motors)

Right: Optical equipment such as edgers, cutters, drills, lensometers, and stock cabinets were carried on the vehicle, while work benches were set up adjacent to it. It had facilities for edging and mounting up to 120 lenses per day. The staffs of these vehicles, however, did not conduct optical exams. (General Motors)

Below: On 30 April 1942, Capt. Joseph R. Harrison, commander of the original mobile optical unit, tests the edging equipment on an optical truck during a demonstration at Southbridge, Massachusetts, home of the American Optical Company, which built the mobile shop. (General Motors)

The stock cabinets on the mobile optical shop could hold a whopping 18,000 pairs of lenses, 8,400 frames, 600 pairs of extra temples, and 1,200 eyeglass cases. The mobile optical shop was designed by Turner Wells, secretary of the American Optical Company. (General Motors)

Mounted on an open-cab CCKW is a mobile optical-shop body. In addition to the red crosses identifying this as a medical vehicle, marked on the body is the caduceus insignia of the U.S. Army Medical Department, above which is stenciled in white "OPTICAL REPAIR / UNIT." (National Archives via Jim Gilmore)

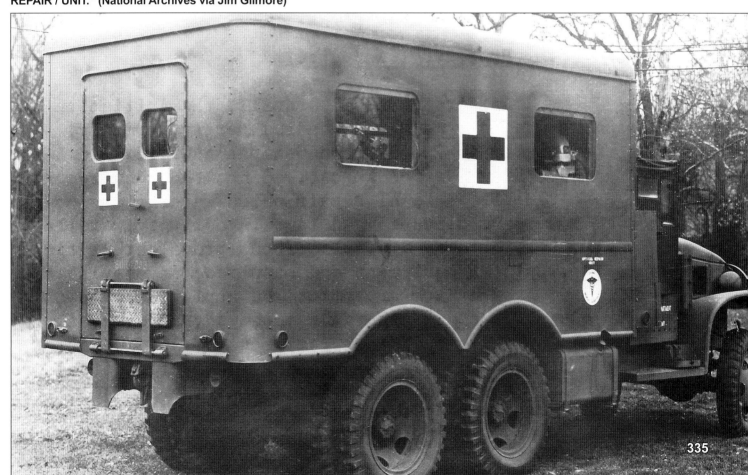

The interior of an optical-shop body is viewed through the rear door. On the bench to the right are lens grinders. Drawers and cabinets held thousands of corrective eyeglass parts, supplies, and tools. At the front of the compartment is a sink, above which is a water tank. (National Archives via Jim Gilmore)

Chapter 26
Ordnance Shop Trucks

The U.S. Army uses a myriad of equipment; beyond those shown on the preceding pages add rifles, tank, artillery, radios and a host of other gear. But for Engineer equipment, the responsibility of maintaining most of this material is the responsibility of the Ordnance Department (renamed the Ordnance Corps 28 June 1950). To perform this mission, a range of specialized shop trucks were developed.

Through the 1930s, these trucks were field-created by the troops as-needed. But in October 1939 the Ordnance Field Service School, using the field-improvised trucks as a guide, designed and procured a series of maintenance trucks. Three types were involved; the Artillery Repair Truck, mounted in a GMC 1½-3-ton COE 4x4 with cargo-type bed; the Small Arms Repair Truck, which utilized the same chassis but featured a school-bus style body; and the Automotive Repair Shop, Machine Shop and Welding Truck, which again used the same chassis, but featured a Brooks raising top body. This body, when raised, was enclosed with canvas side curtains. The generator and welder in this truck were PTO-driven from the GMC's engine.

By December of the following year 1,866 of these trucks were in use in the field, and it was rapidly becoming apparent that the school bus-type enclosed body was superior to the other body styles used. Therefore, work was started on the redesign of these trucks, all utilizing the school bus type body. Ultimately 12 layouts, or "loads" were developed, each of which would equip a vehicle for the repair of various material.

However, these efforts were short-lived, as the 1941 Maneuvers showed that the 1½-ton COE was inadequate for the task at hand.

The vehicles proved to be top-heavy, and thus easily overturned, underpowered, lacked floatation in soft soil, and had inadequate payload capacity. On 14 October Major W. G. Donald of the Ordnance Department wrote to the Quartermaster General requesting that an experimental Ordnance Repair Shop be procured featuring a van-type body mounted on the long-wheelbase CCKW chassis. The Quartermaster would have the van delivered to Raritan Arsenal for installation there of the mounted equipment by the Shops Division.

On 25 November 1941 this project moved ahead, with Yellow Truck and Coach being directed that one truck less body on Contract 10250, previously directed to be delivered to the Buda Company, Harvey, Illinois, was instead to be completed not only without body, but also without the fuel tank, spare tire carrier and battery carrier. This truck was instead to be delivered to Superior Coach Corp., Lima, Ohio. At $676.00, Superior had been the second-lowest bidder for construction of the experimental van body, which was later designated ST-4. The Perley A. Thomas Car Works, of High Point, North Carolina, had been the low bidder, but Superior offered more advantageous delivery time.

Following standard procedure of the time, the Quartermaster Corps was to procure both the chassis and the body when the vehicles were to go into production. However, as fate would have it, Ordnance was directed to procure the bodies themselves. In January 1942, this responsibility fell to Raritan Arsenal, which was also charged with obtaining the tools and equipment to be mounted therein. The van body was changed slightly to include a more efficient gasoline-fired heater, improved lighting and blackout lighting and curtains. The new

Although mobile-shop bodies were mounted on U.S. 4x4 trucks in the late 1930s, the 1940 army maneuvers disclosed a need to develop mobile shops on 6x6 trucks to keep up with the demands of modern warfare. In January 1942 the Ordnance Department received orders to procure such a body, designated the ST-5. (U.S. Army Engineer School History Office)

body was designated ST-5, and it entered production in June 1942.

Seventeen equipment loads were laid out which could be enveloped by the Superior-built ST-5 body. These bodies were under contract 727-ORD-2590 for 2,050 units and 45 more on contract 727-ORD-285.

Listed here are the types, their Standard Nomenclature List numbers, and quantities produced:

Type	SNL	Qty
Artillery Repair, M9	SNL-G-140	124
Automotive Load "A", M8	SNL-G-139	167
Automotive Load "B", M8	SNL-G-13	51
Electrical Repair, M18	SNL-G-149	34
Instrument Repair, Load "A", M10	SNL-G-141	52
Instrument Repair, Load "B" M10	SNL-G-141	23
Machine Shop, Load "A", M16	SNL-G-146	193
Machine Shop, Load "B", M16	SNL-G-146	12
Machine Shop, Load "C", M16	SNL-G-146	14
Machine Shop, Load "D", M16	SNL-G-146	5
Machine Shop, Load "F", M16	SNL-G-146	5
Small Arms Repair, M7	SNL-G-138	264
Small Arms Repair (Signal Corps), M7	SNL-G-138	115
Spare Parts, Load "A", M14	SNL-G-144	51
Spare Parts, Load "B", M14	SNL-G-144	80
Tool and Bench, M13	SNL-G-143	98
Welding Repair, M12	SNL-G-142	190

By July 1942 the Army was making a deliberate effort to reduce the shipping cubage of all their vehicles, and the big, boxy shop vans were a prime target. Raritan Arsenal set out to redesign the van body. The result of this was the ST-6, which while looking very similar to the ST-5, featured a belt about two feet tall, which included the van window area, that could be removed from around the body, stowed inside and the roof reinstalled lower to reduce overseas shipping space. It was intended that once in Theater the belt would be installed in position, and that the truck would spend the rest of its life with the van body in the full-height configuration. The prototype of the ST-6 was displayed at the Army War College in October 1942, and quickly adopted. The ST-6 bodies were produced by Perley Thomas, High Point, NC; Hackney Brothers Body Company, Wilson, NC; Hicks, Lebanon, IN; and Phillips and Buttorff, of Nashville, TN.

The quantities and contracts for these bodies are listed here:

Make	Qty	Contract
Hicks	3,277	727-ORD-3078
Hicks	1,026	294-ORD-2556
Thomas	1,000	727-ORD-3079
Thomas	1,500	727-ORD-3942
Thomas	691	670-ORD-4809
Hackney	354	727-ORD-3943
Hackney	449	727-ORD-3944
Hackney	490	670-ORD-4806
P & B	1,500	727-ORD-3941
P & B	810	294-ORD-2555

The steel shortage that resulted in cargo trucks adopting wooden bodies also led to the design of the composite ST-7 and ST-8 van bodies, but work was halted on these early in the design stage as the steel crisis passed.

Like other special-purpose trucks, the shop trucks were perceived as high-value targets. In order to mask their true purpose, early in the ST-6 production the design was modified. Added near the top of the bodies were brackets which allowed bows to be secured. Over

The ST-5 mobile-shop body was reminiscent of a school-bus body, with its plentiful side windows divided by pillars. The ST-5 body included a gasoline-fired heater, a ventilator, interior lighting, including blackout lights, and blackout curtains. (Fred Crismon collection)

the bows would be installed a canvas tarp, which stretched down the side of the truck, allowing it to masquerade as a cargo truck. This arrangement also had the added benefit of adding another layer of insulation in the winter; in summer, the canvas side flaps could be raised, forming awnings that shielded the van body from the heat of the sun. Philadelphia's Mobile Shop Unit prepared a pilot design of this arrangement in April 1943.

With the adoption of the ST-6 body, the load list was revised. The new list included the following loads, shown here with their Standard Nomenclature List numbers and quantity produced:

Artillery Repair, M9A1	SNL-G-140	259
Automotive Load "A", M8A1	SNL-G-139	547
Automotive Load "B", M8A1	SNL-G-139	256
Electrical Repair, M18A2	SNL-G-149	682
Instrument Repair, Load "A," M10A1	SNL-G-141	624
Instrument Bench, M23	SNL-G-178	199
Machine Shop, Load "A," M16A1 & M16A2	SNL-G-146	1,804
Machine Shop, Load "B", M16A1	SNL-G-146	201
Machine Shop, Load "C", M16A1	SNL-G-146	117
Machine Shop, Load "D", M16A1	SNL-G-146	47
Machine Shop, Load "F", M16A1	SNL-G-146	47
Small Arms Repair, M7A1 & M7A2	SNL-G-138	2,314
Small Arms Repair (Signal Corps), M7A1	SNL-G-138	2,039
Welding Repair, M12A1	SNL-G-142	619
Signal Corps, M30	SNL-G-235	886

The models below were produced only with Hicks and Krieger bodies. Hicks was working under contract 33-008-847; and Krieger, based on Long Island, was under contract 30-069-2568.

Signal Corps, General Repair, M31	SNL-G-229	?
Tire Repair, Load "A", M32	SNL-G-234	20
Tire Repair, Load "B", M32	SNL-G-234	20
Tire Repair Trailer Load "A", M25	SNL-G-234	20
Tire Repair Trailer Load "B", M25	SNL-G-234	20

Hicks and Krieger also produced 12 M23 Instrument Bench trucks and 30 Machine Shop, Load "B," M16A2.

Even the Army felt that this list was growing unwieldy, and in May-June 1943 a conference was held to study the possibility of eliminating some models and placing others in standard cargo trucks rather than in the special van bodies. Included in this study was the ¾-ton Emergency Repair Truck.

This study resulted in the creation of Ordnance Maintenance Sets "A" through "L." These sets replaced or supplemented the Emergency Repair Truck, Spare Parts Truck, Tool and Bend Truck, Artillery Repair Truck, Machine Shop loads C, D, and F, and the welding truck.

The new maintenance sets A and B utilized a ¾-ton truck, while set C had large cabinets and replaced the 2½-ton Spare Parts Truck, Load "B." The new set D had smaller cabinets and replaced the 2½-ton Spare Parts Truck, Load "A." These two loads were developed by the Engineering Division at Raritan Arsenal in July 1942. At about the same time, set "E" was developed to replace the "Tool and Bench Truck, M13." Set F was a replacement for the Artillery Repair Truck.

Further Ordnance Maintenance sets replaced Machine Shop Loads C, D, and F. Ordnance Maintenance Set G had a milling machine, while set H featured a bandsaw and 1-inch floor-mounted drill press, set K featured an air compressor and tools, as well as a 60-ton capacity hydraulic press, and set L was a welding outfit. In addition to creating the sets A through L, the study also resulted in other variants being reclassified as Limited Standard. By the late 1940s the list of shop

An ST-5 shop body is mounted on an open-cab CCKW-353-A2chassis. A key difference between the ST-5 shop body and the later ST-6 shop body was that the ST-6 had highly visible horizontal moldings across the front of the body in line with the tops and the bottoms of the side windows, and theST-5 lacked these moldings.

trucks had been reduced to:

Artillery Repair, M9A1	SNL-G-140
Electrical Repair, M18A2	SNL-G-149
Instrument Repair, Load "A", M10A1	SNL-G-141
Instrument Bench, M23	SNL-G-178
Machine Shop, Load "A", M16A2	SNL-G-146
Machine Shop, Load "B", M16A1	SNL-G-146
Signal Corps, Repair, M7A2	SNL-G-138
Signal Corps, General Repair, M31	SNL-G-229
Tire Repair, Load "A", M32	SNL-G-234
Tire Repair, Load "B", M32	SNL-G-234

By October 1942, the task of outfitting the shop trucks was overwhelming the personnel at Raritan, and interfering with other work there. To rectify this, the Philadelphia Ordnance District contracted with the Thornton-Fuller Company for the outfitting of the shop trucks. To do this work, the company took over the Philadelphia Convention Hall and Commercial Museum. The operation therein was known as the Mobile Shop Depot and Thornton-Fuller worked under the direction of the Industrial Service Division of the Tank-Automotive Center. The facility operated until August 1944. In 1944 and 1945 Krieger Steel Sections, Inc. began turning out the trucks.

The ST-6 was further refined along the way, dividing the group into what was referred to as "old style" and "new style." A subsequent comparison test, Project 2128/8-9-3, was authorized on 19 August 1943, and a study of the two types conducted beginning 7 October 1943. As defined by the report of these tests: "The old type body has single pane safety glass windows and less insulation of the body proper than the new type ST-6 body which has double pane safety glass windows, felt insulating material between the outside body sheets and the internal members, and insulation under the floor." Both were equipped with the Evans Model MV203010 gasoline-fired heater.

This test compared the insulating values of the two types, and it is emphasized that this test compared production examples of both types – indicating that the "new style" was by then in production. The truck with registration number 0019352 was equipped with Hicks Body Company body 4589, while CCKW registration number 0013829 was furnished with Perley Thomas body 13533. A an adjunct to this test, a fabric duct extension was developed, that would direct the warm air flowing from the heater to a point near the floor. This, combined with the improved insulation, partially solved the cold floor problem which had plagued the earlier shop trucks when operating in below-zero conditions.

Raritan Arsenal completed 1,478 shop vans on CCKW chassis and 82 on Studebaker US6 chassis. The Philadelphia Mobile Shop Depot produced considerably more, with 1,455 on the Studebaker chassis, and a whopping 10,631 on the CCKW chassis. Krieger Steel Sections produced 232 complete shops, plus 129 van-only trucks. Hicks Body Company delivered to the Corps of Engineers 519 van only trucks.

The general utility of the van truck itself was such that the vehicle was standardized, without tool equipment, as "Truck, 2½-ton, 6x6, Shop Van, M535, SNL-G-227" per OCM 28591.

The right interior side of the ST-5 body of a Truck, Automotive Repair, M8 (Load A) is viewed in a 29 August 1942 photograph. The bench was a Type 9 Class B. Overhead are lamps and electrical receptacles. Blackout curtain housings are above the windows. (TACOM LCMC History Office)

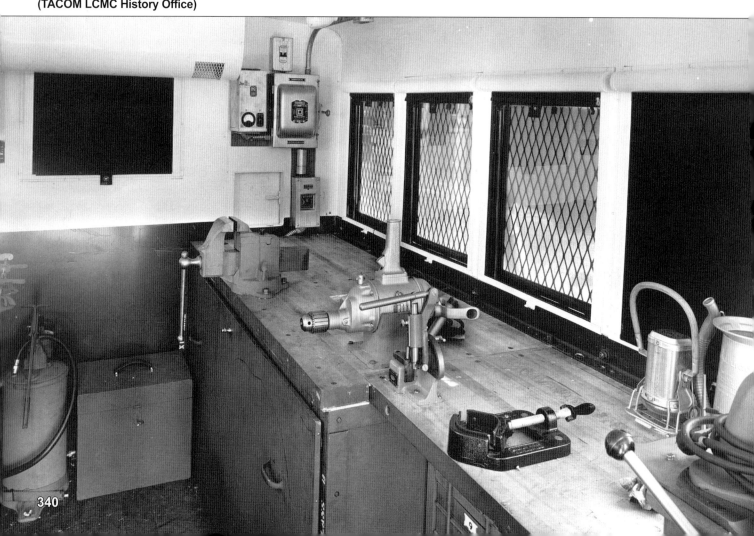

The ST-5 bodies were fitted-out with at least 17 special-purpose variants, carrying a variety of equipment suites called loads, depending on the vehicle's mission. These were dedicated to the specialized repair of automotive systems, small arms, automotive electronics, fire-control instrument, and more. This example was designated Truck, Small Arms Repair (Signal Corps), M7. (TACOM LCMC History Office)

The interior of this Truck, Small Arms Repair (Signal Corps), M7 lacks the portable Homelite generator seen in the forward end of the similar ST-5 body in the preceding photo. On the forward end of the left workbench is ⅜-inch portable drill on a press stand. A bench grinder is partially visible at the front of the right bench, and both benches have a vise. Numbered parts drawers are below the benches. (TACOM LCMC History Office)

The interior of a Truck, Instrument Repair, M10 (Load A) was photographed in August 1942. It was fitted with specialized tools and equipment to repair fire-control instruments in the field. To the front of the bench on the left is a 010-inch bench lathe. (TACOM LCMC History Office)

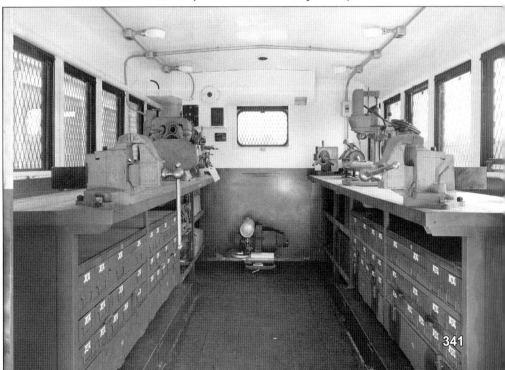

This ST-5 body is configured as a Truck, Automotive Repair, M8 (Load B). A bench and cabinet across the front of the compartment house a welding generator, controls for which are on the cabinet's right side. The shop van's bare wood floor made for bitterly cold working conditions in frigid areas. (TACOM LCMC History Office)

The interior of the Truck, Artillery Repair, M9, had a workbench on the right. The bars below the bench secured the parts drawers shut. On the forward bulkhead were the heater and its control panel. In the left side of the compartment are rope coils and a chain come-along. (TACOM LCMC History Office)

This Truck, Welding, M12, photographed in June 1942, bore U.S. Army registration number 488928. The tire carriers on the ST-5 bodies were a special design with a mounting plate on hinged legs that swung down for ease of retrieving the tire. (Fred Crismon collection)

At the rear of the welding table, to the left, inside the body of this Truck, Welding, M12, is one of two racks for oxy-acetylene bottles. An anvil is on a pedestal fastened the floor. A vise is mounted at the far end of the passenger's side workbench. On the workbench at front is a bench grinder. (TACOM LCMC History Office)

The interior of the ST-5 body of the Truck, Spare Parts, M14, Load A, included cabinets with parts drawers and lockers on each side, for dispensing parts for maintaining and repairing vehicles in the field. In the foreground are cage-type stowage racks. (TACOM LCMC History Office)

This interior pertains to the Truck, Tool & Bench, M13, as photographed on 15 August 1942. To the right is a bench grinder with a lamp. On the floor at the front of the compartment is a portable toolbox. (TACOM LCMC History Office)

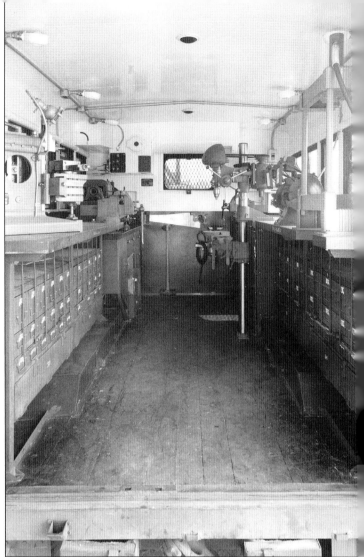

The ST-5 body of the Truck, Spare Parts, M14 (Load B-1) had a row of sheet-metal lockers on each side. They were mounted on stanchions, the bottoms raised off the floor to clear the tops of the wheel wells. The locker doors are marked Type 2 Class A. (TACOM LCMC History Office)

The Truck, Machine Shop, M16 (Load A) featured parts drawers and a workbench on each side of the compartment. Jutting from the forward end of the right workbench is a turret drill press, while to the front of the left workbench is a lathe. (TACOM LCMC History Office)

The Type 5, Class 1 bench and the numbered drawers bench are shown in the Truck, Electrical Repair, M18, which was based on the ST-5 shop body. Under the front end of the bench is a gasoline-engine-driven, 10-kilowatt electrical generator. (TACOM LCMC History Office)

Bolted to the floor of this Truck, Machine Shop, M16 (Load C) are a milling machine and, to the front of it, a band saw. A high-gloss enamel, apparently white or off-white, was used on most of the interior surfaces of the shop body. Parts drawers are to the far right. (TACOM LCMC History Office)

The Truck, Machine Shop, M16 (Load D), as photographed on 22 September 1944, had a floor-mounted drill press, to the front of which was a floor-mounted grinder. Partially visible on top of the parts cabinet to the far right is a 7½-inch horizontal metal shaper. (TACOM LCMC History Office)

French troops unbox a CCKW with a shop body that has been delivered to a dock in Algeria on 17 April 1943. This photo illustrates the greatest liability of the ST-5 shop body as mounted on the CCKW: it was much taller than the enclosed-cab CCKW, and it took up a lot of space when transported on a ship. (National Archives)

Mounted on the floor of the shop body of Truck, Machine Shop, M16 (Load F) is a hydraulic press, to the right of which is an air receiver. In the enclosure at lower front is an air compressor. The V-8 gasoline engine at left drives the compressor at right, which was manufactured from a similar block as the engine. (TACOM LCMC History Office)

Above: To address the problem of efficiently and economically shipping shop-body CCKWs, the ST-6 body was developed. This body had a collapsible roof, as shown here in a 22 November 1942 photo, which rendered the top of the shop body only slightly taller than the roof of the CCKW cab. (National Archives)

Left: The ST-6 body was placed in operating condition by raising the roof and installing windows, pillars, and body panels to support the roof. When the roof was collapsed, the pillars, windows, panels, and doors were stored in boxes inside the body, and a shorter, temporary door was installed in the rear. (Barton College)

CCKW chassis are lined up at a facility for installing shop bodies. U.S. Army registrations visible on vehicles to the left include 0012931, 0013418, and 0012957. The fuel tanks were removed, as the trucks would receive special new ones to accompany the shop bodies. (Barton College)

347

Above: Not all U.S. military equipment losses were the result of enemy action. This photo shows the aftermath of a fire at Hackney Brothers, builders of shop bodies for CCKWs in North Carolina, in which some trucks in the process of receiving the bodies were destroyed. Hackney produced 1,293 ST-6 bodies from March 1943 to April 1944. (Barton College)

Left: A CCKW-353 with an ST-6 shop body is viewed from the rear. The grates over the windows helped protect the glazing from damage. Affixed to the bumperettes were extension plates, each of which was attached with four bolts. (U.S. Army Engineer School History Office)

A wealth of information is stenciled on this shop body, including that the CCKW-353 chassis was serial number 186645-2, powered by GMC 270 engine serial number 270184125, and that the body was the ST-6 model made by the Hicks Body Company, with no designated type assigned as of yet. The heater was by the Evans Products Company. (U.S. Army Engineer School History Office)

A CCKW-353 with an ST-6 shop body is viewed from the rear. The grates over the windows helped protect the glazing from damage. Affixed to the bumperettes were extension plates, each of which was attached with four bolts. (U.S. Army Engineer School History Office)

Above: The same CCKW-353 with an ST-6 shop body seen in the two preceding photos is viewed from the right side. Some ST-6 bodies were fitted with a door at the lower front corner of the right side for accessing an electrical generator inside the body in that area. (U.S. Army Engineer School History Office)

Left: A Truck, Signal Repair, M30 with an ST-6 shop body was photographed at Raritan Arsenal, Metuchen, New Jersey, on 21 June 1944. Much of the work of designing the U.S. Army's shop bodies was carried out at the Raritan Arsenal. (National Archives)

The interior of a Truck, Signal Repair, M30, is viewed through the rear door in a 29 June 1944 photograph. It provided facilities for repairing Signal Corps equipment in the field and was fitted with parts drawers, workbenches, and machinery such as a bench grinder and a portable drill and drill stand. (National Archives)

Left: In this small-arms signal repair truck, the cage that served to guard the drawers from damage and to hold them closed has been removed. In addition, the blackout shades have been drawn. The bench top was made of laminated hardwood. (National Archives)

Right: To cope with the problems of large numbers of tires that required repairing in operational areas around the world, the Truck, Tire Repair, 2½-ton, 6x6, M32 was developed. It was available in Load A and Load B configurations. Hoops were provided on top of the body for a camouflage tarpaulin, since shop trucks were one of the types of vehicles the enemy specifically targeted. (National Archives)

Left: As an accessory for the Truck, Tire Repair, 2½-ton, 6x6, M25, several configurations of 1-ton, two-wheeled trailers were developed to transport equipment essential to tire-repair operations. This M25 (Load A) trailer is transporting an electrical generator. (National Archives)

Another configuration of the M25 (Load A) trailer is shown with racks inserted, and bows on top to support a tarpaulin. A detachable caster wheel on the front of the draw bar supported the hitch when the trailer was not coupled to a truck. (National Archives)

This is the Trailer, Tire Repair, 1-ton, 2-wheel, M25 (Load B), developed for use with the M25 tire-repair truck. A rack is fitted to the trailer, and bows for a tarpaulin are inserted into pockets attached to the tops of the stakes. (National Archives)

A .50-caliber ring-mount machine gun was installed on this ordnance maintenance truck photographed on 28 April 1944. The door with the grille on the lower front corner of the side of the body and the exhaust and grille on the front right side of the body were associated with an onboard generator. (TACOM LCMC History Office)

Left: The same ordnance maintenance truck is viewed from the right side. Ordnance maintenance trucks worked in forward areas to restore to service vehicles and equipment without having to resort to sending the materiel to rear areas for the same services. (TACOM LCMC History Office)

Right: The ordnance maintenance truck is observed from the left rear. The U.S. Army registration number, 6097429, is faintly visible on the right rear door. The louvered panel above the front window of the body is the air intake for the heater. (TACOM LCMC History Office)

Below: The top of the ST-6 shop body of the ordnance maintenance truck was fairly simple, with two lengthwise hat-channel stiffeners. Details of the ring and the three support arms of the .50-caliber machine gun ring mount are also visible. (TACOM LCMC History Office)

Above: In a view of the ordnance maintenance truck from the left side, the spare tire and its holder are below the front of the shop body. Two universal rifle brackets, each with an M-1903 Springfield rifle installed, are visible in the rear of the cab. (TACOM LCMC History Office)

Right: The same ordnance maintenance truck, U.S.A. 6097429, is seen from the front. Visible on the right front of the shop body are the generator exhaust and muffler and a grille for the generator. At the center of the shop body is a window with protective grille. (TACOM LCMC History Office)

Left: Because the ordnance maintenance truck did not have an exposed rear cross sill, which on CCKW cargo trucks housed the tail lights and trailer receptacle, the fixtures were mounted on panels under the body, to the rear of the mud flaps. The rear doors are unequal in size and there is an operating handle on the right door only. (TACOM LCMC History Office)

Left: In a view of the interior of an ordnance truck, a bench lathe is on the forward right workbench. A ½-inch drill press is partway down the right side of the compartment. In the right foreground is a hydraulic push-pull jack. To the right and left, blackout curtains are pulled down on the windows in the doors. (TACOM LCMC History Office)

Right: The right side of the same ordnance maintenance truck is viewed from the rear door, giving a better view of the hydraulic push-pull jack to the far right. Between the jack and the ½-inch drill press is a bench grinder. A handsaw and a sledgehammer are stowed on the front bulkhead. (TACOM LCMC History Office)

Left: The full extent of the benches, cabinets, drawers, and machinery on the right side of the ordnance maintenance truck is shown. To the left is an Ammco 7-inch bench shaper with a lamp on a flex arm. Next to the fire extinguisher to the far left is the guard for the shaper's drive belt. (TACOM LCMC History Office)

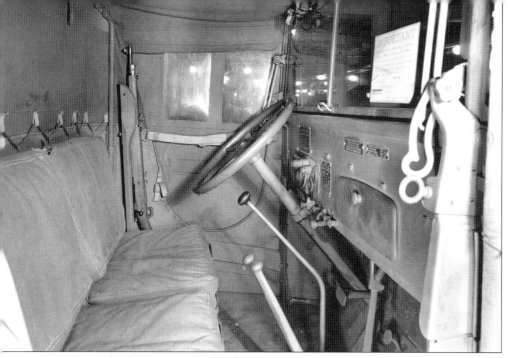

The open cab of an ordnance maintenance truck with the canvas cover and doors installed is viewed from the passenger's door. To the rear of the driver's seat is a universal rifle bracket with an M1 Garand rifle in it. To the right, the right windshield bracket and adjusting arms are shown close-up. (TACOM LCMC History Office)

Above: A mobile tire-repair unit was photographed at Aberdeen Proving Ground on 3 March 1943. Hitched to it was an M25 trailer holding a generator. An awning was rigged to the side of the shop body. Of interest is the liquid-container holder on the side of the trailer to the front of the fender. (National Archives)

Left: This 2 November 1943 photograph taken at Aberdeen Proving Ground documents the failure of the chassis frame of a mobile shop maintenance truck, U.S. Army registration number 6096414. The point of frame failure was between the rear of the cab and the front of the shop body. Squiggly patterns of dark paint have been sprayed on the vehicle, including the tires. (National Archives)

In a September 1943 test of a mobile shop maintenance struck to gauge its durability when heavily loaded at Aberdeen Proving Ground, banded crates and bags full of spare parts were stacked in the compartment, in addition to the vehicle's complement of machinery. (National Archives)

Left: After 259 miles of cross-country operation and 122 miles of highway use, the chassis frame of this mobile shop maintenance truck was bent, as documented in this 6 October 1946 photo. The ST-6 body had been removed, and a straightedge on top of the right side of the frame to the rear of the cab (visible to the right) showed daylight in the center. (National Archives)

Below: A CCKW chassis frame that had been fitted with an ST-6 mobile shop maintenance body was photographed at Aberdeen Proving Ground after 716 miles of cross-country operation using 3x6-inch wooden sills under the shop body. The view is from the front left part of the frame looking aft, showing severe bending of the frame. (National Archives)

357

Left and Below: To correct the occurrences of bending of the frame with the ST-6 body, a fix was developed in the form of a reinforcement welded to the bottom of the frame in the area to the rear of the chassis. The top photo shows a reinforcement from below the frame, and the bottom photo shows it from the outside. (National Archives)

As a result of a tool conference in the spring of 1943 that looked at ways to eliminate unnecessary models of mobile shop trucks and shift their contents into standard cargo trucks, Ordnance Maintenance Sets G, H, K, and L were developed, replacing machine shop loads C, D, and F, and the welding truck. This example represents those ordnance maintenance sets. (National Archives)

Right: As documented in this 1 January 1944 photograph from Aberdeen Proving Ground, a maintenance shop truck with ST-6 body suffered failure of the spare-tire carrier after 3,623 miles of operation. (National Archives)

Left: Simultaneous with recording the failure of the spare-tire carrier, a crack that had developed in the body on the left front corner, inboard of the reflectors, was also documented. (National Archives)

Right: With the tarpaulin removed, the contents of Ordnance Maintenance Set H are visible. Machinery includes a DoAll Model ML vertical band saw, a Buffalo turret drill press with 1-inch capacity, and a bench grinder on a workbench mounted over drawers. (National Archives)

As documented in a 16 March 2944 photograph, Ordnance Maintenance Set K included a 60-ton hydraulic press (foreground: in this case, a K. R. Wilson, manufactured in Buffalo, New York), as well as a 105-cubic-feet air compressor, and an assortment of air tools, including hammers, grinders, and wrenches. (National Archives)

Chapter 27
Signal Corps

The Signal Corps was charged with a range of responsibilities during the war, and incidental to carrying this out, utilized a range of relatively sensitive equipment. To provide sheltered mobility for this gear, a range of specialized van trucks were developed. The basic vehicle employed for this was the K53 van truck.

Standardized on 3 July 1942, and housed within a K-53 was the AN/MRN-1 instrument approach localizer. This unit was used to guide aircraft equipped with the RC-103 receiver to the centerline of a runway.

On 20 July 1942 the Field Artillery Board began testing Mobile Meteorological Station SCM-10-T1. This vehicle consisted of a K-53 van truck housing plotting boards, balloon inflation and observation equipment, and supplied for obtaining and evaluating the accumulated meteorological data. Following these tests, the design was modified and entered production as the Meteorological Station Set SCM-10-T2.

In March 1943, the K-53 was adapted to house the Mobile Meteorological Station SCM-1-T4. The SCM- went on to be used by U.S. forces around the globe, often employed by Mobile Weather Squadrons. The vehicles equipped with the SCM-1-T4 towed a 1-ton Ben Hur-type trailer upon which was a PE-75 Power unit. This unit supplied the electricity for the equipment in the van.

K-53 vans were also used to house the SCR-575 homing beacons.

The K-59, while from ground level resembled the common K-53, housed the RC-153 antenna, which extended above the van roof.

Like shop vans, the Signal Corps van bodies consumed a great deal of shipping space. Unlike the ship vans, a collapsible version of the Signal Corps bodies was not developed. Instead, for many applications the HQ-17 shelter became popular. This shelter could be placed into the cargo bed of any long wheelbase CCKW cargo truck.

Each of the army's first aircraft-detecting radar system SCR-268-B included three K-60 CCKW-based van trucks and a K-56 6-ton 6x6 van. This system was superseded by the SCR-584, and in August 1944, as demand for 6x6s peaked, a number of such radar systems were being scrapped.

The U.S. Army Signal Corps fielded several types of vans based on CCKW chassis, to shelter radio and meteorological equipment and operators. This example, a Truck, K-53, based on CCKW U.S. Army registration number 422636, housed a Meteorological Station Set SCM-13-T1. It was photographed by the Signal Corps General Development Laboratory on 29 May 1942. (Fred Crismon collection)

A 14 August 1944 letter from Brigadier General F. H. Heileman, Director of Supply, A.S.F., elaborated on the topic in this manner:

"1. Attention is invited to basic letter noting the availability of excess Signal Corps vehicles resulting from the dismantling of fifty (50) radio sets SCR-268-B. It will be noted that the number of trucks, K-60, for transfer to Chief of Ordnance is reduced from one hundred fifty (150) to one hundred thirty-seven (137). Attached copy of shipping instructions from Chief of Ordnance gives the number as one hundred fifty (150). This headquarters has authorized the Chief Signal Officer to apply the difference of thirteen (13) vehicles on a special project requirement of the Army Air Forces.

"2. It is desired that the chassis of the trucks, 2-1/2 ton, 6x6, K-60 Van, be made available to meet Ordnancr (sic) requirements for chassis, or that cargo bodies be applied to permit distribution of the vehicles as cargo trucks. The K-60 Van bodies will be made available for administrative use with trucks, 2-1/2 to 5-ton, 6x4, chassis, GMC, or with other suitable chassis. It is believed that trucks, 1-1/2-ton, 4x2, chassis, can be used with the K-60 Van body."

In a similar manner, a further 360 K-60 van trucks became surplus at Camp Stewart on 20 March 1945. These trucks were shipped to Holabird for removal of the Signal Corps gear and subsequent transfer to Ordnance.

The Signal Corps also made use of the similar appearing K-57, K-58 and K-61 vans.

Several Sales Orders were issued for the production of specific van chassis for the Signal Corps. Among them were the following:

1,800 TC-200303
2,935 TC-200435
2,380 TC-200444

Also built for the Signal Corps were these sales orders for CCKW-353 without winch, but no specific end use was noted on the sales orders.

2,252 TC-200502
750 TC-200557
1,423 TC-200558

As is noted in detail elsewhere in this book, GMC and the Detroit Ordnance District agreed to begin producing uniform chassis 17 May 1943, dispensing with the specific chassis types listed above, as well as a host of others. After that date, GMC records no longer reflect what chassis may have ultimately been fitted with Signal Corps van bodies.

The same Meteorological Station Set SCM-13-T1 is observed from the front right. The K-53 truck was developed to provide the Army with a lighter and more mobile meteorological station than its predecessor, the K-55, which was based on a semi-trailer. Mobility was a key point for weather-forecasting units that operated close to the battle fronts. (Fred Crismon collection)

This Truck, K-53, U.S. Army registration number 495768, was photographed at the Signal Corps General Development Laboratory on 15 April 1942. On this version of the body, the windows were fitted with exterior blackout curtains that slid on tracks.

Stored on the rear of the K-53 van body was a spare tire flanked by bottles associated with the M-185 hydrogen generator. The M-185 generated gas for weather balloons, which carried equipment for transmitting by radio information on weather conditions in the upper atmosphere. (Fred Crismon collection)

This Signal Corps van body, on CCKW U.S. Army registration number 434762, had exterior blackout curtains that fitted on brackets at the tops of the windows, instead of the sliding curtains seen in preceding photos. (National Archives)

The same vehicle is viewed from the rear. A diamond-tread plate was mounted vertically on the rear of the vehicle. Above and between the windows was a hood for a ventilation blower. (National Archives)

This plan shows the layout of the interior of a Mobile Meteorological Station SCM-1. The front of the van body is to the left. Inside the double doors on the front left of the body was a mount for a power unit. Other features included a ceiling light projector, a plotting table, a theodolite, a barograph, and other equipment. (Fred Crismon collection)

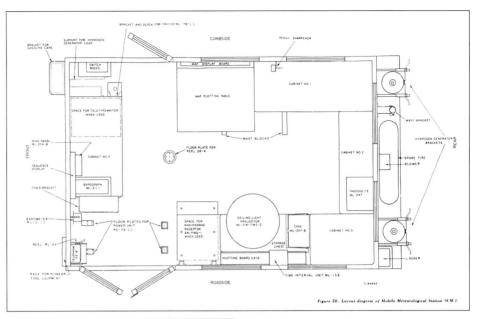

Figure 20. Layout diagram of Mobile Meteorological Station SCM-1.

Truck, K-53, U.S. Army registration number 495768 is viewed from the right, showing the entrance door, below which is the right fuel tank. A ladder was installed on the rear of the vehicle for access to the roof. (Fred Crismon collection)

The Radio Set, AN/MRN-1, was based on the Truck, K-53. This radio set was an instrument-approach localizer used by the U.S. Army Air Forces that guided aircraft equipped with the RC-103 blind-approach set to the centerline of a runway. (Fred Crismon collection)

365

The Signal Corps Truck K-60 featured a windowless van body on a CCKW chassis. Toward the front of the right side of the body was an access door with a piano hinge on top. The K-60 was a multipurpose truck used for a variety of purposes, such as transporting mobile radar and radio units and serving as mobile repair shops. (Fred Crismon collection)

An access door, open here, was provided on the right side of the Signal Corps Truck K-60. The top of the door was fastened to a horizontal piano hinge. (Fred Crismon collection)

Large, double rear doors provided the crew with the means of entering and exiting the K-60. The doors were mounted on piano hinges, and only the right door was equipped with an exterior operating handle. (Fred Crismon collection)

The rear doors of a Signal Corps Truck K-60D are open, allowing a glimpse inside. No equipment has been installed in the interior. Though only faintly visible, on the forward bulkhead are two ventilator openings toward the upper center and three small, round ventilator openings to the lower right. Many of the K-60 bodies were made by Hackney Brothers, of Wilson, North Carolina. (Fred Crismon collection)

The rear doors are closed on this Signal Corps Truck K-60D. This body was manufactured by Wayne Works in Richmond, Indiana. (Fred Crismon collection)

There were no doors on the left side of the Signal Corps Truck K-60. A rub rail fashioned of channels was mounted about halfway up the side of the van body. (Fred Crismon collection)

Chapter 28
Unusual CCKWs

As the U.S. Army's standard 2½-ton truck, it is not surprising that the CCKW was used as the basis for a number of experimental or field-modified vehicles. Some of these seem to be official, but one-off variations, such as the very stylish tanker made from a CCKWX, a vehicle that seems to appear only in builder's photos, and then later, fitted with oversize tires during testing of the latter. Others were likely to be limited-production, depot produced items, such as the CCW-based garbage truck photographed at the Granite City (Illinois) Engineer Depot in the 1950s.

As dependable and versatile as the CCKW, there was little doubt that there was room for improvement. This was the case not just for the CCKW, but for entire army tactical vehicle fleet. Even before VJ-Day the Army had begun a series of conferences that would continue into the late 1940s that defined the attributes desired in the next generation of 2½ ton 6x6. Many of the venerable CCKWs were modified to test some of these concepts.

The automatic transmission, desirable from the standpoint of eliminating clutch maintenance, reduced driver training, and improved off-road operation, was tested by installing a GM Hyrdramatic in a CCKW, that was then tested at Aberdeen. The use of an automatic transmission in a military vehicle was hardly new, as both the M5A1 Stuart and M24 Chaffee light tanks of WWII used automatic transmissions, but the installation in a 2½ ton 6x6 was pioneering. This would become the basis for GMC's Korean War era G-749 (M135/M211) family of vehicles, used by the U.S. military in limited numbers into the 1970s and by Canadian forces a decade beyond that.

Outboard-mounted brake drums were also tested on a CCKW, and subsequently used on the M561 Gama Goat and M656 Mover. Armored cab kits were tried on the CCKW, and were precursors to the heavily armored and armed "gun trucks" that would see service in Vietnam and Iraq. These and other CCKW oddities are presented in the following photos.

Some CCKWs were converted to use as semi-tractors by installing a fifth wheel on the chassis frame. Hitched to this closed-cab CCKW-353 example, a field modification photographed at Fort Benning, Georgia, in March 1942, is a semi-trailer with a special purpose van containing a mobile machine shop. Faintly visible inside the door of the van is what appears to be a lathe. (Fred Crismon collection)

Right: General Motors CCKW-352 483403, converted to a semi-tractor, is displayed without a trailer hitched to the fifth wheel. The fifth wheel is on top of the chassis frame in line between the front and rear tandem wheels. A tow pintle is on the rear of the frame but no bumperettes were installed. The driver had a vacuum hand-control valve to operate the trailer brakes. (U.S. Army Quartermaster Museum)

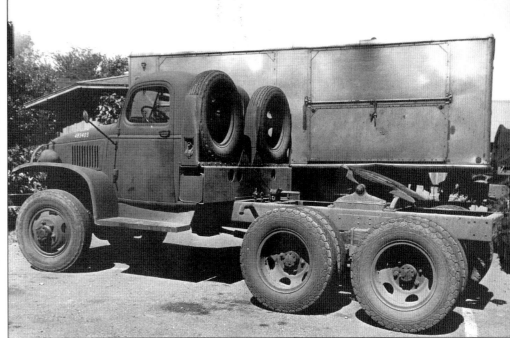

Below: In early 1941, a CCKWX cargo truck features a sleek tanker body.

The mobile artillery observation post had an outrigger on each side below the observer's housing to stabilize the post, apparently to minimize vibrations that would upset the readings of the instrumentation. Mounted on this CCKW chassis, U.S.A. number 465625, was an experimental mobile artillery observation post constructed by the St. Louis Car Company.

Viewed from the front, with the outriggers deployed, is a CCKW-based mobile artillery observation post, which contained facilities and instruments for locating the positions of enemy artillery batteries and directing friendly artillery fire.

Sizeable logs are being loaded onto the body of an open-cab, long-wheelbase CCKW, which will deliver them to a lumber mill. The truck had a very rough wooden bed, including a cab protector at the front. (U.S. Army Engineer School History Office)

This ornate rig on the bed of a closed-cab CCKW-353 appears to have been a mobile airfield control center. The wooden tower on the front half of the steel cargo body had windows on all sides and a glazed roof for all-around visibility. The generator probably supplied power for the four large lights on the rear of the body. (Fred Crismon collection)

Above: The U.S. armed forces employed small drones in World War II for use as targets in gunnery practice. This long-wheelbase CCKW is being employed as a transporter for three drones. Stored on top of the boom are the three wings for the drones. (Fred Crismon collection)

Left: The versatile CCW was put to a seemingly endless procession of uses, so it seems fitting that at least one chassis became host to a garbage-truck body. This example, painted overall in a light color, bore U.S.A. number 4309479. (U.S. Army Engineer School History Office)

Photographed at Aberdeen Proving Ground on 19 December 1946 was this closed-cab CCKW U.S.A. number 4224205. It was being used to test the installation of a Cadillac Hydramatic automatic transmission, as part of the Army's push to adapt automatic transmissions to its trucks during World War II. The reason for the non-powered front axle on this vehicle is not clear, but perhaps the addition of the automatic transmission did not leave enough space for a transfer case. (Fred Crismon collection)

This CCKW-353, U.S.A. number 4916088, was part of Project No. 6341/6-6-8, in which sealed brakes were tested on the truck. The outboard-mounted brake drums are plainly visible. Stenciled on the cab below the door is "AUTO TEST 088." (Fred Crismon collection)

This CCKW-353-A1 was outfitted with an armored cab, including full-length, hinged doors with what appears to have been sliding covers for the windows. The wide window on the frontal armor lacked a cover when this photo was taken. A small light on a post was mounted on each fender. The vehicle was in a display setting, possibly at Fort Eustis. (Fred Crismon collection)

Chapter 29
Field Use During WWII

The ambitious expansion of motorization within the U.S. Army, which included the pioneering ACKWX, would give the leadership experience in managing procurement, maintenance and use of medium tactical vehicles. The CCKWX, although produced in moderate numbers, gave Yellow Truck and Coach and its suppliers the opportunity to refine their production, and troops were given hands-on experience with the vehicles through the Louisiana Maneuvers and the 1941 Tennessee Maneuvers. Those maneuvers in particular pointed to the utility of the 6x6 as the basis for an array of specialized trucks, beyond the basic cargo and tanker configurations.

Once standardized, the CCKW was soon found wherever the American serviceman went. The versatile truck helped push the ALCAN Highway north, and the Ledo Road east. CCKWs operated in virtually every European nation, and on many islands in the Pacific. Fortunate GI's rode the wooden troop seats lining the back of the CCKW, passing their less fortunate comrades who rode the soles of their shoes toward the front. The trucks brought food, fuel, ammunition and supplies to the front. The supplies ranged from boots to doughnuts, brought forward in the special CCKW Clubmobiles.

CCKW-based shop trucks repaired the infantryman's rifle and eyeglasses; the tanker's "office" and the engineer's bulldozer. The GI used a map printed in a CCKW, and drank water purified in a CCKW. On good days, he had a hot meal prepared in a CCKW, eating bread baked in a bakery brought behind one of the versatile GMCs. In another he had work done on his teeth, another brought an operating room to the front, should the worst happen.

The CCKW seemed to be everywhere, yet there were never enough of them. Trucks were delivered on wheels, individually and as pairs in crates, some were even flown in, but still there weren't enough. Trucks were lost on sunken ships, destroyed by landmines, strafing planes and artillery fire. Twenty-six thousand trucks, many of them CCKWs, were sent on one-way trips on the Ledo Road, turned over to Chinese troops at the end of their convoy. Others were simply worn out through the rigors of use, a conscious decision being made to "use up" many trucks in the Red Ball Express, in hopes of advancing swiftly enough to make Germany capitulate.

The trucks poured from the factories in Pontiac, St. Louis and, briefly, Baltimore. While there may never have been enough to meet the demand, the flow was steady, and torrential. The 527,782 6x6 and 23,501 6x4 GMCs would become the most-produced vehicles of their size in the military's history.

General Motors ACKWX-353 U.S. Army registration number 41137 carries a cargo of troops in 1939. Markings for Company I of a Quartermaster regiment are on the driver's door, but the number of the regiment is not visible. (National Archives)

A CCKWX-353, U.S. Army registration number 420707, has been fitted with dual front tires in addition to the standard dual tandem tires in an apparent experiment to improve the vehicle's flotation. This configuration is being put to the test during a crossing of a muddy slough. (Military History Institute)

Right: The Quartermaster Corps maintained a training facility at Fort Francis E. Warren, Wyoming, during World War II. There, a trainee drives a CCKWX-353, U.S.A. number 422498, through water on the difficult-driving course. (Military History Institute)

Below: A line of GMC 2½-ton 6x6 trucks undergo engine checks or servicing in 1940. The two closest vehicles bear on their hoods U.S.A. numbers 416475 and 416217, making them CCKWX-353s built under contract W-398-QM-8266 of 1941. On the door of the closest truck are faint markings that appear to be for Company C, 119th Quartermaster Regiment. (Fred Crismon collection)

An M3 mobile purification unit, U.S. Army registration number 60470, is taking water from the creek in the background, removing impurities from it, and pumping purified water into the holding tank to the left. On the door are the Corps of Engineers insignia and markings for the 7th Engineer Battalion. (General Motors)

Above: In a photograph taken in January 1941, this long-wheelbase GMC 2½-ton 6x6 truck has been outfitted as a field-kitchen vehicle. Stowed on the side of the cargo body is a frame, apparently for the kitchen equipment. Markings for the 53rd Quartermaster Regiment are on the front of the trailer. (Military History Institute)

Right: Among the mobile equipment of U.S. air-defense units was the M1 searchlight trailer, mounting a General Electric 60-inch searchlight installed on a G-221 2-ton trailer. The prime mover for this M1 with the searchlight in the travel position is CCKW-352 443487.

Above: During training maneuvers at an undisclosed location in the continental United States on 8 June 1941, crewmen of M2 light tanks line up for a meal at a field kitchen serviced by a General Motors 2½-ton 6x6. (General Motors)

Left: As troops of the 186th Field Artillery prepare to march from Madison Barracks, New York, to their new base at Fort Ethan Allen, Vermont, in or around June 1941, a CCKW filled with troops in the foreground tows an artillery piece in the foreground. (National Archives)

A CCKW-353 towing a trailer leads a convoy through Manchester, Tennessee, on a rainy day in June 1941. The troop seats in the cargo body are lowered, and the tarpaulin is partially pulled back, probably to the discomfort of the occupants within. (Fred Crismon collection)

A winch-equipped, short-wheelbase CCKW-352, U.S. Army registration number 45781, proceeds through Manchester, Tennessee, during Second Army maneuvers in June 1941. What appear to be reels of wire are visible in the body. (Fred Crismon collection)

During a VII Corps war game in Arkansas on 28 August 1941, A CCKW-352 towing a trailer crosses a pontoon bridge over the Little Missouri River. Painted on the door of the truck is "181st F.A. Btry. C." (General Motors)

This CCKW-352 with oversized sand tires towing an artillery piece was part of a convoy conducting tests for driving on thick sand at dunes near Yuma, Arizona, on 26 October 1942. (Bryce Sunderlin collection)

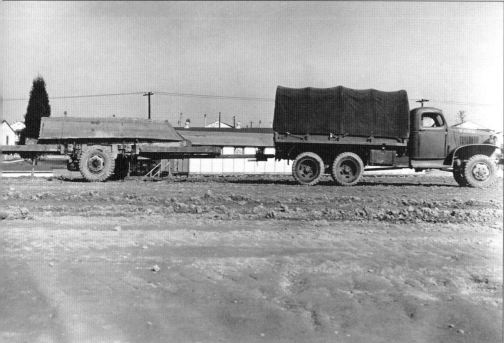

Above: The CCKW-353 made an excellent platform for the SCR-399 radio set. This equipment was housed in the HO-17 shelter, mounted on the cargo body. The K-52 trailer held the PE-35 electrical generator for powering the radio sets. This CCKW, as well as the trailer behind it, have been fitted with oversized tires for desert sand use. (Patton Museum)

Left: This CCKW is towing a bolster trailer holding a pontoon boat for a pontoon bridge. The trailer had a telescoping drawbar to allow long pieces of equipment or materials on the trailer. (U.S. Army Engineer School History Office)

CCKW-353 436147 was a platform vehicle for a SCR-399 radio set enclosed in an HO-17 shelter. Various configurations of radio antennas were installed on these shelters; this example at the Desert Training Center in California in November 1942 has one on the roof and three mounted on the left side of the shelter. (National Archives via Bryce Sunderlin)

Sometime before mid-1942 a CCKW-353 is backed up to a Douglas A-20 Havoc at an airbase. The truck was assigned U.S. Army registration number 495237. Mounted under the front of the left fender is a license plate marked 304ABG30. (General Motors)

To the left, an earth-boring derrick on a 4x4 truck is being used to dig a posthole while several G.I.s hoist a section of tree trunk out of a CCKW-353. Both vehicles have yellow recognition stars on their doors, probably signifying that they were assigned to the Armored Force, which started using such insignia in January 1942. (General Motors)

Two CCKWs are being used in a fruit orchard to transport freshly picked produce somewhere Stateside around 1942. Placards on the grilles identify them as assigned to the 113th Quartermaster Battalion, 38th Infantry Division. (General Motors)

In a photo probably taken during maneuvers in 1942, CCKW-352s of the 138th Field Artillery Battalion, 38th Infantry Division, are parked next to a 105mm howitzer. A pioneer-tool rack has been installed to the rear of the cab of the truck to the left. Installation of these racks was not performed at the factory but was a field modification. (General Motors)

A convoy of CCKW-353s leaves an assembly area during manueuvers in the continental United States in or around 1942. These probably were assigned to a unit of the 38th Infantry Division. (General Motors)

A CCKW-352 used as an artillery prime mover by the 163rd Field Artillery Battalion bears U.S. Army registration number 456007. The small placard on the grille is marked with the battalion designation and the number 38 for 38th Infantry Division. The small A 7 on the placard probably signifies Battery A, 7th vehicle in the order of march. (General Motors)

CCKW-353s of the 38th Infantry Division are backed-up to a loading dock at what appears to be a produce warehouse. The third truck from the left is loaded with fruit crates. Rifle scabbards are strapped to the side panels of the engine compartments. (General Motors)

CCKWs are operating at an unidentified facility in the continental United States around 1942. U.S. Army registration numbers are visible on three of the trucks: 469544, 465481, and 455322. (General Motors)

In a scene that is probably related to the preceding one, two CCKWs are being employed in a supply operation at an unidentified port. To the left is U.S.A. number 486375, while the door is marked "73rd A.D.G." A canvas cover is strapped to the winch drum. (General Motors)

To the right, a long-wheelbase CCKW is partially in view. The cab was the model 1608 with the rear-view mirror mounted on the cowl. To the left is a GMC 4x2 truck. (General Motors)

CCKWs saw use as general-purpose utility vehicles in the U.S. Navy. Naval aviators pose next to a bomb alongside several Consolidated PBY Catalinas. Two men in the body of the long-wheelbase CCKW with U.S. Navy markings in yellow on the door pass down another bomb. (General Motors)

In mountainous terrain in the continental United States, the Diamond T 4-ton wrecker to the left is hoisting the front end of a long-wheelbase CCKW, U.S. Army registration number 479074. In the background is another long-wheelbase CCKW. The occasion most likely was a training exercise or demonstration. (National Archives)

Around 1942, two G.I.s wearing M1917 helmets pose with CCKW-353-A2 U.S. Army registration number 427010. This vehicle was produced in the 1941 model year under contract W-398-QM-8275 and was equipped with the model 1574 cab. (General Motors)

Several CCKWs are visible in this photo of an assembly area at Needles, California, in 1942, including an M3 mobile water-purification unit at the center, with its highly distinctive van body with large side windows. To the front and rear of this vehicle are temporary water holding tanks. (National Archives)

Troops gather around a holding tank as it fills up with water from the M3 mobile water-purification unit to the left. The hose to the left drew water from the creek in the foreground, and hoses from the truck sent purified water into the tank.

Two members of the Women's Army Corps (WACs) wearing chemical suits and masks lay down a decontaminating spray as they stand on the front fenders of a power-driven decontaminating-apparatus truck. This training or practice drill was conducted at Gowen Field, Boise, Idaho, in November 1943. (National Archives)

In late October 1943 a combat engineer cuts a wooden plank with a pneumatic Skilsaw circular saw powered by air supplied by a Leroi motorized compressor. The photo offers a good view of the air receiver above the pioneer-tool rack. On each side of the receiver is a reel for an air hose. (U.S. Army Engineer History Office)

At the Ordnance Operation, General Motors Proving Ground in October 1943, open-cab CCKW-353-A1 4168634 is set up for a dynamometer test. This was part of tests being conducted on the steel radiator. (National Archives)

A Shop, Motorized, General Purpose, U.S.A. number 4153995, is set up for business. The bottoms of the tarpaulin are on supports that formed an awning, and side panels are lowered to provide platforms. Inside is ample storage for parts and tools of many varieties. (General Motors)

Left: Members of the Acorn Training Detachment based at Port Hueneme, California, practice unloading equipment, including pierced-plank matting and pallets, from CCKWs using crawler cranes at Point Mugu, California. The unit was constructing an airfield. (National Archives)

Below: A large proportion of the 500 trucks in the Quartermaster Replacement Center Motor Pool at Camp Lee, Virginia, are visible in this photograph taken in or around 1943, including hundreds of CCKWs. Most of the visible vehicles are closed-cab trucks with steel cargo bodies. (General Motors)

Above: Truck drivers of the Quartermaster Corps get some practice firing the ring-mounted .50-caliber machine guns on CCKWs at aerial targets at Camp Pendleton, near Virginia Beach, Virginia. In the background, a radio operator, airplane spotters, and a control officer monitor the training session. (National Archives via Jim Gilmore)

Right: Trucks of E Company, 33rd Armored Engineer Battalion of the 7th Armored Division cross a river, probably the Colorado, by means of a pneumatic raft at Yuma, Arizona. The nearest truck is CCKW-353 U.S. Army registration number 480557. More trucks await their turn to cross on the other bank. (U.S. Army Engineer History Office)

At the Granite City Engineer Depot in Illinois, CCKW-based shop trucks are parked around a D8 bulldozer at the center. To the left is a mobile shop with an all-metal body. To the right of the bulldozer are two motorized general-purpose shops, as developed by and for the U.S. Army Engineers, with canvas tarpaulins over the body. The truck to the far right has a front-mounted A-frame. (U.S. Army Engineer History Office)

A convoy of GMC 2½-ton 6x6 cargo trucks proceeds along a mountain road during the winter around 1941. On the bluff in the background, several soldiers stand guard with rifles. (National Archives)

In another photo taken at the Granite City Engineer Depot, to the left is a motorized general-purpose shop. Next to it is a 1-ton trailer with 300-amp arc-welding equipment. The trailer had built-in chests for tools, material, welder's masks, and other necessities. To the right is a D8 bulldozer. (U.S. Army Engineer History Office)

Above: A CCKW-353 with a No. 7 wrecker set installed is serving as a field maintenance vehicle. The main feature of this set is a hoist superstructure featuring an I-beam with diagonal braces and a chain hoist on a trolley. A universal-type tow bar is stowed on the side of the body, and a removable ladder is set up against the tailgate. A small vise is attached to the right side of the tailgate. (National Archives)

Right: In a view into the rear of the same maintenance vehicle, chests with tool and parts drawers are visible on each side. To the left is a piece of machinery, apparently an air compressor and air tank. A milk can is on the left side of the tailgate, and a five-gallon liquid container is on a holder on the right mud flap. (National Archives)

At Camp Silbert, Alabama, a chemical decontamination detail demostrate how their CCKW-based mobile decontamination units could be adapted for firefighting. The tank of the decontamination unit on the truck to the right is in view, with much chemical streaking present on it. (U.S. Army Chemical Corps Museum)

Above: Soldiers in overalls pour liquids into galvanized steel garbage cans on the cargo body of a long-wheelbase CCKW which has been equipped as a field kitchen. Three field ranges stretch across the front of the wooden cargo body. More gear and supplies are in the 1-ton trailer coupled to the truck. (Patton Museum)

Left: A mobile communications center is installed on the steel cargo body of a CCKW. Two seats are provided for switchboard operators, and a platform and stairs are set up alongside the cargo body. The Army fielded a number of truck-transportable telephone central office sets or exchanges, such as the TC-1 and TC-10. (National Archives)

A CCKW-based Class 530 fire truck is being used to spray a high-velocity fog of water onto the fire in the background. The centrifugal pump on the front of the vehicle could pump up to 500 gallons per minute of water. (U.S. Army Engineer History Office)

A truck convoy proceeds down a dirt road in the Western United States in or around 1941. The first truck in line is CCKW-353-A1 437767, a 1941 model. A horseshoe and an identification plate are affixed to its grille. (Military History Institute)

At the same location in the preceding photo, the convoy has stopped, displaying a variety of vehicles, including a car, a motorcycle with sidecar, a G-505 Dodge command car, and numerous CCKWs hauling trailers. (Military History Institute)

Hoses from a CCKW Class 530 fire truck are spraying mechanical foam onto a fire. A suction hose is stowed on the fender of the truck; an extension ladder is on the side of the body. Above the rear of the body are two spotlights. (U.S. Army Engineer History Office)

Right: During the World War II era, the military made intensive use of the United States' extensive railroad network to transport its vehicles in-country, thus saving substantial wear and tear on the vehicles. Here, a train is transporting a mix of halftracks and trucks, including CCKWs. (Patton Museum)

Below: In an unidentified city, a display of U.S. Army Quartermaster Corps equipment includes a section dedicated to the truck company. Featured is a long-wheelbase, closed-cab CCKW with a ring mount. A soldier is manning the .50-caliber machine gun on the ring mount. (Military History Institute)

One of the methods of securing a 2½-ton 6x6 truck to a railroad flat car for shipment is demonstrated. Crossbeams serving as wheel chocks are snugged up against the tires. Blocking reinforces the crossbeams, and 2x4s along wheels keep the vehicle from shifting. Wires attached to the wheels and the flatcar completed the rig. (U.S. Army Transportation Museum)

The CCKW was a vehicle of a thousand uses. This one has been put to use as a mobile snack bare. The racks remain in place, and storage chests and counters have been placed in the cargo body. The tarpaulin has been rigged to give the customers standing on the portable stairs a little shade. (National Archives)

Above: In the period from 8 March to 28 October 1942, the 1,387-mile-long Alaska-Canada (or ALCAN) Highway was constructed, largely by the U.S. Army, principally to facilitate military transport from the from the Lower 48 to Alaska. The CCKW played a large role in the highway's construction. Here, at Dawson Creek, British Canada, where the highway began, G.I.s are loading buckets of water from a reservoir into a CCKW. (U.S. Army Quartermasters Museum)

Left: In 1943, a convoy of U.S. Army trucks, including a CCKW towing a trailer in the foreground, negotiate a particularly rough stretch of the Alaska Highway. Over time, the highway would be improved and paved, but at this stage much of it was rudimentary. (General Motors)

Rough and Ready for Action

More than 400,000 GMC "Six by Six" Trucks for Our Armed Forces

There's nothing beautiful about this mud-splashed, war-worn Army truck. But *beauty is as beauty does*, and more of these sturdy 2½-ton, six-wheel drive GMCs are performing more duties for our Armed Forces than any other type of vehicle.

They go ashore with Army Engineers and Navy Seabees, helping to build bases and bridges and bomber strips on newly won territory. They are used by the Air Forces to transport bombs, gasoline and repair equipment. They serve as prime movers for the Artillery's 75 mm and 105 mm guns. They power machine shops for Ordnance and mobile radio stations for the Signal Corps. They transport complete surgical operating units and optical shops for the Medical Corps. They carry countless loads of food and fuel, munitions and materials for the Army Service Forces.

In fact, wherever and whenever Allied Armies need truck transport or truck power, you'll usually find another Army of GMC "six by six" trucks, *Rough and Ready for More Action.*

★ ★ ★

In addition to producing thousands of military trucks and amphibian "Ducks," GMC is now manufacturing several thousand commercial trucks for use in essential civilian occupations. If you are eligible for a new truck, see your GMC dealer first for "The Truck of Value." Remember, too, that your GMC dealer is headquarters for the original truck-saving, time-saving Preventive Maintenance Service.

INVEST IN VICTORY BUY MORE WAR BONDS

Prepared from Front Line Photos from Acme and U. S. Army Signal Corps

GMC TRUCK & COACH DIVISION
GENERAL MOTORS

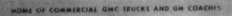

HOME OF COMMERCIAL GMC TRUCKS AND GM COACHES   VOLUME PRODUCER OF GMC ARMY TRUCKS AND AMPHIBIAN "DUCKS"

General Motors, like other large manufacturers of military equipment, took pride in promoting and advertising its products and its contributions to the war effort. This advertisement published in *The Saturday Evening Post* contained an illustration portraying the CCKW's ability to haul troops and cargo through mud, over rivers, and across rough terrain.

Above: On 9 November 1942, the second day of the Operation Torch landings in North Africa, a closed-cab CCKW loaded with supplies disembarks from a landing craft. The tarpaulin was secured directly over the cargo and the racks, dispensing with the use of bows to support the tarpaulin. (National Archives)

Right: Three U.S. Army Air Forces mechanics of the 50th Service Squadron, Staff Sergeants Chlyrta and Anderson and Corporal Matheson, repair a B-17 engine on a portable crane in North Africa in late December 1942. To the left is a CCKW placed into use as a mobile maintenance shop. (National Archives)

A CCKW-352-A1 is being pulled off a landing craft on the North African coast in late 1942. A reel of communications wire is on the front of the vehicle. A weight, height, and length placard is inside the windshield. Duffel bags are piled high in the cargo body, and four five-gallon liquid containers are stowed on the outside of the rack. (General Motors)

U.S. Army engineers repair bomb damage at Youks-Les-Bains Airfield, Algeria, on 15 January 1943. To the left of center, an engineer is operating a paving breaker, more commonly known as a jackhammer, powered by the CCKW-based compressor. In the background is a Bristol Beaufighter with British markings. (National Archives)

Left: A CCKW receives supplies from a USAAF C-47 at an airfield near Buerat, Libya, on 19 January 1943. This truck was part of a fleet of cargo trucks that shuttled supplies to advanced USAAF airfields during the U.S. offensive against Axis forces in North Africa. The truck has been painted a light camouflage color, with the U.S.A. number, 488290, and its surrounding Olive Drab paint, not painted over. (National Archives via Bryce Sunderlin)

Below: Damaged CCKWs are loaded on railroad flatcars on a siding at Tebassa, Algeria, on 18 February 1943. The truck to the right appears to have a buckled frame, and the engine, one of the axles, and many other parts are missing. The second vehicle consists of a steel cargo body and the rear tandem axle and not much else. The third truck is missing the engine, and the frame appears to be buckled aft of the cab. (National Archives)

Above: CCKWs of a quartermaster unit are parked under and adjacent to a highway bridge camouflaged with local foliage at Youks-les-Bains, Algeria, on 18 February 1942. Marked on the door of the CCKW-353 under the far side of the bridge is the name *Willie Mae.* A large number 53 is stenciled on the door of the CCKW at the center. (National Archives)

Right: Technician 5th Class Henry E. Bleckwell of the 3488th Ordnance Company works at a field forge set up alongside a CCK-353 near Tébessa, Algeria, on 7 February 1943. The truck, including the door window and the tarpaulin, has been camouflaged with a slurry of yellow clay, and a crate has been installed atop the cab roof for a stowage bin for five-gallon liquid containers. Boughs are piled on the fender and hood for camouflage. (National Archives)

Personnel of a medical battalion are setting up a mobile surgical unit comprising a CCKW and a tent in North Africa in late March 1943. A spare tire and camouflage netting are lashed to a wooden frame on top of the cab roof, and several boxes are strapped down to the front bumper. (General Motors)

The following sequence documents the assembly of boxed CCKWs by members of the 302nd Ordnance (Base) Battalion at Casablanca, French Morocco, on 2 March 1943. Here, ordnance men stand by ready to go to work as a crane is lifting a box containing CCKW components. A second crate is in the background. (National Archives)

Men of the 302nd Ordnance (Base) Battalion open a twin-unit pack containing two CCKW closed cabs. The paper inside the box helped keep the contents dry during the long sea voyage to North Africa. (National Archives)

A twin-unit pack containing two CCKW chassis has been opened at Casablanca. Two chassis frames were stacked one atop the other. On top of the upper frame were ten tires and wheels, enough for one CCKW. (National Archives)

At a truck assembly area using a crane, personnel of the 302nd Ordnance (Base) Battalion lift a tandem axle assembly from a shipping box at Casablanca on 2 March 1943. The box contained, from the top to the bottom, a tandem axle assembly, two front axles, and a tandem axle assembly: all of the axles for two trucks. (National Archives)

CCKWs are being unpacked and reassembled in Australia on 2 December 1942. In the foreground is a twin pack of chassis frames. Different methods of packing CCKWs were practiced until the procedures were standardized. Here, the two transmissions with their shift levers are stowed on the closer end of the chassis frames. In the background are several reassembled CCKWs. (National Archives via Bryce Sunderlin)

These axles evidently were not shipped as tandem assemblies, as the single Chevrolet "banjo" axle that is being hoisted from a disassembled box is a tandem, not a front, axle. The boom of a Diamond-T wrecker is being used to hoist the heavy axle. (National Archives)

The soldiers seen in the preceding photo are now assembling a tandem-axle unit for installation on a closed-cab CCKW. In this case, the axles are the Timken "split" type. These axles and springs do not look factory-fresh but have the appearance of having seen previous service. (National Archives)

At the 302nd Ordnance (Base) Battalion's truck-assembly area at Casablanca in March 1943, soldiers are easing a CCKW chassis frame down onto the front and tandem axle assemblies. The axles are the Chevrolet type. The engine remained in place on the frame during shipment. In the background to the right of center is a CCKW closed cab awaiting installation. (National Archives)

A truck-mounted crane is lowering a closed cab onto a CCKW chassis at Casablanca. A spreader bar attached to the hoist chain is hooked to the tops of the door openings, and consequently the doors are ajar. The fuel tank on the right side of the chassis frame identifies this as a CCKW-353. (National Archives)

401

The entire assembly line for 6x6 military trucks at the 302nd Ordnance (Base) Battalion area at Casablanca is documented in this 2 March 1943 photograph. To the far right are two unpacked closed cabs. At the center, several chassis are under assembly. In the background are several reassembled CCKWs and the crane that assisted in the operations. (National Archives via Bryce Sunderlin)

This CCKW-353 with a wooden cargo body was configured as a Signal Corps line truck. It carried equipment and supplies necessary for constructing, maintaining, and repairing telephone lines. The photograph was taken in Egypt in late April 1943. (National Archives)

Gasoline trucks were high-priority and easily identifiable targets for the enemy. This CCKW-based 750-gallon gasoline tanker of the 907th Ordnance Company (Heavy Maintenanc), 197th Ordnance Battalion, Fifth Army, in North Africa on 19 May 1943 had a tarpaulin over the tank to camouflage it as a cargo truck. Five-gallon liquid containers are stowed above the tank and on the side and under the front of the body. (Fred Crismon collection)

At an ordnance assembly plant in North Africa in June 1943, workers, including both army and civilian, are installing pintle mounts on closed-cab CCKWs. All of the ring mounts in view are the M32, designed for long-wheelbase CCKWs. In the right distance are some closed-cab CCKWs. (National Archives)

On 11 July 1943, the second day of the invasion of Sicily, vehicles are packed tightly on Green Beach at Gela. These include DUKWs, half-tracks, Jeeps, a ¾-ton Dodge truck to the right, and several CCKWs. To the right of center is a CCKW with a 57mm antitank gun hitched to it; the recognition star on the door has a circle around it, while other vehicles lack the circle around the star. (National Archives via Bryce Sunderlin)

During the U.S. Army's entrance into Palermo, Sicily, on 21 July 1943, a CCKW assigned to I Armored Corps is laden with troops of the 15th Infantry Regiment. The recognition stars on the doors are on dark circles, probably the USAAF-style white star on a blue circle that was used by some units in North Africa. Piled on the cab roof is a folded tarpaulin and camouflage netting. This truck appears to have the Model 1609 cab, set up for a M32 gun mount, but the mount itself is not installed. While GMC prepared the trucks for the mount, the mounts were not shipped from the GMC plants, and were to be installed in the field. (National Archives via Bryce Sunderlin)

The same convoy passing through Palermo, Sicily, is viewed from the rear. The nearest vehicle has two recognition stars on the rear for added emphasis: a plain one on the mud flap and a star in a circle on the tailgate. Also on the tailgate is a tactical or unit symbol: three horizontal bars and the letter M. (National Archives via Bryce Sunderlin)

U.S. Coast Guard crewmen of a transport ship hoist a CCKW-353 over the side of the ship off Paesternum, near Salerno, Italy. The truck would then be lowered to a barge alongside the ship. The bows are stored on top of the front of the racks, and a pioneer tool rack is mounted on the side of the body above the tandem wheels. (General Motors)

Above: CCKWs display their excellent cross-country capabilities while negotiating soft mud in the Volturno River in Italy on 22 November 1943. The first vehicle is an open-cab CCKW-353-2A with a ring mount. Next in line is a closed-cab CCKW, followed by another open-cab CCKW. In the left background is a stockpile of artillery ammunition. (National Archives via Bryce Sunderlin)

Right: At a very muddy USAAF base in Algeria in late November 1943, CCKW-353-B1 U.S. Army registration number 448584 tows a civilian car with the engine and hood removed. The truck has the early-style symmetrical brush guards and GMC logo plate at the top center of the grille. (National Archives)

A CCKW is mired up to its bumper and running boards in deep mud in the Capua Sector in Italy on 22 November 1943. The registration number 4125856 is on the hood. A white recognition star with no circle around it is partially visible on the cab roof. (National Archives via Bryce Sunderlin)

It's muddy going on a road in the La Pesse sector in Italy on 27 November 1943. The combination of a GMC logo on the grille of this CCKW-353 and the asymmetrical brush guards mark this as one of the vehicles produced in January and February 1943, before the GMC logo was deleted from the grille. (National Archives via Bryce Sunderlin)

Left: French General Henri Honore Giraud, next to the bumper, and French and U.S. officers inspects a CCKW undergoing assembly at a huge, open-air assembly area in North Africa in 1943. Curiously, the engine, which usually was shipped installed on the chassis frame, is not present, but the grille with GMC logo and asymmetrical brush guards is in place. (General Motors)

Below: A 700-gallon water tanker truck is parked at a U.S. Army Engineers water point in North Africa. Here, water purified by the late-production M3 purification truck just ahead and above the tanker was stored in temporary holding tanks, awaiting pickup and distribution to army units. (U.S. Army Engineer History Office)

Mechanics of an ordnance company in the 91st Division perform repairs on a GMC CCKW-353, left, and a Dodge ¾-ton truck, right, in the shelter of an arcade under an abandoned hotel in Monghidoro, Italy, on 29 November 1944. The engine is still present in the CCKW but a GMC 270 engine is lying in the mud next to the truck. (National Archives via Bryce Sunderlin)

Left: These five trucks, including a CCKW in the foreground, were destroyed by a German bomb blast at Anzio, Italy, on or before February 8, 1944. The devastation could be significant when vehicles were grouped closely together, as was the case with these trucks. (General Motors)

Below: Vehicle crews of the Fifth Army Mobile American Expeditionary Station take a break along a road in Italy in April 1944. This was a mobile radio unit that brought to troops in the front lines their favorite radio programs and music. There were ten units in the caravan, including Jeeps, trailers, and CCKWs with van bodies, and the unit made much use of captured enemy equipment. The station had a transmitting range of 50 miles. (General Motors)

CCKWs with cargo bodies filled with medium-heavy artillery shells are crowded on the main deck of a landing ship, tank (LST) approaching shore in Anzio Harbor, Italy, on 22 April 1944. From there, the trucks would transport the shells to ammunition dumps on the beachhead. (General Motors)

Trucks of II Corps Headquarters are parked at the Coliseum in Rome on 11 June 1944. To the left is a closed-cab CCKW-352 with a field-installed blackout lamp and brush guard above the left headlight. CCKW-353 4281696 at the center was built in January or February 1943. (National Archives via Bryce Sunderlin)

The boom of an M1 heavy wrecker holds up the front end of an open-cab CCKW-353 as two mechanics of the 911th Ordnance Heavy Automotive Maintenance (HAM) Company repair the burned-out transmission. This muddy scene was near Metz, France, on 17 October 1944. (National Archives via Bryce Sunderlin)

This CCKW-353 went off a bridge and crashed into a creek north of Capua, Italy, on 15 October 1945, resulting in the deaths of a number of U.S. troops. It was recovered from the crash site and is shown here under tow by a truck fitted with a No. 7 wrecker. (National Archives via Bryce Sunderlin)

On a road in the Apennine Mountains of Italy during the Gothic Line Campaign around late summer 1944, a closed-cab CCKW-353 transporting medical personnel is stopped with the hood open, possibly signifying mechanical difficulties. The M49 machine gun ring, installed on M32 mount, has been severely damaged and is no longer round. At least three ambulances are in view: to the right, and along the ridgeline in the right background. (National Archives via Bryce Sunderlin)

American paratroopers are buckling on their parachutes in preparation for a mission in Sicily around 1943. Next to them is a closed-cab CCKW-353 with a wooden cargo body. The white recognition star on the door is surrounded by a yellow circle, interrupted so as not to cover the corner of the three bars painted on the door. Next to the bars is stenciled 4426-A. (National Archives)

A closed-cab CCKW-353-A2 rolls down a street in a town in Mediterranean Theater, possibly in Sicily in 1943. Stenciled on the front of the hood is "HELL DRIVERS / LUCKY TEATER." The star on the door appears to be white on a blue circle and probably has a yellow surround, in keeping with a configuration sometimes seen in the North Africa and Sicily campaigns.

411

During the Italian Campaign, an open-cab CCKW 700-gallon water tanker with Chevrolet axles and snow chains on the tandem tires is parked alongside an interesting structure that may have been a makeshift shower stall, judging from the water cans and vents on the roof and the icicles hanging underneath the hut. The truck bumper bears markings for the 405th Engineer Water Supply Battalion, Fifth Army.

The same 700-gallon water tanker and hut seen in the preceding photo are viewed from the rear of the tanker. On the rear of the tank a white recognition star in a circle is painted on the doors of the equipment chest that held discharge hoses and operating and maintenance tools.

A CCKW dump truck is being loaded with debris from a crane with a bucket during reconstruction activities at the Port of Naples, Italy, following the Allied capture of that city in 1943. CCKWs often played a prominent part in cleanup and rebuilding operations at captured ports: an essential operation in order to keep supplies flowing to the armies. (U.S. Army Engineer History Office)

Although the location of this photograph of CCKWs towing 105mm howitzers into a town is not identified, according to the original Signal Corps caption it shows troops en route to a port of embarkation for "the invasion of Hitler's Europe." The identification star on the closest CCKW's tailgate has what appears to be a unit symbol at the center: a yellow square with horizontal bars. The top of the shield of the howitzer in the foreground is stenciled in yellow "MT. ETNA," a volcano in Italy, and "DJEBEL BERDA," a reference to one of the sites of the fighting between U.S. and Axis forces during the Battle of El Guettar, Tunisia in the early spring of 1943.

In Italy, civilian workers are loading large bags of sugar onto CCKWs for transport to salvage centers, where the sugar will be removed from the torn bags before being forwarded to army units. The nearer truck, backed up to an embankment, displays the amazing flexibility of the tandem wheels. (General Motors)

On a battlefield in North Africa, A CCKW-353 towing a trailer passes knocked-out German PzKpfw IIIs and a Tiger tank. It was the U.S. Army's logistical excellence, largely personified by the CCKW, as much as its firepower that enabled it to prevail over the battle-tested Afrika Korps. (National Archives)

CCKWs of the Fifth Army carrying bridging equipment cross the Po River on a M1 Treadway bridge in May 1945. To cross the Po the Allies built eight bridges, four in the sector of U.S. 5th Army (2 for each Army Corps) and four in the sector British 8th Army (2 for each Army Corps).

MP's in a weary CCKW collect weapons from partisans in Vittoro Emmanuel Square, Bologna, Italy, on 25 April 1945. The left rear outside tire of the open cab, wooden cargo body-equipped truck is missing, while the left front tire is of civilian tread pattern, rather than a cross-country tread. The Army used civilian tread pattern tires on select towed equipment, and tire shortages were chronic in most theaters during the war, making such substitutions not uncommon. (National Archives)

Above: In 1942, the U.S. Army began its buildup in England in preparation for an eventual cross-Channel invasion of France. Toward the end of that year, this CCKW fitted with railroad driving wheels was photographed at Ashchurch, England. It was employed in switching freight cars in a marshalling yard and could pull up to seven loaded cars at a time. (National Archives via Bryce Sunderlin)

Left: A CCKW-based L2 750-gallon fuel or oil servicing truck, developed for delivering fuel and oil to the USAAF aircraft, is secured to the deck of a ship for transport to England on 2 March 1943. Because of the presence of the big fuel tank, this vehicle was non-reducible, meaning it couldn't be partially disassembled and boxed for shipment. Thus, extensive measures had to be taken to secure and protect the truck, including a wooden guard for the closed cab. (National Archives via Bryce Sunderlin)

A U.S. Army Engineers Shop, Motorized, General Purpose, is set up for operation somewhere in England on 18 January 1943. The folding side panels of the body have been lowered, exposing the lathe and drill press inside. A push-broom and a shovel are leaning against the front of the body. (U.S. Army Engineer History Office)

The same motorized general-purpose shop shown in the preceding photo is viewed from the rear. An engineer is operating the lathe to the left. Behind him are drawers for parts and tools. The shop was rigged for electricity, and a bare light bulb is hanging above the bench to the left. (U.S. Army Engineer History Office)

In a heavy-equipment maintenance yard in England on 18 February 1943, a motorized general-purpose shop to the right is available for making repairs. The parts and tool drawers on the right side of the body are in view. The building in the background strongly resembles the one in the preceding photo. (U.S. Army Engineer History Office)

Members of the 50th Field Artillery Battalion on maneuvers at Tidworth, England, on 2 October 1943 are positioning their 105mm howitzer. In the background are two CCKW-352s in use as prime movers; the closer one was U.S.A. number 45697. The bows are leaning against the front racks of the cargo bodies, and camouflage netting is on the cab roofs. (National Archives via Bryce Sunderlin)

Arriving troops in transit in Iceland march past several CCKWs with closed cabs and steel bodies. The vehicles appear to have seen hard use, and the CCKW-353 to the right has a crumpled front bumper. At the center is a CCKW-353. (National Archives)

A civilian car in U.S. Army service that was involved in a crash has been brought into a repair yard in England by a CCKW with a No. 7 wrecker set on 23 December 1943. To the side is an open-cab CCKW containing a mobile machine shop with an ST-6 collapsible body. The door at the front of the body is open, exposing the electrical generator to view. (National Archives)

While Sgt. Melvin C. Sims supervises from the rear of the No. 7 wrecker, Private 1st Class Jack Griffith and Sgt. William C. Bell are pulling the engine of the same car seen in the preceding photo, preparatory to performing a rings-and-bearing job on the engine. The No. 7 wrecker was very handy for lifting jobs of this sort. (National Archives)

In England on the last day of 1943, a U.S. Army officer, center, and a British Army officer, left, give instructions to the lead drivers of a convoy at a point where it has reformed into two columns. The crews of the trucks in the left column apparently were expecting, or had driven through, snow, since their tires are fitted with chains. (Bryce Sunderlin)

At a railroad yard in the European Theater, an AFKWX cab and chassis have been adapted to railroad driving wheels mounted on a frame, for performing switching work, which involved shunting railroad cars around a railroad yard. Two horns and a spotlight are on the cab roof. The flaming grenade symbol of the Ordnance Corps is on the door. (General Motors)

The driver of the AFKWX switcher is easing the vehicle up to a railroad car. The AFKWX switcher has a buffer on each side of the front of its frame, which will engage with buffers on the rear of the railroad car. The switcher had buffers on the rear too. (General Motors)

Troops of the 3899th Quartermaster Gas Supply Company are being transported in a CCKW with a composite cargo body near Bovey Tracey, Devonshire, England, on 20 January 1944. The truck is towing a trailer with a 30-gallon gasoline dispenser and a hose. Quartermaster gas supply companies were responsible for transporting gasoline to frontline units. (National Archives via Bryce Sunderlin)

Left: Under hard use, CCKW chassis frames were susceptible to bending and damage. At Depot 0-616 in Wallasey, England, in January 1944, two mechanics are using an improvised method to correct a bent frame. A straight steel I-beam has been fastened to the top of the frame, and a hydraulic jack on the I-beam is exerting pressure on a chain in order to pull up and correct the left front of the frame. (National Archives via Bryce Sunderlin)

Below: A Piper Cub observation plane with its wings and rudder removed is loaded on a CCKW-353 in preparation for an amphibious exercise at Crown Hill, Devonshire, England, on 12 February 1944. The truck's registration number was 4126494. (National Archives via Bryce Sunderlin)

Two CCKW drivers, Pfc. Millard Webster and Pfc. William Arno, check the tires of their trucks during a pause in a road march near London, England, on 7 March 1944. The word "Whiskee" is painted on the door of the second CCKW, which bears U.S. Army registration number 4276387. (National Archives via Bryce Sunderlin)

An open-cab CCKW-353-B1 with a cargo-dump body, U.S.A. number 4485736, boards a raft with pneumatic pontoons constructed by the 7th Engineer Battalion, assigned to the artillery of the 5th Infantry Division, at Annalong, County Down, Northern Ireland, on 23 March 1944. (National Archives via Bryce Sunderlin)

CCKWs with shop bodies are temporarily assembled at General Store Depot G-25, Cheltenham, England, on 15 February 1944. The trucks are a mix of open-cab and closed-cab types. The first several shop bodies to the left are the ST-6 model in the collapsed position; beyond them are several ST-6 bodies with the roofs raised and windows installed. To the right is a mix of raised and collapsed bodies. (National Archives via Bryce Sunderlin)

Above: In practice for the forthcoming invasion of Normandy, a CCKW-353 with a trailer hitched to it is being ferried on a raft across the Thames River at Pangbourne, Berkshire, England, on 31 March 1944. The raft, operated by the 512th Engineer Light Pontoon Company, was the Class 9 infantry-support raft with five pontoons, and it was powered by two outboard motors. (U.S. Army Engineer History Office)

Left: GMC AFKWXs are in temporary storage at Supply Depot 0-637, Ashton Court, Bristol, England, on 20 March 1944. These are mid-production examples, with open cabs and wooden, 15-foot bodies. The U.S. Army registration numbers of the nearest two trucks are 4548609 and 4550089. Overhead, a barrage balloon provides protection against low-level enemy aircraft attack. (National Archives via Bryce Sunderlin)

On New Year's Day 1944, a truck convoy, including two mid-production AFKWXs in the foreground, is preparing to move out from Supply Depot 0-639 at Maydock Park, England. The side curtain, or door, on the cab of the second AFKWX in line is the early open-cab type, with unequal-sized clear-plastic windows. (National Archives via Bryce Sunderlin)

At an ordnance repair depot in Essex, England, on 8 April 1944, mechanics are salvaging usable parts from a Jeep, left, and a CCKW, right, before the vehicles are scrapped. The charred remnants of the bows and racks in the cargo body of the CCKW indicate that it suffered a fire. (National Archives via Bryce Sunderlin)

Crews of trucks being transported on the main deck of a ship relax on the tops of their vehicles. To the left is a CCKW-based, 400-gallon powered-decontaminating apparatus, with chemical cans stored on the platform to the side of the tank. The closed cab of this truck has an opening for a machine-gun ring mount, but the ring mount itself is not installed. (U.S. Army Chemical Corps Museum)

On D+10, June 16, 1944, U.S. Army trucks are headed to Omaha Beach in Normandy via a long floating dock constructed by U.S. Navy Seabees. To the right, awaiting its turn to head ashore, is a mid-production GMC AFKWX with an open cab and 15-foot wooden cargo body. (National Archives via Bryce Sunderlin)

At an English port, CCKW-353 4151235 backs up the ramp into LST-134 preparatory to the invasion of Normandy. The flexible hose along the left side of the windshield is the carburetor air intake of a permanent fording kit. "Lil' Nellie" is painted in script on the front of the hood, as well as a stencil indicating that Prestone antifreeze was added to the radiator in 1943. (National Archives via Bryce Sunderlin)

Left: In the port of Cherbourg, France, captured by U.S. forces in late June 1944, crawler cranes are being used to unload supplies brought in by DUKW amphibian trucks from Liberty ships in the harbor. In turn, five ACKWXs visible in the photo are prepared to be loaded with those cargoes and transfer them to supply dumps inland. (U.S. Army Engineer History Office)

Below: A broad view is presented of a transfer point on a beachhead in Normandy on 19 July 1944 where cargoes brought ashore by DUKWs were transferred to trucks for transport to supply dumps inland. Lined up waiting their turn to be loaded is a variety of vehicles, including CCKWs and AFKWXs. (National Archives via Bryce Sunderlin)

A CCKW-353 of the 94th Field Artillery, 4th Armored Division, passes through Periers, France, en route to Coutances on 30 July 1944. The placard affixed to the grille reads "RATIONS." The round placard on front of the left bumper contains the vehicle's bridge-weight classification, with the combination classification for the truck and its normally-towed trailer, 9, over the truck-only classification, 7. (National Archives via Bryce Sunderlin)

On the shore at Cherbourg, France, on 29 July 1944, U.S. Army Engineers are working on a marshalling area. Two CCKWs are in view: an open-cab type with a wooden cargo body at the center, and, to the right of it, a closed-cab compressor truck for supplying compressed air for powering pneumatic tools. (U.S. Army Engineer School History Office)

As the Allied forces gained footholds on the European continent, CCKWs were heavily involved in the rebuilding of strategic facilities and infrastructures. Here, on 13 July 1944 during construction of a railroad track spur, a motor shovel is loading a CCKW with a cargo-dump body with soil at a French port, probably Cherbourg. (U.S. Army Engineer School History Office)

A U.S. Army Engineers rock crusher, left, is in operation during road-repair work near Carentan, France, on 11 July 1944. Standing by to the left is CCKW 4486963, equipped with a cargo-dump body. Stowed on the right running board are liquid containers. Marked on the windshield is "Pvt. [?] Gilgunn." (U.S. Army Engineer School History Office)

Above: On a road between Blosville and Saint-Côme-du-Mont in Normandy on 20 July 1944, a CCKW dump truck to the far left is unloading rocks for processing by a screening and secondary-crushing plant. To the front of the CCKW with cargo-dump body in the left foreground is another one that is being filled with gravel. In the right background, men are filling a CCKW with cargo-dump body with gravel by hand. (U.S. Army Engineer School History Office)

Right: CCKWs also were often called on to assist in efforts to clear rubble from war-ravaged French towns and cities. Here, a power shovel prepares to place a load of debris into an open-cab CCKW with a cargo-dump body and a machine-gun ring mount. The location was Alençon, France, on 25 August 1944. (U.S. Army Engineer School History Office)

An open-cab CCKW-353 towing a trailer crosses an M2 steel treadway bridge supported by three inflatable pontoons somewhere in France on 27 August 1944. This combat bridge served to temporarily replace the blown bridge in the background. (U.S. Army Engineer School History Office)

On 18 August 1944, three days after the start of the invasion of Southern France, U.S. Army Engineers are laying a steel-mesh roadway on Beach Alpha Red near Cavalaire-sur-Mer. More rolls of the mesh are on the open-cab CCKW-353 to the right. (Navy History and Heritage Command)

Red Ball Express

One of the most celebrated achievements of the U.S. Army Transportation Corps is the Red Ball Express. The Red Ball Express was a truck convoy system operating between St. Lo and Paris from August through November 1944. Its initial objective was to move 102,000 tons of supplies which had been landed at Normandy to troops advancing across France at an impressive pace. The Red Ball Express transported supplies, not personnel.

To achieve this objective, various roadways were taken over, restricted not only to just military traffic, but specifically to just Red Ball Express traffic, and made one way, the trucks then operating in a massive loop. The name "Red Ball" was taken from the railway term for a fast freight train. The Red Ball Express operated around the clock.

By the end of August, the initial allocation of 118 light and heavy truck companies had been upped to 132 U.S. Army truck companies, and almost 6,000 trucks were involved in the operation.

Light truck companies were typically equipped with 2½ ton GMC 6x6s, either CCKW or AFKWX, often pulling 1-ton trailers. Companies could be formed of either cargo or tanker trucks. Cargo trucks were assumed to be loaded to their 5-ton on-road limit, but were routinely overloaded. A few light truck companies used Chevrolet 1½ ton or Studebaker US6 tractors and 6-ton trailers. The heavy truck companies utilized 4-5 ton truck tractors and 10 or 12-ton trailers.

About 75% of the personnel involved in this operation were black. As the duration of the operation was extended, so was the trip length. By November, the average round trip was 600 miles and Red Ball operations consumed 300,000 gallons of gasoline per day. The total tonnage delivered exceeded 323,000 tons.

Convoy operations began each day at 1800 hours. Initially, each company operated in its own 40 to 48 truck convoy, but this convoy sized proved unwieldy, and subsequently platoon-size 20-truck convoys began to be used. The convoys divided into serials (groups of a minimum of 5 trucks), with the trucks in 60 yard intervals, closing to 15 yards in towns. Each serial had an officer in charge. Each vehicle in Red Ball service was to have a red metal disk, of a size similar to that used for yellow bridge weight classification disks, affixed to the front of the vehicle, usually on the grille. The lead vehicle of the convoy carried a blue flag, with the last vehicle carrying a green flag – if flags were not available a white board with black lettering was used instead. A one-minute gap was allowed between serials, and two minutes between convoys. The maximum speed limit for this "high speed" operation was 25 MPH, and drivers were not permitted to pass. Every two hours a ten-minute break was scheduled, this was be at exactly ten minutes before every even hour. During these breaks the drivers were expected to check and readjust their load bindings, as well as inspect and make running repairs on their trucks – and presumably have some rest. Four 30-minute meal halts were also scheduled, at 0600, 1200, 1800 and 2400 hours. Vehicles which became disabled were to be parked at the side of the road for repair or retrieval by roving "road patrols," usually equipped with 4-ton Diamond T wreckers. Near the end of the Red Ball Express, a round trip took 72 hours, with the trucks running non-stop, the driver and codriver alternating duties. Fatigue, both of men and equipment, lead to many accidents.

The success of the Red Ball Express lead to several similar operations, including the "Red Lion", Green Diamond Express, White Ball Express, the Little Red Ball, and the ABC and XYZ operations, the latter being larger than the Red Ball in terms of tonnage.

As the Allied armies pursued the Germans across France in the late summer and early fall of 1944, those armies struggled to keep sufficient supplies moving forward to meet the requirements of the armies. To meet that need, the Red Ball Express, a huge fleet of cargo trucks that ran around the clock, was formed. Here, an MP directs traffic next to a sign designed to motivate Red Ball Express drivers. (National Archives via Bryce Sunderlin)

During night-driving operations in mid-August 1944, the driver of this AFKWX failed to notice that this bridge had been bombed and drove off it, becoming tightly wedged between the bridge abutments. This undoubtedly posed an interesting problem for a recovery crew and may have necessitated the construction of a pontoon bridge nearby or the rerouting of the truck route. (National Archives via Bryce Sunderlin)

Somewhere in France on 25 September 1944, the MP to the left holds up a column of trucks of the Red Ball Express while a truck pulling a semi-trailer loaded with artillery ammunition advances in the opposite direction to the right. Mounted as a war trophy on the grille of the CCKW to the left is a German stahlhelm or helmet. (National Archives via Bryce Sunderlin)

Right: At a vehicle-servicing area in France, vehicles of the Red Ball Express are stopped for refueling, servicing, and a change of drivers. To the far right, a truck with a No. 7 wrecker kit stands ready for any major lifting operations. Most of the men visible here are African-Americans, who constituted a large proportion of Red Ball Express drivers. (National Archives via Bryce Sunderlin)

Below: Two mechanics of a U.S. Army Ordnance company, Cpl. Doyle Agnas, left, and Pvt. Randall Roberts, are performing an engine change on a closed-cab CCKW at a repair and maintenance depot in France on 6 September 1944. Stenciled on the top of the valve cover of the GMC 270 engine is its type number, 3230, which was a fourth-series 270 engine. (National Archives via Bryce Sunderlin)

At a U.S. Army salvage yard on 1 September 1944, G.I.s sort through reusable scraps in front of a backdrop of dozens of bodies and cabs from wrecked trucks. Recognizable in that mass are some CCKW open cabs and closed cabs and bodies, including mobile shop vans. (National Archives via Bryce Sunderlin)

At the same salvage yard portrayed in the preceding photo, damaged truck cabs are piled up awaiting further disposition. What couldn't be salvaged for replacement assemblies would be relegated to scrap. A notation on this and the preceding photo refers to a location code-named G-25, probably a reference to U.S. Army General Store Depot G-25 at Cheltenham, England. (National Archives via Bryce Sunderlin)

A truck assembly point operated by the 432nd Motor Vehicle Assembly Company, 350th Ordnance Battalion, at La Cambe, France, is documented in a 12 August 1944 photograph. At one point this operation was unboxing and reassembling 100 GMC 2½-ton 6x6 trucks per day. Unlike the two-unit packs used for shipping closed-cab CCKWs, these packs contain a single closed-cab CCKW. (National Archives via Bryce Sunderlin)

At another part of the truck assembly base at La Cambe on 27 July 1944, ordnance personnel are putting together newly arrived open-cab CCKWs. In the foreground is a set of axles on work stands. In the left background, several CCKW-353 chassis are being prepared. In the right background, the cab, the front clip, and the wooden body have been installed on a CCKW-353. (National Archives via Bryce Sunderlin)

The assembly area at La Cambe, France, is shown in an early August 1944 photo. In the foreground, the boxes containing the axles for two-unit packs of CCKWs are being readied. Farther along are wheels ready to be mounted. In the background are chassis frames undergoing work. To the right on roller conveyors are several unboxed twin-packs of chassis frames. (National Archives via Bryce Sunderlin)

At La Cambe, France, in late July 1944, two members of an ordnance company prepare the fender group for mounting on a CCKW. Attached to the inboard edge of the fender is the louvered front fender skirt. In the background are several open-cab assemblies. (National Archives via Bryce Sunderlin)

At a vehicle assembly area in the field, possibly at La Cambe, mechanics make adjustments to a GMC 2½-ton 6x6 chassis with Chevrolet axles. A succession of overhead tracks to support chain hoists was formed from horizontal I-beams mounted on vertical poles. (National Archives via Bryce Sunderlin)

A U.S. Army Ordnance mechanic works on the fan belt of a GMC 270 engine on a 2½-ton 6x6 chassis at a field assembly area. A piece of plywood was fastened to the bottom of the exhaust manifold to keep out moisture and foreign objects. This is an earlier production engine, as denoted by the diecast carburetor. (National Archives via Bryce Sunderlin)

Not far to the west of La Cambe in Normandy was another U.S. Army Ordnance vehicle assembly area, at Isigny, documented in a 25 July 1944 photograph showing CCKW-353 chassis frames being prepared. To the left is a cab on a hoist, ready to be placed on a chassis. In the right background are several trucks and vans under camouflage netting. (National Archives via Bryce Sunderlin)

At a vehicle assembly area in Normandy, members of an ordnance unit are making adjustments to the engine and other components on CCKW frames. During this process, it was necessary to install components that had been removed for shipping and to reconnect electrical wires, fuel lines, brake lines, and so forth. (National Archives via Bryce Sunderlin)

At the La Cambe assembly area on 27 July 1944, Technician 4th Class Raymone Mewes and Pfc. Donald Smith, both hailing from Sheboygan, Wisconsin, are reconnecting the lines on an open-cab CCKW. Although the field-assembly process was not as arduous and complex as the original assembly process of these vehicles, it nonetheless required expertise and methodical work. (National Archives via Bryce Sunderlin)

The vehicle assembly area at Isigny, France, appears to be a study in organized chaos on 25 July 1944. In the left foreground, a man is preparing bows for assembly. At the center is a forklift to assist in lifting and moving heavy components. Farther on, wooden cargo bodies are being prepared, and in the distance, open cabs are lined up. (National Archives via Bryce Sunderlin)

Using a chain hoist on an overhead I-beam, Technicians 5th Class Adrian Stephen William Wiley are lowering an open cab onto a CCKW chassis at the vehicle assembly area at La Cambe, France, on 2 August 1944. Once the cab is in place, the electrical lines and regulator on the firewall will be reconnected. (National Archives via Bryce Sunderlin)

A wooden cargo body is about to be lowered onto the chassis of an open-cab CCKW-353 at the Isigny vehicle assembly area on 25 July 1944. To the right is a subassembly station where front fenders are being attached to the grilles. To the left are several shop trailers. (National Archives via Bryce Sunderlin)

At La Combe on 26 September 1944, vehicle assemblers are lowering a wooden body onto a CCKW-353 chassis. Once the body was in place, the first step was to insert drift pins to secure the front and rear of the body to the frame. Then, hold-down bolts and U-clips were installed, and electrical connections were made. (National Archives via Bryce Sunderlin)

One of the final touches in the assembly of a boxed truck was painting unit codes on the bumpers. At the 83rd Quartermaster Depot, U.S. First Army, at Neblon, Belgium on 2 February 1945, Tech. 5 Harold Bilby, left, holds a stencil while Tech. 5 Chester Skitski applies paint with a stencil brush to the left side of the front bumper of a CCKW. (National Archives via Bryce Sunderlin)

An M1 heavy wrecker, left, unloads a boxed Continental R-975-C1 radial tank engine from the cargo body of a CCKW at a forward supply depot near Hirson, France, on 2 October 1944. More boxed Continental R-975-C1 engines are stored to the right. (National Archives)

The driver of this mired CCKW, Tech. 5 Victor Keller, assesses the prospects of getting his truck recovered and moving again. The vehicle bears markings of Headquarters of Gen. Omar Bradley's Twelfth Army Group, which was located at Verdun, France, at that time. (National Archives via Bryce Sunderlin)

A CCKW-based water purification truck has been set up near a stream. Two temporary water tanks covered with tarpaulins have been set up adjacent to a bridge near Etienne, France, in October 1944. In the foreground next to the trailer is a water pump. (U.S. Army Engineer School History Office)

Privates 1st Class Arthur Burly, left, and Albert Hames of Company A, 133rd Engineers, 35th Division, install chains on the tires of their CCKW with a cargo-dump body, somewhere in France in early November 1944. Stored on the side of the cargo body are M1 antitank mines. (National Archives via Bryce Sunderlin)

Right: A CCKW hauling ammunition in Italy on 1 November 1943 pauses on what looks more like a river of mud than a proper road surface. It was assigned to the 346th Field Artillery Battalion of the 91st Division. For better traction, chains were mounted on the tandem tires. A placard reading "AMMO TRAIN" is on the grille.

Below: The 78th Ordnance Battalion's vehicle-collecting point at Verdun, France, is seemingly awash in mud: the typical scenario most everywhere military vehicles operated in Northwestern Europe in the fall of 1944. Damaged vehicles awaiting further disposition include several open-cab CCKWs with one or more axles missing. The second truck from the left has a cargo-dump body. (National Archives via Bryce Sunderlin)

CCKWs backed up to freight cars to the left are taking on cans of lubricants at Petrol, Oils, and Lubricants (POL) Dump Q-328 at West Moors, Dorset, England, on 22 November 1944. In the background are vast stockpiles of 55-gallon drums. (National Archives via Bryce Sunderlin)

Members of the 80th Infantry Division crowded onto CCKWs are about to depart from an assembly point at the front *en route* to a 30-day furlough back in the States on 11 December 1944. Each of them had been wounded or decorated twice. The message "Hello U.S.A." is spelled out on the sides of the two trucks. (General Motors)

Technician 5th Class James W. Miller, left, and Pfc. Fred J. Wenneman unload a German panzerschreck (bazooka) from the rear of a CCKW filled with captured German equipment near Merzenhausen, Germany, on 4 December 1944. Markings on the bumperettes identify this truck as assigned to Headquarters Company, 82nd Armored Reconnaissance Battalion, 2nd Armored Division, which was in the Ninth Army. (National Archives)

A CCKW assigned to an engineer unit of the 2nd Infantry Division fitted with a plow clears snow from a road near Krinkelt, Belgium, on 13 December 1944. This was the lull before the real storm: in three days the Germans would begin the Ardennes Offensive, and a day later the 12th SS Panzer Division would storm Krinkelt, where it would meet stiff resistance from the American defenders. (General Motors)

At a supply dump in the South of France in late December 1944, G.I.s, mostly African-Americans, are loading rations boxes into CCKWs for transportation to the front. The two nearest trucks are CCKW-352s. The third one is a CCKW-353 with a closed cab and a ring mount. (National Archives via Bryce Sunderlin)

One can imagine the frustration of transportation troops who had to deal with thick, soupy mud like this in Northwestern Europe in late 1944. Here, an open-cab GMC AFKWX is so deeply mired that it is taking a bulldozer to recover it. This was a late-production AFKWX with the extended body and the three-section side racks with, respectively, three, two, and three stakes. (National Archives via Bryce Sunderlin)

French laborers are loading two open-cab AFKWXs with five-gallon gasoline containers from the ship at dockside at Rouen, France, on 4 December 1944. The truck to the right bears U.S. Army registration number 4290788, and marked on the front bumper is "CZMTS 3394 QM (TC) TRK 42." (National Archives via Bryce Sunderlin)

Above: In a photograph probably taken in late 1944 or early 1945, G.I.s shovel sand from the cargo-dump body of a CCKW onto an icy stretch of road to assist vehicles with traction. This open-cab CCKW with a ring mount, U.S.A. number 4498813, was assigned to Gen. George S. Patton's Third Army. (Patton Museum)

Left: Perhaps to replace the bridge in the right background, the U.S. Army Engineers built the ford that the CCKW with a ring mount is driving over in a river in France. The procedure was to put in enough fill for vehicles to drive over, but not so much as to dam the river. (U.S. Army Engineer School History Office)

At an undisclosed location in the European Theater of Operations, a crawler-mounted power shovel dumps a load of soil in a CCKW-353 with a cargo-dump body. The CCKW's U.S. Army registration number, 4490222, is visible on the hood. The folding partition that limited the size of the dump load the body could hold is visible. (U.S. Army Engineer School History Office)

At the Port of Marseilles, France, sometime after the capture of that city in late August 1944, the driver of an AFKWX to the right is backing up his truck. Suspended from the boom on the ship is an open-cab Federal Model 94x43 semi-tractor configured with a fifth wheel for towing a semi-trailer. (National Archives via Bryce Sunderlin)

Constant maintenance and repairs were necessary to keep the U.S. Army's vehicles rolling during the final drive into Germany. Here, two mechanics make adjustments to the engine or accessories of a CCKW. An unusual feature is the presence of a blackout lamp over the right service headlight, with a brush guard welded to the top of the service headlight's brush guard. (National Archives via Bryce Sunderlin)

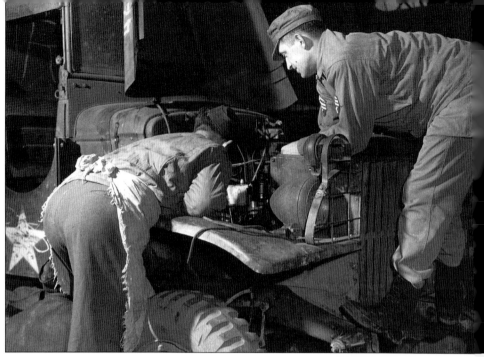

Left: Several G.I.s survey the damage to a destroyed closed-cab CCKW. Many bullet holes are visible on the hood and the cab roof. The left fender is a wreck, and the rear of the chassis appears to have been devastated, with one of the tandem wheels lying to the side of the man to the right. (National Archives via Bryce Sunderlin)

Below: Another devastated CCKW is the object of the curiosity of two G.I.s. The vehicle was a CCKW-352 with an open cab. The fire that engulfed the truck burned the tires, but did not entirely obliterate the markings stenciled on the side of the cab, including "ILLINOIS" and an obsured word that may have been "BOUND." (National Archives via Bryce Sunderlin)

In a scene from the winter of 1944-1945, soldiers are gathered around a tipped-over CCKW with markings on the left bumperettes for the 146th Armored Signals Company, 6th Armored Division. Three soldiers are removing five-gallon liquid containers from the truck and neatly stacking them on the ground. (National Archives via Bryce Sunderlin)

On a narrow, snowy roadway, a column of CCKWs to the right is stopped, while to the left an open-cab CCKW-352 with a ring mount and the word "GASOLiNE" marked on the front of its hood is apparently stuck in a snow bank. The truck to the far right has an unusual location for its pioneer tool rack, on top of the left fender. (National Archives via Bryce Sunderlin)

An open-cab CCKW-353 with a cargo-dump body, U.S. Army registration number 4495595 has been modified with a plow on the front end. This vehicle would have been used to keep roads clear of snow. Snow chains are present on the forward outboard tandem tire only. (National Archives via Bryce Sunderlin)

Two U.S. Army combat engineers are using pneumatic paving breakers to chop through icy ground somewhere in the European Theater during the winter of 1944-1945. A CCKW compressor truck provides the power for these tools. (National Archives via Bryce Sunderlin)

Four soldiers are helping push a CCKW-353-A2 through a difficult stretch of snowy ground. Both of the side curtains, or cab doors, are open, accounting for the odd appearance of the front of the cab. In addition to the five-gallon liquid container on the running board, another container is stowed on the side of the cab. (National Archives via Bryce Sunderlin)

Vehicular traffic swarms around Bastogne, Belgium, in the winter of 1944-1945. This city gained immortality for the U.S. forces's heroic stand there during the Battle of the Bulge. At the bottom, a snow-filled CCKW cargo truck is about to exit Rue de Assenois. In the background is the public plaza now known as McAuliffe Square. (National Archives)

A CCKW-353 is engulfed in flames. A close examination of the photo reveals that the cargo body was full of five-gallon liquid containers, probably filled with gasoline. Some of the containers are scattered on the ground. (National Archives via Bryce Sunderlin)

Mud was an enemy on almost all battle fronts in World War II, and this was the case in the European Campaign. This CCKW, U.S.A. number 4184327, has become deeply mired in mud and will probably need to be recovered by another vehicle. The cargo body was loaded with tires and inner tubes. (National Archives via Bryce Sunderlin)

This CCKW-353 is hopelessly mired in thick mud. Five-gallon liquid containers were stowed in the area below the front of the cargo body where the spare tire normally was located. A pioneer tool rack is mounted horizontally above the tandem wheels, and several shovels are stored on the front of the side of the body. (National Archives via Bryce Sunderlin)

Left: Two G.I.s are beginning to mount metal treads on the tires of a CCKW equipped with dual front tires. Once installed, the treads would form a continuous track around the front tires. On the tandem tires, the tracks wound around the front and rear dual tires as a unit rather around each dual set of tires. (National Archives via Bryce Sunderlin)

Below: It is slow and methodical going as a CCKW-353 tows a 40mm Bofors antiaircraft gun through deep mud somewhere in the European Theater. Two men are standing up in the front of the cargo body, and a .50-caliber machine gun is in the travel position on the ring mount. (General Motors)

Wrecked, damaged and worn vehicles were salvaged to supply parts to maintain the remaining vehicles, or to form a pool of material for large remanufacturing operations commonly known as Depot Rebuilds. Here, an M1A1 wrecker forms the backdrop for a stack of reclaimed CCKW cabs awaiting reuse somewhere in Europe. (National Archives via Bryce Sunderlin)

Captured German soldiers are loading the body of a U.S. soldier into the rear of a CCKW at the site of a suspected massacre on 7 February 1945. At this site, located in the VI Corps area, 57 American closely grouped soldiers were found shot to death, many in the face and head, suggesting that they were massacred. In the background are G.I.s investigating the scene to determine if an atrocity had been committed. (National Archives)

U.S. vehicles pass through a narrow street in a war-torn European town in the final months of World War II. Several troop-carrying CCKWs are in the right lane, including one with markings for the 3597th Quartermaster Truck Company, Third Army. (National Archives via Bryce Sunderlin)

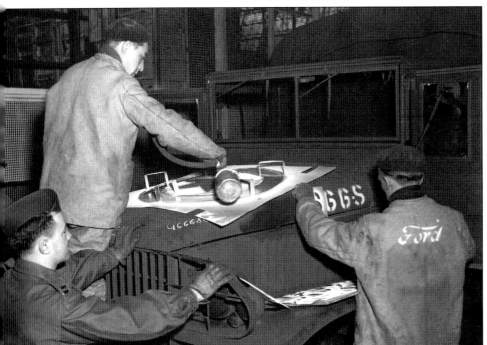

European civilian workers, supervised by a U.S. Army officer, are applying markings to the front clip of a CCKW. One worker is spraying a white identification star and circle on the hood. Handle-like connectors hold the outer part of the stencil to the inner portion. To the right, another worker is using individual stencils to spray on the U.S.Army registration number over an area where the registration number had been oversprayed with Olive Drab paint. (National Archives via Bryce Sunderlin)

A CCKW laden with liquid containers and supply crates and towing a trailer passes what appears to be a laager or encampment area for M4A3E8 medium tanks. Two five-gallon liquid containers are stored on racks on the truck's running board. In the left background is a CCKW with a large load of liquid containers in the cargo body. (National Archives)

Above: A CCKW-353 with a pedestal-mounted, water-cooled .50-caliber machine gun in the cargo body and towing a 40mm Bofors antiaircraft gun precedes an M8 Greyhound scout car across a bridge over the Dill River near Katzenfurt, Germany, near the end of the war in Europe. The two vehicles were assigned to the First Army, and the photo probably was taken at or near the time the First Army broke through the German line along the Dill in late March 1945. (National Archives)

Right: At an assembly area in a mountainous area in the waning days of World War II in the ETO, troops are sleeping in their bedrolls in broad daylight: around noon, judging by the shadows. Two CCKWs are parked by them, one of which has a trailer full of lumber hitched to it. During the rapid drive across Europe, troops of the U.S. Army were often pushed to their limits and had to grab sleep when the opportunity came. (National Archives)

Left: An open-cab CCKW is making a river crossing on a pontoon bridge. The loss of numerous strategic bridges across major rivers on the Allied armies' routes into Germany necessitated the frequent construction of temporary bridges. Pontoon bridges were best suited for spanning wide rivers. (U.S. Army Engineers School History Office)

Below: The First Army's 86th Engineer Heavy Ponton Battalion ferried vehicles across the Rhine River during the March 1945 crossings at Remagen, Germany. Here, a closed-cab CCKW piled high with supplies is in front of an open-cab CCKW, similarly heavily loaded, on a pontoon raft of the 86th. (U.S. Army Engineers School History Office)

A Multiple Gun Motor Carriage M16 armed with a quad .50-caliber machine gun mount stands antiaircraft watch as a closed-cab CCKW packed with captured German troops drives by. (Air Defense Artillery Museum)

A U.S. Army Ordnance officer goes down a checklist at a salvage yard in Europe where G.I.s are stacking discarded vehicle parts and assemblies. To the right of the hood that the two men to the far left are lifting is part of a CCKW open cab. (National Archives via Bryce Sunderlin)

Two CCKWs roll through a destroyed neighborhood during the drive into Germany in the spring of 1945. The nearest vehicle, a CCKW-352 bearing markings of the 904th Field Artillery Battalion of the 79th Infantry Division, is filled with troops and is towing a 105mm howitzer. Stenciled on the front of the hood is "C.E. [or possibly F.] HALL" (National Archives via Bryce Sunderlin)

U.S Army vehicles cross the Alexander Patch Bridge over the Rhine River at Worms. This bridge, named after the commander of the U.S. Seventh Army, was constructed by the 85th Engineer Heavy Ponton Battalion and was 1,047 feet long. On the opposite bank are the remains of the Ernst Ludwig Bridge. (National Archives via Bryce Sunderlin)

At a river-crossing site in Germany in early 1945, the truck-mounted crane to the left is about to lift an inflatable pontoon from a CCKW-353 cargo truck. Although not visible here, the CCKW probably had forward and aft support frames to bear the considerable weight of the pontoon. (U.S. Army Engineer School History Office)

A convoy of U.S. Army Engineer CCKWs crossing a field near Kapfelberg, Germany, are almost dwarfed by the inflatable pontoons they are transporting for bridging the Danube River during the drive to capture the city of Regensburg in April 1945. The trucks had special frames to support the pontoons. (National Archives)

At a facility billed as the world's largest gas station, near Reims, France, the 3939th Gas Supply Company fueled and serviced convoys transporting troops being redeployed from Europe to the Pacific. The 3939th, supplemented by 250 German prisoners, could fuel and service 100 trucks in 15 minutes. (National Archives via Bryce Sunderlin)

Above: In early April 1945, U.S. tanks and trucks, including the CCKW-353s to the left and an M4A3E8 medium tank next to them, are parked at a recently captured Luftwaffe airfield near Muhlhausen, Germany. In the background are various German vehicles and a number of Junkers Ju88G night fighters. (National Archives)

Right: Belgian civilians assist troops of the 430th Tire Repair Company in piling stocks of tires at Depot O-656 in La Louvière, Belgium, on 5 May 1945. These are used tires that have been damaged or worn in service and will be repaired and refurbished at this base. At its highest point, the pile is 56¬ tires high. (National Archives via Bryce Sunderlin)

German prisoners of war are washing U.S. Army trucks, including a Diamond T 4-ton truck to the left and a CCKW-353 to the right, at Camp Washington, near Laon, France, on 19 June 1945. The trucks were being readied for redeployment to the Pacific Theater of War. This camp was one of several under the auspices of the Assembly Area Command, headquartered at Reims, France, which controlled the redeployment of troops in the European Theater. (National Archives via Bryce Sunderlin)

A storage depot officer checks U.S. Army trucks at the staging area at Calas, near Marseille, France, in June 1945. The vehicles were being readied for transfer to the Pacific Theater, where, it was anticipated, they would be needed in a planned invasion of Japan. In the right background are quantities of open-cab CCKWs. (National Archives via Bryce Sunderlin)

In June 1945, a month after the German surrender, CCKWs in Ellrich, Germany, are loaded with displaced persons (DPs), civilians whom the Germans had forcibly brought from their homelands to Germany or its occupied countries for various reasons. The civilians now would be repatriated. (Patton Museum)

At the open-storage and warehouse area of Depot M-407 in Trilport, France, in July 1945, a variety of U.S. Army trucks and vehicles is in view, including an open-cab CCKW-353 towing a trailer in the center foreground and an open-cab CCKW-353 parked next to a closed-cab CCKW in the right foreground. (National Archives via Bryce Sunderlin)

Members of a decontamination unit appear to be treating a mound of earth contaminated with hazardous chemicals. These G.I.s can, if necessary, use the powered decontamination apparatus in the background to spray the area to neutralize the hazardous substances. (U.S. Army Chemical Corps Museum)

What appears to be a civilian service station is being put to use as a light vehicle refueling point for the Seventh Army during its advance through Europe in early 1945. The G.I. to the left appears to be checking the level of fuel in the underground tank while the man just beyond him is pumping gasoline into the underground tank from a CCKW gasoline tanker. The light-colored sign on the rear of the tanker reads "DANGER / GASOLINE." (Fred Crismon collection)

A crew of German laborers conscripted by U.S. Military Government authorities at Stolberg performs repairs to a road in a mountainous area near the western border of Germany, probably in the late winter of 1945. In the right background is a U.S. Army Engineer CCKW compressor truck with what appear to be tire chains draped from the air receiver. To the left of the compressor truck is a CCKW cargo-dump truck. (National Archives via Bryce Sunderlin)

In a town in the European Theater of Operations, a woman walks nonchalantly down a street as U.S. Army vehicles stand by in the background. Two CCKWs are in view. The one at the center is towing a 40mm Bofors antiaircraft gun with a canvas tarpaulin covering most of the mount. (Patton Museum)

Two CCKWs with shop bodies depart from Camp Oklahoma City, one of the Assembly Area Command's bases near Reims, France. At the time this photo was taken, around June 1945, the 87th Infantry Division was gathering here prior to being redeployed to the United States. (National Archives)

An open-cab CCKW with a ring mount crosses a Bailey bridge somewhere in the European Theater of Operations. Named after its British inventor, Donald Bailey, this type of bridge was a prefabricated, modular, truss design that could be erected without the need for heavy equipment or extensive training. (Patton Museum)

Above: At a vehicle repair and maintenance area in the European Theater, several M4 medium tanks are undergoing work, including an M4A1 at the center with its tracks removed and the name *Carolyn Rose* stenciled on the sponson. To the left is the rear end of a mobile repair shop based on an ST-5 shop body mounted on a CCKW. (Patton Museum)

Right: A G.I. guard with an M1 carbine operates the latch of the safety strap on the rear of a CCKW loaded with German prisoners of war. Scenes like this were common in the closing months of World War II, as captured German troops were transported to POW camps. (Patton Museum)

U.S. Army infantrymen file through a town during the waning days of the war in Europe. Signs on the buildings are in German. To the left and in the background are several CCKWs. The closest one has a spare tire stowed on the front end. Despite the very late stage of combat operations in the ETO, a censor has obliterated the unit markings on the fender. (General Motors)

A CCKW with a cargo-dump body and a ring mount, U.S.A. number 4494465, receives a load from a power shovel during clearing operations in a war-torn town in the European Theater. With its low sides and partition limiting the size of the dump load, these trucks could not match the debris-hauling abilities of high-capacity dump trucks. (National Archives)

Another cargo-dump CCKW is being loaded by a crawler power shovel in a ruined European town. Of interest are the field-installed racks between the bumper and the fenders, probably for holding five-gallon liquid containers, and the absence of the flap over the hole in the canvas side curtain or door of the cab for allowing the driver to reach the curtain latches. (National Archives)

460

Combat engineers haul an inflatable pontoon for the pontoon bridge under construction in the background. To their rear is a compressor truck, which would have provided air for inflating the pontoons. Several pontoons in the foreground await inflation. (General Motors)

CCKW-353 U.S.A. number 4124888 has been converted to a railroad switching vehicle by installing steel wheels on the existing wheels. In lieu of buffers, a wooden beam has been bolted to the front of the chassis. To the right is another 6x6 truck converted to a switching vehicle. (Fred Crismon collection)

At a harbor in India in 1942, a closed-cab CCKW-352 has been converted to a semi-trailer by the addition of a fifth wheel on the chassis frame. The semi-trailer hitched to it is being loaded with large bombs from the ship in the background. (General Motors)

At an unidentified port, probably in the Pacific or China-Burma-India Theaters of Operations, a CCKW with a van body is being lowered from a ship onto a dock. The body appears to be a Signal Corps Model K60 mobile radio shelter, as typified by the lack of windows on the side and the presence of the small door with a recessed handle toward the front of the side of the body. (National Archives)

G.I.s load crates of food from freight cars to CCKW cargo trucks in Assam, India, in February 1944. These provisions were earmarked for troops who were building the Ledo Road from India to Burma (today, Myanmar). In Burma, the Ledo Road linked up to the Burma Road which led to the Chinese city of Kunming. (U.S. Army Transportation Museum)

On the Burma Road in China near the Huitong Bridge, equipment for road-construction crews is about to be ferried across the Nujiang River (called the Salween River in Burma). A Jeep and a closed-cab CCKW-353 piled high with supplies are on the raft, whose pontoons are formed of empty 55-gallon drums lashed together.

A native worker holding a checklist observes the work as G.I.s secure a sling to some logs during a clearing operation somewhere in the China-Burma-India Theater on 18 October 1944. In the background is a CCKW in use as a semi-tractor with a semi-trailer full of logs hitched to it. A single spare tire is stowed to the rear of the open cab. The logs were destined for a sawmill.

An International Harvester TD-18 tractor is pulling a CCKW in use as a semi-tractor through thick mud during construction of the Ledo Road in Burma. Work began on this road, also called the Stilwell Road, in December 1942 as an alternate route after the Japanese cut the Burma Road. The CCKW is pulling a semi-trailer loaded with logs. (U.S. Army Engineer School History Office)

In the foreground, a convoy of CCKW cargo trucks departs from the 3538th Ordnance Medium Automotive Company (MAC) vehicle depot. This company arrived in the China-Burma-India Theater in September 1942, and the base in this photo may have been the one at Chabua, India. (U.S. Army Engineer School History Office)

463

Trucks, including the omnipresent CCKWs, are forming up for a convoy at a vehicle depot somewhere in the China-Burma-India Theater. In the background are open-sided warehousing facilities. (National Archives)

Above: At a vehicle depot apparently in the China-Burma-India Theater, Dodge 4x4s predominate, but an open-cab CCKW-353 is in the center foreground, towing an artillery piece. In the background are 6x6 cargo trucks that probably included CCKWs. (National Archives)

Left: In this photo, which appears to be related to the preceding one by dint of their identification numbers, a CCKW-353 towing a field piece precedes a convoy of open-cab CCKW cargo trucks. Unfortunately, no unit markings or registration numbers are visible on the trucks. (National Archives)

At a checkpoint most likely in the China-Burma-India Theater, U.S. and Asian officials go down checklists as a convoy of CCKWs goes through. At least the first two trucks have cargo-dump bodies with the side racks installed. (National Archives)

Above: The sign on the roof of the hut at this checkpoint, probably in the China-Burma-India Theater, identifies it as Military Police Traffic Control Station No. 8. At the front, an MP checks a Jeep, while two CCKW-353s are parked behind it. (National Archives)

Right: An MP communicates on an EE-8-A field telephone set as a convoy of CCKWs passes by, probably in the China-Burma-India Theater. The use of radio and telephone communications to coordinate convoy traffic was one of the key elements in the success of the far-flung transportation networks in the CBI Theater. (National Archives)

A mix of vehicles is in this convoy, including an open-cab CKW-353 to the far left and, to the front of it, an open-cab 353 with a cargo-dump body, towing a trailer with a tarpaulin over it. The next CCKW in line has a cargo-dump body with the front rack removed and what appears to be a machine gun mounted in the body. (National Archives)

Above: Three CCKW-353s make tracks down a dusty road. All three have Model 1608 closed cabs with cowl-mounted rear-view mirrors, steel bodies, symmetrical brush guards, and GMC logos on the top centers of the grilles. All three have pioneer tool racks vertically mounted on the left fronts of the cargo bodies. (National Archives)

Right: A convoy comprising a mix of vehicle models, including ambulances, vans, and 4x4 and 6x6 cargo trucks crosses a pontoon bridge. Partly in view on the rise to the far right is the rear of an engineer CCKW compressor truck. The sides of the compressor are opened, permitting a view inside. (National Archives)

At Mangyou (formerly spelled Mong-yu), near Wanding, Yunnan Province, China, a CCKW towing an artillery piece passes through a ceremonial arch marking the junction of the Burma Road and the Ledo Road on the China-Burma border. The sign to the left signifies that it is 566 miles to Kunming, China, to the left and 478 miles to Ledo, India, to the right. (National Archives)

A CCKW with a SCR-399 radio set passes down a crowded street in a town probably in China. Secured to the cargo body is an HO-17 shelter, which housed the radio equipment and operators. The three whip antennas for the set are not mounted on their bases on the roof of the shelter. (National Archives)

Two sergeants pose by an open-cab CCKW-353 with the tarpaulin decorated to commemorate the first convoy over the Ledo Road. The motto at the bottom of the tarpaulin, "Pick's Pike, Life Line from India to China," was a nod to Gen. Lewis A. Pick, who assumed duties of chief engineer of the Ledo Road in late 1943. Pick led the first convoy over the road, which left Ledo on 12 January 1945 and arrived in Kunming, China, on 4 February.

467

With the assistance of a crane, Indian laborers position a boxed twin-unit pack containing two GMC 2½-ton 6x6 long-wheelbase chassis. Unboxed twin-unit chassis are in the left foreground. A sign inside the building reads, "Sub-Assy. / Front-Rear Axles." (General Motors)

U.S. Army Engineers built this fixed wooden bridge across the Meuse River in or near Sedan, France, in the latter part of World War II. It was the largest fixed bridge constructed by First Army engineers and replaced a bridge blown by the Germans during their retreat through the city in September 1944. Several CCKWs are crossing the bridge.

Private 1st Class Oldrich Safronek fills-up a Jeep at a fueling station in northern Burma in late April 1945. The fuel dispensers, improvised from welded 55-gallon drums, were replenished by a gasoline pipeline that ran along the road. In front of the Jeep is a CCKW fuel or oil servicing truck. (Quartermaster Museum)

Inside a CCKW heavy-machinery shop truck, members of the 967th Engineer Maintenance Company are repairing the clutch of a D7 bulldozer in the India-Burma Theater in August 1945. In the left foreground is a drill press, and in the background is a lathe. The personnel of the 967th arrived in Ledo, India, in April 1944, and their shop trucks joined them two months later. (U.S. Army Engineer School History Office)

Dead-lined, or out of commission, construction equipment awaits repairs at an engineer maintenance base in the India-Burma Theater, August 1945. A CCKW shop truck is among the vehicles to the left, while in the right background, unobstructed from view by other vehicles, is what appears to be an engineer motorized general-purpose shop with its tarpaulin in place and body panels in the travel position. (U.S. Army Engineer School History Office)

A crew of G.I.s is repairing a section of the Ledo Road near Shingbwiyang, Burma, with gravel produced by the rock crusher at the center. Visible in the background is a CCKW air-compressor truck; its air receiver and the left air-hose reel are visible above the man with the shovel bent over at the center of the photo. (U.S. Army Engineer School History Office)

Although hundreds of bridges were constructed on the Ledo and Burma Roads, it was necessary to use ferries to transport trucks across some rivers. Here, at a crossing of the Nujiang River in Yunnan Province, China, a CCKW towing a water trailer embarks on a ferryboat while another CCKW with a water trailer hitched awaits its turn to cross. (U.S. Army Engineer School History Office)

CCKW-353 455422 is being lowered from the attack transport USS *Hunter Liggett* (AP-27) at Tongatabu in the Central Pacific in August 1942. Presumably the landing craft, vehicle (LCV) in the background is about to go into position to receive the truck. (National Archives)

A companion image to the preceding photo documents another phase in an unloading operation involving a CCKW suspended from one of the USS *Hunter Liggett's* booms at Tongatabu in August 1942. Sling cables were hung under the front and the rear of the chassis frame. (National Archives)

A CCKW with a powered decontamination apparatus on the rear of the chassis is being lowered by crane from a ship at Espiritu Santo, New Hebrides, on 23 October 1942. Code-named "Buttons," Espiritu Santo was a key Allied supply and operational base in the Central Pacific Area. (National Archives)

A Higgins tank lighter ferries CCKW 348052 from a transport ship to shore at Espiritu Santo on 25 October 1942. The driver, visible inside the cab, has raised the windshield and opened the door to provide some ventilation in the tropical sun. (National Archives)

Members of Company L, 127th Infantry Regiment, are loading ammunition from a CCKW-353-A2 into a transport plane in Australia in mid-December 1942. The supplies were destined for troops around Buna, New Guinea. The truck was painted in a subtle camouflage scheme of a lighter color sprayed over the base color. A rifle scabbard is strapped above the fender, and a cover is over the grille. (National Archives via Bryce Sunderlin)

On 30 June 1943, D-day on Rendova, an island in the Solomons, a camouflage-painted CCKW wearing tire chains comes ashore, with a wire-mesh roadway to assist in traction on the sand. In the cargo body is a .50-caliber machine gun on a pedestal mount for antiaircraft use. The CCKW's registration number was 474562. (General Motors)

472

A CCKW-353, possibly the same vehicle in the preceding photograph, is poised for an advance on Rendova on 30 June 1943. The tarpaulin is pulled back from the front of the cargo body, revealing that the spare wheel and the rack has been painted in camouflage as well. (General Motors)

Above: Two CCKWs with cargo bodies are set up side by side on New Guinea, serving as a mobile machine shop in late June 1943. The shop was manned by an African-American unit that had been in New Guinea for a year. The tractor to the left is powering a belt that is driving machinery on the left CCKW. (General Motors)

Left: A CCKW-353 that appears to have been taking on supplies from a landing craft, tank, LCT-321, at a beach on Bougainville, in the Southwestern Pacific Area, on 9 November 1943 has become firmly mired in the sand. The chains visible on the tires failed to give the truck sufficient traction in this case. (National Archives via Bryce Sunderlin)

A U.S. Army chemical crew sprays insecticide to control mosquito breeding in a residential neighborhood in the Waikiki area of Honolulu in November 1943. They are using a powered decontamination apparatus on a CCKW to power the sprayers. To the left is Col. George F. Unmacht, the chemical warfare officer of the U.S. Army in Hawaii Territory.

Right: After disembarking from a landing ship, tank, at Cape Gloucester, New Britain, on the day after Christmas 1943, a CCKW with a trailer in tow seems to have become disabled, as it is sitting in the surf with its hood open. The truck is an early CCKW with symmetrical brush guards and the GMC logo plate at the top of the grille. (USMC)

Below: In the Pacific Theater, wherever there was a river to be spanned, the U.S. Navy Construction Battalions, familiarly known as Seabees, were there to erect a bridge, such as this crude but sturdy log example on Cape Gloucester that a CCKW-352 is rolling over. The truck has a Galion dump body built for the U.S. Navy on a U.S. Army contract. Faintly visible on the cab are the number 75 and the horizontal-diamond symbol of the 1st Marine Division. (General Motors)

On a muddy road between the beach and an airfield on New Britain, a CCKW-353 wearing tire chains pauses while a Jeep passes in the other direction. A unit or tactical sign with what appears to be the letter H is on the door of the CCKW. Later on the day this photo was taken, the Seabees turned this muddy trail into a proper road. (USMC)

A CCKW-353 disembarking from a landing ship in the Solomon Islands around January 1944 is carrying a body full of cargo and a trailer full of equipment and supplies for Fleet Air Photographic Squadron 1 (VD-1). This naval unit, which arrived on Guadalcanal in April 1943, flew PB4Y Privateers, providing critical photo-reconnaissance services during the island-hopping offensives in the Central Pacific. (General Motors)

Above: Personnel of the 29th Chemical Company are preparing to spray insecticide to kill mosquitoes to prevent the spread of dengue fever at a residential neighborhood in Honolulu, Hawaii, around late 1943 or early 1944. To accomplish this, they are using sprayers attached to a powered decontamination unit on a closed-cab CCKW. (Chemical Corps Museum)

Right: The African-American crew of the 29th Chemical Company seen in the preceding photo are now spraying down a tree with insecticide, most likely DDT, a popular insecticide in the 1940s that later was found to be highly harmful to the environment and to human health. These men were wearing common overalls and no respirators, leaving them vulnerable to the chemicals they were spraying. (Chemical Corps Museum)

A tractor with a boom is being used to lower 55-gallon drums full of water onto the body of a U.S. Marine Corps CCKW-353 with a cargo-dump body on Saipan on 23 June 1944, eight days after the start of the invasion of that island in the Mariana Islands. The windshield is removed, and the left fender and brushguard met with a mishap and are bent downward. (National Archives)

Marine Corps CCKWs are gathered at Dadi Beach, Guam, in the Mariana Islands during the invasion of that island in the summer of 1944. These included a mix of open- and closed-cab and short- and long-wheelbase versions. Interestingly, all of the headlight housings on these trucks were painted a light color, possibly white. (USMC)

A CCKW-353 outfitted with an A-frame for installing telephone poles in the ground is evidently testing its hoisting capacity by lifting another CCKW. The truck with the A-frame was assigned to the 99th Signal Battalion, Port Moresby, Papua New Guinea, had rollers on frames to the rear of the cab and to the front of the chassis for the winch cable. (General Motors)

Two CCKW-353s disembark from LST-68 onto a prepared sand ramp during the 6th Infantry Division's 30 July 1944 landings at Cape Sansapor, Dutch New Guinea. Both trucks are equipped with permanent fording kits, indicated by the flexible hoses by the left side of the windshields and the stack through the hood of the lead vehicle. (National Archives)

Above: A mired CCKW-353 is being recovered by means of a cable and snatch block on a beach on Morotai in the Halmahera Group on 15 September 1944, the first day of the invasion of that island. The vehicle is equipped with a permanent fording kit. The name "'Little' Johnny" is painted on the side of the cab below a symbol portraying a dump truck, although this truck has a wooden cargo body. (National Archives via Bryce Sunderlin)

Left: Shop bodies on CCKWs sometimes saw use for purposes other than machine and repair shops. On New Caledonia in late September 1944, G.I.s are making use of the services of mobile post office designated Army Post Office (APO) 502, Unit No. 6, Mobile. It was installed in an ST-5 shop body on a CCKW chassis. On the rear door is U.S.A. number 0017983. (National Archives)

At Mar Airfield near Cape Sansapor, Dutch New Guinea, B-25 medium bombers of the 42nd Bomb Group fly overhead on 17 September 1944 as four CCKW 750-gallon fuel or oil servicing trucks stand by. Painted on the tank of the closest truck is "OIL," and "NO SMOKING" is marked in large letters on the side of the body. The third truck in line appears to have "GASOLINE" painted on its tank. (National Archives)

The U.S. Army Engineers operated this water-purification unit on Leyte in the Philippines, shown on 21 October 1944, the day after the invasion landings began. In the background above the portable water reservoir to the left is a CCKW-353 with a cargo body. Hundreds of five-gallon water containers and large and small steel drums await filling with potable water.

A late-production CCKW water purification truck, distinguished by its small side windows, has been set up in a stream by the 1519 Water Supply Company in late April 1945. The scene was near Face Church, Luzon, Philippines. Stenciled at center of the front bumper is the vehicle's 11/9 bridge weight classification, indicating a nominal 9-ton rating for the truck alone, and 11 tons when in combination with its assigned trailer. (National Archives)

The 1519 Water Supply Company has set up this late-production CCKW water purification truck, distinguished by its small side windows, in a stream near Face Church, Luzon, the Philippines, in late April 1945. Stenciled at center of the front bumper is the vehicle's 11/9 bridge weight classification, indicating a nominal 9-ton rating for the truck alone, and 11 tons when in combination with its assigned trailer. (National Archives)

At an excavation site in the Pacific Theater, numerous CCKWs with cargo-dump bodies are transporting the material out. In the background, power shovels are excavating the substance, apparently some type of mineral, and depositing it in the dump trucks. (National Archives)

Military policemen of the 38th Infantry Division guard a group of barefooted Japanese POWs captured in the mountains east of Manila in the Philippines. Two open cab CCKW-353, including one with a ring mount, are standing by to transport the Japanese to a prisoner of war camp. (General Motors)

At the Futenma Vehicle Storage Area on Okinawa after World War II, hundreds of U.S. military vehicles were held until their final disposition was determined. These included Jeeps, ambulances, half-tracks, and trucks of all types. Just beyond the jeep to the right of the line in the center foreground are three CCKWs with ST-6 shop bodies. The one at the center was painted in a three-color camouflage scheme. (National Archives)

A member of the 706th Ordnance Company, 6th Division, operates a bench drill press on a CCKW-353 fitted out as a mobile machine shop on the Kobayashi Line southeast of Manila in mid-March 1945. The racks were hinged to permit using them as work benches, and cabinets and work benches were installed on the floor of the body. Three bows and a framework supported the canvas top. (National Archives)

Another machine-shop CCKW of the 706th Ordnance Company is shown in an 18 March 1945 photograph. On this one, a gasoline-powered air compressor is set up on the rear of the body. Toward the front of the work bench inside are a bench grinder and a vise. An M1 helmet is at the ready in the liquid-container holder on the running board. (National Archives)

Above: At a U.S. Navy mobile radio installation on on Luzon Island on 6 April 1945, the two CCKWs are equipped with shelters housing radio equipment. On the fronts of the shelters are holders for communications cable reels. The trucks' USN registration numbers were 180535 and 198893. (National Archives via Bryce Sunderlin)

Right: At a 500th Bomb Group bomb dump on Saipan on 5 June 1945, personnel are loading M69 napalm bombs onto CCKW bomb-service trucks. The man in the front of the body of the closer truck is operating the hoist winch. Marked on the cab of that truck in large figures is "U.S. ARMY / 500-426." (National Archives)

Right: While the mobile dental lab was used in the ETO during hostilities, this vehicle was the first to see use in the Pacific. Here the vehicle is in use in the Philippines 8 November, 1945, shortly after its arrival in theater. (National Archives)

Below: A fire caused by a gasoline explosion in a U.S. Army motor pool in downtown Manila roars out of control in mid-November 1945. Many trucks and buildings were destroyed and damaged. In the left foreground and background are several CCKWs in various states of repair. (General Motors)

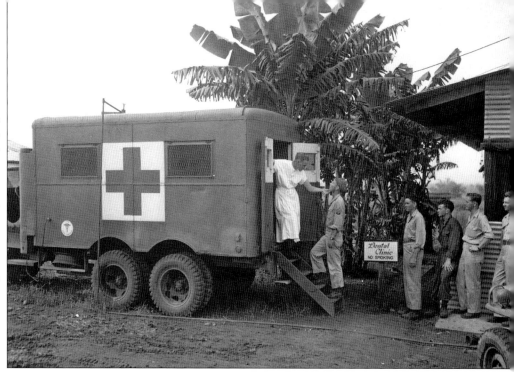

At the end of World War II, the U.S. armed forces had a huge surplus of military vehicles overseas. This posed a large problem in the Pacific Theater, where many of the vehicles were collected at bases at great distances from the United States. One vehicle depot, shown a November 1945 photo, was in New Caledonia. To preserve the vehicles, including CCKWs of various types, waterproofing has been completed. (National Archives via Bryce Sunderlin)

A column of closed-cab CCKWs with a mix of steel bodies and wooden bodies pauses on a mountain road in an undisclosed location. The code 42Q is stenciled on the right side of the bumpers. "U.S. ARMY" with a number over it is painted on the cab doors. (U.S. Army Transportation Museum)

CCKWs probably from the same company as those in the preceding photo carry troops through a mountain pass in an unidentified location. 42Q is marked on the right side of the bumpers and the number 3344 and a number signifying the order of march is on the left side of the bumpers. (U.S. Army Transportation Museum)

CCKW 6046238, mounting a motorized compressor, provides air for pneumatic tools for an engineer unit in the Pacific Theater. The man in the white t-shirt is using a pneumatic drill on a piece of lumber. The unit codes on the truck bumper suggest it was assigned to Headquarters, 2nd Battalion, 534th Engineer Boat and Shore Regiment of the 4th Engineer Special Brigade. This brigade served in New Guinea, the Netherland East Indies, and the Philippines in World War II. (General Motors)

Trucks are queued-up at what seems to be an open-sided warehouse at an unknown location, possibly in the Pacific or the China-India-Burma Theaters in the latter part of World War II. Several CCKWs are along the loading dock, and at the center of the photo is a closed-cab CCKW-353 with an opening in the cab for a ring mount but no mount installed. (Quartermaster Museum)

Chapter 30

Interwar

Even before WWII had drawn to a close, the Army began laying the groundwork for a new generation of wheeled vehicles. A series of Boards were set up which studied the then-current military equipment and considered the attributes needed in the next generation of equipment. These included the 1944 "Armored Equipment Board," the 1945 Army Ground Forces Equipment Review Board – also known as the Cook Board, the 1946 War Department Equipment Review Board, popularly known as the Stilwell Board, and the 1949 Conference on Qualitative Requirements for Tactical Type Ordnance Transport Vehicles.

These reports suggested overall improvements in rust resistance, paint, lighting and other details desired for ALL military vehicles. These vehicles would have vastly interchangeable parts across all sizes as well as all-around increased performance. More specifically to the 2½-ton trucks, it was suggested that the trucks use large single wheels all around, rather than dual rear wheels, preferably with central tire inflation, that the trucks be equipped for fording water at least to the depth of the hood, that sealed brakes be used, that open cabs be convertible to closed cabs, and that automatic transmissions be used, as well as multifuel engines.

The development of the T51, T55 and T55E3 vehicles of the late 1940s and early 1950s was a direct result of the recommendations of these reports. However, as these committees met and engineers crouched over drawing boards, the CCKW soldiered on, not only with U.S. forces, but also with a host of other nations.

The Army's post-WWII CCKW fleet was a hodgpodge of open

After World War II, the U.S. armed services had more military equipment than they needed, including GMC 2½-ton 6x6 trucks, which had been manufactured in the hundreds of thousands. Here, a huge assemblage of army vehicles, including closed-cab CCKW cargo trucks in the foreground, are awaiting sale to the public by the Department of Commerce at the old World's Fair grounds at Flushing, New York.

and closed cab trucks, with both Chevrolet and Timken axles, little changed from the wartime fleet, but for the exchange of a finish of flat olive drab with blue-drab registration numbers for a semigloss olive drab scheme with white markings, which offered better weather protection.

However, the sheer number of CCKWs produced meant that the number of trucks on hand far exceeded the number needed to maintain a peacetime army. Even before VE day surplus trucks were being sold by the Treasury Department – as of 9 April 1945, 50,000 surplus trucks had been sold, with 40 to 50% of those going via dealers to farmers on certificates issued by the Agricultural Adjustment Administration.

Concerns of a massive influx of returned surplus property diluting the market for new vehicles were in part assuaged by Section 33 of the Surplus Property Disposal Act of 1944, which read "It is the policy of this Act to prohibit, as far as feasible and necessary to carry out the objectives of this Act, the importation into the United States of surplus property sold abroad or for export. The Board shall prescribe regulations to carry out such policy, and the importation of surplus property into the United States is hereby prohibited to the extent specified in such regulations. The Secretary of the Treasury is authorized and directed to provide for the enforcement of such regulations." The law made exceptions to this ban on reimportation for members of the armed forces abroad bringing materials back into the U.S. for their own personal use.

In reality, the automotive industry had little to fear with regard to the return of surplus trucks from Europe and Asia. While the U.S. domestic market had been starved for vehicles since early 1942, and the entire civilian commercial and agricultural truck fleets were fatigued from heavy wartime traffic, the U.S. was in far better shape than countries savaged by war. The rebuilding of those nations – not only their truck fleets but even more so their roads, railways, industries and communities would require so many transport vehicles that there would be little to even consider bringing back to the U.S. And, in the U.S. there were ceiling prices imposed by the government, limiting how much vehicles could be sold for, thus leaving little if any profit margin even if one were to attempt to bring the trucks back.

Only well after the war, when inflation took hold, did it become viable to reintroduce surplus into the U.S. A 1951 reimportation of 200 surplus trucks by a West Coast surplus dealer lead to a temporary halt to foreign surplus sales.

More of the CCKWs awaiting sale at Flushing, New York, are viewed. The trucks that are clearly visible are early-production closed-cab CCKWs with GMC logos on the grilles and blackout lamps mounted over the left service headlights. Some examples with ring mounts are present. Bows and racks are stowed inside the steel cargo bodies. Pioneer tool racks are mounted vertically on the front left of many of the bodies.

A woman who has just bought a war-surplus GMC ACKWX-353 cargo truck drives her prize out of Camp Beale, California, on 9 January 1946. The U.S. Army registration number and markings on the bumper had been painted over, and a fresh stencil that probably represented sale information was on the bumper.

Right: A vast U.S. Army surplus-vehicle park at Mourmelon-le-Grand, France, was photographed from above on 14 February 1946. It featured the usual broad mix of vehicle types and models and included many CCKWs. Some with shop bodies are visible, including one at the center and several to the far left.

Below: Surplus U.S. military vehicles assembled at Depot O-644 at Parc du Vincennes, Paris, France, in May 1946, were available for sale to the public. A special office was established at 31 Rue Pauzet where buyers could make the required legal and financial arrangements to purchase vehicles. Once the arrangements were finalized, the vehicle was towed to the front gate, filled with a small amount of gasoline, and transferred to the new owner.

At a U.S. Army Ordnance maintenance and repair shop in Baden-Württemberg, Germany, in January 1946, several German POWs are performing an engine change on a GMC AFKWX. To perform the task, it was necessary to remove the cab. Ordnance personnel instructed the POWs in the procedure. The engine that is being installed appears to be painted light gray, rather than the normal GMC olive.

For Operation Crossroads, the series of atomic tests at Bikini Atoll in July 1946, four Grumman F6F Hellcats were converted to drones to collect air samples and other data near the test site. Two manned planes would control each drone until it approached Roi Island for landing, at which point a ground controller would assume control. Here, during practice for the tests, the man in the seat has taken control of a drone about to land. Behind him is a CCKW with "CROSSROADS" marked on the bumper that contained radio-control equipment in the shelter behind the cab.

U.S. air force personnel decontaminate a WB-29 reconnaissance plane of the 55th Weather Reconnaissance Squadron, McClellan Air Force Base, California, following a 30 April 1952 mission. The plane was conducting air-sampling flights in the government's efforts to detect Soviet nuclear tests. The photo was probably taken in the early 1950s, and the crew is using CCKW-353 60131376 with a powered decontamination apparatus.

At the Yon San Petroleum Tank Farm in Seoul, South Korea, in June 1948, a CCKW-based 750-gallon gasoline tanker is unloading fuel from railroad tankers by means of a pumping unit nicknamed a "milker" on the trailer. The 750-gallon gasoline tankers lacked their own onboard pumping units.

Among the various service vehicles parked around a USAF Douglas C-54 at an unidentified airfield around the late 1940s is a yellow CCKW 750-gallon fuel or oil servicing truck at the center of the photo. The truck was registration number 4238796. "U.S. AIR FORCES" and the number 100 were painted on the tank, and "NO SMOKING WITHIN 50 FEET" was marked on the body.

After the Soviets cut-off the land transportation corridor from West Germany to Berlin in June 1948, the Western Allies organized a massive airlift to provide supplies to the beleagued Allied-controlled sectors of Berlin. Here, CCKW 4261985 is being loaded with supplies from a transport plane at Tempelhof Airport in Berlin.

Above: On a dreary day during the Berlin Airlift, several CCKWs are preparing to shuttle supplies from transport planes to distribution centers. During the 15 months of the airlift, the U.S. Air Force and the Royal Air Force made 278,228 supply flights into Berlin, bringing a total of 2.3 tons of coal, food, and other basic supplies.

Right: A CCKW with a jet engine on a stand in the cargo body is parked next to a USAF C-54 at an unidentified airfield. Next to the jet engine is a large fuel tank, apparently plumbed to the engine, and resting on a form-fitting wooden cradle. This rig probably was the one Master Sgt. Paul G. LeBeau designed, using the exhaust from an engine from a P-80 fighter plane to de-ice aircraft. Seven of these rigs were employed during the Berlin Airlift.

The Karlsfeld Ordnance Center at Munich, Germany, rebuilt many military trucks during the postwar years. Col. C Elford Smith, commander of the center, right, shows the 1,000th 6x6 truck to be rebuilt there, a CCKW, to Brig. Gen. Edward MacMorland, Chief of Ordnance, U.S. European Command (EUCOM), based at Munich, on 25 January 1945. Behind them is a graph showing the progress of GMC truck rebuilds from March 1948 to January 1945. (National Archives)

The Red River Arsenal at Texarkana, Texas, contributed to the effort to refurbish army vehicles for the Mutual Defense Assistance Program, the first U.S. military foreign aid program in the Cold War. This freshly repainted CCKW-353-A2 is in the paint dryer at Red River Arsenal, where it was subjected to 20 minutes under 748 125-watt infrared lamps. (USMC)

A CCKW-353 is fitted with a shelter for an AN/GRC-26 radio set at the base of the 71st Signal Service Battalion in Tokyo on 7 September 1950. Developed around 1950, the AN/GRC-26 evolved from the SCR-399 radio sets of World War II, transmitting and receiving radio teletype signals over a frequency range of 2 to 18 megahertz at a maximum power output of 400 watts. The equipment was housed in an S-55/GRC shelter. (National Archives)

The right side of the interior of a CCKW-based AN/GRC-26 radio set, probably the same one appearing in the preceding photo, is displayed. On the upper shelf to the far right is a Signal Corps frequency-shift exciter. On the lower shelf to the lower left is the teletype equipment. (National Archives)

Left: A bulldozer is required to tow a U.S. Navy Seabees CCKW with a van body ashore from an LST at Blue Beach during Operation Portrex at Vieques, an island off Puerto Rico, in the first quarter of 1950. Operation Portrex was a combined-arms war game to recapture an enemy-occupied island in the Caribbean. (U.S. Army Engineers School History Office)

Bottom: A service-test model of the AN/TFQ-7 laboratory darkroom is installed in a winterized shelter on a CCKW-353 at the Signal Corps Engineering Laboratories on 10 December 1950. The AN/TQF-7 was a mobile processing laboratory for tactical photographic units. Hitched to the truck was a K52 trailer with a PE-95 power unit.

A CCKW-353-B1 with a Hi-lift body is positioned next to a Douglas C-54 at Randolph Field, San Antonio, Texas, in 1950. The ability of this truck to raise its cargo body by means of hydraulic power greatly facilitated the task of loading and unloading cargo planes. The truck is marked with USAF registration number 4235683 and is painted in a high-visibility yellow.

The dark paint of USMC CCKW-353-B2 registration number 4922458 contrasts with the light color of the canvas cab top and tarpaulin. "PULLEY" is stenciled in white on the cab door, and a form-fitting cover is over the ring-mounted .50-caliber machine gun.

A CCKW with an SCR-399 radio set in a HO-17 shelter on the truck body is on display. A sign taped to the rear door explains the nomenclature, Radio Set SCR-399; its weight, 15,000 pounds; the range of the set, 100 to 250 miles; the power unit, the PE-95; and the price, $6,270. Parked to the side of the truck is a trailer containing the PE-95 power unit.

Left: CCKW 4737149 with a bolster body and markings for the Seventh Army is loaded with frame components for an engineer bridge at an unidentified location in the postwar period. The spare tire was mounted on a carrier on top of the rack behind the cab. The special trailer for the bolster truck could carry pontoons or construction materials.

Below: Hitched to CCKW-353 4143177, outfitted with a rail-conversion kit, are a railroad freight car and a flat car. The front axle of this vehicle, which was put to use switching railroad cars, is stenciled "FRONT AXLE" and bears a nomenclature plate headed "AUTO RAILER." Stenciled on front of the hood is information that antifreeze rated to minus 18 degrees Fahrenheit was added to the radiator for the winter of 1949-1950.

Chapter 31

Korea

North Korea's attack on South Korea on 25 June 1950 had the immediate effect of drawing the United States into a war on the Korean peninsula. It also set in motion a series of events that would shape the U.S. tactical vehicle fleet for decades to come. While the CCKW had been literally and figuratively carrying the load of the bulk of the Army's tactical vehicle fleet since World War II, the Army had been experimenting with a series of trucks to replace the wartime motorpool. These "ideal" vehicles would incorporate the features visionaries had requested, and that were outlined in the previous chapter. As this ultimate tactical vehicle fleet was being developed, in 1949 a series of stop-gap, interim designs were created to bridge the anticipated seven-year gap between the war-weary "here and now" and the series production of the "ideal" trucks. Among these interim designs were the M34/M35 2½-ton and the M41/M54 5-ton 6x6 trucks.

The outbreak of the Korean War naturally caused a considerable number of CCKWs, both U.S. Army as well as USMC (which in the interim had been supplied with a number of ex-army CCKWs), to be sent to Korea. While vehicles which had been languishing in long-term storage were hastily given overhauls and sent to front-line units, production of the so-called interim truck designs was ramped up considerably.

Washington feared – to the point of anticipation – that the Korean situation would escalate to a third world war. Efforts began to bring U.S. industry up to full wartime production. Thus, what had been relatively modest orders for the new M34/M35 placed with designer Reo Motors were not only greatly increased, but were augmented with orders for duplicate trucks to be built under license by Studebaker. These vehicles were joined by a new and different General Motors design, the automatic-transmission-equipped M135/M211 family of vehicles.

Fortunately, WW3 did not materialize and the Army was left with not only large numbers of relatively new "interim" vehicles, but also depleted numbers of CCKWs. Not surprisingly, the CCKWs were quickly moved from active units to reserve and National Guard units, and then of course became surplus as ever more new vehicles arrived and the military continued to downsize.

U.S. Army CCKW-353 4705465, assigned to the 8th Engineer Construction Battalion, 1st Cavalry Division, crosses an engineer-built ford on a tributary of the Naktong River in the Republic of Korea in September 1950. At the time, the battalion was constructing a pontoon bridge nearby. Although more modern trucks were beginning to supplant the CCKW by the time of the Korean War, notably the G-742 Eager Beaver and the GMC G-749, the CCKW continued to soldier on for a period.

Japan was a major staging area for the United Nations in their efforts to prevent North Korea from overrunning South Korea. Here, a boom on a transport ship is being used to load CCKW-353 4707187 on board for shipment to South Korea on 2 July 1950, a week after the start of the war. (National Archives via Bryce Sunderlin)

Above: A CCKW heavily camouflaged with evergreen branches takes on cargo from a C-54 at an airfield in South Korea, 28 June 1950. Because of South Korea's isolated position, transporting supplies and materiel to the beleaguered country was a logistical problem in which the CCKW played an important role. (U.S. Army Transportation Museum)

Right: At the Big Five Ordnance Plant in Japan, U.S. Army vehicles were inspected, repaired, and refurbished. In a July 1950 photograph, CCKW hoods are lined up in the foreground for repainting. In the background, fenders from MB/GPW jeeps are on a carousel and are undergoing repainting. (National Archives)

Above: U.S. Army CCKW-352 4548883 kicks up dust as it tows a 105mm howitzer to the front lines in South Korea around dawn on 20 July 1950. Packs are hung on the rear of the rack. The cargo body was wooden. (National Archives via Bryce Sunderlin)

Right: At a tent city that comprised part of I Corps Headquarters on 27 October 1950, a CCKW with an SCR-399 radio set is parked in the foreground. By the buildings in the left background are several machine-shop trucks, and below the knoll in the background is a vehicle park that includes CCKWs. (U.S. Army Quartermaster Museum)

Below: Troops of the 7th Marine Regiment of the 1st Marine Division move up to the front toward Chosin Reservoir on 1 November 1950. To the front of the Jeep to the far left are two CCKWs; the rear one is towing a water trailer, and hitched to the next one is a cargo trailer. (USMC)

With the destruction of many of Korea's bridges during the conflict on that peninsula, the U.S. Army Corps of Engineers kept busy constructing temporary bridges. Here, a CCKW bolster truck and trailer deliver hardware for an engineer bridge in 1950. (U.S. Army Engineer School History Office)

Right: A column of vehicles of the 96th Field Artillery Battalion, U.S. Eighth Army, advances along a sinuous road to support the 8th Cavalry Regiment, 1st Cavalry Division, in an attack on a Communist-held position near Yangui on 26 January 1951. In the foreground are several CCKW-353s towing trailers. (National Archives)

Below: A convoy of trucks assigned to the 7th Quartermaster Company of the 7th U.S. Infantry Division's "Eightball Express" assemble for a last-minute check prior to departing to transport vital supplies to divisional headquarters in Korea on 11 June 1951. Steel-bodied and wooden-bodies CCKW are in evidence. (U.S. Army Quartermaster Museum)

499

Troops prepare 60-inch searchlights for use on 12 September 1951. Mounted in the back of CCKW cargo trucks, the lights, although developed for antiaircraft defense, here will be used instead to expose Communist infantry and positions at night. The power supply for the searchlights is towed behind the truck, as seen in the background. The troop seats, which have been reversed and now extend over the truck sides, form work platforms for the searchlight crew. (National Archives)

Above: Armorers are loading ammunition into an F-80 fighter at an airfield in the Republic of Korea in May 1952. The plane was assigned to the 8th Fighter-Bomber Wing "Hobos" of the Fifth Air Force. To the left is an M27B1 bomb-service truck, hitched to which is a trailer filled with crates. (National Archives)

Left: U.S. Air Force armorers are unloading bombs two at a time from an M27B1 bomb-service truck at a base in the Republic of Korea on 10 September 1952. The bombs are destined for the B-29 Superfortress in the background, *All Shook.* (National Archives)

Sergeant Edward B. Jones checks the dipstick on his CCKW in Korea in 1951. A canvas cover with an adjustable flap in the center is strapped to the front of the grille. Markings on the left side of the bumper indicate the 231st Transportation Truck Battalion, 351st Highway Transportation Group.

A mobile radio set based on CCKW-353 4317718 was photographed at Taegu Base in Korea in October 1950. Although the general shape of the shelter for the radio set is similar to that of the HO-17 shelter frequently seen in this book, this shelter has windows in the front and on the side, unlike the stock HO-17.

Several CCKW-based M27B1 bomb-service trucks are operating at a bomb dump at a USAF airfield in the Republic of Korea in June 1953. To the left, the man in the front of the body has his right hand on the winch control for the hoist. The two other men in the body are attaching the hoist to a bomb; the trolley of the hoist is on the boom directly over them. (National Archives)

501

A CCKW with an ST-6 shop body, U.S.A. number 4867461 of the 205th Signal Repair Company, leads the way across a pontoon bridge across the Han Tan River on Route 19 in the Republic of Korea. (U.S. Army Engineer School History Office)

A knocked-out enemy T-34-85 tank rests along a highway in Korea as a column of U.S. trucks rolls by. Two open-cab CCKW-353s are in the foreground. To the rear of the Jeep following those two CCKWs is another CCKW-353 with what appears to be an armored cab, towing a trailer. (National Archives)

Homeward-bound U.S. Marines packed aboard a CCKW bid farewell to their friends as they embark on the first leg of their journey back to the States. The left side of the windshield has a large crack and a bullet hole in it: testimony to the hazards these hard-working trucks endured in Korea. (USMC)

Chapter 32
Post-Korea

In the 1980s the U.S. military was faced with a minor influx of CCKWs as vehicles which had been loaned to allied nations during the 1950s were returned to U.S. custody. Like their predecessors, these trucks were sold as surplus. However, these trucks, rather than going to work rebuilding war-torn nations, invariably went into the hands of collectors.

Today, no CCKWs are in active military service, and few are found in commercial work, most survivors today being in the hands of collectors who work hard to restore these vehicles as a tribute to the men and women who built and used them to make history.

The final U.S. military service for many CCKWs was as targets. This example is being checked for radiation on 22 March 1952, following an atomic blast at the Nevada proving ground. (National Archives)

This CCKW-353 was photographed 22 April 1952 at Yucca Flats, Nevada, like many trucks used in the desert following World War II, it has been equipped with large single, rather than dual, rear wheels. Because of this ongoing use by the U.S. military, GMC continued to produce CCKW parts in batches well after WWII, even large components such complete engines. Given the large numbers of trucks supplied to Allies, overseas firms as well began to produce parts for the CCKW. Replacement all-steel beds were commonplace, the wartime all-wood beds not holding up to the rigors of use nor weather especially well. Also manufactured in Europe, likely for the French military were exhaust manifolds and cylinder heads. (National Archives)

CCKW Specifications

Model	CCKW-352	CCKW-353
Length	244⅞ inches	256¼ inches
Width	86¼ inches	86¼ inches
Height	93 inches	93 inches
Tire Size	7.50-20	7.50-20
Transmission speeds	5 forward; 1 reverse	5 forward;1 reverse
Transfer speeds	2	2

Engine Data

Engine Make/Model	GMC 270
Number of Cylinders	6
Cubic Inch Displacement	269.5
Horsepower	91.5 @ 2,750 r.p.m.
Torque	216 lb-ft @ 1,400 r.p.m.
Fuel	Gasoline
Governed Speed	2,750 r.p.m.

With over half a million produced, the CCKW was seemingly everywhere that U.S. servicemen went during World War II and Korea. Today but a small percentage of those survive in museums or in the hands of enthusiasts, among them this example from the collection of the late Kevin Kronlund.